**McGRAW-HILL
BOOK COMPANY
INTERNATIONAL**

New York
St. Louis
San Francisco
Auckland
Bogotá
Düsseldorf
Johannesburg
London
Madrid
Mexico
Montreal
New Delhi
Panama
Paris
São Paulo
Singapore
Sydney
Tokyo
Toronto

BRIAN L. SCARFE
Associate Professor of Economics
University of Manitoba

Cycles, Growth, and Inflation
A SURVEY OF CONTEMPORARY MACRODYNAMICS

This book is set in Times New Roman

Library of Congress Cataloging in Publication Data
Scarfe, Brian L.
    Cycles, growth, and inflation.
    1. Economics
    I. Title
    330   HB171   77-30035

ISBN 0-07-055039-5

**CYCLES, GROWTH,
AND INFLATION**
A SURVEY OF CONTEMPORARY
MACRODYNAMICS

1 2 3 4 5   MPMP   7 9 8 7

Printed and bound in the United States of America

To Susan, Andrew, and Adam

CONTENTS

PREFACE

Cycles, Growth, and Inflation is a selective survey of contemporary macrodynamic models. The survey has three parts: Part One—The Trade Cycle, Part Two—The Process of Growth, and Part Three—The Inflation Problem. Essentially, these three separate parts are concerned with stock adjustment models, equilibrium dynamic models, and price adjustment models, respectively. My main reasons for writing this book reflect my concern with the direction in which our macro-economic teaching has developed. Although the analytical core of senior under-graduate and postgraduate courses in macroeconomic theory continues to be based upon the comparative static method, the limitations of this method of analysis have become increasingly apparent. In consequence, numerous economists have contributed to the development of a large variety of specific macrodynamic models, which are taught on a widespread but piecemeal basis at many uni-versities. The behavior of these models can only be explored by using an explicitly dynamic method of analysis. Until the present, no single work has existed which not only develops the dynamic method but also provides a unified framework to which the numerous piecemeal analytical developments may be related. This book attempts to provide a survey which fills this gap in the existing literature.

This book contains a series of explorations in dynamic economic theory. Its most significant features are (a) that it emphasizes the interplay of the various modes of analysis, (b) that it places major emphasis on the analysis of the proper role of prices in a dynamic economy, with special consideration of the inflation problem, (c) that it provides a unified theoretical treatment of macroeconomics for the open, trading economy, and (d) that it provides a framework for analyzing the interplay between resource scarcities and the inflation problem. Thus, this book is designed not only to fill some major gaps in the existing literature on macrodynamic models and their implications for policy analysis, but also to report on some important research results related to three fundamental but inter-related macrodynamic problems, first, the formulation of appropriately co-ordinated stabilization policies in response to cyclical fluctuations, second, the consequences of the existence of scarce and non-renewable natural resources, and, third, the causes and consequences of the problem of inflation. From this it should be evident that the book has broad scope but definite focus.

Unavoidably, a book of this type must rely quite heavily on the mathematical tool of elementary differential equations, aided visually, wherever possible, by the use of phase diagrams. In addition, the verbal analysis is presented in as concise a manner as possible. This "tightness" has been necessitated by space considerations, although it may render the text more difficult to read than a standard textbook. It is hoped that this will not prove to be a deterrent to the serious student. Indeed, it is my fervent hope that all three parts of this book will prove to be very useful to both postgraduate and senior undergraduate students of economic analysis. However, for those who cannot see the relevance of mathematical growth theory, it is possible to skip from any point after the end of chapter 3 through to the beginning of chapter 10 without serious loss of continuity.

Several sections of Part Two of this book derive from my unpublished D. Phil. dissertation, "Capital Accumulation and Comparative Advantage: A Critical Appraisal," Oxford University, 1970, while several sections of Part Three derive from my unpublished monograph, "Inflation and the Exchange Rate," Bank of Canada Research Department, 1974. Much of the writing was completed during a pleasant sabbatical leave spent at Cambridge University in 1974–75. I am indebted, first, to the Rhodes Scholarship Trust and the Canada Council for their financial support of the original dissertation, and, second, to the Bank of Canada for their financial support of the research results underlying Part Three of this book, and, third, to the Canada Council for providing me with a leave fellowship to support my sabbatical leave. This book should in no way be construed to represent the views of any of these institutions. The author remains solely responsible for all opinions expressed in this book.

Space does not permit me to acknowledge my considerable intellectual debt to a whole generation of economists. Nevertheless, I am grateful to my colleagues at the University of Manitoba, C. L. Barber, N. E. Cameron, D. Hum, C. A. Nicolaou, and A. M. C. Waterman, for valuable comments on parts of earlier drafts of this book, and to my former students K. M. Johnston, C. A. Nicolaou, S. K. E. Rahman, and W. G. Tholl for valuable assistance in putting together the final manuscript draft of this book. My biggest debt of gratitude is to my wife and family, on whom the burden of writing this book has chiefly fallen. To them, with my warmest thanks and appreciation, I dedicate this book.

Winnipeg, Canada   B. L. Scarfe
August, 1976

THE TRADE CYCLE

ONE

INVENTORY BEHAVIOR AND STABILIZATION POLICY

A : AN INTRODUCTION TO MACRODYNAMIC ANALYSIS

Economic dynamics is concerned with the study of the behavior of economic variables over time. Such a study usually takes place within the context of models (or equation systems) which are capable of tracing the time paths of these variables from given initial conditions. Following Frisch and Samuelson, "We may say that a system is dynamical if its behavior over time is determined by functional equations in which 'variables at different points of time' are involved in an 'essential' way."[1] In other words, a system or model is dynamic if its functional equations involve both standard variables (like prices and quantities) and the time derivatives or differences of these variables.[2] Systems or models which involve only standard variables and not their time derivatives or differences are usually said to be static systems.

In static systems, model predictions are derived from a comparison of the alternative equilibrium positions which are obtained when some shift occurs in an exogenous variable or policy parameter. This analytical method is known as *comparative statics.* Although the comparative static method is sufficient for many purposes, the analysis of numerous economic issues requires a knowledge of the actual time-paths followed by a model's endogenous variables as they respond to shifts in exogenous variables or policy parameters. To trace these time-paths, as well as to ascertain the stability or instability of any equilibrium position, is a matter of *dynamic analysis.*

1. P. A. Samuelson, *Foundations of Economic Analysis,* Cambridge, Harvard University Press, 1947, p. 314. This formulation can be attributed to R. Frisch, "On the Notion of Equilibrium and Disequilibrium," *Review of Economic Studies,* vol. 3, February 1936, pp. 100–106.

2. In this book, the analysis will be conducted almost exclusively in continuous time and differential equations, rather than in discrete time and difference equations.

In *Capital and Growth*,[3] Hicks distinguishes three classes of macrodynamic models. These three classes are: (a) Price Adjustment or Flex-Price Dynamic Models, (b) Stock Adjustment or Fix-Price Dynamic Models, and (c) Equilibrium Dynamic Models. The fundamental distinctions among these three classes of macrodynamic models depend upon the types of variables or interactions which are *excluded* from them. This principle of selective exclusion is the main simplifying device on which economic analysis proceeds.

Part One of this book is primarily concerned with the analysis of specific stock adjustment or fix price dynamic models. In order to keep the behavioral interactions between stocks and quantity flows sharply in focus, these models simplify by reducing prices to a subordinate role. Although these models are frequently used to describe the cyclical fluctuations in national income (or aggregate monetary demand) that are inherent in stock adjustment processes, and to analyze the problems involved in coordinating appropriate stabilization policies, they do not ordinarily separate out the price effects from the quantity effects implied by national income movements, where national income is a value flow.

Part Two of this book is primarily concerned with the analysis of specific equilibrium dynamic models. These models are appropriate to the analysis of the process of economic growth, and the implications of this process for patterns of comparative advantage in open economies. They trace the long run equilibrium paths of both stocks and prices (as well as quantity flows) on the assumption that both stock adjustments and price adjustments are short run phenomena which are largely irrelevant to the behavior of stocks and prices over the long haul.

Part Three of this book is primarily concerned with the analysis of specific price adjustment or flex-price dynamic models. Particular attention is given to the analysis of the inflationary process, and to the mechanisms through which inflationary impulses are transmitted from one open economy to another in an inherently interdependent world. Although these models simplify by reducing stocks to a subordinate role, they normally incorporate the stock of money as a relevant variable. It should, however, be remembered that, unlike stocks of physical commodities the stock of (pure credit) money does not result from an accumulation of previous net output flows.

Whereas fix-price and flex-price models may be distinguished by the types of variables excluded from them, equilibrium dynamic models are distinguishable from both of the others by the types of interactions that are excluded. Despite the temporal precedence of flex-price models in the history of economic analysis,[4] in this book they are treated last, after the discussion of fix-price models and

3. See J. R. Hicks, *Capital and Growth*, Oxford, Oxford University Press, 1965.

4. See, for example, Hicks, *Op. cit.*, Chapter Six, pp. 58–75, where he associates flex-price models with Wicksell and Lindahl. See K. Wicksell, *Interest and Prices*. London, Macmillan, 1936 (Geldzins und Güterpreise, 1898), and E. Lindahl, *Studies in the Theory of Money and Capital*, London, Allen and Unwin, 1939.

equilibrium dynamic models. Recent research into the behavior of labor markets and the explanation of the rate of change of money wage rates illustrates this resurgence.[5] Thus, in a book designed as a selective survey of contemporary (that is, postwar) macrodynamics, it seems appropriate to treat Cycles first, Growth second, and Inflation third.

Despite its analytical usefulness, the principle of selective exclusion does have some disadvantages. In the post-Keynesian fanfare, with its preoccupation with explanations of cycles and growth in the volume of production, analysis of the proper role of prices in a dynamic economy has been neglected. Were it not for such disadvantages, economists would not find themselves having to ask questions such as "What happens to prices in a Keynesian cumulative process?", since the economic problem would not have been decomposed in this way in the first place. Chapter 11 of this book attempts to provide an answer to this fundamental question.

There can be little doubt that the worldwide problem of inflation has created a crisis for traditional post-Keynesian macroeconomic thinking[6] and for the so-called neo-classical synthesis. The discipline of economics has appeared to be singularly bankrupt in response to the spreading acceleration of inflation. One of the main purposes of this book is to explain how this has come about. Although Part Three of this book is rather different from a modern-dress version of *Prices and Production*,[7] there are some definite similarities. In particular, in chapter 12 an answer is provided to the Hayekian question, "What happens to quantities in a Wicksellian cumulative process?".[8]

This book contains a series of explorations in dynamic economic theory. It is designed to fill some major gaps in the existing literature on macrodynamic models and their implications for policy formulation. First and foremost, an attempt is made throughout to emphasize the interplay of the various modes of analysis. Although the degree of integration or synthesis that is achieved is at times more intuitive than formal, such intuitive integration is very useful when one comes to interpret some of the "stylized facts" of recent economic history. Second, the book places major emphasis on the importance of providing an analysis of the proper role of prices in a dynamic economy. From both the short run and the long run perspective, production and prices are thoroughly integrated. Thirdly, much of the existing literature involves the assumption that the economy under consideration is closed, having no trade or financial linkages with other economies. For open trading nations, however, macroeconomic policies

5. See, for example, E. S. Phelps (ed.), *Microeconomic Foundations of Employment and Inflation Theory*, New York, Norton, 1970.

6. Compare J. R. Hicks, *The Crisis in Keynesian Economics*, Oxford, Blackwell, 1974. See also A. Leijonhufvud, *On Keynesian Economics and the Economics of Keynes*, New York, Oxford University Press, 1968.

7. See F. A. Hayek, *Prices and Production*, London, Routledge, 1935.

8. According to Hicks, this is the fundamental question that Hayek was asking in *Prices and Production*. See Hicks, *Critical Essays in Monetary Theory*, Oxford, Oxford University Press, 1967, p. 205.

are necessarily formulated with one eye on the external constraints imposed by the existence of trade and financial linkages with other nations. If existing macro-dynamic models, originally developed in the context of a closed economy, are to be applicable to the formulation of national economic policies, they must generally be recast in an open economy framework. One of the main purposes of this book is to provide a unified theoretical treatment of the necessary recasting. Finally, this book provides a framework for analyzing the interface between resource scarcities and the inflation problem. In particular, it is concerned with the social consequences of both the atemporal and intertemporal aspects of the resource allocation problem in any economy whose expansion is ultimately limited by the finite nature of the world in which it is embedded. The book begins, however, with the exploration of a simple stock adjustment model.

B: A SIMPLE STOCK ADJUSTMENT MODEL

The purpose of this section and the two following ones is to set out, rather fully, a simple dynamic model of the determinants of aggregate demand. The model chosen is a stock adjustment or fix-price dynamic model of the post-Keynesian variety. It explains aggregate inventory behavior and exhibits the possibility of an inventory cycle. In the final section of this chapter, this model is expanded in order to discuss governmental stabilization policies. The impact of money and interest rates on this model economy is assessed in the following chapter. However, the introduction of price movements into this framework is purposely delayed until chapter 11 of this book.

In the basic stock adjustment model, there are three fundamental structural relationships. The first of these is a multiplier relationship which says that national expenditure, E, is equal to autonomous expenditure, A, plus induced consumption expenditure, cY, where $0 < c < 1$ is the marginal propensity to consume and Y is national output or income. Notice that the marginal propensity to consume is a flow–flow ratio, and, as such, has no time dimension associated with it. The second of these is a definitional relationship which says that the excess of national output, Y, over national expenditure (or sales), E, is equal to *the change* in the level of inventories, DS, where S is the level of these stocks and D is the symbol (or operator) representing the change in a variable, such as stocks, with respect to time t, that is $D \equiv d/dt$. The third of these embodies the assumption that the ratio of *desired* (or target) inventories, S^*, to *expected* (or planned) sales, E^*, is a constant, $h > 0$, which may be called the *desired inventory–sales ratio*. Notice that the desired inventory–sales ratio is a stock–flow ratio and, as such, varies inversely with the length of the time period that is chosen for measuring sales. The three fundamental structural relationships may therefore be written as

$$E = cY + A, \quad DS = Y - E, \quad \text{and} \quad S^* = hE^* \qquad (1B\text{-}1)$$

It can be deduced from the second of these equations that the level of inventories remains constant ($DS = 0$) if and only if output and sales are equal ($Y = E$). When $Y = E$, the first equation implies that $Y = E = A/(1 - c)$, which defines the position of *multiplier equilibrium* for this model. Although the constancy of the level of inventories (or, equivalently, multiplier equilibrium) is a necessary condition for the complete equilibrium of the model, by itself it is not a sufficient condition, since the level of output may not also be "at rest."

In order to pursue the conditions for the complete equilibrium of this model, let it be assumed that total inventory accumulation, $DS = Y - E$, is composed of two additive parts. These two additive parts are *active or planned inventory accumulation*, defined as the difference between output and expected sales, $Y - E^*$, and *passive or unplanned inventory accumulation*, defined as the difference between expected sales and actual sales, $E^* - E$. Active inventory accumulation (decumulation) occurs in order to restore (reduce) the actual level of stocks to their desired level. Passive inventory accumulation (decumulation) occurs because less (more) goods are sold than was expected.

Let active inventory accumulation, $Y - E^*$, be proportional to the difference between desired and actual stocks, $S^* - S$, and let *changes* in expected sales, DE^*, be proportional to the difference between actual sales and expected sales, $E - E^*$. One may then write

$$Y - E^* = \mu(S^* - S) \quad \text{and} \quad DE^* = \lambda(E - E^*) \tag{1B-2}$$

where $\mu > 0$ and $\lambda > 0$ are the two constants of proportionality. The first of these two relationships says that, if desired stocks exceed (fall short of) actual stocks, more (less) output will be produced than is expected to be sold in an attempt to expand (reduce) stocks towards their desired level. This *stock adjustment principle* specifies the way in which the system adjusts to stock disequilibrium ($S \neq S^*$). The second of these two relationships says that, if actual sales exceed (fall short of) expected sales, expected sales will be adjusted upwards (downwards). This *adaptive expectations hypothesis* specifies the way in which the system adjusts to flow disequilibrium ($E \neq E^*$).

Implicit in the previous specification are the notions of *stock equilibrium*, defined by the equation of desired and actual stocks, $S^* = S$, and *flow equilibrium*, defined by the equation of expected and actual sales, $E^* = E$. The complete equilibrium of the model can now be seen to require both stock equilibrium and flow equilibrium. Such an equilibrium implies $S = S^* = hE^* = hE = hY = hA/(1 - c)$, so that the equilibrium level of output, $\bar{Y}$, and the equilibrium level of inventories, $\bar{S}$, are, respectively,

$$\bar{Y} = A/(1 - c) \quad \text{and} \quad \bar{S} = hA/(1 - c) \tag{1B-3}$$

The complete equilibrium of the model therefore requires that *both* active inventory accumulation be zero (the stock equilibrium condition) *and* passive inventory accumulation be zero (the flow equilibrium condition) and *not* just that the sum of these two be zero (multiplier equilibrium). Thus, multiplier equilibrium is a necessary but not sufficient condition for full equilibrium.

Using the five equations of (1B-1) and (1B-2), one may eliminate S^* and E^*, leaving the three equations[9]

$$E = cY + A, \quad DS = Y - E, \quad \text{and} \quad DY = \lambda\mu(hE - S) - (\lambda + \mu)(Y - E) \quad \text{(1B-4)}$$

Finally, the first of these three equations may be used to eliminate E in the second and third equations. One may then write

$$DY = -\{(1 - c)(\lambda + \mu) - ch\lambda\mu\}\{Y - A/(1 - c)\} - \lambda\mu\{S - hA/(1 - c)\}$$

$$\text{and} \quad DS = \{1 - c\}\{Y - A/(1 - c)\} \quad \text{(1B-5)}$$

What do these two equations tell us? Given the level of autonomous expenditure, A, they tell us how the flow of output, Y, *and* the stock of inventories, S, *change* through time. That is to say, if we know Y and S at any particular point of time, such as the initial time $t = 0$, these equations determine for us the levels of Y and S at any other point of time. They trace, therefore, the complete dynamic time paths followed by output and inventories as time passes, given, of course, the level of autonomous expenditure.

C: THE BEHAVIOR OF INVENTORY CYCLES

It is useful to examine the time paths followed by output and inventories diagrammatically. This may be done in terms of the *phase diagram* given in Fig. 1C-1. In this phase diagram, the level of output, Y, is measured on the horizontal axis while the level of inventories, S, is measured on the vertical axis. We have drawn a vertical line from the point of multiplier equilibrium, $Y = A/(1 - c)$. This line represents the locus of all points at which there is no change in the level of inventories. Consequently, this line has been labelled $DS = 0$ in the diagram. If Y exceeds $A/(1 - c)$, the second equation of (1B-5) tells us that the level of inventories must be rising, $DS > 0$. This rise is represented in the phase diagram by the arrows pointing vertically upwards in the quadrants (or phases) labelled (a) and (b), which together include all points lying *to the right* of the line $DS = 0$, or, equivalently, all points at which $Y > A/(1 - c)$. If Y falls short of $A/(1 - c)$, the second equation of (1B-5) tells us that the level of inventories must be falling, $DS < 0$. This fall is represented in the phase diagram

---

9. The last equation of (1B-2) may be written as $E^* = (D + \lambda)^{-1}\lambda E$, whence one may write the last equation of (1B-1) as $S^* = (D + \lambda)^{-1}\lambda hE$. Substituting these two equations into the first equation of (1B-2) yields

$$Y - (D + \lambda)^{-1}\lambda E = \mu(D + \lambda)^{-1}\lambda hE - \mu S \quad \text{or} \quad (D + \lambda)Y = (\lambda + \lambda\mu h)E - \mu(D + \lambda)S.$$

Using the second equation of (1B-1) to eliminate DS, this expression becomes $(D + \lambda + \mu)Y = (\lambda + \mu + \lambda\mu h)E - \lambda\mu S$, which may be rearranged to generate the third equation in (1B-4) above.

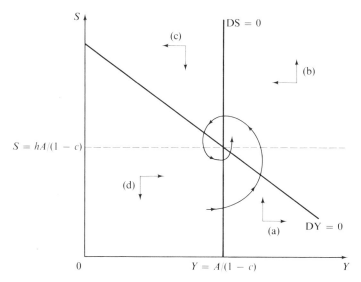

Figure 1C-1 Phase diagram for an inventory cycle.

by the arrows pointing vertically downwards in the quadrants (or phases) labelled (c) and (d), which together include all points lying *to the left* of the line $DS = 0$, or, equivalently, all points at which $Y < A/(1 - c)$.

Although changes in the level of inventories depend only on the deviations of actual output, Y, from its equilibrium level, $A/(1 - c)$, changes in the level of output depend not only upon these deviations *but also* upon the deviations of actual inventories, S, from their equilibrium level, $hA/(1 - c)$. This is made evident in the first equation of (1B-5). Thus, it is only when both output and inventories attain their equilibrium levels that the complete system can remain at rest. This *stationary point* is the point of intersection between the vertical line and the downward sloping line in the phase diagram. The downward sloping line has been labelled $DY = 0$ since it represents the locus of all points at which there is no change in the level of output. Its downward slope depends crucially upon the assumption that $(1 - c)(\lambda + \mu) - ch\lambda\mu$ is *positive*, an assumption which is discussed at length in the next section. If it were otherwise assumed that $(1 - c)(\lambda + \mu) - ch\lambda\mu$ is *negative*, the locus $DY = 0$ would be upward sloping, though the resulting phase diagram would be similar in appearance.

At all points on the downward sloping line $DY = 0$, any given deviation of output from its equilibrium level, $Y - A/(1 - c)$, implies a unique deviation of inventories from their equilibrium level, $S - hA/(1 - c)$. If, given $Y - A/(1 - c)$, $S - hA/(1 - c)$ is in excess of this level, then output must be falling since $DY < 0$. The reason for this is the negative sign of the coefficient $(-\lambda\mu)$ attached to $S - hA/(1 - c)$ in the first equation of (1B-5). Thus, at all points *above* the line $DY = 0$, output must be falling. This fall is represented in the phase diagram by the arrows pointing horizontally to the left in the quadrants (or phases) labelled

(b) and (c). On the other hand, if, given $Y - A/(1 - c)$, $S - hA/(1 - c)$ is smaller than the level required for $DY = 0$, then output must be rising since $DY > 0$. Thus, at all points *below* the line $DY = 0$, output must be rising. This rise is represented in the phase diagram by the arrows pointing horizontally to the right in the quadrants (or phases) labelled (d) and (a).

In any particular quadrant of the diagram, the *combination* of arrows explains the direction of output and inventory movement in that quadrant. Thus, in quadrant (a), both output and inventories are rising, leading the system in a north-east direction. In quadrant (b), output is falling and inventories are rising, leading the system in a north-west direction. In quadrant (c), both output and inventories are falling, leading the system in a south-west direction, and, in quadrant (d), output is rising and inventories are falling, leading the system in a south-east direction.

When these movements are combined into a single story, it becomes evident that *oscillations* in the levels of output and inventories are likely. These oscillations characterize an *inventory cycle*. This cycle is represented in the phase diagram by the *counter-clockwise* inwards spiral towards the stationary equilibrium point. Such an inventory cycle has four chronological phases which occur in the following sequence: (a) a late expansionary phase with growing output ($DY > 0$) and growing stocks ($DS > 0$) led by *active* inventory accumulation, (b) an early recessionary phase with falling output ($DY < 0$) but growing stocks ($DS > 0$) because of *passive* inventory accumulation, (c) a late recessionary phase with falling output ($DY < 0$) and falling stocks ($DS < 0$) led by *active* inventory decumulation, and (d) an early expansionary phase with growing output ($DY > 0$) but falling stocks ($DS < 0$) because of *passive* inventory decumulation. This cyclical phasing is evident in the phase diagram.

It is particularly important to note that, in this cyclical process, the fluctuations in inventory stocks appear *to lag* behind the fluctuations in output flows by one phase. The time sequence follows this particular chronological order, with output leading inventories by one phase, and *not* the reverse. This *lead-lag* relationship is explained by the fact that cycles in inventory *accumulation* (DS) and in output (Y) are coincident. The *change* in inventories reaches its maximum (minimum) at the same time as output reaches its maximum (minimum). The *level* of inventories, however, reaches its maximum (minimum) when output passes through its equilibrium level on the downswing (upswing). The lead-lag relationship is related to the fact that inventory accumulation and decumulation are of two types: active or planned inventory accumulation and passive or unplanned accumulation. The first type arises from the attempt to adjust actual stocks to desired stocks, while the second type arises from the imperfection of foresight about the level of sales.

The oscillations in output and inventories generated by the model occur in a smooth, regular manner. This smooth regularity is artificial, since it is based not only upon the linearity of the model but also upon a constant unchanging level of autonomous expenditure, A. Once A is allowed to shift through time, it is clear that the equilibrium levels of both output flows and inventory stocks will be shifting through time. Such disturbances to the equilibrium point around which the system cycles will also disturb the course of the cyclical process. This is particularly the case if the disturbances in the level of autonomous expenditure are partly random.

Figure 1C-1 indicates that the oscillations tend to become smaller in scale (or *amplitude*) as time proceeds. This *damping* of the cyclical process depends crucially on the assumption that $(1 - c)(\lambda + \mu) - ch\lambda\mu$ is positive. Given this assumption, the oscillations would ultimately disappear if autonomous expenditure, A, remained constant forever. However, "random shocks" in the level of autonomous expenditure tend to rejuvenate the cyclical process. Indeed, it appears that any change in the equilibrium position will set in motion a damped cyclical oscillation around the new equilibrium solution. The path to equilibrium is characterized by fluctuations in the levels of output and inventories. These conclusions are not entirely general, however, and the restrictive mathematical conditions on which they are based are outlined formally in the following section.

D : THE MATHEMATICS OF OSCILLATIONS

It is now time to explore our earlier assumption that $(1 - c)(\lambda + \mu) - ch\lambda\mu$ is positive, or, equivalently, that the locus $DY = 0$ is downward sloping. It turns out that the slope of the locus $DY = 0$ is crucial to the *stability* of the equilibrium solution. Indeed, if $(1 - c)(\lambda + \mu) - ch\lambda\mu > 0$, the equilibrium solution is *stable*, while if $(1 - c)(\lambda + \mu) - ch\lambda\mu \le 0$, the equilibrium solution is *unstable*. For present purposes, stability implies that the system ultimately converges to its equilibrium solution if this solution remains undisturbed, while instability implies that the system diverges from equilibrium as time passes. This may be demonstrated by formally solving the equation system (1B-5).

To find the general time dependent solution to the equation system (1B-5), one may first note that DY and DS are both linear combinations of $Y - A/(1 - c)$ and $S - hA/(1 - c)$, the deviations of Y and S from their respective equilibrium levels. The solution must, therefore, depend upon a functional form for which the time derivative is proportional to the level. Since the exponential is such a functional form, one may let $Y(t) - A/(1 - c)$ and $S(t) - hA/(1 - c)$ be equal to $\{Y(0) - A/(1 - c)\}\, e^{\rho t}$ and $\{S(0) - hA/(1 - c)\}\, e^{\rho t}$, respectively, where $e = 2.71828\ldots$ is the base of natural logarithms, $Y(t)$ and $S(t)$ are the levels of output and inventories at time t, $Y(0)$ and $S(0)$ are the given initial levels of output and inventories at time $t = 0$, and the exponent ρ is a constant still to be found. Given $DA = 0$ by assumption, it follows immediately that $DY = \rho\{Y(0) - A/(1 - c)\}\, e^{\rho t}$ and $DS = \rho\{S(0) - hA/(1 - c)\}\, e^{\rho t}$. Substitution into expression (1B-5) yields the matrix equation

$$\begin{bmatrix} \rho + (1 - c)(\lambda + \mu) - ch\lambda\mu & +\lambda\mu \\ -(1 - c) & \rho \end{bmatrix} \begin{bmatrix} Y(0) - A/(1 - c) \\ S(0) - hA/(1 - c) \end{bmatrix} = \begin{bmatrix} 0 \\ 0 \end{bmatrix} \qquad (1\text{D-1})$$

after cancellation of $e^{\rho t} \neq 0$. One obvious solution to this matrix equation is that the system is initially in equilibrium with $Y(0) = A/(1 - c)$ and $S(0) = hA/(1 - c)$. However, if the initial situation is not one of equilibrium, it is clear that the 2×2 matrix on the lefthand side of expression (1D-1) must be singular. Setting the determinant of this matrix equal to zero, one obtains the *characteristic equation* of the system, namely

$$\rho^2 + \{(1 - c)(\lambda + \mu) - ch\lambda\mu\}\rho + (1 - c)\lambda\mu = 0 \qquad \text{(1D-2)}$$

The two solutions of this quadratic equation, ρ_1 and ρ_2, are given by

$$\rho_1, \rho_2 = -\tfrac{1}{2}\{(1 - c)(\lambda + \mu) - ch\lambda\mu\} \pm \tfrac{1}{2}\sqrt{[\{(1 - c)(\lambda + \mu) - ch\lambda\mu\}^2 - 4(1 - c)\lambda\mu]}$$

$$\text{(1D-3)}$$

with one root taking the plus sign and the other the minus sign.[10] These two values are called the *characteristic roots* of the system.

Since there are two values of ρ that satisfy Eq. (1D-2), the general solutions for $Y(t)$ and $S(t)$ will be linear combinations of the two exponential functions, $e^{\rho_1 t}$ and $e^{\rho_2 t}$.[11] Thus, the general solution to the pair of equations (1B-5) may be written as[12]

$$Y(t) = A/(1 - c) + B_1 e^{\rho_1 t} + B_2 e^{\rho_2 t}$$
$$S(t) = hA/(1 - c) + C_1 e^{\rho_1 t} + C_2 e^{\rho_2 t} \qquad \text{(1D-4)}$$

where B_1, B_2, C_1, and C_2 are arbitrary constants which depend upon the initial output and inventory levels at time $t = 0$.[13] It is clear that the behavior of output and inventories over time depends crucially upon the values obtained by the two characteristic roots, ρ_1 and ρ_2, and therefore upon the four parameters, c, h, λ, and μ.

In the stable case with $(1 - c)(\lambda + \mu) - ch\lambda\mu > 0$, the system moves towards equilibrium since the characteristic roots, ρ_1 and ρ_2, are either (i) real *negative*

---

10. The two solutions to any quadratic equation $k_2\rho^2 + k_1\rho + k_0 = 0$ are given by

$$\rho_1, \rho_2 = \{-k_1 \pm \sqrt{(k_1^2 - 4k_2k_0)}\}/2k_2.$$

11. An exception is made in the special case $\rho_1 = \rho_2 = \rho$, for which the general solution is a linear combination of the two exponential functions, $e^{\rho t}$ and $t \cdot e^{\rho t}$.

12. Compare, for example, R. G. D. Allen, *Mathematical Economics*, London, Macmillan, 1960, chapter 5.

13. That is to say,

$$B_1 + B_2 = Y(0) - A/(1 - c)$$
$$\rho_1 B_1 + \rho_2 B_2 = -\{(1 - c)(\lambda + \mu) - ch\lambda\mu\}\{(Y(0) - A/(1 - c)\} - \lambda\mu\{S(0) - hA/(1 - c)\}$$
$$C_1 + C_2 = S(0) - hA/(1 - c)$$

and $\quad \rho_1 C_1 + \rho_2 C_2 = \{1 - c\}\{Y(0) - A/(1 - c)\}$

where $Y(0)$ and $S(0)$ are the initial output and inventory levels, respectively, and where (by assumption) $DA = 0$ and $\rho_1 \neq \rho_2$.

numbers if $4(1 - c)\lambda\mu \leq \{(1 - c)(\lambda + \mu) - ch\lambda\mu\}^2$ or (ii) conjugate complex numbers with *negative* real parts if $4(1 - c)\lambda\mu > \{(1 - c)(\lambda + \mu) - ch\lambda\mu\}^2$. If (i) is the case, the motion towards equilibrium is *direct*, while if (ii) is the case the motion towards equilibrium follows a damped oscillatory path. This latter path is illustrated in Fig. 1C-1 as the counter-clockwise inwards spiral. In the *unstable* case, with $(1 - c)(\lambda + \mu) - ch\lambda\mu < 0$, the system moves away from equilibrium since the characteristic roots, ρ_1 and ρ_2, are either (iii) real *positive* numbers if $4(1 - c)\lambda\mu \leq \{(1 - c)(\lambda + \mu) - ch\lambda\mu\}^2$ or (iv) conjugate complex numbers with *positive* real parts if $4(1 - c)\lambda\mu > \{(1 - c)(\lambda + \mu) - ch\lambda\mu\}^2$. If (iii) is the case, the motion away from equilibrium is *direct*, while if (iv) is the case, the motion away from equilibrium follows an explosive oscillatory path. This latter path would be illustrated in a phase diagram by a counter-clockwise outwards spiral. Finally, in the borderline case, where $(1 - c)(\lambda + \mu) - ch\lambda\mu = 0$, and the two characteristic roots have no real parts, the oscillations neither damp out nor explode through time, but since equilibrium is unattained this case of regular oscillations is also said to be unstable.

Why must oscillations occur when the characteristic roots are conjugate complex numbers? Putting the non-oscillatory cases on one side, for the remaining oscillatory cases the conjugate complex roots may be written as $\rho_1, \rho_2 = \alpha \pm i\omega$, where $\alpha = -\frac{1}{2}\{(1 - c)(\lambda + \mu) - ch\lambda\mu\}$, $\omega = \frac{1}{2}\sqrt{[4(1 - c)\lambda\mu - \{(1 - c)(\lambda + \mu) - ch\lambda\mu\}^2]}$, and i is the imaginary unit. It is then not difficult to show that the solution (1D-4) may be written in the form:

$$Y(t) = A/(1 - c) + B e^{\alpha t} \cos(\omega t - \varepsilon)$$

and

$$S(t) = hA/(1 - c) + C e^{\alpha t} \cos(\omega t - \eta)$$

(1D-5)

where B, C, ε, and η are arbitrary constants that depend upon the initial conditions.[14] In expression (1D-5), the sinusoidal function $B e^{\alpha t} \cos(\omega t - \varepsilon)$ represents damped, regular or explosive oscillations over time in the symmetrical (cosine) form. Its features are indicated by the four parameters, α, ω, B, and ε. Of these four parameters, α and ω depend upon the underlying structural parameters of the model via the two characteristic roots, whereas B and ε depend upon the initial conditions. The parameter α is the damping factor indicating damped oscillations when $\alpha = -\frac{1}{2}\{(1 - c)(\lambda + \mu) - ch\lambda\mu\} < 0$, regular oscillations

14. $Y(t) - A/(1 - c) = B_1 e^{(\alpha + i\omega)t} + B_2 e^{(\alpha - i\omega)t}$

$$= B_1 e^{\alpha t}(\cos \omega t + i \sin \omega t) + B_2 e^{\alpha t}(\cos \omega t - i \sin \omega t)$$

$$= (B_1 + B_2) e^{\alpha t} \cos \omega t + (B_1 - B_2)i e^{\alpha t} \sin \omega t$$

Now let $B_1 + B_2 = B \cos \varepsilon$ and $(B_1 - B_2)i = B \sin \varepsilon$. Thus, one has

$$Y(t) - A/(1 - c) = B e^{\alpha t} \cos \omega t \cos \varepsilon + B e^{\alpha t} \sin \omega t \sin \varepsilon$$

$$= B e^{\alpha t} \cos(\omega t - \varepsilon)$$

as is given in (1D-5) in the text above. A similar treatment is possible for

$$S(t) - hA/(1 - c) = C_1 e^{\rho_1 t} + C_2 e^{\rho_2 t}$$

when $\alpha = 0$, and explosive oscillations when $\alpha > 0$. The parameter ω is the frequency parameter giving a frequency of oscillations equal to $\omega/2\pi$ and a period equal to $2\pi/\omega$. The parameter B measures the initial amplitude of the oscillations, whereas the parameter ε represents the phase angle of the oscillations and implies that peaks occur at multiples of time $t = \varepsilon/\omega$. A similar treatment is possible for $C\, e^{\alpha t} \cos(\omega t - \eta)$.

It follows from this analysis that the relations of a linear model are such that any oscillatory variation of sinusoidal form runs through the model with unchanging and identical period and damping factor for all of the endogenous variables in the model, though the initial amplitude and phase angle may differ between variables. Despite its mathematical convenience, however, the linearity of the model gives rise to at least three problems of economic interpretation. Discussion of these three problems is postponed until chapter 4.

Which of these various cases and associated motions will occur depends upon the configuration of parameters: the marginal propensity to consume (c), the desired inventory–sales ratio (h), the response proportion or "speed of response" of the stock adjustment mechanism (μ), and the response proportion or "speed of response" of the expectation-adjustment mechanism (λ). Since the marginal propensity to consume is a flow–flow ratio its size is independent of the time unit chosen. However, the sizes of the other three parameters are not. The desired inventory–sales ratio is a stock–flow ratio. Its size diminishes as the time unit chosen is lengthened. For example, a stock–flow ratio of 2.0 with quarterly time units is a stock–flow ratio of 0.5 with annual time units. On the other hand, both "speed of response" parameters expand as the time unit chosen lengthens. That is to say, the proportion of the discrepancy between desired and actual stocks that is worked off in a unit time period increases as the length of the unit period is increased. Similarly, the degree to which expected sales adjust towards actual sales in a unit time period increases as the length of the unit period is increased. Because of this, we are *free to choose* the unit time period in such a way that *one* of h, μ, or λ is unity. The choice made here is that h is unity. Thus, the unit period is defined to be that length of time which makes the desired inventory–sales ratio precisely one. Given the marginal propensity to consume, the course of the system depends upon the sizes of μ and λ *when measured* in these time units.

Generally speaking, the smaller are the speed of response parameters and the marginal propensity to consume, the more likely it is that the system will be stable. The reasons for this are as follows. Let us assume that the system is initially in equilibrium and experiences a sudden, once and for all, movement in autonomous expenditure to a new higher level. In terms of the phase diagram, Fig. 1C-1, the system finds itself in phase (d). The immediate impact is an increase in total expenditure or sales (E) and an unplanned fall in the level of inventories ($DS = Y - E < 0$). Taken by itself, this unplanned fall in the level of inventories would lead to an increase in output in the ensuing period. In addition, however, the increase in sales leads to an increase in both expected sales and desired inventories, which together lead to an even larger increase in output in the ensuing period. The size of the total increase in output in response to the given initial increase in autonomous expenditure depends upon the response proportion of the expectation adjustment mechanism (λ) and the response proportion of the stock-adjustment mechanism (μ). The smaller is λ, the smaller will be the increase in expected sales, and thus in desired inventories. The smaller is μ the smaller will be the increase in output generated by these increases *and* by the fall in actual stocks. Thus, the output repercussions of a given change in A will be smaller, the smaller are λ and μ.[15]

This is not, however, the end of the story, for these output (and income) repercussions change the level of consumption expenditures, and hence total expenditures, via the marginal propensity to consume (c). The smaller is c, and, hence, the smaller is the multiplier, the smaller will these resulting changes in expenditure be. There is, therefore, a positive feedback from total expenditure changes to further total expenditure changes. This positive feedback is represented by the term $ch\lambda\mu$. However, there are also leakages from the circular flow of income (output) and expenditure in the form of savings. These leakages exert a dampening influence on this process, which is represented by the negative feedback term $(1 - c)(\lambda + \mu)$. If this dampening influence is powerful enough, that is, if $(1 - c)(\lambda + \mu) > ch\lambda\mu$, the system will be stable. On the other hand, if this dampening influence is weak, the system will be unstable.

It follows from the previous argument that if the responsiveness of planned inventory investment to stock disequilibrium is rather slow and if, in addition, the responsiveness of expected sales to flow disequilibrium is also rather slow, the inventory cycle will be stable.[16] Unless it is disturbed by "random shocks" in the level of autonomous expenditure, the system will follow a damped cyclical oscillation as illustrated by the counter-clockwise inwards spiral in Fig. 1C-1. Equilibrium will eventually be reached, but the process of attaining equilibrium will not, in general, be a direct one; on the contrary, it will normally exhibit cyclical fluctuations in the levels of output and inventories. These fluctuations are characterized by an inherent tendency for output movements to appear to lead inventory movements by one cyclical phase. Peaks and troughs in the level of output precede peaks and troughs in the level of inventories. Finally, the

---

15. Indeed, if $\mu = 0$, then Y may be taken as equivalent to E^*. In this case, the system reduces to the simple multiplier model, $E = cY + A$ and $DY = \lambda(E - Y)$ with solution $Y(t) = A/(1 - c) + \{Y(0) - A/(1 - c)\} e^{-(1 - c)\lambda t}$. The process implied by this equation is obviously stable; moreover, $Y(t)$ converges on its equilibrium value, $A/(1 - c)$, in a direct manner. It follows that the accelerator mechanism, or the attempt by producers to adjust stocks to a desired level that depends upon expected sales, is ultimately responsible for both cyclical behavior and potential instability.

16. If the stable case prevails, the more similar are the two speeds of response, λ and μ, the less likely will a non-oscillatory solution be. Indeed, this stable non-oscillatory case (in which the movement towards equilibrium is direct) is impossible if $\lambda = \mu$. Moreover, if the unstable case prevails, very high values of the marginal propensity to consume and the speed of response parameters would be necessary to generate a non-oscillatory solution. Thus, it may be argued that oscillations will normally occur in the model, though these oscillations may be damped (the stable case discussed in the text) or explosive (the unstable case).

equilibrium of the complete system requires both *flow equilibrium* (expected sales = actual sales) and *stock equilibrium* (desired stocks = actual stocks).

E: AN INTRODUCTION TO STABILIZATION POLICY

The previous sections of this chapter explored a simple stock adjustment model. This model portrayed an inventory cycle in which the levels of output and inventories oscillated around their equilibrium levels. Building on this basic stock adjustment model, the present section discusses the question how government expenditure policies might be used to stabilize such a model economy. There are two aspects to this stabilization policy. First, how can government expenditure policies be used to move the equilibrium levels of output and inventories to some desired *target* levels. Second, how can government expenditure policies be used to reduce or remove the cyclical momentum in such an economy around its equilibrium position. Stabilization policy therefore entails that the actual levels of output and inventories be made to converge on their target levels with a minimum amount of cyclical fluctuation.

If government expenditure is added to the basic stock adjustment model of the previous section, the level of national expenditure must be redefined to be

$$E = cY + A + G \qquad (1\text{E-}1)$$

where G is the level of government expenditure.[17] Since all the other elements in the model remain unchanged, the complete model may now be written as

$$DY = -\{(1-c)(\lambda+\mu) - ch\lambda\mu\}\{Y - (A+G)/(1-c)\} - \lambda\mu\{S - h(A+G)/(1-c)\}$$

and $\qquad (1\text{E-}2)$

$$DS = \{1-c\}\{Y - (A+G)/(1-c)\}$$

which directly parallels expression (1B-5). The only difference between Eqs. (1E-2) and (1B-5) is that A has been replaced by $A + G$.

Let it now be assumed that, prior to time $t = 0$, the economy is in equilibrium at the *target* level of national output or income. By convention, this target level may be defined to be the position $Y = 0$, with $A = 0$ and $G = 0$. Now let it be assumed that, at time $t = 0$, the level of autonomous expenditure shifts to some level $A \neq 0$. This shift changes the equilibrium level of national income to $Y = A/(1 - c)$, which is no longer equal to the target level of national income $Y = 0$. It also sets in motion an inventory cycle around the level $Y = A/(1 - c)$, a cycle which may be either damped or explosive depending upon the actual configuration of parameters, c, h, λ, and μ. The question for government expenditure policy is then whether G can be varied in such a way as to remove the

---

17. Taxation is ignored in this section, though it may be thought of as a negative component of G which could then be redefined as the government deficit.

discrepancy between $Y = A/(1 - c)$ and the target level $Y = 0$, *and* to reduce the amplitude of cyclical fluctuations so that rapid convergence to $Y = 0$ occurs.

Three possible forms for government expenditure policy (or the level of official demand) may now be considered. These three forms are (a) proportional stabilization policy, (b) integral stabilization policy, and (c) derivative stabilization policy.[18] Proportional stabilization policy implies that government expenditure is proportional to *the current shortfall or deficiency* in national output or income below its target level. Since by convention the target level is zero, such a policy may be denoted by $g_p(0 - Y) = -g_p Y$, where g_p is the proportion of the current shortfall (which may be positive or negative) that the government intends to fill. Integral stabilization policy implies that government expenditure is proportional to *the accumulated shortfall or deficiency* in national output or income below its target level over time. Since the target level at all points of time is zero, such a policy may be denoted by $-g_i \int_0^t Y(\tau)\, d\tau$, where g_i is the proportion of the accumulated shortfall that the government intends to fill. Derivative stabilization policy implies that government expenditure is proportional to *the change in the shortfall or deficiency* in national output or income below its target level at a given point of time. Such a policy may be denoted by $-g_d D Y$, where g_d is the proportion of the change in the shortfall that the government intends to fill.

Whichever form or combination of forms that government expenditure takes, it is reasonable to assume that there exists a lag before it can be expected to affect the level of national expenditure or aggregate demand. There are several reasons for the existence of such a lag. First, there is a recognition lag; it takes time for the government to become aware that national income is failing to attain its target level. Second, there is an implementation lag; it takes time from the moment of recognition for the appropriate expenditure policies to be designed and put in place. Third, there is an effectiveness lag; it takes time from the design of appropriate expenditure policies for these policies to have their effect on the level of national expenditure. Treating these three lags as a single exponential lag with speed of response $\gamma > 0$, the equation for total government expenditure, G, becomes in the general case

$$(D + \gamma)G = -\gamma \left\{ g_p Y + g_i \int_0^t Y(\tau)\, d\tau + g_d D Y \right\} \tag{1E-3}$$

which implies that G is continuously being adjusted towards the level

$$-\left(g_p Y + g_i \int_0^t Y(\tau)\, d\tau + g_d D Y \right)$$

18. The analysis here follows that of A. W. Phillips, "Stabilisation Policy in a Closed Economy," *Economic Journal,* vol. 64, June 1954, pp. 290–323, and R. G. D. Allen, *Macro-Economic Theory,* London, Macmillan, 1967, chapter 18. However, the basic stock adjustment model into which these three possible policy responses are inserted differs from that considered in these sources. The main difference is that the linear multiplier–accelerator model employed herein incorporates circulating capital and inventory adjustments rather than fixed capital and plant-size adjustments.

If expression (1E-3) were combined with expression (1E-2) in such a way as to eliminate S and G, one would discover that the resulting equation contains terms in D^3Y, D^2Y, DY, Y, and $\int_0^t Y(\tau)\,d\tau$. Explicitly, this equation has the form

$$k_4 D^3 Y + k_3 D^2 Y + k_2 DY + k_1 Y + k_0 \int_0^t Y(\tau)\,d\tau = z \qquad (1E\text{-}4)$$

where $\quad k_4 = 1$

$$k_3 = \gamma + \{(1 - c)(\lambda + \mu) - ch\lambda\mu\} + \gamma g_d(\lambda + \mu + \lambda\mu h)$$

$$k_2 = \gamma\{(1 - c)(\lambda + \mu) - ch\lambda\mu\} + \lambda\mu(1 - c) + \gamma g_p(\lambda + \mu + \lambda\mu h) + \gamma g_d \lambda\mu$$

$$k_1 = \gamma\lambda\mu(1 - c) + \gamma g_i(\lambda + \mu + \lambda\mu h) + \gamma g_p \lambda\mu$$

$$k_0 = \gamma g_i \lambda\mu$$

and $\quad z = \{\lambda + \mu + \lambda\mu h\}\{D + \gamma\}DA + \lambda\mu(D + \gamma)A$

or $\lambda\mu\gamma A$ for A constant. Allowing for the integral, such an equation is a fourth order differential equation in Y. The coefficients of this equation are complicated functions of the underlying structural parameters of the model, c, h, λ, μ, γ, g_p, g_i, and g_d. Although a detailed analysis of this equation is difficult to pursue, in broad outline the behavior of the level of national income over time may be readily summarized.

It is useful to begin the summary on the assumption that only proportional stabilization policy is applied. In this case, $g_i = g_d = 0$, and the system reduces to a third order differential equation in Y since the integral $\int_0^t Y(\tau)\,d\tau$ disappears. The first thing to be noticed about this reduced system is that it has a stationary equilibrium solution at the position,

$$Y = A/(1 - c + g_p), \quad S = hA/(1 - c + g_p), \quad \text{and} \quad G = -g_p Y \qquad (1E\text{-}5)$$

This equilibrium solution is obtained by setting $DY = DS = DG = 0$ in expressions (1E-2) and (1E-3), given $g_i = g_d = 0$. It is immediately obvious that the solution for Y lies between the original equilibrium level without government expenditure, $Y = A/(1 - c)$, and the target level, $Y = 0$. Proportional stabilization policy only succeeds in moving the equilibrium level of national income part of the way towards the target level. Only partial or incomplete correction is obtained. This conclusion is, of course, also true for all non-discretionary "built-in stabilizers" of the taxation or transfer payment variety which are dependent upon the *level* of national income. It gives rise to the need for discretionary stabilization policies, which will be discussed in later sections of this book.

Not only does the use of proportional stabilization policy by itself fail to achieve complete correction of the equilibrium level of national income, but also it may not succeed in reducing the amplitude of oscillations in the system. For both these reasons, proportional stabilization policy should be coupled with other forms of stabilization policy. In particular, integral stabilization policy is required in order to obtain complete correction of the level of national income, while derivative stabilization policy is required in order to ensure that the amplitude of oscillations damps towards zero rapidly.

When integral stabilization policy is added to proportional stabilization policy, the equilibrium level of national income becomes $Y = 0$, the target level, so that complete correction can be obtained. The mathematical reason for this is that, on differentiating Eq. (1E-4) in D^3Y, D^2Y, DY, Y, and $\int_0^t Y(\tau)\,d\tau$ to remove the integral, there remains no constant term (as long as A is taken to be given). The equation becomes homogeneous in the dependent variable, Y, with stationary solution $Y = 0$. The intuitive reason is that the value of the integral, $\int_0^t Y(\tau)\,d\tau$, must be continuously changing through time as long as Y is not equal to zero, and from Eq. (1E-3) it is evident that this will lead to continuous changes in the level of government expenditure, G. Thus, in order to prevent integral stabilization policy from generating perpetual changes in G, the gap between the equilibrium level and the target level of national income must be zero continuously. Moreover, in stationary equilibrium, it is evident that the value of G must be equal to $-A$, so that $A + G = 0$. Of course, if this stationary solution is unstable, it will not be attained as time passes.

Since integral stabilization policy increases the order of the differential equation, it also increases the likelihood of oscillations. Indeed, a strong enough integral stabilization policy can change a situation of damped oscillations into a situation of explosive oscillations. That is to say, "A mixed proportional and integral stabilization policy, applied to a multiplier-accelerator system after an initial fall in demand, succeeds in correcting fully for the deficiency in demand but at the cost of increased oscillation."[19] It is for this reason that derivative stabilization policy is required, to offset the possible explosive tendencies inherent either in the initial unregulated system or in the system with proportional and integral policies. For derivative stabilization policy always takes the form $-g_d DY$, and therefore acts to reduce the speed of motion of the system. Such a reduction lessens the tendency of the system to "overshoot" the target level of national income by diminishing the amplitude of oscillations.

It should be evident from the foregoing discussion that the economic regulation of even the simplest economy is by no means an easy task. Even the stabilization of an economy whose unregulated behavior is describable by a second order differential equation, and for which changes in autonomous expenditure take the form of simple shifts, requires the appropriate coordination of proportional, integral, and derivative stabilization policies. That is to say, stabilization policy requires, *first*, a recognition not only of (a) where the economy is now in relation to targets, but also (b) where the economy has been in relation to targets over a considerable period of time, and (c) how fast the economy is now moving in relation to targets, and, *second*, the implementation of a coordinated set of policy responses in the light of such recognition. For a complex economy with several targets and several possible instruments, and with more complicated time forms for its lagged responses, this becomes an exceedingly difficult task.

19. Allen, *Macro-Economic Theory*, p. 361.

TWO

THE RATE OF INTEREST AND
REAL STOCK ADJUSTMENTS

A : THE RATE OF INTEREST

So far, our discussion of stabilization policy has concentrated on the regulation of inventory cycles with government expenditure policies. No consideration has been given to the role of cycles in fixed capital investment in the complete cyclical process. Nor has any mention been made of the use of monetary policy and interest rates for regulatory purposes. In order to expand the model discussed so far to allow for fixed capital investment, one may redefine S^* and S to be the desired and actual stocks of short term investment goods, respectively, where these goods now include capital equipment of fairly short economic life, such as machinery, as well as inventories of various forms. Short term investment goods are therefore to be distinguished from long term investment goods, or capital assets of long economic life, such as buildings, roads, etc.

Anyone who finds this distinction unpalatable is at liberty to continue thinking of S^* and S as desired and actual inventories, thus keeping the distinction between fixed and circulating capital goods reasonably pure. Indeed, as will be seen, the analysis of prices in a Keynesian cumulative process in chapter 11 maintains the traditional distinction between fixed and circulating capital. For present purposes, however, one is more concerned with drawing a distinction between accelerator induced investment and autonomous investment than between investment in circulating and fixed capital. In any case, chapter 4 presents a more traditional analysis of fixed capital investment in linear and non-linear multiplier–accelerator models of the trade cycle.

Keeping this distinction in mind, let the desired stock of capital goods of short economic life, S^*, be a function of the expected level of sales, E^*, and the rate of interest, r. Let this function be written as

$$S^* = H(E^*, r) \quad \text{with} \quad H_{E^*} > 0 \quad \text{and} \quad H_r < 0 \qquad (2A\text{-}1)$$

where H_{E^*} and H_r are the partial derivatives of the H-function with respect to E^* and r, respectively. Thus, one has generalized the simple linear relationship, $S^* = hE^*$, of Eq. (1B-1), to a non-linear function with S^* depending positively on E^* and negatively on the rate of interest, r. As expected sales increase, so does the desired capital stock, given the rate of interest. As the rate of interest increases, the desired capital stock decreases for any given level of expected sales. The reason for this is that the present discounted value of the future stream of earnings generated by capital assets over their life decreases as the discount rate (or rate of interest) is increased. Alternatively, the rate of interest is an important element in the carrying cost of inventory stocks and capital assets in general; as it increases, desired stocks fall.[1]

Given the *capital stock adjustment principle* (or "flexible accelerator") relating planned investment to discrepancies between the desired and actual stocks of capital goods of short economic life, it is now clear that planned investment expenditure on these goods becomes a positive function of E^*, the expected level of sales, and a negative function of both S, the actual capital stock, and r, the rate of interest. This function may be written as

$$Y - E^* = \mu\{H(E^*, r) - S\} \tag{2A-2}$$

which is a generalization of the simple linear relationship $Y - E^* = \mu\{hE^* - S\}$ implicit in expression (1B-2). As before, one also has the relationships

$$E^* = (D + \lambda)^{-1}\lambda E, \quad DS = Y - E \quad \text{and} \quad E = cY + A(r, a) + G \tag{2A-3}$$

where autonomous expenditure, A, has been generalized to the function $A(r, a)$ to reflect the fact that A includes a component of investment expenditure on capital assets of long economic life. This long term investment expenditure is taken to depend negatively on the rate of interest, r, and positively on a shift parameter, a, reflecting the state of long term expectations. It follows that $A_r < 0$ and $A_a > 0$, where A_r and A_a are the partial derivatives of $A(r, a)$ with respect to r and a, respectively. It is generally to be assumed, however, that the elasticity

---

1. In neo-classical investment theory, the desired capital stock is given by

$$S^* = (\alpha\pi/q)^\sigma E^*$$

where $0 < \alpha < 1$ is the distribution parameter attached to capital inputs in the production function, $\sigma > 0$ is the elasticity of substitution of the production function, π is the product price, and q is the user cost of capital or implicit rental price of capital services supplied by the firm to itself. If taxation is ignored,

$$q = p(\delta + r - p^{-1}\,dp^e/dt)$$

where p is the price of capital goods, $p^{-1}\,dp^e/dt$ is the expected proportional capital gain in holding these goods, δ is the depreciation coefficient, and r is the rate of interest. Taxation of the return to capital complicates the formula for q, but does not alter the fact that q depends directly on r and, therefore, that S^* is inversely related to r. On these points, compare for example D. W. Jorgenson and J. A. Stephenson, "Investment Behaviour in U.S. Manufacturing, 1947–1960," *Econometrica*, vol. 35, April 1967, pp. 169–220.

of investment expenditure on long term capital assets with respect to the rate of interest is considerably greater than the corresponding elasticity for investment expenditure on short term capital assets. Notice that, as before, national output or income, Y, will exceed national expenditure (or absorption), E, by the amount of output retained within the "business sector" in the form of net accumulation of short term capital assets. Although this is not a customary convention, it is useful for our present purposes.

Since an additional variable, the rate of interest, has now been added to the model, it is necessary to explain how this variable is determined. In order to do so, one must consider the demand and supply of money. In traditional post-Keynesian monetary theory, it is usual to answer the question "Why do people hold money?" by suggesting that there are three basic reasons or "motives" for individual decision making units to hold money, namely (a) a transactions motive, (b) a precautionary motive, and (c) a speculative motive. The first of these "motives" arises from the non-synchronous nature of an individual's receipts and payments, when coupled with the existence of transactions costs. This transactions motive demand for money is related to two of the basic functions of money, namely as a means of payment and as a standard of value. The second of these "motives" arises from the desire to maintain sufficient liquidity to avoid financial embarrassment in the event of unforeseen and unavoidable expenditures occurring. This pre-cautionary demand for money is related to the third basic function of money, namely as a store of value, though contingency reserves would not be held in this form were it not for the fact that money also functions as a means of payment. The third of the "motives" for holding money arises if there is sufficient risk aversion in the face of uncertainty about the future value (or yield) of alternative assets. This speculative demand for money is also a demand for money as a store of value, though it is unlikely that money would be held in this manner in conditions in which it is not a reliable standard of value. Indeed, the basic theory of liquidity preference is itself dependent upon the stability of the expected rates of return on alternative investment portfolios, and this is only likely if money prices remain reasonably stable.[2]

In accordance with post-Keynesian monetary theory, the demand for money may be taken to be a positive function of the expected level of sales, E^*, a negative function of the rate of interest, r, and a negative function of the shift parameter, a, reflecting the state of long term expectations with respect to the prospective yield on long term investment goods. As the expected level of sales (or the expected level of national expenditure) increases so does the volume of money required to facilitate this expected level of expenditure, given the rate of interest and the state of long term expectations. As the rate of interest increases, the demand for money decreases for a given level of expected sales and state of

2. On the points raised in this paragraph, compare J. R. Hicks, *Critical Essays in Monetary Theory*, Oxford, Oxford University Press, 1967, Chapters 1–3. The impact of inflation on the demand for money and for alternative capital assets is discussed at length in Chapter 10, Section C, of this book.

long term expectations. The reason for this is that the higher the rate of return on interest bearing assets such as bonds the more attractive they become to hold in comparison with non-interest bearing money. Alternatively, higher rates of interest reduce a person's preference for liquidity or money. Finally, given E^* and r, an optimistic shift in the state of long term expectations (an increase in a) not only augments the volume of long term investment expenditure, it also reduces the degree of liquidity preference, or the demand for money. On the other hand, a pessimistic shift in the state of long term expectations (a decrease in a) not only reduces the volume of long term investment expenditure, it also augments the degree of liquidity preference, or the demand for money. Letting L represent the demand for money, one may write the money demand function as

$$L = L(E^*, r, a) \quad \text{with} \quad L_{E^*} > 0, \quad L_r < 0 \quad \text{and} \quad L_a < 0 \qquad (2A\text{-}4)$$

where L_{E^*}, L_r, and L_a are the partial derivatives of the L-function with respect to E^*, r, and a, respectively.[3] It is to be noted that this expression is similar to Eq. (2A-1), $S^* = H(E^*, r)$, which determined the desired stock of capital assets of short economic life. However, it also includes the shift parameter, a, which also affects the volume of investment expenditure on capital assets of long economic life, $A(r, a)$.

On the supply side, it is assumed that the supply of money, M, is under the control of the monetary authorities.[4] Supply of money, M, is, therefore, taken to be an exogenous policy parameter. Given M and L, the rate of interest, r, is assumed to adjust in such a way as to bring M and L into equality with each other. This adjustment may well take time. One may, therefore, write

$$Dr = v\{L(E^*, r, a) - M\} \qquad (2A\text{-}5)$$

where $v > 0$ is the speed of response of the adjustment mechanism. Thus, the rate of interest rises whenever there is excess demand for money ($L > M$), and falls whenever there is excess supply ($L < M$).

The complete set of equations before any consideration is given to governmental stabilization policies affecting either or both of G and M is given by Eqs. (2A-2), (2A-3), and (2A-5). Given a, G, and M, therefore, there are five simultaneous equations in the five endogenous variables, Y, E, E^*, S, and r. These equations contain three non-linear elements in the form of the functions, $H(E^*, r)$, $A(r, a)$, and $L(E^*, r, a)$. Of these equations, two do not include the differential operator, D, while the other three include D taken in each case to the first power. The system may therefore be reduced to a third order differential equation system in one of the variables.

Rather than proceed with this reduction in a direct way, we shall analyze

---

3. The fix price mode of analysis does not require one to distinguish the demand for nominal money balances from the demand for real balances. This distinction will, however, become crucial in Part Three of this book, and especially in chapters 10 and 13.

4. This assumption is relaxed in later sections of this book.

the system in the following sections under certain simplifying assumptions. Three points should, however, be noted here. First, given a, G, and M, the system of equations generates a unique stationary equilibrium solution (when all the D's are zero) as follows:

$$\bar{E}^* = \bar{E}, \quad \bar{S} = H(\bar{E}, \bar{r}), \quad L(\bar{E}, \bar{r}, a) = M$$

and

$$\bar{E} = \bar{Y} = \{A(\bar{r}, a) + G\}/(1 - c) \qquad (2A\text{-}6)$$

where a bar over a variable is used to denote the equilibrium value of that variable. Second, the system of equations may be linearized around its stationary equilibrium solution. Letting $Y(t) = \bar{Y} + \hat{Y}\,e^{\rho t}$, $E(t) = \bar{E} + \hat{E}\,e^{\rho t}$, and similarly for the other variables, where $\hat{Y}$ and $\hat{E}$ are arbitrary constants which depend upon the initial conditions, one may write the five basic simultaneous equations as

(a) $\quad \bar{Y} + \hat{Y}\,e^{\rho t} - \bar{E}^* - \hat{E}^*\,e^{\rho t} = \mu\{H(\bar{E}^* + \hat{E}^*\,e^{\rho t}, \bar{r} + \hat{r}\,e^{\rho t}) - \bar{S} - \hat{S}\,e^{\rho t}\}$

(b) $\quad \bar{E} + \hat{E}\,e^{\rho t} = c(\bar{Y} + \hat{Y}\,e^{\rho t}) + A(\bar{r} + \hat{r}\,e^{\rho t}, a) + G$

(c) $\quad \rho\hat{E}^*\,e^{\rho t} = \lambda(\bar{E} + \hat{E}\,e^{\rho t} - \bar{E}^* - \hat{E}^*\,e^{\rho t})$

(d) $\quad \rho\hat{S}\,e^{\rho t} = \bar{Y} + \hat{Y}\,e^{\rho t} - \bar{E} - \hat{E}\,e^{\rho t}$

and

(e) $\quad \rho\hat{r}\,e^{\rho t} = v\{L(\bar{E}^* + \hat{E}^*\,e^{\rho t}, \bar{r} + \hat{r}\,e^{\rho t}, a) - M\} \qquad (2A\text{-}7)$

The linearization procedure implies the following approximation (for example)

$$L(\bar{E}^* + \hat{E}^*\,e^{\rho t}, \bar{r} + \hat{r}\,e^{\rho t}, a) = L(\bar{E}^*, \bar{r}, a) + L_{E^*}\hat{E}^*\,e^{\rho t} + L_r\hat{r}\,e^{\rho t} \qquad (2A\text{-}8)$$

Given (i) the use of this form of approximation for all three of the non-linear expressions in the equation system (2A-7), (ii) the definition of the equilibrium solution, and (iii) the fact that $e^{\rho t} \neq 0$ may be cancelled from the equations, the five equations imply the matrix expression:

$$\begin{bmatrix} +1 & 0 & -(1 + \mu H_{E^*}) & +\mu & -\mu H_r \\ -c & +1 & 0 & 0 & -A_r \\ 0 & -\lambda & \rho + \lambda & 0 & 0 \\ -1 & +1 & 0 & \rho & 0 \\ 0 & 0 & -vL_{E^*} & 0 & \rho - vL_r \end{bmatrix} \begin{bmatrix} \hat{Y} \\ \hat{E} \\ \hat{E}^* \\ \hat{S} \\ \hat{r} \end{bmatrix} = \begin{bmatrix} 0 \\ 0 \\ 0 \\ 0 \\ 0 \end{bmatrix} \qquad (2A\text{-}9)$$

Setting the determinant of the 5×5 matrix equal to zero yields the cubic characteristic equation

$$\rho^3 + [(1 - c)(\lambda + \mu) - cH_{E^*}\lambda\mu - vL_r]\rho^2$$

$$+ [(1 - c)\lambda\mu - \{(1 - c)(\lambda + \mu) - cH_{E^*}\lambda\mu\}vL_r - (A_r + cH_r\mu)\lambda vL_{E^*}]\rho$$

$$- [\lambda\mu v\{(1 - c)L_r + A_r L_{E^*}\}] = 0 \qquad (2A\text{-}10)$$

where the partial derivatives H_{E^*}, H_r, L_{E^*}, L_r, and A_r are all evaluated at the stationary equilibrium solution ($\bar{Y}$, $\bar{E}$, $\bar{E}^*$, $\bar{S}$, and $\bar{r}$).

Third, the dynamic behavior of the system in the neighborhood of equilibrium depends upon the solution values (or characteristic roots) to the cubic characteristic Eq. (2A-10). In particular, the system will be locally stable if and only if all the characteristic roots have negative real parts. Local stability, however, does not imply that the stationary equilibrium solution is eventually reached from all meaningful initial positions, only those within a small neighborhood of the equilibrium solution. Local stability does not imply global stability. In addition, it is not generally possible to infer the global behavior of a non-linear system of differential equations from the characteristic roots the Jacobian matrix of the linearized system unless some sort of regularity condition holds.[5] Such a regularity condition might well include the assumption that the Jacobian determinant of the system be strictly one-signed everywhere, an assumption satisfied by the majority of the non-linear dynamic models discussed in this book. As a result of this mathematical problem, however, when the disequilibrium motions of non-linear dynamic models are discussed in this book, the discussion is, in general, only strictly valid for motions in the neighborhood or locality of the equilibrium solution.

B: THE HICKS–HANSEN PROTOTYPE

In order to proceed with the qualitative analysis of the system outlined in the previous section and with the incorporation of stabilization policy into this framework, it is useful to consider three simplified prototypes. The first of these is obtained by assuming that the rate of interest does not change. This case may occur either (a) in the very unlikely event that the speed of response of the interest rate adjustment mechanism is very small relative to the other speeds of response in the model, so that $v \to 0$, or (b) in the event that the money supply is always instantaneously adapted to the demand for money that is forthcoming at a particular target interest rate. In either event, the rate of interest may be taken to be an exogenous variable, and the system collapses to the second order stock adjustment model of Secs. B, C, and D of the previous chapter. The only change is that the partial derivative H_{E^*} replaces the simple coefficient h. Thus, the first prototype is simply the *inventory cycle* model that has already been fully discussed.

The second prototype is obtained by assuming that the speed of response of the stock adjustment mechanism is very small relative to the other speeds of response in the model, so that $\mu \to 0$ and Y and E^* may be taken to be identical because of Eq. (2A-2). That is to say, if there is no planned inventory accumulation,

---

5. For more detail, see for example K. Ogata, *State Space Analysis of Control Systems*, Englewood Cliffs, Prentice-Hall, 1967, chapter 8, pp. 437–526.

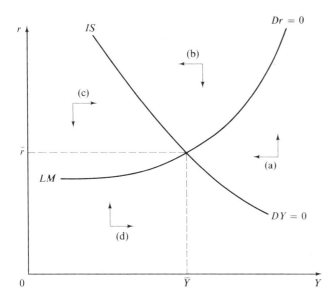

Figure 2B-1 Phase diagram for the *IS–LM* prototype.

output and expected sales will be equal. In this case, the system collapses to

$$DY = \lambda(E - Y), \quad E = cY + A(r,a) + G, \quad \text{and} \quad Dr = v\{L(Y,r,a) - M\} \quad \text{(2B-1)}$$

with quadratic characteristic equation[6]

$$\rho^2 + \{\lambda(1 - c) - vL_r\}\rho - \lambda v\{(1 - c)L_r + L_Y A_r\} = 0 \quad \text{(2B-2)}$$

where the partial derivatives are again evaluated in the neighborhood of the stationary equilibrium solution, in this case $\bar{E} = \bar{Y} = \{A(\bar{r},a) + G\}/(1 - c)$ and $L(\bar{Y},\bar{r},a) = M$. This prototype may readily be recognized as a dynamic version of the *Hicks–Hansen IS–LM* model.[7]

Figure 2B-1 presents the phase diagram for this *IS–LM* prototype. In this diagram, the level of national income, Y, is measured on the horizontal axis while the rate of interest, r, is measured on the vertical axis. The equilibrium levels of national income and the rate of interest are given as the coordinates, $\bar{Y}$ and $\bar{r}$, respectively. The downward sloping line or singular curve labelled $DY = 0$ is the familiar investment–savings equilibrium locus, or *IS* curve, representing all combinations of the level of national income and the rate of interest at which

---

6. This equation may be derived either by linearizing the reduced system around its stationary equilibrium point or, equivalently, by setting $\mu = 0$ in Eq. (2A-10), and discarding the zero root.

7. Since production is set equal to expected sales without reference to the existing level of inventory stocks, the dynamic processes of the Hicks–Hansen *IS–LM* model must be based on the assumption that the system never runs out of stocks.

the commodity market is in *flow equilibrium* in the sense that expected sales $(E^* = Y)$ are equal to actual sales (E). The equation for this singular curve is $Y = \{A(r, a) + G\}/(1 - c)$. Its negative slope depends upon the assumption that the volume of new investment expenditure on capital assets of long economic life is negatively related to the rate of interest, that is $A_r < 0$. Higher values for government expenditure, G, and for the shift parameter, a, are associated with $DY = 0$ curves which lie further to the north-east, while lower values of G and a are associated with $DY = 0$ curves lying further to the south-west.

To the right of the $DY = 0$ locus, where $Y > \{A(r, a) + G\}/(1 - c)$, national income (output) exceeds national expenditure and output must be falling $(DY < 0)$. This is represented in the phase diagram by the leftwards arrows in phases (a) and (b). To the left of the $DY = 0$ locus, where $Y < \{A(r, a) + G\}/(1 - c)$, national income (output) falls short of national expenditure and output must be rising $(DY > 0)$. This is represented in the phase diagram by the rightwards arrows in phases (c) and (d).

The intersection of the downward sloping IS curve with the upward sloping line labelled $Dr = 0$ is the stationary equilibrium point $(\bar{Y}, \bar{r})$. The singular curve $Dr = 0$ is the familiar liquidity–money equilibrium locus, or LM curve, representing all combinations of the level of national income and the rate of interest at which the money market is in *stock equilibrium* in the sense that the demand for money (L) is equal to a given supply of money (M). Higher values for the money supply, and for the shift parameter, a, are associated with LM curves which lie further to the south-east. Lower values for the money supply, and for the shift parameter, a, are associated with LM curves which lie further to the north-west.

At all points below the LM curve, there is excess demand for money $(L > M)$ and the rate of interest must be rising $(Dr > 0)$. This is represented in the phase diagram by the upwards arrows in phases (a) and (d). At all points above the LM curve, there is excess supply of money $(L < M)$ and the rate of interest must be falling $(Dr < 0)$. This is represented in the phase diagram by the downwards arrows in phases (b) and (c).

It is evident both from the phase diagram and from the characteristic Eq. (2B-2) that, given a, G, and M, the stationary equilibrium solution of the IS–LM prototype is (at least) locally stable. From any point in the neighborhood of the stationary equilibrium solution, the system will converge towards equilibrium. Since the two characteristic roots which describe motion in the neighborhood of the stationary equilibrium solution will be either (a) real negative numbers or (b) conjugate complex numbers with negative real parts, the approach to equilibrium will either be direct (non-oscillatory) or oscillatory. In the oscillatory case, the cyclical fluctuations occur in a *counter-clockwise direction*. Thus, if the system oscillates, peaks and troughs in the level of national income (output) will appear to lead peaks and troughs in the rate of interest by one cyclical phase. The rate of interest is, therefore, a lagging cyclical indicator.

The effect of interest rate repercussions is to dampen down the scale of multiplier responses to changes in autonomous expenditure. In the full model, they will also be seen to dampen down the oscillations caused by multiplier–accelerator interactions. There is, however, one kind of shift which offsets the normal dampening effect of interest rate movements on output movements. This is a shift in the state of long term expectations. More especially, monetary factors may enhance the rapidity of a cyclical downswing if a pessimistic shift in the state of long term expectations (a fall in a) causes a financial crisis (a leftward shift in LM) to follow upon a real crisis (a leftward shift in IS). Although the model treats such shifts as being simultaneous, one is reminded that "Liquidity-preference, except those manifestations of it which are associated with increasing trade and speculation, does not increase until *after* the collapse in the marginal efficiency of capital."[8] Further comments on expectational shifts and the place of monetary factors in the trade cycle are to be found in chapters 4, 10, and 13 of this book.

C: THE FLOW EQUILIBRIUM PROTOTYPE AND THE GENERAL CASE

In the *IS–LM* prototype, one has, of course, lost sight of the accelerator mechanism and the importance of real stock adjustments. The third prototype reinstates these features of the model. Unlike the *IS–LM* prototype, in which there was no *planned* accumulation or decumulation of stocks of capital assets of short economic life (inventories), the third prototype assumes that there is no *unplanned* accumulation or decumulation of stocks. The basic simplification of this prototype is that the model is in flow equilibrium at all points of time. That is to say, it is assumed that expectations are always realized, that $E^* = E$. It is *not*, however, assumed that the model is in *stock* equilibrium, so that S is not necessarily equal to S^* and L is not necessarily equal to M.

Under these assumptions, the model generates a sequence of momentary *flow* equilibria which may or may not eventually converge to a position of stock equilibrium, depending upon whether the sequence is stable or unstable. From an empirical point of view, the usefulness of these assumptions depends upon the relative sizes of various speeds of response. Indeed, the fundamental assumption of this prototype is that the speed of response in the expectational adjustment process is so large relative to the speeds of response in the stock adjustment and interest rate adjustment mechanisms that the expectational lag can safely be ignored (that is that $\lambda \to \infty$, or $\rho + \lambda \to \lambda$). Expectational adjustments are completed within the unit period and the model behaves as if its economic actors had "perfect foresight," that is, as if their expectations of the magnitudes of flow variables were exactly realized. It is evident that such an assumption does considerable violence to reality, and later in this section it will be dropped.

8. J. M. Keynes, *The General Theory of Employment, Interest and Money*, London, Macmillan, 1936, p. 316. See also J. R. Hicks, *A Contribution to the Theory of the Trade Cycle*, Oxford University Press, 1950, chapters 11 and 12, pp. 136–168.

The effect of this assumption on the equation system outlined in the previous sections is to reduce it to the four equations

$$DS = Y - E = \mu\{H(E,r) - S\}, \quad E = cY + A(r,a) + G$$

and

$$Dr = v\{L(E,r,a) - M\}$$

(2C-1)

with quadratic characteristic equation[9]

$$\{1 - c - cH_E\mu\}\rho^2 + \{\mu(1 - c) - (1 - c - cH_E\mu)vL_r - (A_r + cH_r\mu)vL_E\}\rho$$
$$- \mu v\{(1 - c)L_r + A_rL_E\} = 0 \qquad (2C-2)$$

where the partial derivatives are again evaluated at the stationary equilibrium solution, $\bar{S} = H(\bar{E}, \bar{r})$, $L(\bar{E}, \bar{r}, a) = M$, and $\bar{E} = \bar{Y} = \{A(\bar{r}, a) + G\}/(1 - c)$.

The first point that should be noticed about this prototype is that the locus $Y = \{A(r,a) + G\}/(1 - c)$ is a *stock equilibrium* locus for capital goods of short economic life, rather than a *flow equilibrium* locus (the *IS* curve) for commodity outputs in general as it was in the *IS–LM* prototype. Indeed, if $Y > \{A(r,a) + G\}/(1 - c)$, the stock of capital assets of short economic life is rising $(DS > 0)$, while if $Y < \{A(r,a) + G\}/(1 - c)$ the capital stock is falling $(DS < 0)$.

In the present case, the *IS* curve is not relevant since flow equilibrium in the commodity market is maintained at all points of time. Moreover, in the complete model without "perfect foresight" the positioning of any flow equilibrium locus in Y, r space would shift around with different stock situations. Indeed, the present analysis makes it clear that the *IS* curve formulation is based upon the implicit assumption that stocks do not affect production decisions, as in the Hicks–Hansen prototype.

The second point that should be noticed is that the condition $(1 - c - cH_E\mu) > 0$ is crucially important to the stability of the system. If this condition is met in the neighborhood of the stationary equilibrium point (that is, when H_E is evaluated at the stationary point), then this point is locally stable. Formally speaking, the two characteristic roots (the solutions to Eq. 2C-2) which describe motion in the neighborhood of the stationary equilibrium solution will be either (a) real negative numbers or (b) conjugate complex numbers with negative real parts.

On the other hand, if the stability condition is *not* met and $(1 - c - cH_E\mu) < 0$, the system will diverge from equilibrium in a non-oscillatory fashion from almost all points in the neighborhood of equilibrium. The stationary equilibrium point is now said to be a *saddle point*, where for present purposes a saddle point may be defined to be an equilibrium solution for which the characteristic roots which describe motion in the neighborhood of this solution are real and opposite

---

9. This equation may be derived either by linearizing the reduced system (2C-1) around its stationary equilibrium point or, equivalently, by dividing Eq. (2A-10) through by λ and taking the limit as $\lambda \to \infty$.

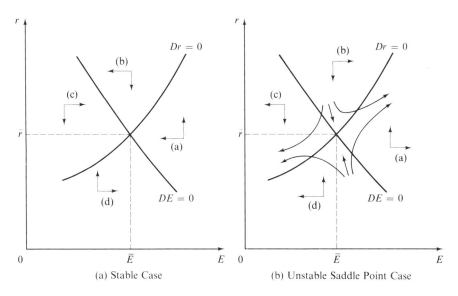

(a) Stable Case (b) Unstable Saddle Point Case

Figure 2C-1 Phase diagram for the flow equilibrium prototype.

in sign.[10] The stable and unstable cases are illustrated by the two phase diagrams of Fig. 2C-1.

In these two phase diagrams, the level of national expenditure, E, has been placed on the horizontal axis and the rate of interest, r, on the vertical axis. The $Dr = 0$ locus is, once again, the familiar LM curve (though with the demand for money depending upon $E^* = E$ rather than $E^* = Y$). The $DE = 0$ locus has been drawn to be downward sloping. It is equally possible that it is upward sloping, or, indeed, that it changes its slope from positive to negative at some point(s). What matters for our purposes, however, is the fact that it intersects the $Dr = 0$ locus in the general manner described in the diagrams.

The stability condition $(1 - c - cH_E\mu) > 0$ for the flow equilibrium prototype can be compared with the stability condition for the original inventory adjustment model outlined earlier, namely $(1 - c)(\lambda + \mu) - ch\lambda\mu > 0$. From this comparison and the fact that the partial derivative H_E corresponds to the constant h, it is easy to see that the new condition implies the old since $(\lambda + \mu) > \lambda$. However, once it is remembered that the flow equilibrium assumption implies that the speed of response in the expectational adjustment process becomes infinitely large relative to the speed of response in the stock adjustment mechanism, it is evident that in the limit $\lambda + \mu$ approaches λ and the two conditions reduce to the same thing.

10. It is worth noting in passing that many of the equilibrium dynamic models discussed in Part Two of this book also possess steady-state equilibria which exhibit the saddle point property. Moreover, the main reason why they do so is the unrealistic assumption of "perfect foresight." On this point, see chapter 8.

In both the original inventory adjustment model and the present flow equilibrium model that includes monetary and interest rate effects, stability occurs whenever the effects on the system of the shifts that occur in the desired capital stock in response to changes in national income (or output) are small, that is, if the combination $cH_E\mu$ is small relative to $(1 - c)$. Since $cH_E\mu$ may be called the propensity to invest and $(1 - c)$ is the propensity to save, stability of the multiplier process involves only that the propensity to invest be smaller than the propensity to save. Induced investment implies that the desired capital stock shifts as the system attempts to get into equilibrium, and it is these shifts that may lead to the overshooting of equilibrium and thus to instability.

In the flow equilibrium prototype, monetary parameters do not affect the criterion for stability. This is, however, a conclusion which is definitely misleading since it is entirely the result of the unrealistic assumption that the system is in flow equilibrium at all points of time. Indeed, monetary parameters can affect the stability of the complete model, whose properties will now, at long last, be analyzed.

The analysis starts from the characteristic equation given as Eq. (2A-10). For convenience, this expression may be repeated here as

$$k_3\rho^3 + k_2\rho^2 + k_1\rho + k_0 = 0$$

where $\quad k_3 = 1, \quad k_2 = [(1 - c)(\lambda + \mu) - cH_{E*}\lambda\mu - vL_r]$

$$k_1 = [(1 - c)\lambda\mu - \{(1 - c)(\lambda + \mu) - cH_{E*}\lambda\mu\}vL_r - (A_r + cH_r\mu)\lambda vL_{E*}]$$

and $\quad k_0 = -[\lambda\mu v\{(1 - c)L_r + A_r L_{E*}\}]$ $\hfill$ (2C-3)

The first point to be noticed about this equation is that imbedded in two of its coefficients is the familiar term $(1 - c)(\lambda + \mu) - cH_{E*}\lambda\mu$. If this term is *positive,* all the coefficients attached to the powers of ρ in the equation, namely k_3, k_2, k_1, and k_0, are necessarily positive, given the sign constraints imposed on the various partial derivatives in the model. Applying Descartes' Rule of Signs,[11] it is easy to see that the equation cannot then possess any real non-negative roots. Thus, if the system is unstable in the neighborhood of the stationary equilibrium solution, it must be cyclically unstable, given $(1 - c)(\lambda + \mu) - cH_{E*}\lambda\mu > 0$. However, even if $(1 - c)(\lambda + \mu) - cH_{E*}\lambda\mu$ is *negative,* the system need not be unstable, though it *is* necessary for stability that the other terms in coefficients k_2 and k_1 be sufficiently large to ensure that all the k's remain positive.

Unfortunately, the condition that all the k's be positive is not a sufficient condition for stability. Indeed, the system will be stable if and only if all its characteristic roots are either real negative numbers or conjugate complex numbers with negative real parts. This will be so if and only if the so-called Routh-Hurwitz

---

11. Descartes' Rule of Signs says that the number of real positive roots to a polynomial is equal to the number of sign changes in the coefficients of this polynomial less an even integer (which may be zero). Thus, if all the coefficients are positive, there can be no real positive roots. Indeed, in the present case, there can be no real non-negative roots since $k_0 > 0$.

conditions hold.[12] In the present situation, an exploration of the Routh-Hurwitz conditions does not reveal any particularly useful economic results, even if (as a borderline case) the simplifying assumption that $(1 - c)(\lambda + \mu) = cH_{E^*}\lambda\mu$ is made. Nevertheless, whether or not the condition $(1 - c)(\lambda + \mu) > cH_{E^*}\lambda\mu$ is satisfied, monetary parameters must enter into the criteria for the stability of the system. Moreover, it remains generally true that movements in the rate of interest tend to reduce the power of the multiplier–accelerator mechanism, thereby reducing the amplitude of cyclical fluctuations.

Finally, in so far as cyclical fluctuations do occur, the oscillations are such that peaks (troughs) in Y appear to precede peaks (troughs) in both S and r. Not only do cycles in the level of national income lead cycles in the level of stocks of capital goods with short economic life, but also they lead cycles in the rate of interest. The complete model is more likely to be stable if the degree to which cycles in r lag cycles in Y is shorter in comparison with the degree to which cycles in S lag cycles in Y than if it is longer. For in this case, it is more likely that the positive feedback effects of E^* on S^* through $H_{E^*} > 0$ can be offset by the negative feedback effects of r on S^* through $H_r < 0$.

D: MONETARY AND FISCAL POLICY

The previous sections of this chapter analyzed the behavior of a simple macro-dynamic model under alternative specifications of the magnitudes of various speed of response parameters. The basic model incorporated both monetary adjustments and real stock adjustments simultaneously. Its novelty, therefore, consisted of the addition of real stock adjustments of the accelerationist type to a dynamic version of the *IS–LM* framework, or, equivalently, the addition of monetary adjustments to a multiplier–accelerator framework.

In the present section, the effects on this model economy of monetary and fiscal policy are discussed. Consider, first, fiscal policy. From our earlier discussion in Sec. E of the previous chapter, it is clear that, in addition to a proportional component of the "built-in stabilizer" variety, fiscal policy must include an integral component if complete correction of the level of national income is to be attained. It must also include a derivative component if the possibility of

---

12. The Routh-Hurwitz conditions state that the characteristic roots of the cubic equation $k_3\rho^3 + k_2\rho^2 + k_1\rho + k_0 = 0$ all have negative real parts if and only if the three principal minors of the matrix

$$\begin{bmatrix} k_1 & k_0 & 0 \\ k_3 & k_2 & k_1 \\ 0 & 0 & k_3 \end{bmatrix}$$

are all positive, provided (as may legitimately be assumed) $k_0 > 0$. That is to say, the necessary and sufficient conditions are $k_1 > 0$, $k_1 k_2 > k_0 k_3$, and $k_1 k_2 k_3 > k_0 k_3 k_3$, which, given $k_0 > 0$, imply $k_i > 0$, all $i = 0,\ldots,3$. On these points, see for example J. V. Uspensky, *Theory of Equations,* New York, McGraw-Hill, 1948, p. 304, or Ogata, *op. cit.,* p. 448–9.

unstable motions is to be reduced, particularly if $cH_{E*}\lambda\mu$ is large relative to $(1 - c)(\lambda + \mu)$, leading to a powerful accelerator effect. These results carry over to the present model without modification.

When monetary policy is considered, it is clear that an additional instrument is now available for stabilizing the level of national income around its target level. While changes in G shift the multiplier equilibrium relation, $Y = \{A(r, a) + G\}/(1 - c)$, making it possible to attain the target level of Y if there exists an attainable $r > 0$ such that $L(E^*, r, a) = M$ when E^* equals target Y, changes in M shift the money market equilibrium locus, $L(E^*, r, a) = M$, making it possible to attain the target level of Y if there exists an attainable $r > 0$ such that $Y = \{A(r, a) + G\}/(1 - c)$ at the target Y. However, just as fiscal policy required an integral component to achieve complete correction of the level of national income, so too does monetary policy. That is to say, the money supply must adjust in response to the time integral of the discrepancies between the target and actual levels of national income, or, equivalently, *changes* in the money supply must adjust in response to the current discrepancy.

It may well be, however, that there also exists a target level for the rate of interest (or, equivalently, given a target Y, for the actual stock of capital of short economic life). In this case, both monetary and fiscal policy are required to achieve the two separate targets, and both policies must have an integral component. For example, one might adjust the money supply towards the time integral of the discrepancies between the actual and the target interest rates.

It follows from the previous analysis that monetary policy may be a useful device for stabilizing the level of national income (or output) for an economy in transition. The main features of the model that lead in a disequilibrium dynamic situation to fluctuations in national income are the changes in planned investment that occur in response to changes in the level of national income. In so far as these changes can be offset by appropriate adjustments in the rate of interest, monetary policy serves a useful purpose in stabilizing the economy. This is particularly important if the combined recognition, implementation, and effectiveness lags in the application of fiscal policy are longer than the similar lags that occur in the application of monetary policy. The essence of sound monetary policy in a closed economy is to maintain interest rates at such a level that the forthcoming volume of planned investment expenditure does not lead to an excessive rate of expansion or contraction of the level of national income or expenditure. This is, however, no easy task if the volume of planned investment expenditure moves in a volatile fashion, particularly if the feedback effects through $H_{E^*} > 0$ are large relative to the feedback effects through $H_r < 0$.

From time to time, therefore, one may misjudge the appropriate monetary policy and subject the system to destabilizing monetary shocks. For example, if from an initial position of stock and flow equilibrium one increases the money supply, the equilibrium rate of interest falls, while both the equilibrium capital stock and the equilibrium level of national income rise. Even if this new equilibrium position is stable, the process of transition towards it may well be cyclical, with cycles in Y appearing to lead cycles in S and r. If this is so, then the process of accumulating capital assets of short economic life may well lead to a cyclical phase in which rising interest rates appear to squeeze the accumulation of capital assets of long economic life (and especially the volume of new housing construction). Whether or not this is so, it is clear that changes in monetary policy may well affect some sectors of the economy more than others. In particular, their impact may well be greatest in the residential construction sector. Fundamentally, therefore, movements in the rate of interest alter the allocation of investment across alternative forms of capital assets. Monetary disturbances may lead to structural imbalances in the economy.

Finally, although monetary and fiscal policy may be used as separate instruments, in the long run the stock equilibrium implications of (a) investment in capital assets of long economic life and (b) the manner in which government expenditures are financed (that is, the compounded effects over time of the governmental budget constraint) must be considered. The consequential interdependence of monetary and fiscal policy in the long run leads to the conclusion that for any given state of long term expectations there may well be one and only one level of the rate of interest which is consistent with the maintenance of the target level of national income and expenditure over the long run. This rate of interest may be called *the natural rate of interest*. Of course, the state of long term expectations (as well as the targets) will undoubtedly have changed before such a long run situation is attained. This discussion will be continued in the final section of the following chapter, and in Part Three of this book.

AGGREGATE DEMAND, TRADE, AND PAYMENTS

A : MONETARY ADJUSTMENT UNDER FIXED EXCHANGE RATES

The discussion in the previous chapters has concentrated entirely on a closed economy, with no trade and financial linkages with other economies. The time has come to consider an extension of the analysis to the situation of an open economy. The extension begins from the dynamic version of the Hicks-Hansen *IS–LM* prototype. That is to say, real stock adjustments are ignored in the following analysis. Because of the seminal contributions of Mundell to this particular area of economic analysis,[1] the resulting system may be referred as the Hicks-Hansen-Mundell model.

To begin with, the *IS–LM* prototype may be reformulated as

$$DY = \lambda Z(Y,r,G) \quad \text{and} \quad Dr = vL(Y,r,M) \tag{3A-1}$$

where $Z(Y,r,G)$ represents the volume of excess demand in the commodity market (that is, $E - Y$, in the *IS–LM* prototype), and $L(Y,r,M)$ represents the volume of excess demand in the money market. For simplicity, the shift parameter, a, representing the state of long term expectations, has been dropped from the notation. In terms of the earlier notation for the *IS–LM* prototype, the partial derivatives of $Z(Y,r,G)$ correspond to $Z_Y = -(1-c)$, $Z_r = A_r$ and $Z_G = 1$. Thus, it is appropriate to assume that $Z_Y < 0$, $Z_r < 0$, and $Z_G > 0$, though, of course, with export and import flows in the model the partial derivative Z_Y must necessarily be somewhat more complicated than the simple term $-(1-c)$.[2] The partial

---

1. See especially R. A. Mundell, *International Economics,* New York, Macmillan, 1968.

2. In particular, if there are leakages from the circular flow of income and expenditure into both tax revenues and imports as well as private savings, then $Z_Y = -\{s(1-t) + t + m\} = -\{1 - c(1-t) + m\}$, where $s = 1 - c$ is the marginal propensity to save, t is the marginal propensity to tax, and m is the marginal propensity to import.

derivatives of $L(Y, r, M)$ are, as before, $L_Y > 0$ and $L_r < 0$, with the additional derivative $L_M < 0$ since it is equal to -1. Given G and M, the equation system (3A-1) may be linearized around its stationary equilibrium solution $Z(Y, r, G) = 0$ and $L(Y, r, M) = 0$. This linearization procedure yields the fundamental characteristic equation,

$$\rho^2 - (\lambda Z_Y + v L_r)\rho + \lambda v(Z_Y L_r - L_Y Z_r) = 0 \qquad (3A\text{-}2)$$

where the partial derivatives are all evaluated in the neighborhood of the stationary equilibrium solution. This equation corresponds exactly to Eq. (2B-2).

When this model economy is opened up to foreign trade and payments, two additional variables are required, namely (a) the home currency value of the stock of foreign exchange reserves (R), and (b) the home currency value of one unit of foreign exchange $(1/\pi)$. Since $1/\pi$ is the price of foreign exchange, it follows that π is the *exchange rate* defined as the value of one unit of home currency in terms of foreign exchange. Throughout this book, the term exchange rate (π) will refer to the reciprocal of the price of foreign exchange, so that an appreciation of the home currency is associated with higher values of π, while a depreciation of the home currency is associated with lower values of π. For the moment, however, it will be assumed that the exchange rate is fixed. The possibility of flexibility in π will be considered in Secs. C and D of this chapter.

Let the expression $F(Y, r)$ refer to the *surplus* on the balance of payments expressed in terms of home currency, excluding official sales and purchases of foreign exchange. Negative values of $F(Y, r)$ may be taken to represent a balance of payments deficit. Since imports will rise as national income increases, and exports may fall, it may be assumed that the partial derivative F_Y is negative. Since net capital inflows will rise as the domestic interest rate increases (given foreign interest rates), it may be assumed that the partial derivative F_r is positive. Notice, however, that to assume that each particular interest rate differential implies a continuous net capital inflow (or outflow) of a constant amount does not appropriately capture the true flavor of an international portfolio adjustment model. Nevertheless, for ease of exposition, the simple flow model of international capital movements is used herein rather than the more complicated stock adjustment model.

The counterpart of a surplus on the balance of payments, $F(Y, r) > 0$, will necessarily be a rise in the volume of foreign exchange reserves, while the counterpart of a deficit, $F(Y, r) < 0$, will necessarily be a fall in exchange reserves. It follows that the level of foreign exchange reserves may be represented by the integral of $F(Y, r)$. Thus, without loss of generality, one may write

$$R(t) = \int_{-\infty}^{t} F\{Y(\tau), r(\tau)\}\, d\tau \qquad (3A\text{-}3)$$

To close the system, it is now simply necessary to consider the possible responses of the model economy to movements in $R(t)$.

The first possibility that may be considered is the gold standard case. Under a strict gold standard, foreign exchange consists entirely of gold. Moreover, the rules of the gold standard game tie the domestic money supply directly to the gold stock. Given a fixed ratio of the money supply to the gold base, the money supply must necessarily adapt to the level of foreign exchange reserves. Let $m > 0$ be the required ratio of the money supply to the gold stock (the reciprocal of the reserve ratio or the reserve multiplier). Then, with instantaneous adaptation, one may write

$$M = mR \qquad (3A-4)$$

Given this relationship, it follows immediately from differentiation of Eq. (3A-3) that changes in the money supply must reflect the state of the balance of payments. Thus, one has

$$DM = mF(Y, r) \qquad (3A-5)$$

which is sufficient to close the system, given an exogenous level of government expenditure, G.[3] Indeed, putting Eq. (3A-5) together with Eq. (3A-1) yields a system of three first order non-linear differential equations in the three unknowns, Y, r, and M.

It is useful to analyze this system with the aid of a diagram, Fig. 3A-1. In this diagram, the level of national income, Y, is measured along the abscissa, while the rate of interest, r, is measured along the ordinate. The downward sloping line $DY = 0$ is the locus $Z(Y, r, G) = 0$ or the IS curve. The upward sloping line $Dr = 0$ is the locus $L(Y, r, M) = 0$ or the LM curve. Finally, the upward sloping line $DM = 0$ is the locus $F(Y, r) = 0$, which may be called the foreign balance locus or BF curve. The equilibrium levels of Y and r (and implicitly M) are given by the common intersection point of the three curves, $Y, \bar{r}$. In this diagram, the BF curve has been drawn steeper than the LM curve at their intersection point, though this need not be so. It will be so if $-F_Y/F_r > -L_Y/L_r$ or $F_Y L_r > L_Y F_r$, that is if the LM curve is relatively more sensitive than the BF curve to changes in r (and relatively less sensitive to changes in Y), where the partial derivatives are evaluated in the neighborhood of the intersection point. On the other hand, the BF curve is less steep than the LM curve at their intersection point if $F_Y L_r < L_Y F_r$, that is, if international capital flows are very sensitive to relative interest rates. The relationship between the slopes of the LM and BF curves, however, is rather unimportant in the following analysis.

From an initial position of equilibrium (say $\bar{Y}$, $\bar{r}$, and the associated M), let it be assumed that there is a rise in foreign interest rates which leads to smaller capital inflows (or larger capital outflows) and shifts the BF curve to BF',

---

3. Of course, one might well expect the adaptation of M to R to take time. If the resulting lag is taken to be of a simple exponential form with speed of response $\eta > 0$, then one may write $(D + \eta)M = \eta m R$, or $(D + \eta)DM = \eta m F(Y, r)$. For simplicity, however, it is assumed that $\eta \to \infty$. In either event, M adjusts to the integral of $F(Y, r)$, an integral adjustment process.

as illustrated in Fig. 3A-1. In consequence, the equilibrium level of national income falls to Y' and the equilibrium rate of interest rises to $\bar{r}'$.[4] Assuming stability, the adjustment towards the new equilibrium position occurs in the following manner. The initial reduction in net capital inflows with its associated shift in the BF curve, generates a deficit in the balance of payments, which leads to a contraction in the gold stock and in the domestic money supply. The contraction in the domestic money supply implies a leftward shift in the LM curve which continues until it intersects the IS and BF curves at the new equilibrium position, Y' and $\bar{r}'$. Thus, the adjustment process takes the form of a Humean specie-flow mechanism. This specie-flow mechanism is characterized by monetary adjustments which carry the LM curve to the intersection of the IS and BF curves.

Analysis of the stability of equilibrium requires a consideration of the characteristic equation of the system, which may be written as

$$\rho^3 - \{\lambda Z_Y + vL_r\}\rho^2 + \{\lambda v(Z_Y L_r - L_Y Z_r) - vmL_M F_r\}\rho + \lambda vmL_M\{Z_Y F_r - F_Y Z_r\} = 0$$

$$(3A\text{-}6)$$

where the various partial derivatives are evaluated in the neighborhood of the equilibrium solution.[5] The first point to be noticed about this equation is that it cannot possess any real non-negative characteristic roots, since all of its coefficients are positive (Descartes' Rule of Signs). If the system in unstable, it must necessarily be cyclically unstable. The second point to be noticed is that the Routh-Hurwitz conditions reduce to the inequality[6]

$$-(\lambda Z_Y + vL_r)(Z_Y L_r - L_Y Z_r) > -mL_M\{F_Y Z_r + \lambda^{-1}vF_r L_r\} \qquad (3A\text{-}7)$$

Equilibrium will be locally stable if and only if this condition holds in the neighborhood of the equilibrium position. Given the signs of the various partial

---

4. An initial fall in foreign national income leading to a decrease in export demand would shift *both* BF and IS curves to the left, but for reasons parallel to those discussed in Sec. C of this chapter, the horizontal shift in BF will exceed that in IS. In consequence, Y will again be lower and r higher in the new equilibrium position.

5. Equation (3A-6) is obtained in the following way. Let $Y = \bar{Y} + \hat{Y} e^{\rho t}$, $r = \bar{r} + \hat{r} e^{\rho t}$ and $M = \bar{M} + \hat{M} e^{\rho t}$. Then, the linearization procedure allows one (for example) to write

$$Dr = \rho\hat{r} e^{\rho t} = vL(Y, r, M) = vL(\bar{Y}, \bar{r}, \bar{M}) + vL_Y \hat{Y} e^{\rho t} + vL_r\hat{r} e^{\rho t} + vL_M \hat{M} e^{\rho t}$$

Remembering that $L(\bar{Y}, \bar{r}, \bar{M}) = 0$, and that $e^{\rho t} \neq 0$ may be cancelled from this expression (and the other similar expressions), one may write the system in matrix form as

$$\begin{bmatrix} \rho - \lambda Z_Y & -\lambda Z_r & 0 \\ -vL_Y & \rho - vL_r & -vL_M \\ -mF_Y & -mF_r & \rho \end{bmatrix} \begin{bmatrix} \hat{Y} \\ \hat{r} \\ \hat{M} \end{bmatrix} = \begin{bmatrix} 0 \\ 0 \\ 0 \end{bmatrix}$$

Setting the determinant of the 3 × 3 matrix equal to zero yields the cubic characteristic equation given as Eq. (3A-6) in the text.

6. The Routh-Hurwitz conditions for the cubic case may also be written as $k_i > 0$, $i = 0, \dots, 3$, and $k_1 k_2 > k_0 k_3$. Since all the k_i's are positive, the inequality given as expression (3A-7) is simply this latter condition after cancellation of some terms. See footnote 12 (chapter 2).

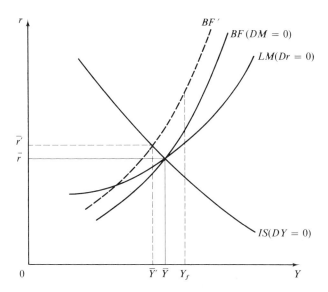

Figure 3A-1 The *IS, LM,* and *BF* curves.

derivatives, the lefthand side of the inequality (3A-7) is necessarily positive, and the righthand side is negative if and only if $F_Y Z_r + \lambda^{-1} v F_r L_r$ is negative. In this case, the inequality is necessarily satisfied. Moreover, even if $F_Y Z_r + \lambda^{-1} v F_r L_r$ is positive, a sufficiently small value of m in relationship to λ and v will still permit the inequality to be satisfied. Thus, given instantaneous changes in the money supply in response to the state of the balance of payments, stability is more likely the larger are the other speed of response coefficients, λ and v, and the smaller is the reserve multiplier, m. Even in the stable case, however, the approach to equilibrium may well entail damped cyclical oscillations in Y, r, and M as the Humean specie-flow adjustment mechanism partially overshoots the mark. On the other hand, cyclical instability in the form of explosive oscillations will occur if the inequality (3A-7) is reversed, as it will be if the monetary response is both large and rapid (in comparison with the other speeds of response in the model).

The specie-flow adjustment mechanism of the gold standard case necessarily entails that no attempt is made to prevent inflows and outflows of gold from affecting the domestic money supply. That is to say, no sterilization of gold flows occurs. Since changes in the money supply reflect the state of the balance of payments, the Humean adjustment mechanism is likely to imply a position of equilibrium which is undesirable from the point of view of internal balance. That is to say, the equilibrium level of national income will differ from an internal target level of national income, which for present purposes may be taken to be the level of national income which generates full employment, say Y_f. On the other hand, if an attempt is made to sterilize inflows and outflows of gold and prevent them from affecting the domestic money supply, the balance of payments disequilibrium will be perpetuated, an undesirable situation from the point of view of external balance. Quite evidently, therefore, an additional instrument is required in order to achieve the two targets of internal and external balance simultaneously. Fiscal policy must be added to the model.

For simplicity, fiscal policy may be assumed to take the form

$$DG = g(Y_f - Y) \tag{3A-8}$$

Changes in government expenditure are taken to be proportional to the gap between full employment, national income, and the actual level of national income, where $g > 0$ is the constant of proportionality. Notice that this specification implies integral stabilization policy, though for simplicity the lags in the adjustment of government expenditure policy have been ignored.[7]

If fiscal policy is introduced, both internal balance and external balance may be achieved simultaneously *provided that* the external balance locus $F(Y,r) = 0$ intersects the internal balance locus $Y = Y_f$, which has been illustrated in Fig. 3A-1 by the vertical dotted line at Y_f. Given that such a combined target point exists, the resulting system may be linearized around this point yielding the fourth order characteristic equation[8]

$$\rho^4 - (\lambda Z_Y + \nu L_r)\rho^3 + \{\lambda\nu(Z_Y L_r - L_Y Z_r) - \nu m L_M F_r + \lambda g Z_G\}\rho^2$$
$$+ \{\lambda\nu m L_M (Z_Y F_r - F_Y Z_r) - \lambda\nu g Z_G L_r\}\rho - \lambda\nu m g Z_G L_M F_r = 0 \tag{3A-9}$$

where the various partial derivatives are all evaluated in the neighborhood of the combined target point, $F(Y,r) = 0$ and $Y = Y_f$, when equilibrium prevails at this point, that is $Z(Y,r,G) = L(Y,r,M) = 0$. Applying Descartes' Rule of Signs, one discovers that this characteristic equation cannot possess any real non-negative characteristic roots since all of its coefficients are positive. Again non-cyclical instability is ruled out. Unfortunately, the Routh-Hurwitz conditions are not particularly revealing in this case.[9] In the following section, this system is analyzed under certain simplifying assumptions, and the so-called principle of effective market classification is discussed.

---

7. As suggested in chapter 1 (especially expression 1E-3), integral stabilization policy with lagged adjustment may be written as $(D + \gamma)G = \gamma g_i \int_0^t \{Y_f - Y(\tau)\}\, d\tau$, where γ is the speed of response of the adjustment lag. Differentiating this expression one has $(D + \gamma)DG = \gamma g_i(Y_f - Y)$, which (dropping the i subscript) reduces to expression (3A-8) as $\gamma \to \infty$. On this point, compare footnote 3 of this chapter.

8. This expression is obtained by combining Eqs. (3A-8) with (3A-1) and (3A-5), and linearizing the resulting system around the combined target point to obtain the matrix equation

$$\begin{bmatrix} \rho - \lambda Z_Y & -\lambda Z_r & 0 & -\lambda Z_G \\ -\nu L_Y & \rho - \nu L_r & -\nu L_M & 0 \\ -mF_Y & -mF_r & \rho & 0 \\ g & 0 & 0 & \rho \end{bmatrix} \begin{bmatrix} \hat{Y} \\ \hat{r} \\ \hat{M} \\ \hat{G} \end{bmatrix} = \begin{bmatrix} 0 \\ 0 \\ 0 \\ 0 \end{bmatrix}$$

Setting the determinant of the 4×4 matrix equal to zero one obtains the quartic characteristic Eq. (3A-9) above.

9. In the quartic case, the Routh-Hurwitz conditions state that the characteristic roots of the

B: EFFECTIVE MARKET CLASSIFICATION AND THE ASSIGNMENT PROBLEM

The previous section contained an analysis of the response of the domestic money supply to balance of payments disequilibria. Following the rules of the gold standard game, it is evident that money supply responses are assigned to the correction of the balance of payments situation. When an internal full employment target is introduced, fiscal policy responses are assigned to correct the level of national income. This assignment of instruments to targets is also appropriate in other less rigid fixed exchange rate regimes, where foreign currency and credits may also serve as exchange reserves, such as a gold exchange standard or even a dollar standard.

The purpose of this section is to explore the question why one should assign monetary policy to the correction of the balance of payments and fiscal policy to the correction of the level of national income, rather than the reverse assignment. The answer is shown to depend upon the relative stability of the system under alternative assignment rules. It follows that particular markets may be effectively classified with respect to the instrument that should be assigned to them in order to bring about a stable adjustment of the system towards its target levels. The *Tinbergen principle* that the number of instruments must be at least as great as the number of targets may then be augmented by the *effective market classification principle,* which uses stability analysis as a guide to the appropriate assignment of instruments to targets.[10]

In order to proceed, it is useful to simplify the fourth order system outlined at the end of the previous section. For present purposes, let it be assumed that flow equilibrium in the commodity market and stock equilibrium in the money market are maintained continuously so that $Z(Y,r,G) = L(Y,r,M) = 0$ at all points of time. This is equivalent to the assumption that λ and v both approach infinity. On this assumption, Y and r are always at the point of intersection of the *IS* curve and the *LM* curve, though shifts in G and M may alter this intersection

---

equation $k_4\rho^4 + k_3\rho^3 + k_2\rho^2 + k_1\rho + k_0 = 0$, all have negative real parts if and only if the four principal minors of

$$\begin{bmatrix} k_1 & k_0 & 0 & 0 \\ k_3 & k_2 & k_1 & k_0 \\ 0 & k_4 & k_3 & k_2 \\ 0 & 0 & 0 & k_4 \end{bmatrix}$$

are all positive, given $k_0 > 0$. If all the k_i's are positive for $i = 0,\ldots,4$, the Routh-Hurwitz conditions reduce to the inequality $(k_1k_2 - k_0k_3)k_3 > k_1k_1k_4$. See Uspensky, *op. cit.,* p. 304.

10. A thorough theoretical investigation of the effective market classification principle and the "comparative advantages" of particular instruments in guiding the system towards particular targets is to be found in P. Fortin, "Can Economic Policy Pair Instruments and Targets? (Or Should It?)," *Canadian Journal of Economics,* vol. 7, November 1974, pp. 558–577.

point. Thus, the system may be simplified to the following second order system,

$$Z(Y, r, G) = 0, \quad L(Y, r, M) = 0$$

with

$$DM = mF(Y, r) \quad \text{and} \quad DG = g(Y_f - Y) \tag{3B-1}$$

with quadratic characteristic equation[11]

$$\{Z_Y L_r - L_Y Z_r\}\rho^2 + \{mL_M(Z_Y F_r - F_Y Z_r) - gZ_G L_r\}\rho - mgZ_G L_M F_r = 0 \tag{3B-2}$$

where the partial derivatives are evaluated in the neighborhood of the combined target point, $F(Y, r) = 0$ and $Y = Y_f$.

Since all of the coefficients in this second order characteristic equation are strictly positive, the real parts of the two characteristic roots are necessarily negative. It is therefore implied that the combined target point must be approached from all points in its immediate neighborhood. Thus, the assignment of monetary policy to the balance of payments target and fiscal policy to the full employment target is necessarily a stable assignment of instruments to targets, given the simplifying assumption that $Z(Y, r, G) = L(Y, r, M) = 0$.

Of course, in the more general fourth order system, cyclical instability may be possible, although it can be averted by choosing combinations of m and g that allow the Routh-Hurwitz conditions to be satisfied. Since this will probably imply relatively small values of m and g, it seems important for stability that there be sufficient foreign exchange reserves to absorb $F(Y, r) < 0$ and sufficient political reserves to absorb $Y < Y_f$ for some period of time, if, for example, a balance of payments deficit is coupled with unemployment.

What would happen, however, if controls were crossed, and monetary policy were assigned to the full employment·target and fiscal policy to the balance of payments? In this case, one may write the system as

$$Z(Y, r, G) = 0, \quad L(Y, r, M) = 0$$

with

$$DM = m(Y_f - Y) \quad \text{and} \quad DG = gF(Y, r) \tag{3B-3}$$

with m and g suitably redefined. It is evident that one should take m to be positive, but the sign of g may not be determined until the relative slope of the LM and BF curves is known. If BF is steeper than LM in the neighborhood of the combined target point so that $F_Y L_r > L_Y F_r$, fiscal expansion will tend to reduce the surplus on the balance of payments (or increase the deficit) since the current account effects resulting from an increase in Y will dominate the capital account effects resulting from an increase in r. On the other hand, if BF is less steep than LM in this neighborhood so that $F_Y L_r < L_Y F_r$, fiscal expansion will tend to increase the surplus on the balance of payments (or reduce the deficit) since the current account effects will be dominated by the capital account effects.

---

11. This equation may be derived either by linearizing the reduced system around the combined target point or, equivalently, by dividing Eq. (3A-9) through by λv and taking the limit as $\lambda v \to \infty$.

Unlike a monetary expansion which increases Y and decreases r and therefore leads unambiguously to a reduction in the balance of payments surplus, the effect of fiscal policy on the balance of payments is ambiguous. Monetary policy is, therefore, much more powerful as a corrective to balance of payments disequilibria than is fiscal policy, a fact which is directly associated with the relative stability of alternative assignments.

It follows from the previous analysis that, if it is known that $F_Y L_r - L_Y F_r > 0$, one should let g be positive in the crossed controls case. On the other hand, if it is known that $F_Y L_r - L_Y F_r < 0$, one should let g be negative. There are, therefore, two possibilities to consider when one expands the characteristic equation of the system. This equation may be written as

$$(Z_Y L_r - L_Y Z_r)\rho^2 + \{gZ_G(F_Y L_r - L_Y F_r) + mL_M Z_r\}\rho + mgZ_G L_M F_r = 0 \qquad (3B\text{-}4)$$

where the partial derivatives are again evaluated in the neighborhood of the combined target point $F(Y, r) = 0$ and $Y = Y_f$.

If $g > 0$, it is immediately obvious that the last coefficient of the quadratic characteristic Eq. (3B-4) is negative. Since the first coefficient is necessarily positive, there must be exactly one change in the sign of the coefficients of the equation. By Descartes' Rule of Signs, there is then exactly one real positive characteristic root (and one real negative root). Thus, the combined target point is a *saddle point,* and the system will diverge in a non-oscillatory fashion from almost all starting positions in the neighborhood of this point. With $g > 0$, the assignment of monetary policy to the full employment target and fiscal policy to the balance of payments target is definitely an unstable assignment. Moreover, this result carries over without modification to a more general fourth order system in which $Z(Y, r, G)$ and $L(Y, r, M)$ are not taken to be equal to zero at all points of time.

On the other hand, if $g < 0$ *and* $F_Y L_r - L_Y F_r < 0$, all the coefficients of Eq. (3B-4) are positive, and the crossed controls assignment will be stable. This result may not, however, carry over to the more general fourth order system. Moreover, this assignment is more likely to lead to oscillations (albeit damped) than the opposite assignment of monetary policy to the balance of payments objective and fiscal policy to the full employment objective. Furthermore, a more appropriate portfolio adjustment approach to international capital flows suggests that $F_Y L_r - L_Y F_r$ is unlikely to remain negative over the longer run since F_r must fall as the process of adjustment towards portfolio equilibrium proceeds.

The main problem with this assignment is, of course, that in the short run the relative slopes of LM and BF may not be known. If $g < 0$ when BF is steeper than LM and $F_Y L_r - L_Y F_r > 0$, then instability may well reappear, though in this case there will be two roots with positive real parts so that explosive oscillations are possible. Since the main reason for assigning particular instruments to particular targets is to allow policy makers "to grope" their way towards the specified targets in a situation in which quantitative information about slope parameters and speeds of response is scarce and unreliable, an assignment whose stability may depend upon the precise magnitudes of these parameters is not particularly desirable. Thus, one concludes that under fixed exchange rates monetary policy should be directed towards the balance of payments objective and fiscal policy should be directed towards the full employment objective.

C: THE FLEXIBLE EXCHANGE RATE CASE

In the previous sections of this chapter, it has always been assumed that the external balance locus, $F(Y,r) = 0$, intersects the vertical internal balance locus $Y = Y_f$ at some feasible $r > 0$ so that external and internal balance can be achieved simultaneously. If, however, there is no $r > 0$ such that $F(Y,r) = 0$ *and* $Y = Y_f$, the two targets of external and internal balance are incompatible. To ensure their compatibility it is necessary to change the foreign exchange rate, π. More generally, if the authorities also have an objective with respect to the *composition* of the balance of payments, they must be free to alter the value of $r > 0$ at which $F(Y,r) = 0$ and $Y = Y_f$. To do so requires that the exchange rate be allowed to adjust, thus shifting the $F(Y,r) = 0$ locus (and with it the $Z(Y,r,G) = 0$ locus) to a more suitable position.

The purpose of this section is to explore the case in which the exchange rate is taken to be flexible. Under a regime of flexible exchange rates, π must be included as an argument in both the function representing excess demand in the commodity market, $Z(Y,r,\pi,G)$, and the function representing the balance of payments surplus, $F(Y,r,\pi)$. It is assumed that both Z_π and F_π are negative. As long as the so-called Marshall-Lerner elasticity condition[12] is satisfied, an appreciation of the domestic currency (an increase in π) will reduce the surplus (or increase the deficit) on the current account of the balance of payments. In addition, as long as speculation is stabilizing, the higher value of the currency will increase the volume of capital outflows (or reduce capital inflows).[13] In combination, both of these forces necessarily produce a negative value for F_π. The negativity of Z_π follows from the repercussions of the fall in the current account surplus on excess demand in the commodity market.

If one ignores day to day smoothing operations, one may assume that with flexible exchange rates the change in the level (R) of foreign exchange reserves (expressed in domestic currency) is either zero or perhaps equal to a constant target amount.[14] It follows immediately from expression (3A-3) that if DR is

---

12. When trade is initially balanced and supply elasticities are infinite, the Marshall-Lerner condition may be expressed as $|\eta_x| + |\eta_m| > 1$, where η_x is the foreign demand elasticity for exports and η_m is the domestic demand elasticity for imports. Somewhat more complicated expressions are required if trade is not initially balanced and if supply elasticities are not infinite. On these points see, for example, C. P. Kindleberger, *International Economics,* Homewood, Irwin, 1963, Appendix D, pp. 656–658. The importance of the Marshall-Lerner elasticity condition is discussed in considerable detail in chapter 10 of this book.

13. As indicated in the following section, this effect is only likely to be temporary since expected and actual exchange rates must converge in the longer run.

14. Revaluations of the existing stock of foreign exchange reserves when π changes are ignored.

equal to zero then $F(Y, r, \pi)$ must necessarily be equal to zero, and if DR is constant $F(Y, r, \pi)$ must be constant. Thus, π will adjust in such a way as to maintain balance of payments equilibrium (where any constant target change in foreign exchange reserves may be subsumed within this equilibrium). Without loss of generality, therefore, the basic equation system for the flexible exchange rate case may be written as

$$DY = \lambda Z(Y, r, \pi, G), \quad Dr = \nu L(Y, r, M), \quad \text{and} \quad F(Y, r, \pi) = 0 \qquad (3C\text{-}1)$$

where M and G may be taken to be given exogenously.

It is useful to analyze this system with the aid of another diagram in Y, r space, Fig. 3C-1. In this diagram, the upward sloping line $Dr = 0$ is the locus $L(Y, r, M) = 0$ or the LM curve. The IS and BF curves are sketched in as before on the assumption that the exchange rate is given. However, given the Marshall-Lerner elasticity condition (and the absence of destabilizing speculation), an appreciation of the currency (an increase in π) will shift both curves to the left, whereas a depreciation shifts both curves to the right. It follows that, as the exchange rate changes, a *locus of intersection points* between the IS and BF curves is traced out. This IS–BF intersection locus (or exchange locus) is the downward sloping line labelled $DY = 0$ in the diagram. It is established by solving $F(Y, r, \pi) = 0$ for π in terms of Y and r and substituting the resulting value of π into $DY = \lambda Z(Y, r, \pi, G)$, thus tracing out an implicit $DY = 0$ locus in Y, r space, given G, of course. Higher values of π are associated with points along this locus which lie further to the north-west, whereas lower values of π are associated with points lying further to the south-east.

Figure 3C-1 Flexible exchange rates and the IS–BF intersection locus.

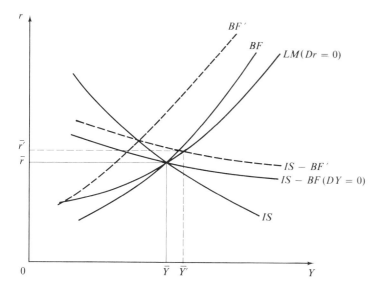

The downwards slope of the *IS–BF* intersection locus requires further explanation. Assuming that G is constant, $Z(Y, r, \pi, G) = 0$ and $F(Y, r, \pi) = 0$ may be differentiated totally and, when $d\pi$ is eliminated across the two equations, one obtains

$$dr/dY = \frac{-(F_\pi Z_Y - Z_\pi F_Y)}{(F_\pi Z_r - Z_\pi F_r)} \tag{3C-2}$$

On the standard assumptions, with $mps > 0$ and $mpm > 0$ representing the marginal propensities to save and import, respectively, the partial derivatives included in this expression take the following form: (a) $Z_Y = -(mps + mpm) < 0$, $Z_r < 0$, and $Z_\pi = \partial(\text{exports} - \text{imports})/\partial\pi < 0$ if the Marshall-Lerner elasticity condition holds, and (b) $F_Y = -(mpm) < 0$, $F_r > 0$, and $F_\pi = \partial(\text{exports} - \text{imports} + \text{capital inflows})/\partial\pi < 0$ if the Marshall-Lerner elasticity condition holds *and* currency speculation is not destabilizing. It follows immediately from these conditions that the denominator of Eq. (3C-2) must be positive. Moreover, since $-Z_Y > -F_Y$ and $-F_\pi \geq -Z_\pi$, it is evident that $F_\pi Z_Y$ must be greater than $Z_\pi F_Y$. Hence, $F_\pi Z_Y - Z_\pi F_Y > 0$ and the numerator of Eq. (3C-2) is negative. It follows that $dr/dY < 0$. The *IS–BF* intersection locus must be downward sloping.[15]

From an initial position of equilibrium (say $Y, \bar{r}$ in Fig. 3C-1), let it be assumed that there is a rise in foreign interest rates which leads to smaller capital inflows (or larger capital outflows) and (if the exchange rate were to be held constant) would shift the *BF* curve to *BF'* and the *IS–BF* intersection locus to *IS–BF'*, as illustrated in Fig. 3C-1. In consequence, with M and G held constant, the equilibrium level of national income and the equilibrium rate of interest rise to $\bar{Y}'$ and $\bar{r}'$, respectively.[16] Assuming stability, the adjustment towards the new equilibrium position occurs in the following manner. The rise in foreign interest rates leads to a capital outflow. Whereas under a fixed exchange rate regime this would have created a balance of payments deficit, under flexible exchange rates the capital outflow leads to a depreciation of the domestic currency. Given that the Marshall-Lerner elasticity condition holds, the fall in π is associated with an increase in the current account balance and leads to an expansion in the level of national income, although this expansion is limited by the consequential rise in the domestic interest rate which must occur if the money supply remains constant. Under flexible exchange rates, therefore, the adjustment process implies exchange rate changes which carry the intersection of the *IS* and *BF* curves onto the *LM* curve. This adjustment process may be sharply distinguished from the Humean specie-flow adjustment mechanism which characterizes a rigid gold standard regime. In particular, it should be noticed that the effect of a change

15. The introduction of a marginal propensity to tax does not alter this conclusion qualitatively. An alternative way of deriving the slope of the *IS–BF* intersection locus is presented in chapter 10.

16. An initial fall in foreign national income leading to a decrease in export earnings is fully offset in this model by a depreciation of the domestic currency, which leaves both Y and r unchanged. This result may not carry over to other models in which the fix price assumption is abandoned.

in foreign interest rates on domestic income goes in opposite directions under the fixed and flexible exchange rate regimes, though this result must be qualified once price repercussions are permitted. Indeed, in the more robust context of chapter 10 in which price effects and output effects can be appropriately separated, it is demonstrated that under flexible exchange rates the price effects of a rise in foreign interest rates are positive, *but the output effects are likely to be negative* (as in the fixed exchange rate case). One may therefore conclude that there is a basic inconsistency in the attempt to handle flexible exchange rates in a fix-price framework, an inconsistency which can easily lead to results that are misleading if not erroneous.

Analysis of the stability of equilibrium requires a consideration of the characteristic equation of the system given in expression (3C-1). This equation may be written as

$$-F_\pi \rho^2 + \{\lambda(F_\pi Z_Y - Z_\pi F_Y) + v F_\pi L_r\}\rho + \lambda v\{(F_\pi Z_r - Z_\pi F_r)L_Y$$
$$- (F_\pi Z_Y - Z_\pi F_Y)L_r\} = 0 \qquad (3C-3)$$

where the partial derivatives are again evaluated at the equilibrium point, namely $Z(Y, r, \pi, G) = L(Y, r, M) = F(Y, r, \pi) = 0$, given M and G. Since $F_\pi Z_Y - Z_\pi F_Y > 0$, it is not difficult to establish that all the coefficients of this quadratic characteristic equation are positive. Therefore, there can be no characteristic roots with non-negative real parts. The equilibrium point is necessarily locally stable, though it may well be approached through damped cyclical oscillations. In terms of Fig. 3C-1, these oscillations would occur in a counter-clockwise direction, with peaks (troughs) in the level of national income appearing to precede peaks (troughs) in the rate of interest by one cyclical phase, similarly to the original *IS–LM* prototype for a closed economy.

In this model, instability is only likely to occur if (a) the elasticities of export and import demand are so low in the short run that the Marshall-Lerner condition fails, or (b) currency speculation is sufficiently destabilizing, thus making the sign of F_π positive (and with it $Z_\pi > 0$ if the Marshall-Lerner condition fails). If F_π is positive in the short run, the only sensible response that the authorities have to an increase in foreign interest rates is to raise the domestic rate of interest, thus preventing capital outflows from increasing and the exchange rate (π) from falling. This can most effectively be achieved by a reduction in the domestic money supply, in which case the flexible exchange rate regime turns out to behave very much like the fixed rate regime.

D: STABILIZATION POLICY IN AN OPEN ECONOMY

Under fixed exchange rates, a small open economy cannot maintain an independent monetary policy. The attempt to do so despite shifts in foreign monetary policies must have a substantial impact on the state of the balance of payments. Since changes in foreign exchange reserves will be difficult to sterilize if international capital flows are interest elastic, shifts in foreign monetary policies are sooner or later bound to generate changes in the domestic money supply.

Under flexible exchange rates, it is theoretically possible to maintain an independent monetary policy. For example, a small open economy that is concerned about its dependence on long term capital inflows may attempt to reduce the deficit on the current account of its balance of payments by maintaining a monetary policy which is loose enough to ensure a low external value of the currency. From an initial position of unemployment, such a policy will also aid the achievement of full employment. Thus, in this case, both a short run employment objective and a balance of payments composition objective are served, it may be argued, by an easier monetary policy.[17] Of course, both monetary and fiscal policy must normally be used to achieve these two objectives simultaneously, implying as they do the existence of a target rate of interest. In particular, contractionary fiscal policy *must* be used in conjunction with expansionary monetary policy if the current account balance is to be improved without moving aggregate output or employment from its target level. In this case, however, the assignment question is rather unimportant. Indeed, under the simplifying assumption that $Z(Y, r, \pi, G) = L(Y, r, M) = 0$ used in Sec. B of this chapter, it can easily be shown that either assignment of monetary and fiscal policy to interest rate and national income targets is stable (given F_π and Z_π negative).

Although the possibility of maintaining an independent monetary policy is considerably enhanced under flexible exchange rates, the degree to which this is so depends strongly on the stability of the foreign exchange market. If the foreign exchange market is unstable the authorities are bound to intervene, with consequences similar to the fixed exchange rate case, especially if the resulting changes in foreign exchange reserves are difficult to sterilize because international capital flows are interest elastic. In this case, the independence of domestic monetary policy is heavily circumscribed, and the exchange rate regime becomes one of *managed flexibility*.

Since in reality substitution effects do take considerable time, the Marshall-Lerner condition may well fail in the short run. In such a situation, depreciation of the domestic currency will lead to a temporary *fall* in the current account surplus (or a rise in the deficit) which is eventually reversed as substitution effects come into operation. If lags of this sort cause the initial trade balance effects of currency depreciation to be perverse, the stability of the foreign exchange market under flexible exchange rates must depend upon the existence of stabilizing speculation.

To be stabilizing, the behavior of private speculators must be governed by expectations which are inelastic in the short run. That is to say, speculators must behave as if there exists a normal or customary level of the exchange rate

---

17. It is pointed out in chapter 13 of this book that, once the inflationary repercussions of such a policy are taken into account, this conclusion is likely to be misleading if not fallacious.

which responds only slowly to underlying economic conditions.[18] This will generally be the case, for example, if exchange rate expectations are adaptive; that is,

$$D\pi^* = \delta(\pi - \pi^*), \quad \text{or} \quad \pi^*(t) = \int_{-\infty}^{t} \delta\, e^{\delta(\tau - t)}\, \pi(\tau)\, d\tau \qquad (3D\text{-}1)$$

where π^* is the expected or "normal" exchange rate, π is the actual exchange rate, and $\delta > 0$ is the speed of response of the adaptive expectations mechanism.[19] It is evident from this equation that the normal exchange rate is a "weighted average" of all past values of the actual exchange rate, with the weights declining exponentially with time.

There can be little doubt that the existence of stabilizing speculation must itself depend upon the experience of a previous history of roughly constant exchange rates. Thus, if the Marshall-Lerner condition fails in the short run, the possibility of an independent monetary policy that is promised by flexible as opposed to fixed exchange rates depends for its continuity on the implementation of monetary policies which are not very different from one's trading partners'. Moreover, even if fundamentally different monetary policies are temporarily pursued, the short run inelasticity of exchange rate expectations will reduce the impact of these policies on both the actual exchange rate and the level of national income. Thus, from the point of view of stabilization policy, the inelasticity of exchange rate expectations (just like the maintenance of a fixed exchange rate) is highly beneficial if the external environment remains stable and if disturbances are domestic in origin. However, when large scale disturbances are occurring in the world economy, these expectations (like the maintenance of a fixed exchange rate) make it more difficult to stabilize the economy through the use of the

18. For example, the expectation that the US dollar exchange rate will remain roughly constant through time may well be deeply rooted in Canadian traditions. It is associated with the fact that the Canadian economy has experienced and is expected to continue experiencing common overall movements with the US economy. Although this expectation of a roughly constant exchange rate may make it difficult to insulate the Canadian economy from *external* shocks, it may well be an important element in the stability of the economy in response to *internal* shocks. This point is well illustrated by the monetary instabilities created in 1961–62 when the all too successful attempt by the government to "talk" down the exchange rate undermined this firmly entrenched expectation. On this point, compare R. M. Dunn, *Canada's Experience with Fixed and Flexible Exchange Rates in a North American Capital Market,* Canadian–American Committee, Washington, D.C., May, 1971, pp. 61–62.

19. It is not difficult to show that the two expressions in (3D-1) are equivalent. Since $\delta\, e^{-\delta t}$ is independent of the integral, the second expression may be written as

$$(\delta\, e^{-\delta t})^{-1} \pi^*(t) = \int_{-\infty}^{t} e^{\delta\tau}\, \pi(\tau)\, d\tau$$

Differentiating this expression with respect to time, one obtains

$$e^{\delta t}\, \pi^*(t) + \delta^{-1}\, e^{\delta t}\, d\pi^*(t)/dt = e^{\delta t}\, \pi(t)$$

Dividing through by $e^{\delta t} \neq 0$ and rearranging, one obtains (dropping the t-arguments) the first expression in (3D-1) above.

exchange rate as an insulating device. A more extensive elaboration of this conclusion can be found in chapters 10 and 11 of this book.

Throughout this chapter, real stock adjustments of the inventory variety have been ignored. Once they are reinstituted, however, the accelerator mechanism comes back into operation, though it is important to note that the additional leakage from the income–expenditure stream into imports is likely to reduce the amplitude of oscillations and render the model more stable. In addition, fluctuations in foreign exchange reserves may be seen to play an important buffer stock role. Indeed, the counterpart to active inventory accumulation (decumulation) may well be a fall (rise) in the level of foreign exchange reserves. Thus, the value sum of inventory stocks and foreign exchange reserves is likely to be considerably more stable (in a relative sense) than either inventories or the stock of exchange reserves when these are taken separately.

E: SOME LIMITATIONS OF THE ANALYSIS

In previous sections, the nominal stock of money outstanding, M, has been taken to be determined either exogenously or by the reaction function of the monetary authorities to the state of the balance of international payments. We did not explicitly link the nominal stock of money to governmental borrowing requirements, although this could easily have been done. Indeed, the reaction function of the monetary authorities might well be written as

$$DM = m_0 + m_1 F(Y, r, \pi) + m_2 G \qquad (3E\text{-}1)$$

where M is the nominal stock of money, $F(Y, r, \pi)$ is the overall balance of payments *surplus*, G is the governmental budgetary *deficit*, m_0 is a shift parameter, $m_1 > 0$ measures the extent to which the balance of payments surplus becomes monetized, $m_2 > 0$ measures the proportion of the governmental budgetary deficit which is financed by new money creation, and $D \equiv d/dt$ is the differential operator as before. The balance of payments surplus, $F(Y, r, \pi)$, may again be specified as an increasing function of the nominal interest rate ($F_r > 0$) and a decreasing function of both the level of national income in nominal terms ($F_Y < 0$) and the foreign exchange rate ($F_\pi < 0$), though once price effects are allowed the $F(Y, r, \pi)$ specification of the balance of payments surplus must be amended.

There is no reason to suppose that m_0, m_1, and m_2 are constant; indeed, a good case can be made for supposing that m_1 and m_2 are both increasing functions of the nominal interest rate, r. If the nominal interest rate is already high in relationship to given foreign interest rates, the less likely is it that the monetary authorities will try to sterilize inflows of foreign exchange. In addition, the higher is the nominal interest rate and thus the cost of servicing the governmental budgetary deficit if it is financed by issuing new debt obligations (government bonds) to the public, the greater will be the pressure on the authorities to monetize G. If this is so, changes in the nominal money supply are unambiguously a positive function of the price of money, namely the nominal rate of interest, r.

Although the monetary authorities may be able to control the nominal supply of money, the volume of money outstanding is unlikely to be determined exogenously once the reaction function of the monetary authorities is considered. The reaction function given in Eq. (3E-1) is robust with respect to exchange rate regimes, and is particularly appropriate in a regime of *managed flexibility*. It may be coupled with the two excess demand functions,

$$DY = \lambda Z(Y, r, \pi, G) \quad \text{and} \quad Dr = vL(Y, r, M) \tag{3E-2}$$

that were introduced earlier in this chapter. Given the governmental budgetary deficit, G, there remains at most one degree of freedom in the model which allows the authorities to choose between alternative combinations of M and π, with high values of M being associated with low values of π, and *vice versa*.

It follows that the nominal money supply may well have to be treated as an endogenous variable. This conclusion does not simply depend upon the usual notion that there is some interest elasticity to primary–secondary relationships if commercial banks hold excess reserves. Rather, it rests upon the interest elasticity of the supply of primary money operating through the reaction function of the central banking authorities.

Finally, in an economy operating with a flexible exchange rate (and *a fortiori* in an inflationary economy regardless of exchange rate regime), the fix-price line of approach that has been followed so far is severely limited since it gives no means of separating out the price repercussions from the quantity repercussions that occur when nominal national income shifts. Moreover, it does not distinguish real balances, M/P, from the nominal stock of money, M, where P measures the domestic price level. There appear to be two ways of proceeding. One of these is to examine the long run equilibrium dynamic consequences of an expanding nominal stock of money in a context in which the rate of resource utilization (and associated unemployment percentage) remains constant (presumably at its natural rate), and in which expectations (including inflationary expectations) are always realized. This is the equilibrium dynamic line of approach of the so-called "money growth" models.[20] The other, and more difficult, way is to integrate formally the demand for real cash balances and the determinants of the nominal stock of money with the kinds of models discussed in chapters 11 and 12 of this book, thus providing a monetary theory of inflation which is fully integrated with variations in overall rates of resource utilization.

However one proceeds, it is important to realize that control by the monetary authorities over the nominal money supply does not imply control over the total volume of real balances that individual decision making units wish to hold, since

---

20. For a brief but lucid treatment of these models see R. M. Solow, *Growth Theory: An Exposition*, Oxford, Oxford University Press, 1970, chapter 4, pp. 58–76. This route is left largely unexplored in this book since it surely fails to capture the fundamental "monetary nature" of a monetary economy.

the price level remains a free variable. Indeed, changes in the price level are one of the means by which the actual volume of real cash balances that is outstanding at a given point of time is eventually brought into equality with the volume of real cash balances that the community desires to hold. Variations in nominal (and real) interest rates as well as overall rates of resource utilization will, of course, be observed on route. Themes of this kind are explored more fully in Part Three of this book.

FOUR

FIXED CAPITAL AND ECONOMIC FLUCTUATIONS

A: LINEAR AND NON-LINEAR ACCELERATORS

In chapter 1 of this book, a linear multiplier–accelerator model incorporating circulating capital and inventory adjustments was analyzed in some detail. Mention was made in chapter 2 of the possibility of treating other investment goods in the same way. In the present chapter, however, we present a more traditional analysis of fixed capital investment and plant size adjustments in linear and non-linear multiplier–accelerator models of the trade cycle.

The story begins with the assumption that inventory adjustments can be ignored so that (as in the case of the *IS–LM* prototype discussed in Sec. B of chapter 2) output and expected sales are identical. Once again, output (or expected sales) adjusts towards actual sales (or aggregate expenditure) via an exponentially distributed lag function with speed of response $\lambda > 0$. Thus,

$$DY = \lambda(E - Y) \tag{4A-1}$$

where Y is output and E is expenditure. Expenditure is assumed to be the sum of induced consumption expenditure, cY, autonomous expenditure, A, and accelerator induced net investment expenditure, I. Thus, one has[1]

$$E = cY + A + I \tag{4A-2}$$

The multiplier–accelerator model may be completed by letting I adjust towards a target level which depends upon *changes* in the level of output. If this target

---

1. Notice that our simple expenditure function has now been augmented by the I term. If this term were ignored, the system would reduce to the simple multiplier model with solution

$$Y(t) = A/s + \{Y(0) - A/s\} \, e^{-\lambda st}$$

where $s = (1 - c)$ is the marginal propensity to save, $Y(0)$ is the initial level of output, and $Y(t)$ is the level of output at time t. The process implied by this equation is obviously stable.

level of net investment expenditure is given by $I^* = f(vDY)$, with $v > 0$ and $f' > 0$, then one may write

$$DI = \eta \{ f(vDY) - I \} \tag{4A-3}$$

where $\eta > 0$ is the speed with which actual investment responds to its target level, $f(vDY)$.

Substituting from expressions (4A-2) and (4A-3) into expression (4A-1), one obtains the fundamental differential equation

$$(D + \lambda)Y = \lambda \left\{ cY + A + \frac{\eta}{D + \eta} f(vDY) \right\} \tag{4A-4}$$

The solution to this differential equation depends upon the functional form assumed for $f(vDY)$. In particular, if $f(vDY) = vDY$ for a constant value of the accelerator coefficient, v, then a simple *linear* multiplier–accelerator model results. In the remainder of this section, this linear version will be analyzed. Since various problems arise in its economic interpretation, in the following section two alternative specifications of a non-linear multiplier–accelerator model are outlined and compared. These two alternative specifications are due, respectively, to Hicks and Goodwin.[2]

In the case of a linear accelerator mechanism with $f(vDY) = vDY$, the general solution to Eq. (4A-4) for constant A may be written as

$$Y(t) = A/s + B_1 e^{\rho_1 t} + B_2 e^{\rho_2 t} \tag{4A-5}$$

where $s = 1 - c$ is the marginal propensity to save, B_1 and B_2 are arbitrary constants which depend upon the initial conditions,[3] and ρ_1 and ρ_2 are the characteristic roots of the equation,

$$T\rho^2 + (T + s - v)\rho + s = 0$$

namely

$$\rho_1, \rho_2 = \frac{(v - s - T) \pm \sqrt{\{(v - s - T)^2 - 4sT\}}}{2T} \tag{4A-6}$$

---

2. See J. R. Hicks, *A Contribution to the Theory of the Trade Cycle*, Oxford, Oxford University Press, 1950, and R. M. Goodwin, "The Non-Linear Accelerator and the Persistence of Business Cycles," *Econometrica*, vol. 19, January 1951, pp. 1–17. The original analysis is to be found in P. A. Samuelson, "Interaction between the Multiplier Analysis and the Principle of Acceleration," *Review of Economics and Statistics*, vol. 21, May 1939, pp. 75–78.

3. That is to say, B_1 and B_2 may be derived from the two equations:

$$B_1 + B_2 = Y(0) - A/s \quad \text{and} \quad B_1\rho_1 + B_2\rho_2 = DY(0)$$

It should be noted that the value assigned to $DY(0)$ in the second of these two equations is equal to $-\lambda s \{ Y(0) - A/s \}$ if it is assumed that $I(0) = 0$, so that the accelerator mechanism has not yet come into operation at time 0.

In deriving Eq. (4A-6), it has been assumed that the length of the investment lag is unity ($\eta = 1$) to normalize the lag parameters, and that $T \equiv 1/\lambda$ where T may be called the time constant of the output lag. On these assumptions, $T < 1$ is associated with an output lag which is shorter than the investment lag, whereas for $T > 1$ the output lag is longer than the investment lag. In addition, the normalization rule allows one to treat the accelerator coefficient, v, as an implicit inverse measure of the length of the investment lag. Thus, a long investment lag will be associated with a small value for v, whereas for a short investment lag one generally expects a large value for v.

Given expression (4A-6), it is not difficult to show that there are four possible ways in which the model can respond to a shift in A which disturbs an initial equilibrium situation. If $v < (\sqrt{T} - \sqrt{s})^2$, both characteristic roots are real and negative, and the response function is characterized by a damped non-oscillatory movement towards the new equilibrium position, much like the simple multiplier case. If $(\sqrt{T} - \sqrt{s})^2 < v < T + s$, the characteristic roots are conjugate complex numbers with negative real parts, and the response function is characterized by damped cyclical oscillations around the new equilibrium position. If $T + s < v < (\sqrt{T} + \sqrt{s})^2$, the characteristic roots are conjugate complex numbers with positive real parts, and the response function is characterized by explosive cyclical oscillations around the new equilibrium position. Finally, if $(\sqrt{T} + \sqrt{s})^2 < v$, both characteristic roots are real and positive, and the response function is characterized by an explosive non-oscillatory movement which overshoots the new equilibrium position and diverges away from it in perpetuity.

Putting the non-oscillatory cases on one side, for the remaining oscillatory cases the conjugate complex roots may be written as $\rho_1, \rho_2 = \alpha \pm i\omega$, where $\alpha = (v - s - T)/2T$, $\omega = \sqrt{\{4sT - (v - s - T)^2\}}/2T$, and i is the imaginary unit. As demonstrated in Sec. D of chapter 1, it is then not difficult to show that the solution (4A-5) may be written in the form:

$$Y(t) = A/s + B\,e^{\alpha t}\cos(\omega t - \varepsilon) \tag{4A-7}$$

where B and ε are arbitrary constants that depend upon the initial conditions.[4] Despite its mathematical convenience, this solution, which is dependent upon the linearity of the model, gives rise to at least three problems of economic interpretation.[5]

In the first place, trade cycles are more or less regular; they tend neither to damp out nor explode through time. However, regular oscillations can only occur in the linear multiplier–accelerator model if $v = s + T$, which is a highly unlikely configuration of parameters. Thus, there is a problem of non-regular amplitude, making it necessary to assume either that the trade cycle is basically damped but is kept alive by "random or erratic shocks" in autonomous expenditure, or

4. More exactly, $B\cos\varepsilon = B_1 + B_2$ and $B\sin\varepsilon = (B_1 - B_2)i$, where B_1 and B_2 are explained in footnote 3 of this chapter. See also Sec. D of chapter 1, especially footnote 14 of chapter 1.
5. The analysis at this point follows closely that of Allen, *Macro-economic Theory*, pp. 364–369.

that the trade cycle is basically explosive but is constrained by the existence of "ceilings and floors" in a manner which is well illustrated by the Hicks and Goodwin models outlined in the following section.

In the second place, trade cycles do not appear to be symmetric: the upswing often tends to be longer than the downswing. Although it is possible to generate this effect in a linear model by grafting it onto a growing trend in autonomous expenditure, this solution seems somewhat *ad hoc*. Thus, there remains a problem of cyclical symmetry.

In the third place, trade cycles appear to have an intrinsic amplitude, rather than an arbitrary amplitude based simply upon initial conditions. Thus, there is a problem of arbitrary amplitude. The purpose of the following section is to illustrate how non-linear multiplier-accelerator models can avoid these problems of economic interpretation that arise in the linear case.

B: THE HICKS AND GOODWIN MODELS: A COMPARISON

In his model of the trade cycle, Hicks assumes that the multiplier-accelerator mechanism is basically explosive as implied by values of the accelerator coefficient, v, which exceed $s + T$. The explosive nature of the accelerator is kept in check by the imposition of a capacity constraint or ceiling, which, although it may be rising through time, puts a limit on the upswing of any particular cyclical movement. Thus, the investment process associated with the upswing is limited by the capacity of the capital goods trades. In addition, the accelerator mechanism is allowed to go out of operation in the downswing when there is excess capacity. Indeed, the disinvestment process associated with the downswing is limited by the scrapping rate for capital goods.

Let M represent the scrapping rate for capital goods, and $L + M$ represent the gross investment capacity of the capital goods trades. Then L is the net investment capacity of the capital goods trades. Using this notation, Hicks' non-linear accelerator may be represented by

(a) $\qquad\qquad$ if $\ DY \geq 0, \ f(vDY) = vDY \leq L$

and $\hfill$ (4B-1)

(b) $\qquad\qquad$ if $\ DY < 0, \ f(vDY) = -M$

In the upswing ($DY \geq 0$), target gross (induced) investment is equal to $M + vDY$ provided this does not exceed $M + L$, and target net (induced) investment is equal to vDY provided this does not exceed L. In the downswing ($DY < 0$), target gross investment is zero and target net investment is $-M$. Thus, gross investment is constrained to lie between $L + M$ and 0, whereas net investment is constrained to lie between L and $-M$. There are, therefore, two distinct equations representing the behavior of the system in the upswing and the downswing, respectively. These two equations are

(a) $$(D + \lambda)Y = \lambda \left\{ cY + A + \frac{\eta}{D + \eta}(vDY) \right\}, \quad \text{if} \quad vDY \leq L$$

and (4B-2)

(b) $$(D + \lambda)Y = \lambda \left\{ cY + A + \frac{\eta}{D + \eta}(-M) \right\}$$

The first of these equations has the characteristic roots given in expression (4A-6) herein assumed to be conjugate complex numbers with positive real parts, whereas the second of these equations has characteristic roots $-\eta$ and $-\lambda s$, which are obviously both real and negative.

The system behaves in the following way. Let an initial equilibrium situation with $Y = A/s$ be disturbed by a short lived burst in autonomous expenditure represented by a temporary increase in A. In consequence, output must begin to increase, thus bringing the accelerator into operation. An upswing ensues which may or may not peak before the ceiling (where net output is equal to $(A + L)/s$) is reached. In either case, output eventually ceases to rise and the accelerator mechanism goes out of operation. Since, however, the level of output is then necessarily above its equilibrium level it cannot be sustained and a slump develops. This slump carries net output down towards a level equal to $(A - M)/s$, the scrappage of capital equipment then acting like negative autonomous expenditure. However, as long as there is some limit to this disinvestment process, as there necessarily must be if autonomous expenditure has a slowly rising trend through time, the slump must necessarily give way to an upswing which carries the level of output past its equilibrium level A/s towards the ceiling. Whether or not the ceiling is reached, the level of output must eventually cease to rise and the cycle turns over once again.

The Hicks model of the trade cycle avoids the three basic problems of economic interpretation that linear multiplier–accelerator models present. First, the amplitude of cyclical fluctuations is approximately regular. This is especially so for strong booms where the cyclical upswing is broken by the capacity ceiling rather than petering out of its own accord. Second, the cycle is asymmetric because the upswing is likely to be shorter than the downswing unless autonomous expenditure has a fairly rapidly rising trend. Once monetary repercussions are incorporated, though, the real crisis which occurs as the boom turns over is likely to be accompanied by a monetary crisis, the expectational consequences of which are associated with a temporary fall in the level of autonomous expenditure which speeds up the fall in output. Indeed, we have encountered this possibility in Sec. B of chapter 2. Third, the cyclical fluctuations have an intrinsic amplitude which is basically determined by the economic variables, L and M, rather than simply by the historical initial conditions.

Using this same L and M notation for the net investment capacity of the capital goods trades and the scrapping rate for capital goods, respectively, the

Goodwin model of the trade cycle incorporates an accelerator mechanism of the form

$$f(vDY) = M\left[\frac{L+M}{Le^{-vDY}+M} - 1\right]$$

or (equivalently)

$$\frac{L-f(vDY)}{L} = \frac{M+f(vDY)}{M}e^{-vDY} \qquad (4B-3)$$

This mechanism, which explains the target level of net investment expenditure $f(vDY)$, has the following properties:

(a)   as $vDY \to \infty$, $f(vDY) \to L$ and $f'(vDY) \to 0$

(b)   as $vDY \to 0$, $f(vDY) \to 0$ and $f'(vDY) \to ML/(L+M)$ (4B-4)

(c)   as $vDY \to -\infty$, $f(vDY) \to -M$ and $f'(vDY) \to 0$

It follows that $f(vDY)$ has the functional form of a logistic curve and may be graphed as illustrated in Fig. 4B-1. Once again, target net investment is constrained to lie between L and $-M$, with target gross investment lying between $L+M$ and 0.

If A is constant, and the output lag is very short relative to the investment lag so that $\lambda \to \infty$ and $D + \lambda \to \lambda$, one may write the fundamental differential Eq. (4A-4) as

$$Y - \frac{A}{s} = \frac{f(vDY) - sDY}{s} \qquad (4B-5)$$

provided that the speed of response of the investment lag is taken to be unity ($\eta = 1$). Alternatively, an identical expression may be obtained if the investment lag is very short relative to the output lag so that $\eta \to \infty$ and $D + \eta \to \eta$, provided that the speed of response of the output lag times the marginal propensity to save is taken to be equal to unity ($\lambda s = 1$). On either of these two assumptions, the resulting expression (4B-5) indicates that the deviation of net output from its equilibrium level, A/s, depends simply upon the difference between target induced investment, $f(vDY)$, and induced savings, sDY.

Let $sDY = (vDY)s/v$ be represented by the upward sloping straight line in Fig. 4B-1, and let it be assumed that sDY intersects $f(vDY)$ three times as illustrated in the diagram. This is equivalent to the assumption that the accelerator mechanism would be explosive in the neighborhood of the origin ($vDY = 0$), though as we shall see the accelerator never operates on this unstable middle section of the $f(vDY)$ locus; rather, it operates in the two stable sections of the $f(vDY)$ locus, contained between points a and c and between points d and f

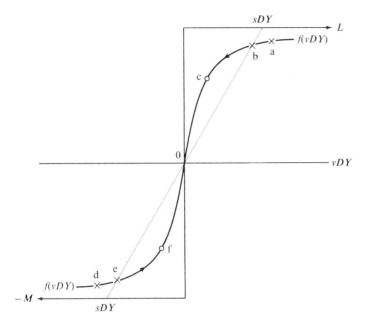

Figure 4B-1 The logistic function $f(vDY)$.

in the diagram, and jumps from c to d at cyclical peaks and from f to a at cyclical troughs.

To illustrate the cyclical mechanism involved, suppose that output is initially beginning to expand out of a cyclical trough at point a in Fig. 4B-1. At this point, $Y < A/s$, $DY > 0$ and $f(vDY) < sDY$. Output proceeds to rise but at an ever-diminishing rate through point b at which $Y = A/s$ until point c is reached. Thus, the arc from a to c represents a cyclical upswing. At point c, $f(vDY) - sDY$ is maximal, implying that $Y - A/s$ is also maximal by Eq. (4B-5). A peak is reached at which point DY falls instantaneously to zero. But from Eq. (4B-5) it cannot be zero with $Y \neq A/s$, so that it must in fact fall instantaneously to a level at which it is sufficiently negative to generate the required positive discrepancy between $f(vDY)$ and sDY. This point is represented by d in Fig. 4B-1. At this point, $Y > A/s$, $DY < 0$, and $f(vDY) > sDY$. Output proceeds to fall but at an ever-diminishing rate through point e at which $Y = A/s$ until point f is reached. Thus, the arc from d to f represents a cyclical downswing. At point f, $f(vDY) - sDY$ is minimal, implying that $Y - A/s$ is also minimal by Eq. (4B-5). A trough is reached at which point DY rises instantaneously to zero. But from Eq. (4B-5) it cannot be zero with $Y \neq A/s$, so that it must in fact rise instantaneously to a level at which it is sufficiently positive to generate the required negative discrepancy between $f(vDY)$ and sDY. This point is represented by a in Fig. 4B-1. The cyclical process thus continues in the sequence a, b, c, d, e, f. Along this process, although $Y - A/s$ is a continuous function of time, the switching of regime between the upswing and the downswing (and *vice versa*) is associated with sharp discontinuities in DY. Finally, the story is only altered in rather insignificant ways if both the output and the investment lags are taken to have finite speed of response parameters.

Like the Hicks model, the Goodwin model of the trade cycle avoids the three basic problems of economic interpretation that linear multiplier–accelerator models present. First, the amplitude of cyclical fluctuations is definitely regular, though net output oscillates between narrower limits than $(A + L)/s$ and $(A - M)/s$. Second, the cycle will be asymmetric as long as L and M are unequal. In particular, the upswing will be longer (but slower) than the downswing if the net investment capacity of the capital goods trades, L, is smaller than the scrapping rate for capital goods, M. Third, the cyclical fluctuations have an intrinsic amplitude which is entirely determined by the economic variables, L and M, in conjunction with the fundamental structural parameters of the model, especially s and v.

Both the Hicks and Goodwin models are therefore superior to the simple linear model from the point of view of economic interpretation. Although both models include non-linear accelerator mechanisms, their underlying behavior is rather different. In particular, the time shape for output in the Hicks model still retains something of the sinusoidal form characteristic of linear models; indeed, on the upswing, the model takes the same path as the linear multiplier–accelerator mechanism until the ceiling is reached, although the downswing takes a path that is similar to the simple multiplier process. On the other hand, the time shape for output in the Goodwin model produces sharp peaks and troughs with the rate of output expansion falling throughout the upswing and the rate of output contraction falling throughout the downswing. Finally, both models incorporate some of the particular economic reasons why the period or frequency of the trade cycle is fairly constant.[6] In particular, they both emphasize capacity constraints, especially in the capital goods trades, as well as the economic life of durable capital goods, via the introduction of the scrappage rate. Neither model, however, considers the impact of the degree of capacity utilization on prices, a topic which will be considered in detail in Part Three of this book.

Although both the Hicks and Goodwin models avoid the interpretation problems inherent in the simple linear model, they need to be supplemented by a discussion of (a) the place of money and prices in the business cycle, (b) the distinction between autonomous and induced investment, (c) the relationship between growth trends and cyclical fluctuations, and (d) the role of psychology

---

6. Compare Keynes, *The General Theory*, p. 317, where he says: "The explanation of the *time-element* in the trade cycle, of the fact that an interval of time of a particular order of magnitude must usually elapse before recovery begins, is to be sought in the influences which govern the recovery of the marginal efficiency of capital. There are reasons, given first by the length of life of durable assets in relation to the normal rate of growth in a given epoch, and secondly, by the carrying-costs of surplus stocks, why the duration of the downward movement should have an order of magnitude which is not fortuitous, which does not fluctuate between, say, one year this time and ten years next time, but which shows some regularity of habit between, let us say, three and five years."

and expectational shifts in the whole process.[7] Some attempt has been made to discuss these matters in chapter 2 of this book, and further aspects are taken up in Part Three. There can be no doubt, however, that the multiplier–accelerator interaction process (linear or non-linear) is too mechanical to describe adequately the cyclical process in any actual economy. Nevertheless, it is difficult to see any other process serving better as the analytical core to a more general model of the business cycle.

C: THE HARROD MODEL AND THE "KNIFE EDGE" PROBLEM

As a link to Part Two of this book, it is useful to consider what happens to the fundamental differential Eq. (4A-4) when both the output and the investment lags are ignored. Suppose, then, that both speeds of response are infinitely large, that is $D + \lambda \to \lambda \to \infty$ and $D + \eta \to \eta \to \infty$. On this assumption, Eq. (4A-4) reduces to

$$sY = A + f(vDY) \qquad (4\text{C-}1)$$

If, in addition, autonomous expenditure is set equal to zero ($A = 0$) and the accelerator mechanism is taken to be linear, one obtains the following flow equilibrium (savings equal investment) condition

$$sY = vDY, \quad \text{with solution} \quad Y(t) = Y(0)\,e^{gt}, \quad \text{where} \quad g = s/v \qquad (4\text{C-}2)$$

The equilibrium growth path of the system implies that output grows at the rate g. Indeed, $g = s/v$ is Harrod's famous equation for *the warranted rate of growth*.[8]

The warranted rate of growth is defined to be "that over-all rate of advance which, if executed, will leave entrepreneurs in a state of mind in which they are prepared to carry on a similar advance."[9] It is equal to the savings propensity (s) divided by the incremental capital requirements ratio or accelerator coefficient (v), where both s, the proportion of output (or income) that is saved, and v are assumed to be constant.

An alternative way of deriving Eq. (4C-2) is due to Domar.[10] Whereas Harrod starts from the capital requirements or accelerator condition $I = vDY$ and equates investment with savings $S = sY$ to obtain $sY = vDY$, Domar starts with a full capacity utilization condition of the form $K = bY$, where K is the existing capital stock, Y is aggregate output as before, and b is the reciprocal

7. The interested reader should consult both Hicks, *A Contribution to the Theory of the Trade Cycle*, and N. Kaldor, "Hicks on the Trade Cycle," pp. 193–209 in Kaldor, *Essays on Economic Stability and Growth*, London, Duckworth, 1960.

8. See R. F. Harrod, *Towards a Dynamic Economics*, London, Macmillan, 1948, p. 81.

9. *Ibid.*, p. 82.

10. See E. D. Domar, "Capital Expansion, Rate of Growth, and Employment," *Econometrica*, vol. 14, April 1946, pp. 137–147.

of the capacity output–capital ratio or simply the capital–output ratio. Since investment (ignoring depreciation) is simply the increase in the capital stock, the flow equilibrium condition that investment equals savings yields $DK = sY$. It follows that

$$DK = \frac{sK}{b}, \quad \text{or} \quad K(t) = K(0)\,e^{(s/b)t} \tag{4C-3}$$

and the capital stock grows exponentially at the rate s/b. Moreover, it must then be implied by the full capacity utilization condition that output also grows at the rate s/b, given that s and b are taken to be constant. Along the equilibrium growth path, capital and output must grow at the same rate, $g = s/b$.

It is obvious from a comparison of expression (4C-2) and (4C-3) that the formal mathematical structure of the Harrod and Domar models, when expressed in continuous time, is identical. Indeed, the two models coincide with $v = b$ and, thus, $g = s/b$. There is, however, a difference in interpretation which is best illustrated by the use of analogous discrete time period models. In the Harrod version, the accelerator relationship may best be approximated by the backward difference $I(t) = v\{Y(t) - Y(t-1)\}$. In order to obtain the growth rate equation $\{Y(t) - Y(t-1)\}/Y(t-1) = s/v$, it is necessary to associate this accelerator relationship with a proportional savings function relating savings to past output, $S(t) = sY(t-1)$. In the Domar version, the full capacity utilization condition may best be approximated by the forward difference $I(t) = b\{Y(t+1) - Y(t)\}$. In order to obtain the growth rate equation $\{Y(t+1) - Y(t)\}/Y(t) = s/b$, it is necessary to associate the full capacity utilization condition with a proportional saving function relating savings to current output, $S(t) = sY(t)$. Other combinations lead to differences in the mathematics of the two versions, and different specifications of the warranted growth rate. Despite these (and, no doubt, other) differences in economic interpretation, the system as outlined may be referred to as the Harrod-Domar growth model.

For the system to be continuously on the warranted growth path, two conditions are necessary: (a) initial stock equilibrium, that is $K(0) = bY(0)$ and (b) continuous flow equilibrium, that is $DK = dK(t)/dt = sY(t)$, at all $t \geq 0$. Suppose, as an example of disequilibrium, that the initial capital stock, $K(0)$, is not equal to the desired capital stock at time zero. That is to say suppose that $K(0) \neq bY(0)$; the initial capital stock is not appropriately adjusted to the initial output. Suppose, however, that the savings–investment equilibrium condition is retained.[11] Is it now the case that the system converges back to a situation in which the ratio of K to Y is equal to b, and both grow at the warranted rate, g? In other words, does the system converge to a steady-state growth path with growth rate $g = s/b$?

Let the notion of the desired capital stock at time t be denoted $K^*(t)$.

---

11. It is easy to show that the addition of an output lag will not alter the conclusions of this section.

Then, by the earlier formulation, $K^*(t) = bY(t)$. Now suppose that desired investment at time t is equal to the investment that would be required if the system
were growing at the warranted rate, g, that is gK, plus some proportion $\mu > 0$
of the discrepancy between the desired capital stock and the actual capital stock
at time t. Moreover, let there be an exponentially distributed lag function with
speed of response $\eta > 0$ between actual investment (DK) and desired investment.
Then, one may write

$$DK = \frac{\eta}{D + \eta} \{gK + \mu(K^* - K)\} \qquad (4C\text{-}4)$$

Given the definition of the desired capital stock and the savings–investment
flow equilibrium condition, it follows that $K^* = bY = (b/s)DK$. Using the Harrod
equation $g = s/b$ and letting $x \equiv DK/K$, one may write expression (4C-4) as

$$Dx = \frac{\eta}{g}(g - \mu)(g - x) \qquad (4C\text{-}5)$$

with solution

$$x(t) = g + \{x(0) - g\} \, e^{\{(\mu - g)\eta/g\}t} \qquad (4C\text{-}6)$$

Notice that if $x(0) - g = 0$, $x(t) = g$. In other words, if the initial growth rate
of the capital stock is precisely equal to the warranted growth rate, the system
remains in steady-state equilibrium. However, if the initial growth rate is not
equal to the warranted growth rate, it will only converge back to this rate if the
second term in expression (4C-6) converges to zero as t increases. This occurs if
and only if $(\mu - g)\eta/g < 0$, or $g > \mu$. The error adjustment mechanism indicates
that steady-state growth in the capital stock at the warranted rate g is stable
if and only if $g > \mu$. On the other hand, it is unstable if and only if $g \le \mu$.

How is this result to be interpreted? Clearly, the smaller is μ the more
likely is the system to be stable. But what plausible values could one put on
μ? It is to be remembered that μ is the proportion of a given discrepancy
between desired and actual capital stock that producers plan to eliminate at time
t, or, in period analysis, in one period. The quicker, therefore, that producers
react to a surplus or deficiency in the actual capital stock, the larger is μ, and
the more likely is it that steady growth at the warranted growth rate is unstable.
The reciprocal of μ may be considered to be a measure of the length of the
investment planning interval or horizon. Hence, the shorter is this horizon, the
more likely is the model unstable.

How likely is stability? Consider $0.1 \le s \le 0.2$, and $2.0 \le b \le 4.0$ on annual
data. Then $0.025 \le g \le 0.10$. Suppose that $g = 0.025$. Then steady growth at the
warranted rate is stable if and only if the investment planning horizon exceeds
40 years. Moreover, even if $g = 0.10$, steady growth at the warranted rate is
stable if and only if the investment planning period exceeds 10 years. Since
these lengths of investment planning periods are unreasonably long, it is usually

concluded that any divergence from a path dictated by the warranted rate of growth is unlikely to be corrected. Indeed, the divergence between the actual and warranted growth rates is likely to grow through time and growth at the warranted rate is dynamically unstable. Hence, warranted growth paths of the Harrod-Domar growth model are usually characterized as "knife edge" paths.

The "knife edge" instability problem implies that if the initial growth rate of the capital stock, $x(0)$, is in excess of the equilibrium growth rate, g, because of an initial shortfall of the actual capital stock below the desired capital stock, then the positive difference $x(t) - g$ will increase with the passage of time. On the other hand, instability also implies that if $x(0)$ is less than g because of an initial excess of actual capital stock then the negative difference $x(t) - g$ will increase in absolute size with the passage of time. A disturbance associated with deficient capital stock is inflationary, while a disturbance associated with redundant capital stock is deflationary and normally leads to unemployment of the Keynesian type.

D: THE EXISTENCE PROBLEM

So far, however, nothing has been said about the supply of labor. Let it be assumed that the supply of labor is growing at a fixed rate, n, and that technological progress of the Harrod-neutral[12] or labor augmenting form is occurring at the fixed rate, m. Then the "effective stock of labor," $L(t)$, is growing at the rate $m + n$, or

$$\bar{L}(t) = L(0)\, e^{(m+n)t} \tag{4D-1}$$

which measures the supply of labor in efficiency units (or units of constant efficiency) at all points of time. Following Harrod, $m + n$ may be called *the natural rate of growth*.[13]

Now if the underlying technology or production function for output as a whole exhibits fixed technical input coefficients, to produce one unit of output will require b units of capital and (say) c efficiency units of labor.[14] Unless the capital–labor ratio is exactly equal to b/c, both capital and labor cannot be fully employed. Moreover, continuous full employment in the labor market

---

12. Technological change is said to be Harrod-neutral if and only if it leaves the capital–output ratio undisturbed at a constant rate of profit. It therefore leaves equilibrium factor shares unchanged at a constant rate of profit. See Harrod, *op. cit.*, p. 23. On this definition, technical progress is said to be capital saving (biased against the share of capital) if the capital–output ratio falls when the rate of profit is constant, and it is said to be labor saving (biased against the share of labor) if the capital–output ratio rises when the rate of profit is constant.

13. See Harrod, *op. cit.*, p. 87.

14. As indicated in Part Two of this book, the same result may be obtained with any linearly homogeneous production function for output as a whole, provided that for some reason the rate of profit is held constant.

requires that $Y(t) = c^{-1} L(0) e^{(m+n)t}$ for all $t \geq 0$, whereas continuous equilibrium in the capital market requires that $Y(t) = b^{-1} K(0) e^{gt}$ for all $t \geq 0$, where $g = s/b$. These two conditions can be satisfied simultaneously if and only if (a) $K(0)/L(0) = b/c$ and (b) $g = m + n$. A full capacity, full employment equilibrium growth path is possible only if $g = s/b = m + n$, that is, only if the warranted and natural rates of growth are equal. If this is not the case, such a growth path does not exist. If b, c, s, and $m + n$ are given constants, it is only by accident that the complete model has an equilibrium solution. Note, however, that if by accident g is equal to $m + n$, the equilibrium growth path is a *steady-state* growth path. That is to say, output, capital, and "the effective stock of labor" all grow at the same rate, $g = m + n$.

It has, therefore, been shown that in general a solution to the Harrod–Domar growth model satisfying the three conditions, (a) full employment of labor, (b) full capacity utilization, and (c) savings equals investment, does not exist. All three conditions cannot be satisfied at once unless $g = s/b = m + n$. The possibility that an equilibrium growth path need not exist, however, has nothing whatsoever to do with the instability of the warranted growth path. The problem of reconciling the warranted and natural rates of growth and the "knife edge" problem are conceptually quite separate. The former is a question of existence, and the latter is a question of stability. The two problems may, however, interact in the following way.

First, suppose that the warranted rate of growth exceeds the natural rate of growth. Then the warranted rate of growth cannot be achieved over a long run period. The actual growth rate of the system must fall short of the warranted rate and, given instability, cannot return to the warranted rate. The excess capital stock does not get worked off and the actual growth rate continues to fall. The actual growth rate must also fall short of the natural growth rate and Keynesian unemployment is generated. The result is secular stagnation, once thought to be characteristic of mature capitalistic economies.

Second, if the warranted growth rate is less than the natural growth rate, any attempt to increase employment without also increasing the savings ratio or decreasing the capital–output ratio will not succeed. Since the capital stock deficiency that would be created by an attempt to increase employment will not be corrected if the warranted growth path is unstable, the outcome is likely to be a chronically inflationary situation with persistent Marxian unemployment. Such a situation may be considered to caricature some heavily populated less developed economies.

In order to get around the existence problem it is necessary to reconcile the natural and warranted rates of growth by relaxing one or more of the assumptions that lead to their rigidity. If the assumption that the effective stock of labor grows at a fixed exogenous rate, $m + n$, is retained, reconciliation requires that either s or b or both be variable so that they can be adapted to satisfy the equation $g = s/b = m + n$. Generally speaking, a flexible s can be generated by assuming that saving is not only a function of income itself, but also a function of the way in which income is divided between profits and wages, that is, of income distribution.[15] On the other hand, a flexible b can be generated by assuming that there is no longer a rigidly fixed coefficients production function; rather, one may assume that there is some possibility of substituting capital for labor, and therefore a choice of technique. The first way of reconciling the warranted and natural growth rates (the flexible savings ratio) follows Robinson and Kaldor.[16] The second way (the flexible capital–output ratio) follows Solow and Swan,[17] and leads to the single sectoral neo-classical growth model which is discussed in the first section of chapter 5 of this book. It should, however, be noted that *both* methods of reconciliation require sufficient flexibility in overall rates of profit.

Finally, it may well be foolish to assume that the natural rate of growth is constant. Not only may the growth rate of the labor force vary for underlying demographic reasons, but also some of these reasons may be endogenous. Moreover, the rate of technological progress may vary through time. Technological discoveries may occur in waves, or they may result from investments in "research and development" or from the experience of "learning by doing." Furthermore, resource constraints and environmental problems may seriously undermine the concept of the natural rate of growth. All of these important qualifications are discussed in Part Two of this book.

15. Alternatively, if intertemporal consumption choices are consistent with the life cycle savings hypothesis the overall savings rate will vary with the age distribution of the population and, therefore, with the rate of population growth. This possibility is incorporated in the optimal growth discussion that appears in chapter 5 of this book.

16. See J. Robinson, *The Accumulation of Capital*, London, Macmillan, 1956, and N. Kaldor, "A Model of Economic Growth," *The Economic Journal*, vol. 67, December 1957, pp. 591–624.

17. See R. M. Solow, "A Contribution to the Theory of Economic Growth," *Quarterly Journal of Economics*, vol. 70, February 1956, pp. 65–94, and T. W. Swan, "Economic Growth and Capital Accumulation," *The Economic Record*, vol. 32, November 1956, pp. 334–361.

THE PROCESS OF GROWTH

FIVE

CAPITAL ACCUMULATION IN A NEO-CLASSICAL FRAMEWORK

A : NEO-CLASSICAL GROWTH MODELS

Most recent growth models are based upon an underlying theory of production which simply embodies an hypothesis about the way in which technological constraints relate input combinations to output combinations, and a further hypothesis about the way in which these technological constraints may change over time. Growth in output is therefore in part a consequence of growth in factor inputs and in part a consequence of growth in factor productivities through technological change; that is, outward shifts in the volume of output that can be achieved from given inputs.

The most simple of recent growth models assume that the technological constraints may be summarized by a single macroeconomic or aggregate production function which shifts through time according to a simple rule. On the one hand, it may be assumed that there is only a single homogeneous commodity being produced and that this commodity may either be consumed or saved (and therefore used to increase future production). On the other hand, it may be assumed that all relative commodity prices are fixed so that value sums refer to quantity aggregates, and, hence, that heterogeneous commodity outputs can be reduced to a single measure of overall output by aggregating at the fixed prices. In either case, output is treated as if it were homogeneous. Models of this kind are called single sectoral growth models. Both the Harrod-Domar growth model and the single sectoral neo-classical or Solow-Swan growth model belong to this class.

Other recent growth models treat output at any point of time as if it were homogeneous, but differentiate current output from the saved-up portion of past outputs. That is to say, new and old capital goods are assumed to differ in their technological specification. Such models are known as vintage models. Still other models separate output into two types, consumption goods and capital goods, each type being assumed to be homogeneous. The technology of these models consists of two separate production functions, and the models themselves are known as two sectoral growth models. In the present chapter and the two following ones, variations of these three types of models: (a) single sectoral growth models, (b) vintage models, and (c) two sectoral growth models, are outlined and discussed.

The present chapter discusses the single sectoral neo-classical growth model from three points of view. In this section, an explicit savings function is assumed. In the following section, one asks the question "Is there an optimal rate of savings?", thus shifting the discussion from descriptive growth models to optimal growth models. Complications arising from the existence of non-renewable resources are introduced into the optimal growth framework in the last two sections of this chapter. Throughout the discussion, however, a single aggregate production function of the neo-classical variety is assumed to exist.

In the single sectoral neo-classical growth model, both the specification of the underlying technology or production function, and (in the descriptive version) the set of rules which govern the growth of factor supplies, are very simple. Aggregate output is assumed to be a continuous function of capital and labor inputs. That is,

$$Y(t) = F\{K(t), \bar{L}(t)\}, \quad \text{all} \quad t \geq 0 \tag{5A-1}$$

where $Y(t)$ is output, $K(t)$ is capital input, and $\bar{L}(t)$ is the effective labor input, all variables taken at time t. If Harrod-neutral technical progress is occurring at the fixed rate m, then $\bar{L}(t) = L(t) e^{mt}$, and the shifting production function in terms of natural labor units, $L(t)$, may be condensed into a stationary production function in terms of effective labor units, $\bar{L}(t)$. It is this stationary production function which is given in expression (5A-1).

Introducing the savings–investment flow equilibrium condition of the product market, and the full employment condition, one has (assuming no depreciation)

$$DK(t) = sY(t), \quad \text{all} \quad t \geq 0, \quad \text{and} \quad \bar{L}(t) = L(t) e^{mt} = L(0) e^{(m+n)t} \tag{5A-2}$$

where s is the propensity to save and n is the growth rate of the labor supply in natural units. Substituting from this expression into the full capacity utilization condition or production function, one obtains a first order differential equation in $K(t)$, namely

$$DK(t) = sF\{K(t), L(0) e^{(m+n)t}\} \tag{5A-3}$$

This equation is the fundamental differential equation of the single sectoral neo-classical growth model. Its general solution depends upon the form and properties of the production function chosen and upon the determinants of the propensity to save.

Two properties are imposed upon the production function. First, it is assumed to be twice differentiable and to exhibit first degree homogeneity or constant returns to scale. The property of constant returns to scale allows the production function to be written as

$$y(t) = f\{k(t)\}, \quad \text{all} \quad t \geq 0 \tag{5A-4}$$

where $y(t) = Y(t)/\bar{L}(t)$ is output per unit of the effective stock of labor at time t, and $k(t) = K(t)/\bar{L}(t)$ is capital per unit of the effective stock of labor at time t. In consequence, the fundamental differential equation may be written in the form[1]

$$Dk = sf(k) - (m + n)k \tag{5A-5}$$

where for simplicity the time subscripts have been omitted.

Second, the production function is assumed to be well behaved, where a well behaved production function has

(a) $f'(k) > 0$, (b) $f''(k) < 0$, (c) $f(k) \rightarrow 0$ and $f'(k) \rightarrow \infty$ as $k \rightarrow 0$

and $\tag{5A-6}$

(d) $f(k) \rightarrow \infty$ and $f'(k) \rightarrow 0$ as $k \rightarrow \infty$

where $f'(k)$ and $f''(k)$ refer to the first and second derivatives of the production function with respect to k, respectively. In consequence, it can be shown for a wide range of savings behavior that there exists a unique steady-state solution with constant k. This solution is obtained from expression (5A-5) by setting $Dk = 0$, thus implying the existence of a capital–output ratio $b \equiv k/f(k)$ which satisfies the Harrod-Domar consistency condition,

$$(m + n) = s/b, \quad \text{or} \quad (m + n) = sf(k)/k \tag{5A-7}$$

Moreover, this steady-state solution is the asymptotic state to which all equilibrium dynamic paths converge. That is to say, the steady-state solution is stable in the sense that it will be approached asymptotically by all paths satisfying the fundamental differential equation given as expression (5A-5).

Let us begin by considering the case of a proportional savings function in which s is assumed to be a positive constant. This case is illustrated in Fig. 5A-1(a). Since it is assumed that the production function is well behaved, the slope of $y = f(k)$ declines continuously through all positive values as k increases. Moreover, the slope of any chord (such as the straight line with slope $(m + n)/s$ in Fig. 5A-1) also declines continuously through all positive values as k increases. Hence, there exists one and only one point satisfying $y = f(k)$ such that the slope of the chord to this point is precisely $(m + n)/s$. In Fig. 5A-1(a), this is the point with coordinates k^*, y^*. This point is therefore the unique steady-state solution of the system. Capital, output, and the effective stock of labor all grow at the steady rate $m + n$. Capital and output per unit of the effective stock of labor

---

1. This expression follows directly from (a) the fact that constant returns to scale allows one to write Eq. (5A-3) as $DK = sL(0) e^{(m+n)t} f(k)$, and (b) the fact that the rule for the differentiation of a quotient allows one to write $Dk + (m + n)k = DK/L(0) e^{(m+n)t}$.

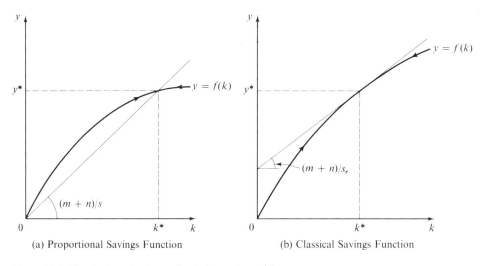

Figure 5A-1 (a) Proportional Savings Function   (b) Classical Savings Function

Figure 5A-1 The single sectoral neo-classical growth model.

remain constant. Capital and output per head of labor (measured in natural units) grow at the rate m, the rate of Harrod-neutral technical progress. Assuming factor pricing according to the conditions of competitive equilibrium, the rate of profit equals the marginal productivity of capital (the slope of the function $y = f(k)$) and remains constant over time. The real wage rate per efficiency unit of labor also remains constant, and the wage rate per man (or per man-hour) grows at the rate m.

The steady-state configuration of the system is somewhat altered if savings depend upon the distribution of income so that[2]

$$s = s_w + (s_r - s_w)kf'(k)/f(k) \tag{5A-8}$$

given that the rate of profit (r) is equal to the marginal productivity of capital, $f'(k)$, and that s_w and s_r refer to the propensities to save out of wage income and profit income, respectively. Substituting from Eq. (5A-8) into the fundamental differential equation, Eq. (5A-5), yields

$$Dk = s_w f(k) + (s_r - s_w)kf'(k) - (m + n)k \tag{5A-9}$$

2. This equation may be derived in the following way. Suppose that income, Y, is divided into wages, W, and profits, P, and that total savings, $S = sY$, depends upon the sum of savings out of wages and savings out of profits. Then $Y = W + P$ and $S = sY = s_w W + s_r P$, where s_w is the propensity to save out of wages, and s_r is the propensity to save out of profits. It follows that $sY = s_w(Y - P) + s_r P$, and $s = s_w + (s_r - s_w)P/Y$. The share of savings in income varies with the share of profits in income as long as $s_w \neq s_r$. Normally, it is assumed that the propensity to save out of profits exceeds the propensity to save out of wages, so that $0 \leq s_w \leq s_r \leq 1$. Since with all prices equal to unity, $P = rK$, where r is the rate of profit, the distribution of income may be made to depend either upon an externally given profit rate or upon the marginal productivity of capital derived from a continuous production function as in the text above.

In the special classical savings function case, where $s_w = 0$ and $0 < s_r \leq 1$, expression (5A-9) reduces to

$$Dk = s_r k f'(k) - (m + n)k \qquad (5A\text{-}10)$$

Similarly to Eq. (5A-5), Eq. (5A-10) also may be shown to have a unique steady-state solution. This solution is obtained by choosing the unique value of k for which $Dk = 0$, so that

$$m + n = s_r f'(k) \quad \text{or} \quad m + n = s_r r \qquad (5A\text{-}11)$$

Whereas the proportional savings function case with $s_w = s_r = s$ has a unique steady-state solution in which k takes a value such that the *average productivity of capital*, $1/b$, times the savings propensity, s, is equal to $m + n$, the classical savings function case has a unique steady-state solution in which k takes a value such that the *marginal productivity of capital*, r, times the savings propensity, s_r, is equal to $m + n$. The classical savings function case is illustrated in Fig. 5A-1(b).

The steady-state properties of the neo-classical single sectoral growth model with a classical savings function are very similar to those of the proportional savings function case. In both cases, the savings propensity has no effect on the steady-state growth rate, $m + n$, which is entirely given from the labor side alone. The steady-state values of capital per head and output per head are, however, directly related to the savings propensity in both cases. It follows that, although factor shares are constant in any given steady-state, across alternative steady-states with differing savings propensities factor shares will generally differ depending upon the elasticity of substitution of the production function. Since across alternative steady-states with a given growth rate, $m + n$, a higher s or s_r is always associated with a lower rate of profit, r, a higher savings propensity will be associated with a higher share of capital if the elasticity of substitution is greater than unity and with a lower share of capital if the elasticity of substitution is less than unity. In the Cobb-Douglas case, where the elasticity of substitution is unity, factor shares are identical across alternative steady-states.

It has therefore been shown that if (a) the underlying production function exhibits constant returns to scale and is well behaved, and (b) technological progress is Harrod-neutral and occurs at a constant rate, m, then there exists a unique steady-state solution to the neo-classical single sectoral growth model with either a proportional or a classical savings function (or indeed with the more general differential savings function of expression 5A-9). Moreover, it is not difficult to show that this steady-state solution must be stable, given the conditions imposed on the production technology.

For the proportional savings function case, this may be readily seen by examining Fig. 5A-1(a) in conjunction with Eq. (5A-5). Starting from an initial capital–output ratio below the steady-state value, the system must necessarily accumulate capital at a faster rate than $m + n$ until the rise in k allows the capital–output ratio to reach its steady-state value, $k^*/f(k^*)$. More formally, if $f(k)/k$ exceeds $(m + n)/s$, then Dk must be positive and $f(k)/k$ must fall towards its steady-state value. On the other hand, starting from an initial capital–output ratio above the steady-state value, the system must necessarily accumulate capital at a slower rate than $m + n$ until the fall in k allows the capital-output ratio to reach the steady-state value, $k^*/f(k^*)$. That is to say, if $f(k)/k$ falls short of $(m + n)/s$, then Dk must be negative and $f(k)/k$ must rise towards its steady-state value. The steady-state solution is therefore stable in the sense that any equilibrium dynamic path from arbitrary initial conditions converges through time to a steady-state path with constant k. For the classical savings function case, a similar story may be told by examining Fig. 5A-1(b) in conjunction with Eq. (5A-10).

Nothing that has been said herein relates to the stability of the equilibrium dynamic path itself, that is, whether or not a disturbance of this path is corrected through time. This is a question of disequilibrium dynamics rather than equilibrium dynamics, and the answer to it is likely to depend upon the particular error adjustment mechanism that is chosen.[3] Nevertheless, at least for well-behaved technologies, a steady-state path is the asymptotic growth path of any equilibrium dynamic path. Other than this, the most important equilibrium dynamic property of the system is that along any equilibrium dynamic path a higher savings propensity (either proportional or classical) *is* associated with a higher rate of growth of the capital stock. It is therefore also associated with a higher rate of growth of output, since the rate of growth of output is simply a weighted average of the rate of growth of capital and the rate of growth of the effective stock of labor, the weights depending upon factor shares via the implicit function theorem.

B: OPTIMAL PATHS OF CAPITAL
   ACCUMULATION

In this section, we address ourselves to the question: given (a) the state of technology embodied in the simple neo-classical production function, $y(t) = f[k(t)]$, (b) the natural rate of growth, $m + n$, and (c) an initial value of the ratio of capital to the effective stock of labor, $k(0)$, does there exist a rate of savings that is capable of generating a path of capital accumulation[4] which is optimal from the point of view of some intertemporal criterion function? Another way of putting this question is to ask whether there exists an optimal growth path, and, if so, what are its characteristics.

The objective (or criterion) function used in this and subsequent sections is an intertemporal utility function in which at any point of time the instantaneous utility (or felicity) attained by society is equal to $L(t)U\{C(t)/L(t)\}$, where $L(t)$ is the number of heads (taken to be equivalent to the labor force in natural units) and $C(t)$ is the aggregate consumption of society at time t. Thus, the instantaneous

---

3. On this point, see F. H. Hahn, "The Stability of Growth Equilibrium," *Quarterly Journal of Economics,* vol. 74, May 1960, pp. 206–226.

4. The analysis of this section follows R. M. Solow, *Growth Theory, An Exposition,* Oxford, Oxford University Press, 1970, chapter 5, pp. 77–91, quite closely.

utility attainable by the average individual in society depends upon the level of consumption per head, and the total utility attainable by society is this level multiplied by the number of heads. The utility function, $U\{C(t)/L(t)\}$ is assumed to be continuous and twice differentiable, with $U' > 0$ and $U'' < 0$. Marginal utility is positive but diminishing.

Assuming that society has a positive time preference rate, ρ, the intertemporal utility function may be expressed as the present value of all future felicities. Since this present value is the integral of discounted future felicities, the objective of society is to maximize V, where

$$V = \int_0^\infty e^{-\rho t} L(t) U\{C(t)/L(t)\}\, dt \qquad (5B\text{-}1)$$

The constraints under which this maximization must be carried out may be summarized as:

$$Y(t) = F\{K(t), L(t)\, e^{mt}\}$$

$$L(t) = L(0)\, e^{nt} \qquad (5B\text{-}2)$$

and

$$C(t) = Y(t) - DK(t)$$

Output depends upon capital inputs and effective labor inputs via a neo-classical production function which is assumed to be homogeneous of degree one; the number of heads grows at the rate n; and consumption is the difference between output and the volume of capital accumulation. There exists a formal trade-off between consumption today and consumption tomorrow, and our problem is one of the calculus of variations.

Let $c(t) = C(t)/L(t)$ be the level of consumption per head and let $k(t) = K(t)/L(t)\, e^{mt}$ be the amount of capital available per efficiency unit of labor. Then our formal problem may be re-expressed as[5]

Maximize

$$V = \int_0^\infty e^{(n-\rho)t} L(0) U\{c(t)\}\, dt$$

$$(5B\text{-}3)$$

Subject to

$$c(t)\, e^{-mt} = f\{k(t)\} - (m+n)k(t) - Dk(t)$$

This problem may be solved by setting up the Lagrangian expression,

$$g(t) = e^{(n-\rho)t} L(0) U\{c(t)\} - \lambda(t)\left[c(t)\, e^{-mt} - f\{k(t)\} + (m+n)k(t) + Dk(t)\right]$$

$$(5B\text{-}4)$$

---

5. This reduction of the problem follows from the facts that:

(a) $\qquad DK(t) = F[K(t), L(t)\, e^{mt}] - C(t) = L(0)\, e^{(m+n)t}\{f[k(t)] - c(t)\, e^{-mt}\}$

and

(b) $\qquad DK(t) = L(0)\, e^{(m+n)t}[Dk(t) + (m+n)k(t)].$

where $\lambda(t)$ is a Lagrange multiplier. The Euler necessary conditions for a maximum are

$$\partial g(t)/\partial c(t) = e^{(n-\rho)t} L(0)U'_c - \lambda e^{-mt} = 0$$

$$\partial g(t)/\partial k(t) = -\lambda(m + n - f'_k) = -d\lambda/dt = d/dt\,\{\partial g(t)/\partial Dk(t)\} \quad (5B\text{-}5)$$

and $\qquad \partial g(t)/\partial \lambda(t) = f\{k(t)\} - (m + n)k(t) - Dk(t) - c(t)e^{-mt} = 0$

If the first of these equations is differentiated with respect to time, t, it is possible to eliminate $\lambda^{-1}\,d\lambda/dt$ across the first two equations, thus generating the relationship

$$m + n - \rho + (U''_c/U'_c)\,dc(t)/dt = \lambda^{-1}\,d\lambda/dt = m + n - f'_k \quad (5B\text{-}6)$$

Finally, this expression may be simplified and put together with the last equation of (5B-5) to obtain the two fundamental differential equations which describe the optimal growth path, namely

$$Dk(t) = f\{k(t)\} - (m + n)k(t) - c(t)e^{-mt}$$

and $\qquad\qquad\qquad\qquad\qquad\qquad\qquad\qquad\qquad\qquad\qquad (5B\text{-}7)$

$$\beta Dc(t) = (f'_k - \rho)c(t)$$

where $\beta = -c(t)U''_c/U'_c$ is the absolute value of the elasticity of marginal utility with respect to consumption per head. This elasticity may or may not be constant. However, in the following analysis it will be useful to regard it as a constant.[6]

The two fundamental differential equations may be analyzed in terms of the phase diagram presented as Fig. 5B-1. In this diagram, the locus $Dk(t) = 0$ is the locus of all points at which the ratio of capital to the effective stock of labor is constant. The equation of this locus is $e^{-mt}c(t) = f\{k(t)\} - (m + n)k(t)$. Given the properties of a well-behaved neo-classical production function, this locus first rises then falls as $k(t)$ increases, reaching a maximum at that value of $k(t)$ where $f'_k = m + n$ as illustrated in Fig. 5B-1. The locus $D\{e^{-mt}c(t)\} = 0$ is the locus of all points at which the ratio of consumption to the effective stock of labor is constant, or at which consumption per head rises at the steady-state rate m, the rate of Harrod-neutral technological progress. The equation of this locus is $f'_k = \rho + \beta m$.

The intersection of these two singular curves at $k^*(t)$, $e^{-mt}c^*(t)$ in the phase diagram (Fig. 5B-1) indicates the existence of an *optimal steady-state situation* in which $k(t)$ and $e^{-mt}c(t)$ both remain constant. This optimal steady-state has the property that the marginal product of capital, f'_k, is equal to $\rho + \beta m$, which may

---

6. The corresponding utility function in this case would be

$$U(c) = c^{1-\beta} \quad \text{with} \quad 0 < \beta < 1$$

Thus $U'_c = (1 - \beta)c^{-\beta}$ and $U''_c = -\beta(1 - \beta)c^{-\beta-1}$, so that $-cU''_c/U'_c = \beta$, an expression which may easily be identified as the absolute value of the elasticity of marginal utility with respect to consumption per head.

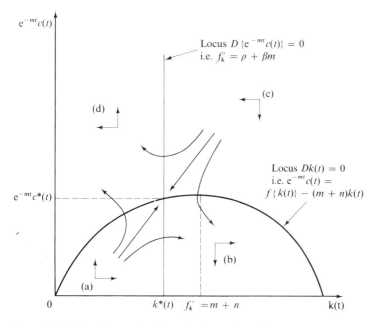

Figure 5B-1 Phase diagram for the optimal growth model.

be identified as the *social rate of discount*. The social rate of discount, or rate of interest, depends upon three underlying parameters of the model: (a) the basic time preference rate, ρ, (b) the absolute value of the elasticity of marginal utility with respect to consumption per head, β, and (c) the steady-state growth rate of consumption per head, m. Thus, if it is known that consumption per head can grow at the rate m in steady-state equilibrium, then the social rate of discount $(\rho + \beta m)$ must exceed the pure time preference rate (ρ) by an amount which allows for the diminishing marginal utility of consumption that goes with increasing consumption per head (βm). If future generations are going to be richer than the present generation simply through the force of technological progress which depends only on the elapse of time, then the social rate of discount should allow for this fact.

In the optimal steady-state, the associated ratio of capital to the effective stock of labor, $k^*(t)$, falls short of the ratio which would maximize steady-state consumption per efficiency unit of labor. Indeed, it is clear from Fig. 5B-1 that steady-state consumption per efficiency unit of labor would be maximized if $f_k' = m + n$, whereas the optimal steady-state is attained when $f_k' = \rho + \beta m$. Moreover, if the original integral $V = \int_0^\infty e^{(n-\rho)t} L(0) U\{c(t)\}\, dt$ is to converge when $U\{c(t)\} = c(t)^{1-\beta}$ and $c(t)$ grows at the steady-state rate m, it is both necessary and sufficient that $n - \rho + m(1 - \beta)$ be negative, or that $\rho + \beta m > m + n$. If the original problem is to have an appropriately bounded solution, the social rate of discount must exceed the natural rate of economic growth. Thus, if an

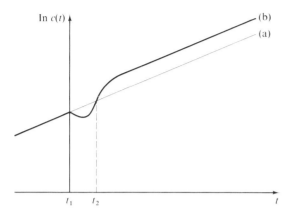

Figure 5B-2 Intertemporal trade-off relationships.

optimal path of capital accumulation exists, in steady-state equilibrium accumulation will stop short of the level of $k(t)$ which maximizes consumption per efficiency unit of labor. To push accumulation further would involve a sacrifice of current consumption which would not be warranted in terms of future consumption gains.

This point may be further analyzed in terms of Fig. 5B-2, a diagram which also serves to illustrate the fundamental questions of intergenerational equity involved in the trade-off between consumption today and consumption tomorrow. In Fig. 5B-2, the natural logarithm of consumption per head, $\ln c(t)$, is measured on the vertical axis and time, t, is measured on the horizontal axis. Two conceivable paths of consumption per head are illustrated in Fig. 5B-2. Path (a) is one along which consumption per head grows steadily at the rate m. Path (b) diverges from path (a) in that between time t_1 and t_2 present consumption is sacrificed in order "to buy" a strip of future consumption, which is greater in perpetuity after time t_2 on path (b) than on path (a). Both paths, of course, ultimately have steady-state growth rate m. The question being asked in the present section is effectively, "When does it pay to follow path (b) rather than path (a)?" The answer to this question depends upon the relative weight attached by society to consumption today and consumption tomorrow as embedded in an intertemporal utility function. An optimal steady-state is one in which accumulation has proceeded to the point at which it no longer pays to choose (b) over (a).

In an optimal steady-state, the savings ratio, s^*, is equal to $(m+n)k^*/f(k^*)$ where $f'_{k^*} = \rho + \beta m$. Moreover, for any well-behaved neo-classical production function, $k/f(k)$ and f'_k bear a strictly inverse relationship to each other. It is then not difficult to sign the following partial derivatives, namely $\partial s^*/\partial \rho < 0$, $\partial s^*/\partial \beta < 0$, and $\partial s^*/\partial n > 0$. However, the sign of $\partial s^*/\partial m$ is unclear. Comparing two otherwise identical societies, the society with the higher rate of time preference will save less, the society with the higher absolute value of the elasticity of marginal utility with respect to consumption per head will save less, the society with the higher rate of population and labor force growth will save more, and the society with the higher rate of technical change may save more or less depending upon the other underlying parameters of the model.

The economic reasons for these comparative steady-state conclusions are fairly obvious. First, the higher is ρ the lower is the value that society places on future consumption relative to present consumption; and a more myopic society is less likely to save for the future. Second, the higher is β the quicker diminishing marginal utility sets in as consumption per head rises in response to technological progress. In consequence, a smaller present value is placed upon this additional consumption and the less willing is society to save. Third, the higher is n the larger will be both the number of mouths to feed and the number of workers to equip tomorrow. In order to provide future generations with sufficient capital resources, society must increase its propensity to save. Notice, therefore, that demographic factors which affect the natural rate of growth also affect the warranted rate of growth in the same direction. Fourth, if the equilibrium share of capital $\alpha = f_k' k / f(k)$ is roughly constant along the production function, then higher values of m will be associated with higher values of s^* if $\rho > \beta n$ and with lower values of s^* if $\rho < \beta n$. There appears to be no clear intuitive reason for this result. Finally, the optimal steady-state savings ratio, s^*, is less than the equilibrium share of capital, since $s^* = (m + n)k^* / f(k^*) = (m + n)\alpha / f_k' = (m + n)\alpha/(\rho + \beta m) < \alpha$ if the utility integral is to converge. This is an arithmetical consequence of the social rate of discount exceeding the natural rate of economic growth.

So far, we have discussed the properties of the optimal steady-state without discussing whether there exists an optimal trajectory which leads from an arbitrary initial ratio of capital to the effective stock of labor, $k(0)$, to the steady-state position. In order to discuss this question, it is necessary to return to the phase diagram, Fig. 5B-1. At all levels of $e^{-mt} c(t)$ below the $Dk(t) = 0$ locus, it is clear from the first equation of (5B-7) that $Dk(t)$ is positive, which accounts for the rightward horizontal arrows in phases (a) and (b) of Fig. 5B-1. At all levels of $e^{-mt} c(t)$ above the $Dk(t) = 0$ locus, $k(t)$ must be falling; this is indicated by the leftward horizontal arrows in phases (c) and (d) of the diagram. On the other hand, if $f_k' > \rho + \beta m$, it is clear from the second equation of (5B-7) that $c(t)^{-1} Dc(t)$ exceeds m so that $e^{-mt} c(t)$ must be rising. Since high values of f_k' are associated with low values of $k(t)$, this accounts for the upwards vertical arrows in phases (a) and (d) of Fig. 5B-1. Finally, if $f_k' < \rho + \beta m$, falling values of $e^{-mt} c(t)$ are implied as illustrated by the downwards vertical arrows in phases (c) and (b) of the diagram.

Once these forces of motion are combined into a single story, it becomes obvious that the optimal steady-state solution is a *saddle point*. Given any initial value, $k(0)$, almost all paths eventually *diverge* from the optimal steady-state solution. If society initially consumes too much and continues in this fashion it will inevitably eat up its whole capital stock as illustrated by trajectories leading into phase (d). If society initially consumes too little and continues in this fashion, it will inevitably accumulate only for the sake of accumulation and experience falling consumption per efficiency unit of labor, as illustrated by trajectories leading into phase (b). It is obvious, therefore, that society should never follow a trajectory that enters either phase (d) or phase (b). To avoid such errant paths, the trajectory chosen must lie entirely within either phase (a) or phase (c) of the diagram. Indeed, for any given initial ratio of capital to the effective stock of labor, $k(0)$, there exists a unique choice of initial consumption per efficiency unit of labor (or per head), $e^{-m0} c(0)$, such that the economy sets out on a trajectory which leads to the optimal steady-state solution. Such a trajectory is an *optimal path of capital accumulation*. Thus, on our present assumptions, there exists a unique optimal path of capital accumulation from $k(0)$ to $k*(t)$.

What are the properties of such a path? If the economy starts from a position in which the marginal product of capital, f_k', exceeds the social rate of discount or rate of interest, $\rho + \beta m$, then $k(0) < k*(t)$ and the economy has under-sufficient capital. In this case, it pays society to accumulate capital and consequently to increase consumption so that *both* $k(t)$ and $e^{-mt} c(t)$ increase through time towards $k*(t)$ and $e^{-mt} c*(t)$, respectively. The excess productivity of capital should be used to expand the relative size of the capital stock, thus permitting an increasing time stream of consumption per efficiency unit of labor to be followed. Notice, however, that initial consumption per efficiency unit of labor (and per head) must be set below *both* its final steady-state value and the value it would obtain if the system were allowed to remain in steady-state equilibrium at $k(0)$. In this case, to follow the optimal trajectory requires some sacrifice of present consumption per head. Thus, if $f_{k(0)}' > \rho + \beta m$, then the initial savings propensity, $s*(0)$, must exceed $(m + n)k(0)/f\{k(0)\}$ to generate $Dk(0) > 0$.

On the other hand, if the economy starts from a position in which the marginal product of capital, f_k', falls short of the social rate of discount or rate of interest, $\rho + \beta m$, then $k(0) > k*(t)$ and the economy has over-sufficient capital. In this case, it pays society to decumulate capital and consequently to decrease consumption so that *both* $k(t)$ and $e^{-mt} c(t)$ decrease through time towards $k*(t)$ and $e^{-mt} c*(t)$, respectively. The deficient productivity of capital should be worked off by a relative contraction in the size of the capital stock, and an associated decreasing time stream of consumption per efficiency unit of labor. Notice, however, that initial consumption per efficiency unit of labor (and per head) must be set above *both* its final steady-state value *and* the value it would obtain if the system were allowed to remain in a steady-state equilibrium at $k(0)$. In this case, to follow the optimal trajectory entails an initial feast. Thus, if $f_{k(0)}' < \rho + \beta m$, then the initial savings propensity, $s*(0)$, must fall short of $(m+n)k(0)/f\{k(0)\}$ to generate $Dk(0) < 0$.

In general, the optimal savings propensity will vary along the traverse to the optimal steady-state, but remain constant once this steady-state is attained. Despite this, however, to follow a rule of maintaining a constant savings propensity along the traverse may not lead to too large a welfare loss over time, provided that (a) the constant savings propensity chosen is the one appropriate to the optimal steady-state, namely $s* = (m + n)k*/f(k*)$, where $f_{k*}' = \rho + \beta m$, and (b) the initial situation is reasonably close to the optimal steady-state. At least it is known from the previous section that, while not generally optimal, trajectories with constant savings propensities do converge on steady-state equilibrium.

Finally, attention should be directed to the central role played by the social rate of discount or rate of interest, $\rho + \beta m$, in the previous analysis. This variable measures the intertemporal terms of trade, and summarizes everything of importance to society's intertemporal choices. The issue whether or not a myopic society with a high rate of time preference, and consequently with a high social rate of discount and a low rate of savings will be judged with hindsight to have been unfair to future generations raises important questions of intergenerational equity, questions that are largely hidden within the concept of the social rate of discount. These questions are of crucial importance in an economy which may be incapable of positive growth in consumption per head because its production processes are based upon the continuous absorption of non-renewable resources. Our discussion of optimal savings is extended into the context of such an economy in the following section. Further issues concerning intertemporal choices and inter-generational equity are raised in the first section of chapter 6 of this book.

C: OPTIMAL ECONOMIC GROWTH WITH NON-RENEWABLE RESOURCES

The process of economic growth has involved the continuous substitution of non-human energy for human energy in basic production processes. Since many sources of non-human energy are non-renewable, the process of economic growth is ultimately limited;[7] indeed, eventual economic decline may be inevitable. The purpose of this section is to broaden our understanding of growth theory so that we are able to evaluate critically this underlying message of the "energy crisis." Of course, energy resources are not the only ones which may be non-renewable; although they are often the non-renewable resource which comes to mind, the analysis of this section is applicable to any non-renewable resource, and, in particular, to non-renewable resources in the aggregate.

The analysis begins by postulating once again an intertemporal utility function of the form

$$V = \int_0^\infty e^{-\rho t} L(t) U\{C(t)/L(t)\} \, dt \qquad (5C\text{-}1)$$

which is identical to expression (5B-1). The constraints under which this utility function is to be maximized are generalized to

$$Y(t) = F\{K(t), L(t) e^{mt}, R(t)\}$$
$$L(t) = L(0) e^{nt}$$
$$C(t) = Y(t) - DK(t) \qquad (5C\text{-}2)$$

---

7. The analysis of this section follows J. E. Stiglitz, "Growth with Exhaustible Natural Resources: Efficient and Optimal Growth Paths," *Review of Economic Studies,* Symposium on the Economics of Exhaustible Resources, Special Issue, 1974, pp. 123–137, quite closely. Several other papers in this symposium also have relevance for this section.

and
$$\int_0^t R(t)\, dt = Z(0) - Z(t), \quad \text{or} \quad R(t) = -DZ(t)$$

Output depends upon capital inputs, effective labor inputs, and inputs of non-renewable resources, $R(t)$, via a neo-classical production function which is assumed to be homogeneous of degree one; the number of heads grows at the rate n; consumption is the difference between output and the volume of capital accumulation; and the use of non-renewable resources leads to a reduction in their available stock, $Z(t)$, whose initial supply $Z(0)$ is assumed to be given and finite. Thus, the production function has been generalized to include inputs of non-renewable resources. Since these inputs lead to a depletion of the existing stock of non-renewable resources, an additional constraint has been added.

Our problem, once again, is one of the calculus of variations. It may be simplified by letting $c(t) = C(t)/L(t)$ be the level of consumption per head, $k(t) = K(t)/L(t)\, e^{mt}$ be the amount of capital input per efficiency unit of labor, $r(t) = R(t)/L(t)\, e^{mt}$ be the volume of resource input per efficiency unit of labor, and $z(t) = Z(t)/L(t)\, e^{mt}$ be the remaining stock of non-renewable resources per efficiency unit of labor. With this change in notation, our formal problem may be rewritten as[8]

Maximize
$$V = \int_0^\infty e^{(n-\rho)t} L(0) U\{c(t)\}\, dt$$

Subject to
$$c(t)\, e^{-mt} = f\{k(t), r(t)\} - (m+n)k(t) - Dk(t) \tag{5C-3}$$

and
$$r(t) = -\{Dz(t) + (m+n)z(t)\}$$

This problem may be solved by setting up the Lagrangian expression,

$$g(t) = e^{(n-\rho)t} L(0) U\{c(t)\} - \lambda_1(t)[c(t)\, e^{-mt} - f\{k(t), r(t)\} + (m+n)k(t) + Dk(t)]$$
$$- \lambda_2(t)[r(t) + (m+n)z(t) + Dz(t)] \tag{5C-4}$$

where $\lambda_1(t)$ and $\lambda_2(t)$ are Lagrange multipliers. The Euler necessary conditions for a maximum are

$$\partial g(t)/\partial c(t) = e^{(n-\rho)t} L(0) U_c' - \lambda_1\, e^{-mt} = 0$$

$$\partial g(t)/\partial k(t) = -\lambda_1(m+n-f_k') = -d\lambda_1/dt = d/dt\{\partial g(t)/\partial Dk(t)\}$$

$$\partial g(t)/\partial r(t) = \lambda_1 f_r' - \lambda_2 = 0$$

$$\partial g(t)/\partial z(t) = -\lambda_2(m+n) = -d\lambda_2/dt = d/dt\{\partial g(t)/\partial Dz(t)\}$$

---

8. This reduction follows exactly as the reduction involved in moving from Eqs. (5B-1) and (5B-2) to Eq. (5B-3) in the previous section. In addition, one requires the facts that

$$\text{(a)} \quad DZ(t) = -R(t) = -L(0)\, e^{(m+n)t} r(t)$$

and

$$\text{(b)} \quad DZ(t) = L(0)\, e^{(m+n)t} [Dz(t) + (m+n)z(t)]$$

$$\partial g(t)/\partial \lambda_1(t) = f\{k(t), r(t)\} - (m+n)k(t) - Dk(t) - c(t)\,e^{-mt} = 0 \qquad (5C\text{-}5)$$

and $\quad \partial g(t)/\partial \lambda_2(t) = -\{r(t) + (m+n)z(t) + Dz(t)\} = 0$

where f_k' and f_r' are the partial derivatives of $f\{k(t), r(t)\}$ with respect to its two arguments. Eliminating λ_1 and λ_2 across the six equations, one obtains the four fundamental differential equations of the system, namely

$$Dk(t) = f\{k(t), r(t)\} - (m+n)k(t) - c(t)\,e^{-mt}$$

$$\beta Dc(t) = (f_k' - \rho)c(t)$$

$$(f_r')^{-1}\,df_r'/dt = f_k' \qquad\qquad\qquad (5C\text{-}6)$$

and $\qquad\qquad Dz(t) = -\{r(t) + (m+n)z(t)\}$

where $\beta = -c(t)U_c''/U_c'$ as defined in the previous section.

The first and last of these four equations are simply the constraint functions of the system. Moreover, the first and second equations exactly parallel the two Eqs. (5B-7) of the previous section. The derivation and interpretation of the third equation require further comment, however. First, with regard to derivation, the third equation of (5C-5) implies $f_r' = \lambda_2/\lambda_1$, while the second and fourth equations imply $\lambda_2^{-1}\,d\lambda_2/dt - \lambda_1^{-1}\,d\lambda_1/dt = f_k'$. It follows immediately that *the growth rate of f_r' must be equal to f_k'*. This condition is known as the *transversality condition*. It is a fundamental efficiency condition which must hold along any optimal path of the system. Second, with regard to interpretation, it says that the rate of return obtained from the use of capital equipment in the production process, f_k', must be equal to the rate of return obtained from the withholding of resource stocks from the production process, or the proportional capital gain from resource ownership, $(f_r')^{-1}\,df_r'/dt$. Put differently, this fundamental efficiency condition says that the rate of return on both assets must be the same, where the rate of return on capital is simply the marginal product of capital and where the rate of return on resource ownership is the rate of change of the marginal product of the resource.

Of the four fundamental differential equations of the system, the last is decomposable from the rest, so that in order to proceed one must effectively solve the first three equations for $k(t)$, $c(t)$, and $r(t)$. Given this solution, the time path for $z(t)$ may readily be obtained from the remaining fourth equation. However, little progress can be made without more explicit knowledge of the form of the production function, $f\{k(t), r(t)\}$, and its two partial derivatives.

In order to proceed, it will be assumed that the production function takes the familiar Cobb-Douglas form.

$$f\{k(t), r(t)\} = k(t)^\alpha r(t)^\delta \qquad (5C\text{-}7)$$

where $\alpha > 0$ and $\delta > 0$ are the elasticities of output with respect to capital inputs and resource inputs, respectively, and where $1 - \alpha - \delta > 0$ is the elasticity of output with respect to effective labor inputs.[9] Thus, the production function is homogeneous of degree one in capital, labor, and resource inputs. It is also well behaved. The assumption of a Cobb-Douglas production function does, however, tend to generate rather specialized results. Some part of the following section of this chapter is devoted to this lack of generality, and to the consequences of relaxing the Cobb-Douglas assumption.

Given the Cobb-Douglas form to the production function, it is evident that $f_k' = \alpha k(t)^{\alpha-1} r(t)^{\delta}$ and $f_r' = \delta k(t)^{\alpha} r(t)^{\delta-1}$. It follows immediately that the first three equations of (5C-6) may be rewritten as

$$Dk(t) = k(t)^{\alpha} r(t)^{\delta} - (m+n)k(t) - c(t)\,e^{-mt}$$

$$\beta Dc(t) = \{\alpha k(t)^{\alpha-1} r(t)^{\delta} - \rho\}\, c(t) \tag{5C-8}$$

and

$$\alpha k(t)^{-1} Dk(t) + (\delta - 1) r(t)^{-1} Dr(t) = \alpha k(t)^{\alpha-1} r(t)^{\delta}$$

It is now not difficult to show that an *optimal steady-state solution* exists, and that the steady-state growth rates of consumption per head, capital (and output) per efficiency unit of labor, and resource inputs per efficiency unit of labor are, respectively,

$$c(t)^{-1} Dc(t) \equiv \theta = \{(1 - \alpha - \delta)m - \delta\rho\}/(1 - \alpha - \delta + \delta\beta) \lessgtr 0$$

$$k(t)^{-1} Dk(t) = \theta - m = -\delta(\rho + \beta m)/(1 - \alpha - \delta + \delta\beta) < 0 \tag{5C-9}$$

and $\quad r(t)^{-1} Dr(t) = \delta^{-1}(1-\alpha)(\theta - m) = -(1-\alpha)(\rho + \beta m)/(1 - \alpha - \delta + \delta\beta) < 0$

The derivation of these growth rates proceeds as follows. Let θ be the steady-state growth rate of consumption per head. Then, from the first equation of (5C-8), one may write

$$c(t)\,e^{-\theta t} = e^{(m-\theta)t}\{k(t)^{\alpha} r(t)^{\delta} - (m+n)k(t) - Dk(t)\} \tag{5C-10}$$

Now, by definition, the lefthand side of this expression is constant in steady-state equilibrium. Therefore, the righthand side must be constant, which will be so if both $k(t)$ and $k(t)^{\alpha} r(t)^{\delta}$ grow at the rate $\theta - m$. Since the growth rate of $k(t)^{\alpha} r(t)^{\delta}$ is $\alpha k(t)^{-1} Dk(t) + \delta r(t)^{-1} Dr(t)$, one therefore has

$$\alpha(\theta - m) + \delta r(t)^{-1} Dr(t) = \theta - m \tag{5C-11}$$

But from the second and third equations of (5C-8), one also has

$$\alpha(\theta - m) + (\delta - 1)r(t)^{-1} Dr(t) = \rho + \beta\theta \tag{5C-12}$$

---

9. The original production function may therefore be written $Y(t) = K(t)^{\alpha}\{L(t)\,e^{mt}\}^{1-\alpha-\delta} R(t)^{\delta}$, with equilibrium factor shares for capital, labor, and resources being α, $1 - \alpha - \delta$, and δ, respectively.

These two equations may be solved simultaneously for θ and for $r(t)^{-1}Dr(t)$, giving the solution values of Eq. (5C-9).

The most important conclusion which may be drawn from these solution values is that the growth rate of consumption per head may be positive or negative depending upon the sign of $(1 - \alpha - \delta)m - \delta\rho$. Indeed,

$$\theta \lessgtr 0 \quad \text{if and only if} \quad (1 - \alpha - \delta)m/\delta \lessgtr \rho \qquad (5\text{C-}13)$$

where $(1 - \alpha - \delta)m/\delta$ may be defined to be *the rate of resource augmenting technological progress* implied by the Cobb-Douglas production function. Thus, the steady-state growth rate of consumption per head will be positive (negative) if and only if the rate of resource augmenting technological progress exceeds (falls short of) the pure time preference rate of the society in question.

Before commenting on this conclusion, it is useful to write the first equation of (5C-9) in the form

$$(1 - \alpha)\theta + \delta\{\rho - (1 - \beta)\theta\} = (1 - \alpha - \delta)m \qquad (5\text{C-}14)$$

It is known, however, that the original welfare integral will converge if and only if $\rho - n - (1 - \beta)\theta > 0$, or $\rho - (1 - \beta)\theta > n$. It therefore follows that

$$(1 - \alpha)\theta + \delta n < (1 - \alpha - \delta)m \qquad (5\text{C-}15)$$

and a *necessary* (but not sufficient) condition for θ to be positive is that $(1 - \alpha - \delta)m/\delta > n$. Thus, if the rate of population growth is positive, a necessary condition for it to be possible to sustain at least a constant level of consumption per head is that the rate of resource augmenting technological progress must exceed the rate of population growth. If this condition does not hold, θ *must* be negative. However, even if this condition holds, θ may still be negative by choice if $\rho > n$, that is if society is sufficiently myopic.

In summary, it has been shown that an optimal steady-state growth path exists. Along this path, the growth rate of consumption per head cannot be positive unless the rate of resource augmenting technological progress exceeds the rate of population growth. Even if this necessary condition holds, the growth rate of consumption per head will be positive only if society's time preference rate is sufficiently small, that is smaller than the rate of resource augmenting technological progress. In the optimal steady-state, the savings ratio, s^*, is given (from the first equation of 5C-8) by

$$s^* = 1 - \frac{c(t)e^{-mt}}{k(t)^\alpha r(t)^\delta} = \frac{(\theta + n)\alpha}{\rho + \beta\theta} \qquad (5\text{C-}16)$$

which is less than the equilibrium share of capital, α, by virtue of the convergence condition.

This section has addressed itself to the question whether or not an economy using non-renewable resources in its basic production processes is capable of steady-state growth in consumption per head at a non-negative rate. The answer to this question depends upon four underlying features of the economy: (a) the rate of population growth, (b) the shape of the social welfare function and particularly society's time preference rate, (c) the rate of technological progress, and (d) the shape of the underlying technology and particularly the degree of substitutability between resources, on the one hand, and capital and labor on the other. Other things being equal, the higher are the rate of population growth and society's time preference rate, the more likely it is that the optimal steady-state will be associated with falling consumption per head, $\theta < 0$; whereas the higher are the rate of technological progress and the degree of substitutability, the more likely it is that a steady-state path with $\theta \geq 0$ is possible. Even if a steady-state path with $\theta \geq 0$ is technically possible, a myopic society may not opt to follow such a path, with serious implications for the consumption possibilities of future generations. The question of intergenerational equity is much more acute in the context of non-renewable resources than in the previous context (Sec. B of this chapter) in which resource constraints were absent.

Finally, we observe that the consumption possibilities available to future generations depend upon the time honored race between diminishing returns and technological change. These possibilities may be widened by greater saving and smaller consumption in the present, so that increased capital inputs may to some degree substitute for reduced resource inputs in the future. Nevertheless, a society which neglects the resource constraints of the future will necessarily consume too much in the present, perhaps following for a time a path of rising consumption per head, a path whose economic costs are imposed upon future generations as the time stream of consumption per head eventually decreases.

D: RESOURCE CONSTRAINTS AND THE GROWTH PROCESS

The conclusions reached in the previous section depended upon the assumption of a Cobb-Douglas production function. It is well known that such a production function embodies the property that the elasticity of substitution (σ) between each pair of inputs is unity. This section begins with a discussion of the rationale lying behind the assumption of a unitary elasticity of substitution, and of the consequences resulting from abandoning it.

It is useful to proceed by re-examining the production function given as the first equation of (5C-2). If this production function is differentiated logarithmically, one may write

$$g_Y = \alpha g_K + (1 - \alpha - \delta)(m + n) + \delta g_R \qquad (5D-1)$$

where g_Y, g_K, $m + n$, and g_R are the growth rates of output, capital, labor, and resource inputs into the production process, and α, $(1 - \alpha - \delta)$, and δ are the equilibrium factor shares of capital, labor, and resource inputs, respectively. These factor shares only remain constant as the growth rates vary if the elasticity of factor substitution (σ) is unity, as it is in the case of a Cobb-Douglas production function. If the system is in steady-state equilibrium, then $g_Y = g_K = g_C$ where g_C is the growth rate of consumption. On steady-state assumptions, it follows from expression (5D-1) that

$$(1 - \alpha)(gc - n) = (1 - \alpha - \delta)m + \delta(g_R - n) \tag{5D-2}$$

Combining Eqs. (5C-11) and (5C-12) and using the convergence condition, it is easy to show that $g_R = r(t)^{-1}Dr(t) + (m + n) = -(\rho + \beta\theta) + (\theta + n) < 0$. It follows immediately from expression (5D-2) that a necessary (but not sufficient) condition for $g_C - n = \theta$ to be positive is that $(1 - \alpha - \delta)m - \delta n > 0$, as before. Moreover, the more negative g_R is, the greater is the amount by which this inequality must be satisfied if the time stream of consumption per head is to be a rising one. Of course, since $g_R = -(\rho + \beta\theta) + (\theta + n)$, it is evident from Eq. (5D-2) that $g_C - n = \theta = \{(1 - \alpha - \delta)m - \delta\rho\}/\{(1 - \alpha - \delta) + \delta\beta\}$, as before, and that the necessary and sufficient condition for $\theta > 0$ is $(1 - \alpha - \delta)m - \delta\rho > 0$.

If the elasticity of substitution is *greater* than unity, α and $(1 - \alpha - \delta)$ will rise relative to δ as the process evolves. The importance of resource inputs in the production process declines through time, making it more likely that the condition $(1 - \alpha - \delta)m/\delta > \rho > n$ can be satisfied through time. But in this case, we have a non-renewable resource which is *inessential* to the production process. Indeed, if the elasticity of substitution is greater than unity everywhere on the production surface, output can be positive when resource inputs are zero. Since this phenomenon defies any conceivable definition of what is meant by an essential resource, this optimistic case is put on one side.

If the elasticity of substitution is *less* than unity, α and $(1 - \alpha - \delta)$ will fall relative to δ as the process evolves. The importance of resource inputs in the production process rises through time, making it eventually impossible to satisfy the condition $(1 - \alpha - \delta)m/\delta > \rho > n$. If population growth remains positive, the only viable long run paths have declining consumption per head. In this case, we have a non-renewable resource whose marginal and average products are *bounded* from above, so that diminishing returns to capital and labor inputs set in with a vengeance as the stock of resources moves towards exhaustion and resource inputs decline. As resource depletion occurs, the equilibrium share of resources in the production process increases towards unity, and no amount of substitute capital inputs can save the day. This scenario captures the pessimistic doomster view of the world.[10]

Although the analysis of the preceding section was cast in the framework of the important Cobb-Douglas borderline case in which the elasticity of substitution is unity, it is evident that the degree of substitutability between resource inputs, on the one hand, and capital and labor inputs on the other is of crucial importance to the evolution of a resource using economy. Indeed, "The easier it is

---

10. On these points compare G. Rosenbluth, "Economists and the Growth Controversy," *Canadian Public Policy,* vol. 2, Spring 1976, pp. 225–239.

to substitute, and the more important is the reproducible input, the more one wants to substitute the reproducible resource for the exhaustible one."[11] Unless there is sufficient substitutability, however, the only viable steady-state paths with non-renewable but essential resources have declining consumption per head. Substitutability is therefore of paramount importance to the resource scarcity problem, as intuitive reasoning suggests.

In the previous discussion, we have combined the existence of non-renewable resources with the existence of population growth. The greater is the extent to which renewable or recyclable resources can be substituted for those resources which are non-renewable, and the closer is the society in question able to approximate zero population growth, the more favorable become the prospects that future generations will be able to maintain or surpass the consumption standards of the present generation. In some sense, therefore, we have cast the problem of intergenerational equity in a framework which is excessively constrained through neglecting (a) the substitution possibilities between alternative forms of resource inputs and (b) the possibilities of a demographic transition towards lower rates of population growth. On the other hand, the possibilities of substituting capital inputs for resource inputs are perhaps overstated by the assumption of a Cobb-Douglas technology. Finally, if the non-renewability of certain resource inputs (and particularly energy inputs) does carry the implication that future generations may well be poorer than the present generation, then serious questions of intergenerational equity are raised by the highly opulent consumption standards of many citizens of the Western world, especially when it comes to the consumption of fossil fuels, which are necessarily non-renewable.[12] We shall have more to say on this matter in later sections of this book.

11. P. Dasgupta and G. M. Heal, "The Optimal Depletion of Exhaustible Resources," *Review of Economic Studies*, Symposium on the Economics of Exhaustible Resources, Special Issue, 1974, p. 12.

12. On this point, see R. M. Solow, "Intergenerational Equity and Exhaustible Resources," *Review of Economic Studies*, Symposium on the Economics of Exhaustible Resources, Special Issue, 1974, pp. 29–45. See also K. Boulding, "The Economics of the Coming Spaceship Earth," pp. 3–14 in H. Jarrett (ed.), *Environmental Quality in a Growing Economy*, Baltimore, Johns Hopkins Press, 1966, and R. U. Ayres and A. V. Kneese, "Economic and Ecological Effects of a Stationary Economy," *Resources for the Future, Inc.* Reprint 99, Washington D.C., 1972.

SIX

CAPITAL THEORY AND VINTAGE MODELS

A: CENTRAL ISSUES IN CAPITAL THEORY

One of the fundamental properties of recent models of capital accumulation and economic growth is the notion that capital is not a primary factor of production. Capital is produced within the economic system for further use by the economic system. Not only is it non-permanent, it is also reproducible and therefore augmentable. As a produced factor of production, capital is neither "disembodied waiting" nor a stock of homogeneous "machines." Fundamentally, capital is "waiting" embodied in a large variety of different types of machines, buildings, inventories, etc. Capital is, therefore, a generic label for a collection of heterogeneous and specific capital goods.

The fundamental choices which affect the process of economic growth are intertemporal choices, choices, that is, between today and tomorrow. How much of today's production should be held back from consumption today (or saved) in order to increase production tomorrow? In what forms should this saving be held; that is, how should investment be allocated among alternative capital assets? Indeed, one of the main problems involved in formulating a theory of capital in which capital goods are allowed to be heterogeneous concerns the whole question of the allocation of new investment among alternative capital assets and the appropriateness of this allocation when viewed from a later point of time.

The central capital-theoretic idea of intertemporal choice has been conceptualized in some detail in the previous chapter. The fundamental variable measuring the intertemporal terms of trade is the rate of interest, which may be associated with "the price of capital." But what is capital? It will be useful in exploring the nature of capital, to proceed in a slightly roundabout way, that is by distinguishing between traditional capital theory[1] and modern capital theory

---

1. Compare D. Usher, "Traditional Capital Theory," *Review of Economic Studies*, vol. 32, April 1965, pp. 169–186.

(or the theory of growth equilibrium). Traditional capital theory is the theory of a single time consuming economic process, associated with the production and use of a single type of capital good, or produced means of production, which is the means by which production can be adapted to the choices made by the community among the alternative time streams of consumption that are available to it. Capital, then, refers to the stock of capital goods or the stock of non-permanent and augmentable resources which enable production to be maintained permanently at a higher level than would be possible without them.[2] Capital is a non-primary factor of production. It is the physical embodiment of society's decisions to postpone until a future date the consumption of services which are provided by the primary resources available today.

The irreversibility of time is important to capital theory. For capital accumulation, the accumulation of non-permanent and augmentable resources, is a necessary prerequisite for a permanent increase in *per capita* production and income (ignoring the fact that certain types of technological progress could increase *per capita* production and income without any capital accumulation occurring). Capital is that factor of production which allows the present services of some primary resources to be postponed until tomorrow, whereas the services of tomorrow's primary resources cannot generally be brought forward to today or anticipated. (Of course, the services of tomorrow's potential capital resources — that is, today's or yesterday's primary resources — can be brought forward to today, simply by not investing today or by running down the existing capital stock inherited from yesterday. But this is a separate matter.) Nevertheless, capital is neither "disembodied waiting," as in the "period of production" approach to capital theory, nor a "machine," as in the "real capital" approach to capital theory. It is a curious mixture of both, neither the one nor the other. It is "waiting" embodied in a vast variety of specific capital goods. It is therefore important to distinguish between physical concepts of capital and fund concepts of capital — that is to say, between capital defined as the number of (homogeneous) machines of which there may be more than one type (that is, types of capital goods), and capital defined by its value in terms of some commodity (such as a consumption good or homogeneous labor) as numeraire.

Traditional capital theory does not, however, recognize the diversity or heterogeneity of capital goods. As already indicated, it is concerned with the production and use of a single type of capital good and, hence, with a single time consuming process; indeed, the main point to be noticed about traditional capital theory is that it is concerned only with the functioning of a *single* time consuming process. It is fundamentally a *microeconomic* theory. Within any given time consuming process, however, it is recognized that the production process associated with the production of a capital good is different from the production process associated with its use — that is, the production process of the

2. Compare F. A. Hayek, *The Pure Theory of Capital,* London, Routledge and Kegan Paul, 1941, pp. 52–56.

consumption goods producing sector. Indeed, it is only in specific singular cases that the two production processes of the whole time consuming process may be unambiguously aggregated into a single production process, and output may be treated as if it were homogeneous since the relative price of capital goods does not change in response to changes in the rate of profit. Thus, traditional capital-theoretic models are inherently two sectoral.

Modern capital theory, or the theory of economic growth, tries to go further and to discuss several time consuming processes at once. Indeed, it also tries to incorporate new time consuming processes as they come into being through technological progress. If these processes and the capital goods associated with them can be consistently or unambiguously aggregated into a smaller set of processes, so much the better. In general, however, this may not be possible. There is, nevertheless, an inherent tendency for modern capital theory to assume that aggregation difficulties can be overcome and to "go macro" by assuming that all output can be treated as homogeneous or as being produced on the same production function as in one sectoral growth models, or, at least, by assuming that all capital goods produced at any one time are homogeneous but distinct from consumption goods as in two sectoral growth models. Much of the remainder of this section and the following one is concerned with the legitimacy of these homogeneity assumptions. In order to proceed, it is useful to examine the concept of equilibrium as it applies to capital-theoretic models.

The notion of the equilibrium of any model, whether static or dynamic, may be associated with "a position of rest." To some extent, the definition of equilibrium is arbitrary. However, it is useful to have a fairly precise definition. An equilibrium position is defined as a position in which the set of variables within the system or model bear such a relationship to each other that there is no inherent tendency for them to change. Notice that since the variables themselves may be rates of change of more basic variables, there is nothing in the above definition that confines it to the stationary equilibrium positions that are characteristic of static systems.

To follow Machlup, "We may define *equilibrium,* in economic analysis, as a *constellation of selected interrelated variables so adjusted to one another that no inherent tendency to change prevails in the model which they constitute.* The basic model as well as its equilibria are, of course, mental constructions (based on abstraction and invention)."[3] Equilibrium is a characteristic of a model and is defined *in relation* to the variables included in the model. The model may include many variables or few; it may ignore long run interactions or short run interactions. Whatever are the purposes for which a model is built, there is a basic freedom of choice as to which variables are included in the model. To quote Machlup again: "It is chiefly this freedom of choice which makes it often almost meaning-less to declare a concrete economic situation in the real world, identified by

---

3. Fritz Machlup, "Equilibrium and Disequilibrium: Misplaced Concreteness and Disguised Politics," *The Economic Journal,* vol. 68, March, 1958, p. 9.

historical time and geographic space but not specified with regard to the variables selected, as a position of equilibrium or disequilibrium."[4] It is hence a dangerously long jump from an analytical concept of equilibrium, as has been defined, to a descriptive concept of equilibrium characterizing a concrete historical situation. The assumption of equilibrium, or of a strong tendency towards equilibrium, must not be taken for granted just because we, as economists, are so used to it.

The equilibrium positions of economic analysis are usually based on the supposition that the various decision making units of the system will make choices that maximize under the constraints of the system some monotonic increasing function of their own "well-being." Of course, actual human beings do not always behave as if they were maximizing such a function. In consequence, when any piece of economic analysis incorporating the fundamental assumption of equilibrium is applied to the real world, there are likely to be discrepancies between model predictions and actual happenings for this reason, among several other reasons. But to analyze anything, some assumptions must be made. The assumption that an equilibrium position corresponds to a maximum (or minimum) position can be justified in two ways. First, it has been a most fruitful hypothesis for the discovery and formulation of meaningful theorems about how the market system functions. Second, there is no equally precise and definite assumption to put in its place. The assumption of maximizing behavior (and the identification of maxima or minima with equilibrium positions) is the fundamental methodological tool or working hypothesis of economic analysis.[5]

So far, it has been suggested that the notion of equilibrium requires that each of the decision making units of the system or model be in a preferred position, having solved a basic problem of either maximization or minimization under constraints. In an unchanging static system, equilibrium is stationary. However, in a dynamic system, the preferred position will normally be changing through time so that the equilibrium time path is one of moving equilibrium. The notion of the equilibrium of a dynamic system – or of an equilibrium dynamic system – does, however, generate some basic problems. For an equilibrium dynamic system is one which traces out a time path for which at every point of time the system is in equilibrium in the sense that all the decision making units of the system are always in the position that they prefer to be in at every particular point of time and in terms of the constraints then ruling. But these constraints may themselves depend upon previous decisions, decisions that were made on the basis of expectations that were held at an earlier point of time. It therefore appears that the equilibrium of a dynamic system will normally require something more than the usual maximizing assumption. For whenever there is more than one form in which wealth can be held, that is, there is more than one form of capital asset in the system, then dynamic equilibrium requires

4. *Ibid.*, p. 6.
5. On these points, compare Hicks, *Capital and Growth,* pp. 15–16.

the assumption of perfect foresight. To follow Hicks, the assumption of perfect foresight entails that

> . . . the expected prices on which current actions are based are the *right* prices – the prices which will in fact equilibrate the market when the time comes. . . . It is not implied that people know what they expect to happen will in fact happen. We are simply asking what are the prices which, if they were expected with perfect certainty and then realized, would generate the process under consideration. (Notice that the prices are expected with perfect certainty; risk, and its offspring liquidity, are some of the imperfections which are here taken right out.)[6]

As a necessary condition for dynamic equilibrium,[7] perfect foresight implies that the expectations held at any point of time are certain and consistent, so that the transactions that are planned on the basis of these expectations are exactly those that when executed equilibrate all markets at the prices that were expected. The equilibration of the expected rates of return on all investments results in the equilibration of the actual rates of return. Perfect foresight implies the complete compatibility, consistency, or harmony of *ex ante* plans so that the *ex post* situation can be identical to the *ex ante*, that all plans are realized, and that all expectations are right and not wrong.

Perfect foresight is, however, only a necessary condition for dynamic equilibrium. Not only does dynamic equilibrium require that the future is not uncertain when viewed from the present, but also it requires that the present itself was not uncertain when viewed from the past and, moreover, that no allocative mistakes that may have been made in the past are affecting the present. Dynamic equilibrium therefore requires the assumption that the model's irrevocable past has bequeathed a set of initial conditions that are exactly appropriate to the current set of expectations about the future. In particular, the actual capital stock, specified component by component, is exactly that set of fossils that is desired at the beginning of the current period in terms of the expectations then ruling. In other words, full dynamic equilibrium requires both stock equilibrium and flow equilibrium at all points of time.

Perfect foresight is a within period, flow equilibrium condition. Starting from an initial position of stock equilibrium, the absence of flow equilibrium in a particular period results in stock disequilibrium at the end of the period. Thus,

6. Hicks, "A 'Value and Capital' Growth Model," *Review of Economic Studies,* vol. 26, June, 1959, p. 160.

7. It is, of course, possible to rig up assumptions that make perfect foresight unnecessary to dynamic equilibrium; but these assumptions will ensure that no foresight is needed at all. Swan's "meccano sets" or "ectoplasm" are of this nature; that is, all capital is infinitely durable and instantaneously adaptable to any productive sector or technique. In general (and apart from the case of fixed coefficient Leontief dynamic models for which the absence of choice leads to odd properties of its own), only homogeneous capital models, where capital follows some simple law of depreciation which is independent of age such as "exponential decay," and where capital can be instantaneously shifted between sectors, can avoid the assumption of perfect foresight. Compare Swan, "Economic Growth and Capital Accumulation," *The Economic Record,* vol. 32, November 1956, pp. 334–361.

stock disequilibrium carries the impact of flow disequilibrium forward to the next period. If, however, one started out in stock disequilibrium and the within period flow equilibrium condition held, then the final position would exhibit either stock equilibrium or stock disequilibrium depending upon whether or not the time period of analysis was long enough to allow the initial stock disequilibrium to be worked off (if, indeed, reactions to disequilibrium are such that this is possible). It is concluded, therefore, that the equilibrium over time of any (non-trivial) dynamic system requires both appropriate initial conditions (initial stock equilibrium) *and* perfect foresight (the consistency of plans).

The notions of perfect foresight and dynamic equilibrium are, of course, not particularly plausible. In particular, the notion of a special class of dynamic equilibria known as steady-state equilibria is also somewhat implausible. A steady-state solution may be defined as an equilibrium in which the relative quantities of all goods produced and consumed, and the relative prices of these goods, remain constant through time. All quantities grow at the same unique growth rate. A steady-state solution may therefore be called a regularly progressive or balanced growth solution. As a general equilibrium of microvariables which expands, or contracts, through time, it may be said to be a generalization of the neo-classical stationary state to conditions of a non-zero growth rate. The steady-state therefore corresponds to the stationary long run equilibrium solution of a static system.

Whether or not a time path of moving equilibrium traced out by an equilibrium dynamic system from arbitrary initial conditions approaches or converges to a steady-state solution is a question of the stability of steady-state equilibrium. The question of the stability of any equilibrium position is always a question of dynamics. The present question is answerable entirely in terms of equilibrium dynamics. True stability is, however, normally a question of disequilibrium dynamics. That is to say, whether or not a system returns to a given equilibrium position (or path) or moves away from it if the system is disturbed from its equilibrium can only be analyzed by setting out an explicit model of reactions to disequilibrium, that is, a disequilibrium dynamic model. This is true whether the system under analysis is itself a static system or an equilibrium dynamic system. Indeed, the analysis of any system (static or dynamic) that is out of equilibrium is always a question of disequilibrium dynamics.

The major usage of the concept of steady-state equilibrium or of a regularly progressive economy is for the purpose of comparative dynamics (though, in a sense, the comparison of alternative *steady-state* equilibria may be said to be comparative statics, for it is the *states* of two equilibria that are compared, the unique growth rates of the equilibria being a part of these states). It can be used to answer questions such as "Does a higher growth rate entail a higher or a lower rate of profit?" The crucial assumption of this type of analysis is, of course, that the two situations under comparison must be equilibrium positions. Since, however, both prices and quantities will normally be different in the two equilibrium situations under comparison, to compare the quantity of an aggregate such as capital in one situation with the quantity in the other situation will involve a cross-sectional index number problem of the type encountered throughout economic analysis.

In reality, the growth of one economic quantity usually entails the decline of another. Growth is fundamentally the consequence of the multisectoral interaction of microeconomic processes, where the growth path of one economic quantity, though interdependent with the growth path of another, diverges from it. Economic growth is a process which is anything but regularly progressive. Nevertheless, for some purposes it is useful to have a long period general equilibrium model which is not confined to the conditions of a stationary state. Steady-state growth equilibrium provides such a model.

One may think of any actual economy as being in a state of dynamic traverse between two steady-state paths. Even if this traverse could also be conceived to be occurring in equilibrium conditions, an index number technique would still be required to calculate the quantity of an aggregate such as capital, and to say how much of gross investment is net investment, because prices and quantities would both be changing along the traverse. Since the growth paths of the various microeconomic processes of the system are diverging along the traverse (that is to say, the degrees of freedom of the variables of the system are far less severely constrained than they are in the case of the regularly progressive economy—indeed, they are normally limited only by the optimal conditions of production and exchange), it becomes difficult to deal with them all at once unless they can be aggregated into a smaller system. As will be seen in chapter 8, the conditions for this aggregation to be consistent or unambiguous are pretty stringent.

It is difficult, however, to conceive of such a traverse occurring in equilibrium, for as we have seen this would require two conditions to be fulfilled. The first condition is a stock equilibrium condition; the initial set of capital goods must be exactly appropriate to the current set of expectations about the future course of the economy. The second is a flow equilibrium condition; the set of expectations on which current plans are based must be certain and consistent, so that all plans can be realized, and the *ex post* situation can be identical to the *ex ante* situation. This is the assumption of perfect foresight.

Now it is quite evident that these two conditions are unlikely to be met in reality. Since they are not, the historic cost of existing items of the capital stock is out of line with their value based on expected future earnings. Moreover, the actual capital stock is out of line with the desired capital stock. Any modern attempt to explain investment behavior will, of course, start from this point and incorporate an adjustment function relating investment to some measure of the gap between desired capital stock and actual capital stock. To explain investment behavior, the determinants of the desired capital stock must be investigated. Be that as it may, there is still an index number problem resulting from the passage of time to add to the cross-sectional one, though this latter would occur whether or not foresight were perfect.

It follows from these brief comments that dynamic equilibrium models of a growing economy, and *a fortiori* their steady-state properties, are unlikely to be of much direct applicability to the real world. They are not, and cannot be, a description or photograph of the historical growth of actual economies. They are, at best, a framework of reference against which any analysis of an actual growing economy can be checked to find out whether or not the analysis incorporates any fundamental logical errors. The real world counterparts of the flow variables of these models, which are almost invariably aggregative in some way, and usually aggregative over some set of commodities, some set of individual decision makers, and some period of time, are slippery animals. The stock variables may be even worse because of the greater influence of expectational chops and changes upon them. It is to the conundrums of capital measurement that the following section turns.

B: THE TWO PROBLEMS OF CAPITAL MEASUREMENT

The problem of measuring capital is fundamentally an index number or aggregation problem and hence generally admits of no completely clear-cut solution. As has been suggested in the previous section, the index number problem underlying capital measurement has two distinct components. The first component is associated with *the* problem of dynamic economics, that is the problem of time and uncertainty. The second component is associated with *the* problem of comparative equilibrium analysis, that is the problem of coordinating measurements made at different equilibrium positions. The two components are distinct because the first component is consequential upon the absence of perfect foresight and the presence of disequilibrium, and hence does not arise in equilibrium dynamic systems. In this section, these two components of the problem of capital measurement will be discussed in turn, although detailed analysis of the second component is reserved for chapter 8.

Solow has summed up the fundamental problems associated with the evaluation of the capital stock as follows:

> Capital problems are inevitably bound up with questions of uncertainty, limited foresight, and reactions to the unexpected. One must admit that economics has barely scratched the surface here. Yet without a satisfactory account of behaviour under uncertainty we cannot have a complete theory of capital.[8] ... The real difficulty of the subject comes not from the physical diversity of capital goods. It comes from the intertwining of past, present and future, from the fact that while there is something foolish about a theory of capital built on the assumption of perfect foresight, we have no equally precise and definite assumption to take its place.[9]

Perhaps Solow is right when he makes the methodological point that, in the context of capital theory, "The fundamental difficulty of uncertainty cannot

8. R. M. Solow, *Capital Theory and the Rate of Return*, (F. DeVries Lectures), Amsterdam, North-Holland, 1963, p. 13.

9. R. M. Solow, "The Production Function and the Theory of Capital," *Review of Economic Studies*, vol. 23, no. 61, 1955–56, p. 102.

really be dodged; and since it cannot be faced, it must simply be ignored."[10] Nowhere does the present treatment face up to the problem of uncertainty, and in this regard its tone agrees with Solow's methodological point. It is, however, quite a separate question whether or not capital-theoretic models should be based upon the assumption of perfect foresight. For the absence of uncertainty simply implies that expectations are single valued. It does not also imply that these expectations are correct. Indeed, single valued expectations may in fact turn out to be either right or wrong. It is the assumption of perfect foresight that constrains them to be not only single valued (or certain) but also realized (or correct). It will be seen in chapter 8 that there are serious reasons for suggesting that by abandoning the assumption of perfect foresight, while at the same time retaining the assumption of single valued expectations (no uncertainty), the usefulness of capital-theoretic models may be enhanced considerably.[11]

All economic variables are affected to some extent by expectations, since they depend upon decisions to buy or to sell which in turn depend upon expectations as to the future use value of the items bought or sold. These expectations may turn out to be right or wrong; but in any case there is always a distinction to be made between the *ex ante* and the *ex post,* between the expected outcome (on which the decision is based) and the actual outcome. The importance of this distinction is most evident with regard to the problem of calculating the value of a stock of partly used durable goods or service yielding capital assets, whose future service stream is measured in terms not only of the quantity of service alone but also of the price at which these services may be sold.

It is only in conditions of equilibrium that an unambiguous measure of the stock of capital is possible, though, of course, a measure appropriate to one equilibrium position may be inappropriate to another. The value of capital is only an exact determinant magnitude in conditions of equilibrium because it is only in equilibrium that there exists an unambiguous value yardstick, given by the equilibrium prices of the system, for aggregating heterogeneous capital assets into a single stock. Equilibrium is a necessary condition for the so-called backward looking and forward looking concepts of the value of capital to be equivalent. The backward looking concept treats capital as a stock output of the production process and measures it by the compounded value of the past stream of inputs from which it was created. It is thus a cost measure. The forward looking concept treats capital as a stock input into the production process and measures

10. R. M. Solow, *Capital Theory and the Rate of Return,* p. 15.

11. If the assumption of perfect foresight yields a "first approximation" model, the assumption of single valued but not necessarily correct expectations yields a "second approximation" model. To go further towards a "third approximation" model by introducing multivalued expectations or uncertainty will, of course, require the introduction of revised decision rules. For example, in investment decisions, the maximization of the discounted value of the expected cash flow returns (present value maximization) must be replaced by the maximization of the discounted value of "certainty equivalent" cash flow returns (or the maximization of the discounted value of the expected utilities of the cash flow returns—the Bernouilli hypothesis as applied to an additively separable intertemporal utility function).

it by the discounted value of the future stream of outputs that it is expected to generate netted of the discounted value of the future stream of cooperative labor (and other) costs. It is thus a productivity measure. In equilibrium the rate of interest is such as to equate the productivity and cost measures. Equilibrium, therefore, entails that the supply price of partly worn equipment, which may be defined as its initial cost accumulated up to the present date at compound interest minus its gross earnings also accumulated from the dates at which they accrued up to the present, is equal to its demand price or present value defined as its expected future earnings discounted back to the present, appropriate market rates of interest being used throughout. Perfect foresight and initial stock equilibrium ensure that all relevant past *and* future expectations are not only single valued but also correct. It is no longer necessary to use rules of thumb or arbitrary conventions such as the accountants' "at cost or market, whichever is the lower" when evaluating stocks of various goods, since dynamic equilibrium entails that the "cost" and "market" measures coincide. It is uncertainty and lack of foresight that break the link, expressed by a common rate of profit equal to the rate of interest, by which the backward and forward concepts of the value of capital may be made to coincide and by which the past, present, and future may be amalgamated into an eternal present.

It is obvious, then, that in normal circumstances the forward looking and backward looking concepts of capital will not coincide. The "who's who" of capital goods "is not just what it would have been if all those concerned in the past had known what expectations about the future would be held to-day."[12] Since past expectations are bound to have been to some extent mistaken, "the historic cost of existing equipment is out of gear with its value based on expected future earnings, and that value is clouded by the uncertainty that hangs over the future."[13] How much out of gear depends upon the degree to which expectations have been falsified by the passage of time, and upon the speed with which market forces act to bring about consistent changes in capital combinations through informational diffusion. In short, the time uncertainty or fossilization problem underlying capital measurement pervades the whole gamut of difficulties inherent in analyzing the process of movement towards dynamic equilibrium in a system of interlocking markets.

The first, or disequilibrium, component of the problem of capital measurement has now been outlined. Since the second, or equilibrium, component will be analyzed in detail in chapter 8, it will suffice herein to suggest briefly why it occurs. The second component is a pure cross-sectional index number problem that arises when two situations that are distinguished by more than infinitesimal differences are compared. It is associated with the comparison of different general equilibria; from one equilibrium to the next both prices and quantities will differ,

---

12. J. Robinson, "Some Problems of Definition and Measurement of Capital," *Collected Economic Papers,* vol. II, Oxford, Blackwell, 1960, p. 198.

13. J. Robinson, *The Accumulation of Capital,* London, Macmillan, 1956, p. 117.

and to isolate price differences from quantity differences at an aggregative level usually involves an index number manipulation. Such a manipulation will involve a formula error; that is to say, for comparative purposes some set of relative prices will be multiplied by an incongruent set of relative quantities, that is, quantities pertaining to a different equilibrium situation than that to which the prices pertain. It may also involve a homogeneity error; that is to say, the specific components of an aggregate relating to one equilibrium position may differ qualitatively from the components of an aggregate relating to another equilibrium position.[14]

In the two sectoral growth model to be discussed in Sec. A of chapter 7, it will be indicated that the relative price of capital goods will normally change in response to changes in the wage–rental ratio (w/r). This change in the relative price of capital goods is known as the Wicksell Effect.[15] The Wicksell Effect is positive if the relative price of the capital good rises in association with an increase in w/r (that is, if the production of capital goods is labor intensive). It is negative if the relative price of the capital good falls in association with an increase in w/r (that is, if the production of capital goods is capital intensive). Notice that in the two sectoral model an unambiguous measure of output exists if and only if there is no Wicksell Effect (that is, if the capital intensities of consumption goods production and capital goods production are identical), in which case the two commodities are one for all relevant purposes.

The fact that the Wicksell Effect may be either positive or negative implies that there is no necessary correlation between the value of capital in terms of the consumption good and the wage–rental ratio. Between two alternative (static or dynamic) equilibria, the value of capital in terms of the consumption good will differ both because of differences in the quantity of capital and differences in its price in terms of the consumption good. This latter price component is the Wicksell Effect. It follows that

> . . . there is no simple relation between a sum of value of capital and any kind of index of physical capital. The relation between output per unit of labour and the value of capital per head is not a purely technical one. It combines the effects (in various proportions in different situations) of technical relations with the effects of differences in factor prices.[16]

---

14. There is, of course, a third type of error associated with actual index number manipulations, and that is, sampling error, which is a measurement error that must be considered in its own right. However, the concern here is with conceptual errors of measurement, and these are of two types: formula error and homogeneity error.

15. Cf. J. Robinson, *The Accumulation of Capital*, p. 396, where she says: "Wicksell points out (Knut Wicksell, *Value, Capital and Rent*, Allen and Unwin, 1954, p. 137) that the length of the period of production does not by itself determine the ratio of capital to labor, because the value of capital required for a given method of production depends on the real-wage rate." A fuller treatment of the Wicksell Effect is to be found in Swan, *op. cit.*, and J. Robinson, "The Real Wicksell Effect," *Collected Economic Papers*, vol. II, pp. 185–190.

16. J. Robinson, "Accumulation and the Production Function," *Collected Economic Papers*, vol. II, p. 137.

When there is more than one capital good, not only is there an index number problem of comparing aggregate output between alternative equilibria, but also there is an index number problem of comparing the "quantity" of capital between alternative equilibria. Both the relative prices and the relative quantities of the various capital goods may differ between the equilibria. An index of the "quantity" of capital can only be found from a measure of the value of capital in terms of some numeraire by removing the "price" component in an approximate sort of way—that is to say, by a standard index number manipulation. Probably the most useful type of index number for this purpose is a chain index.

Finally, the concept of the Wicksell Effect may be generalized to include all movements in relative commodity prices in response to changes in factor prices (or in the wage–rental, w/r, ratio). If such movements occur for a group of commodities over which aggregation has been carried out, then the resulting aggregate will be ambiguous, and it may behave in a manner opposite to or at least different from the behavior that would be expected of it if it were in fact a homogeneous entity.

In summary, the previous two sections have suggested that capital using processes relate particular time streams of primary resource inputs to corresponding time streams of consumption goods outputs. As such, the use of capital equipment has dimensions in time that tie together the past, present, and future. The present is tied to the past through its inherited capital stocks, while the future affects the present through the impact of expectations. Intractable capital-theoretic problems arise whenever the inherited stocks are inappropriate to the existing expectations. The remaining sections of this and the three following chapters are concerned with a more detailed consideration of capital-theoretic models, and in particular with the vintage aspects, multisectoral aspects, and capital measurement aspects of the process of capital transmutation, a process whereby the capital stock of an economy gradually changes in form and function as time passes, perhaps partly in response to the substitution effects set in motion by the uneven evolution of technological developments in various sectors of the economy. We begin in the remaining two sections of this chapter with a discussion of vintage models. Chapters 7 and 8 then proceed to develop the multisectoral approach to the process of capital accumulation, and the discussion culminates in chapter 9 whose first section is entitled Technological Progress and Capital Transmutation.

C: TECHNOLOGICAL PROGRESS AND VINTAGE MODELS

In previous sections, the idea of Harrod-neutral technological progress has been introduced. A technical change is said to be Harrod-neutral if and only if at a constant rate of profit it leaves the capital–output ratio (and therefore equilibrium factor shares) unchanged. Since Harrod-neutral technological change only affects the relationship between labor inputs and output, while leaving the relationship between capital inputs and output unchanged, it may be referred to as labor augmenting. Harrod-neutral or labor augmenting technological progress is obviously consistent with the maintenance of a constant capital–output ratio, one of the requirements necessary for the existence of a steady-state growth path. Indeed, if technological progress is not Harrod-neutral, a regularly progressive or steady-state growth equilibrium path is not, generally speaking, possible.

So far, technological progress has been treated as if it were completely disembodied. That is to say, technical developments do not need to be embodied in the form of new capital goods in order to have an effect on the economy. In this section, this assumption is dropped in favor of one in which technical developments affect only new capital goods, and not old ones. Technological progress may then be said to be embodied or "capital augmenting." The quality of capital equipment is improving, vintage by vintage, at a constant rate which depends upon the speed with which technical developments can be embodied in new capital goods. Technological progress influences the economy only through new investment.

The economy to be considered may be characterized as one which at any point of time, t, produces a single homogeneous output, part of which is turned into machines of the latest vintage, τ, with $\tau = t$. The capital equipment in use at any point of time, t, is not homogeneous. It consists of equipments with vintage numbers $\tau \leq t$. Machines of any vintage only embody the technological developments that have occurred up until the time at which they are new, but do not benefit from any further technological progress after they have been produced.

It is assumed that from vintage to vintage the underlying production functions differ in a simple Harrod-neutral fashion. However, the production function associated with each vintage of equipment is assumed to be of the Cobb-Douglas form. It will be seen that the Cobb-Douglas assumption is herein crucial, for it is only on this assumption that technological progress is both "capital augmenting" and compatible with the existence of a steady-state solution (which requires technical change to be Harrod-neutral or labor augmenting). Finally, it is assumed that there is no physical depreciation of capital goods of any vintage.

Two classes of vintage models may be distinguished. The first class may be called "putty-putty" models. In "putty-putty" models, the production function associated with the use of any given vintage of machines permits capital–labor substitution not only when the machines of that vintage are about to be built (that is *ex ante*) but also after the machines of that vintage have been constructed (that is *ex post*). In other words, the *ex post* production function associated with the use of any given vintage of machines is identical to the *ex ante* production function. In such a model, machines are never completely scrapped through the force of obsolescence, though they may be scrapped through the force of depreciation or physical wear and tear. This suggests that if the physical life of machines is infinite (machines last forever), so is the economic life of machines. As the wage rate rises in response to technological progress, old machines become more and more costly to operate and are manned by smaller and smaller labor crews. But so long as their physical life is infinite, old machines are never completely scrapped.

The second class of vintage models may be called "putty-clay" models. In "putty-clay" models, it is assumed that there exists an *ex ante* production function which allows the capital intensity of new machines to be chosen, but once a machine is constructed there is no further (or *ex post*) possibility of capital–labor substitution. Once a machine of any vintage is constructed, it must be operated with a fixed labor crew if it is to be used at all. Capital is putty *ex ante* and clay *ex post*. If the wage rate rises through time in response to technological progress, old machines will eventually be scrapped because they become obsolete and can no longer earn a positive quasi-rent. The economic life of machines, T, is now an important variable, so long as machines do not wear out before they would otherwise become obsolete.

In the remainder of this section and the following one, these two types of vintage models are discussed in turn.[17] Taking the putty-putty case first, let $K_\tau(t)$ be the number of machines of vintage τ in existence at time t. Notice that $K_\tau(t) = K_\tau$ in the putty-putty case, given no physical depreciation. Let $L_\tau(t)$ be the number of men used in conjunction with machines of vintage τ at time t, and let $Y_\tau(t)$ be the output obtained from the operation of machines K_τ with labor crew $L_\tau(t)$ at time t according to a Cobb-Douglas production function with constant returns to scale. The newer is a machine (the higher is its vintage number, τ), the more efficient it is. It is assumed that the efficiency differences between machines simply affect their associated production functions by the scalar exponential function, $e^{m(1-\alpha)\tau}$, where m is the rate of Harrod-neutral technical progress and $(1 - \alpha)$ is the elasticity of output with respect to labor inputs. The production function for each vintage is therefore of the form

$$Y_\tau(t) = e^{m(1-\alpha)\tau} K_\tau^\alpha L_\tau(t)^{1-\alpha}, \quad \text{for} \quad \tau \le t \tag{6C-1}$$

Now let it be assumed that labor is optimally allocated among vintages, so that the wage rate, $w(t)$, is the same on all vintages. Then

$$\partial Y_\tau(t)/\partial L_\tau(t) = (1 - \alpha) Y_\tau(t)/L_\tau(t) = w(t) \quad \text{for each} \quad \tau \le t \tag{6C-2}$$

Eliminating $Y_\tau(t)$ and $L_\tau(t)$ in turn from Eqs. (6C-1) and (6C-2) there results

$$L_\tau(t) = \{(1 - \alpha)/w(t)\}^{1/\alpha} e^{m'\tau} K_\tau \quad \text{and} \quad Y_\tau(t) = \{(1 - \alpha)/w(t)\}^{(1-\alpha)/\alpha} e^{m'\tau} K_\tau$$

where

$$m' = m(1 - \alpha)/\alpha \tag{6C-3}$$

---

17. There is also a third class of vintage model, namely a "clay-clay" model, but this class will be omitted from our discussion.

It follows from Eq. (6C-3) that both output per machine of a given vintage and labor per machine of a given vintage fall in response to a rising wage rate through time since labor is continuously reallocated to machines of latest vintage as they appear. Integrating the two expressions of Eq. (6C-3) over all existing vintages yields

$$L(t) = \int_{-\infty}^{t} L_\tau(t)\, d\tau = \{(1-\alpha)/w(t)\}^{1/\alpha} \int_{-\infty}^{t} e^{m'\tau} K_\tau\, d\tau$$

$$Y(t) = \int_{-\infty}^{t} Y_\tau(t)\, d\tau = \{(1-\alpha)/w(t)\}^{(1-\alpha)/\alpha} \int_{-\infty}^{t} e^{m'\tau} K_\tau\, d\tau$$

and hence

$$w(t) = (1-\alpha)\frac{Y(t)}{L(t)} \tag{6C-4}$$

where $Y(t)$ is total output from all vintages at time t, and $L(t)$ is the total employment of labor at time t, or, given full employment, the total labor supply at time t.

Now let the effective stock of capital at time t be defined as $\bar{K}(t)$, where

$$\bar{K}(t) = \int_{-\infty}^{t} e^{m'(\tau-t)} K_\tau\, d\tau \tag{6C-5}$$

Using this definition and Eq. (6C-4), the aggregate production function may be written as

$$Y(t) = e^{m(1-\alpha)t}\, \bar{K}(t)^\alpha\, L(t)^{(1-\alpha)} \tag{6C-6}$$

That the aggregate production function, Eq. (6C-6), may be written implies that aggregation over vintages is possible. Aggregation over vintages is carried out by measuring capital as an "effective stock" in which new machines are weighted more heavily than old machines. The weights are incorporated into the aggregate, $\bar{K}(t)$, through the $e^{m'(\tau-t)}$ component of Eq. (6C-5). They reflect the declining marginal productivity of old machines relative to new machines. Such a decline may occur for two reasons: economic obsolescence as a consequence of embodied technical changes, and physical wear and tear or depreciation, the latter of which has been assumed away herein. If, however, both of these are occurring, the weights, which are based upon relative marginal productivities or marginal rates of substitution between capital goods of different vintages, must reflect them both.[18]

---

18. Thus, one should write $\bar{K}(t) = \int_{-\infty}^{t} e^{m'(\tau-t)} K_\tau(t)\, d\tau = \int_{-\infty}^{t} e^{(m'+\delta)(\tau-t)} K_\tau(\tau)\, d\tau$, where $K_\tau(t) = K_\tau(\tau)e^{\delta(\tau-t)}$ is the number of surviving machines of vintage τ that is used in production at time t and δ is the "exponential decay" depreciation rate, which is assumed to be the same for every vintage.

Aggregation into an "effective stock of capital" is consistent (or unambiguous) so long as the production function for each vintage is homogeneous of the first degree; that is, each and every underlying production function should exhibit constant returns to scale.[19] If this is the case (as assumed), then the marginal rates of substitution between the various vintages of capital goods depend only upon the times at which the capital goods were produced and not upon the amount of labor in use with them. Aggregation therefore obeys the Leontief–Solow condition for consistent aggregation.[20]

It remains, therefore, to select a "numeraire" vintage. One way of doing this would be to choose the vintage $\tau = 0$ that was new at time $t = 0$ as numeraire. If this vintage were given a weight of unity in the aggregate, each successive set of new machines of vintage later than $\tau = 0$ would be marked up by a "productivity improvement factor," $e^{m'\tau}$. In the measure $\bar{K}(t)$, however, the latest vintage of machines at any point of time is selected as the "numeraire." This formulation measures the capital stock always in terms of "equivalent new machines." Old machines are thus marked down in value by the weights $e^{m'(\tau - t)}$ as technical progress proceeds. The convenience of choosing the latest vintage as the numeraire, and hence the measure $\bar{K}(t)$, may be explained as follows. If the weights are always calculated in relation to the productivity of the capital goods of the latest vintage so that the weights of all the older capital goods are smaller than unity and decline with age, then in perfect foresight equilibrium the effective stock of capital, $\bar{K}(t)$, is equal to the value of capital in terms of the consumption good (that is current output).[21] This formulation takes account of the fact that the productivity of new machines is rising through time by marking down the value of old machines in consequence of their increasing obsolescence.

Given the aggregate production function, Eq. (6C-6), the model may be completed by adding the savings–investment equilibrium condition and the full employment equilibrium condition when the labor supply grows at the fixed exogenous rate, n. Assuming a proportional savings function,[22] savings–investment equilibrium implies

$$K_t = sY(t) \tag{6C-7}$$

19. See F. M. Fisher, "Embodied Technical Change and the Existence of An Aggregate Capital Stock," *Review of Economic Studies*, vol. 32, October, 1965, pp. 263–288.

20. See R. M. Solow, "The Production Function and the Theory of Capital," *Review of Economic Studies*, vol. 23, no. 61, 1955–56, p. 108. The Leontief-Solow condition simply asserts that an unambiguous index of the quantity of capital inputs into a production process can be found if and only if the marginal rate of substitution of each type of capital good for any other type is independent of the amount of labor in use.

21. See R. M. Solow, "Investment and Technical Progress," in K. J. Arrow, S. Karlin, and P. Suppes, *Mathematical Methods in the Social Sciences*, Stanford, Stanford University Press, 1960, p. 100. See also M Brown, *On the Theory and Measurement of Technological Change*, Cambridge University Press, 1966, p. 85, and Allen, *Macro-Economic Theory, A Mathematical Treatment*, London, Macmillan, 1967, pp. 290–292.

22. A classical savings function could equally well have been assumed and the subsequent analysis would have been virtually unchanged, for in Cobb-Douglas conditions, $s = s_r \alpha$, where s_r is the propensity to save out of profits and α is the share of profits in income.

where K_t is the number of machines of vintage $\tau = t$ produced. But from the definition of $\bar{K}(t)$, given in Eq. (6C-5),

$$e^{-m't}\,d/dt\{e^{m't}\,\bar{K}(t)\} = e^{-m't}\,d/dt\left\{\int_{-\infty}^{t} e^{m'\tau}K_\tau\,d\tau\right\} = K_t \qquad (6C\text{-}8)$$

It follows from the aggregate production function and the assumption that $L(t) = L(0)\,e^{nt}$ that one may write

$$e^{-m't}\,d/dt\{e^{m't}\,\bar{K}(t)\} = s\,e^{(m+n)(1-\alpha)t}\,\bar{K}(t)^\alpha\,L(0)^{1-\alpha} \qquad (6C\text{-}9)$$

This first order differential equation may be written in the form

$$\{e^{m't}\,\bar{K}(t)\}^{-\alpha}\,d/dt\{e^{m't}\,\bar{K}(t)\} = s\,e^{m't+n(1-\alpha)t}\,L(0)^{1-\alpha} \qquad (6C\text{-}10)$$

since $m' = m(1-\alpha)/\alpha$ as before. Integrating this expression and multiplying through by $(1-\alpha)\,e^{-m'(1-\alpha)t}$, one obtains

$$\bar{K}(t)^{1-\alpha} = \frac{s}{n+m/\alpha}\,L(0)^{1-\alpha}\,e^{(m+n)(1-\alpha)t} + \left\{\bar{K}(0)^{1-\alpha} - \frac{s}{n+m/\alpha}\,L(0)^{1-\alpha}\right\}e^{-m'(1-\alpha)t}$$

$$(6C\text{-}11)$$

Expression (6C-11) indicates that if $\bar{K}(0)$ takes on the precise initial value $L(0)\{s/(n+m/\alpha)\}^{1/(1-\alpha)}$ then the system will proceed on a steady-state path where the value of capital in terms of output, $\bar{K}(t)$, grows at the rate $m + n$, the natural rate of growth. On this path, output $Y(t)$ also grows at the rate $m + n$, so that the capital–output ratio remains constant.

It may therefore be concluded that the putty-putty vintage model with a linearly homogeneous Cobb-Douglas production function is consistent with steady-state growth at the natural rate, $m + n$. Moreover, the steady-state properties of the putty-putty vintage model are much the same as those of the neoclassical model with disembodied technical progress that was discussed in Sec. A of the previous chapter. The savings propensity does not have any effect on the steady-state growth rate since this is given by the natural growth rate, $m + n$. The savings propensity does, however, affect the level of capital per head, $\bar{K}(t)/L(t)$, and output per head, $Y(t)/L(t)$, that the steady state attains. Finally, in steady-state equilibrium it can be shown that the average age of a balanced (or steady-state) stock of machines is $(m + n)^{-1}$ or the reciprocal of the steady-state growth rate.[23]

Suppose, however, that the initial value $\bar{K}(0)$ is not appropriate to a steady-state path. Then, expression (6C-11) also indicates that as $t \to \infty$, $\bar{K}(t)$ approaches a path of steady growth at the rate $m + n$. It follows that any non-steady equilibrium dynamic path of the putty-putty vintage model with a linearly homogeneous Cobb-Douglas production function converges through time to a

---

23. See R. G. D. Allen, *Macro-Economic Theory*, p. 290.

steady-state equilibrium path from arbitrary initial conditions. The steady-state path is stable in the sense of equilibrium dynamics.

It has therefore been shown that the properties of the capital augmenting embodied progress model and the traditional disembodied model are equivalent when technical progress can be taken in the Harrod-neutral form. However, capital augmenting technical progress is neutral in the sense of Harrod if and only if the individual vintage production functions, and hence the aggregate production function, are of the Cobb-Douglas form. A unitary elasticity of factor substitution is required if technical progress is to be both capital augmenting and Harrod-neutral. It follows that some of the properties of the traditional disembodied model do not carry over to the model with embodied progress when the elasticity of substitution is not equal to unity and technical progress is not neutral. That is to say, the equivalence in equilibrium of the two models is only complete under Cobb-Douglas conditions.[24]

D: "PUTTY-CLAY" AND NON-MALLEABLE CAPITAL

The putty-clay case is somewhat different from the putty-putty case. In particular, it differs in mathematical form because integrals must be taken not from $-\infty$ to t, but from $t - T$ to t, where T is the economic life of machines. The integrals are therefore truncated because actual scrapping is now necessary in order to release labor crews to operate new machines. If technical progress occurs and the wage rate rises through time the fixed *ex post* labor crew with which machines of a given vintage must be operated implies that these machines earn a falling quasi-rent through time and are scrapped when this quasi-rent becomes zero. There are now two margins of choice: (a) the intensive margin or the choice of the capital intensity of machines when they are new, and (b) the extensive margin or the choice of the time at which machines are scrapped.

It is easy to show that the economic life of machines of vintage t, T, is determined by the fact that when the machines are scrapped the wage rate must be equal to the *average* productivity of labor since the quasi-rent earned by the machines is then zero. Put differently, the wage rate must be equal to the average productivity of labor on machines of the oldest vintage still in operation, or the marginal vintage. That is, if Y_t is the output obtained from machines that were new at time t and if L_t is the fixed labor crew with which these machines can be operated, then

$$Y_t/L_t = w(t + T) = w(t)\,e^{\beta T} \tag{6D-1}$$

24. See the discussion between Phelps and Matthews in the *Quarterly Journal of Economics*; E. S. Phelps, "The New View of Investment: A Neoclassical Analysis," vol. 76, November 1962, pp. 548–567, R. C. O. Matthews, "The New View of Investment: A Comment," vol. 78, February, 1964, pp. 164–172, and E. S. Phelps and M. E. Yaari, "Reply," vol. 78, February, 1964, pp. 172–176.

if the wage rate, $w(t)$, grows at the exponential rate β. Hence, the economic life of machines of vintage $\tau = t$ is given by

$$T = \beta^{-1} \ln \{Y_t/w(t)L_t\} \qquad (6D\text{-}2)$$

where ln is the natural logarithmic operator. The economic life of machines (the extensive margin) is therefore longer the smaller is the rate of growth of the wage rate (β) and the larger is the capital intensity decided upon when the machines were new (the intensive margin) as measured by the reciprocal of the share of wages in output when the machines were new, $w(t)L_t/Y_t$.

Let it be assumed that when a machine is to be newly installed its specification depends upon choosing the most appropriate capital intensity on the basis of an *ex ante* production function of the Cobb-Douglas type. Then

$$Y_\tau = e^{m(1-\alpha)\tau} K_\tau^\alpha L_\tau^{1-\alpha} \qquad (6D\text{-}3)$$

where K_τ, L_τ, and Y_τ are all fixed for all t such that $t - T \leq \tau \leq t$. If $\tau > t$ the machines have not yet been invented, and if $\tau < t - T$ the machines have already been scrapped. Assuming investment–savings equilibrium and full employment one may write

$$K_t = sY(t) = s \int_{t-T}^{t} Y_\tau \, d\tau \quad \text{and} \quad L(t) = \int_{t-T}^{t} L_\tau \, d\tau = L(0) e^{nt} \qquad (6D\text{-}4)$$

where $Y(t)$ is aggregate output (or income) at time t and $L(t)$ is the total labor supply at time t.

It may now be shown quite easily that a steady-state solution exists. In steady-state equilibrium one should have

$$Y_{t-T} = Y_t e^{-(m+n)T} \quad \text{and} \quad L_{t-T} = L_t e^{-nT} \qquad (6D\text{-}5)$$

It follows from Eq. (6D-5) that since the wage rate must be equal to the average productivity of labor on machines about to be scrapped

$$w(t + T) = Y_t/L_t = Y_{t-T} e^{(m+n)T}/L_{t-T} e^{nT} = w(t) e^{mT} \qquad (6D\text{-}6)$$

The wage rate must grow at the rate of technical progress in steady-state equilibrium; hence, $\beta = m$. It also follows from Eqs. (6D-4) and (6D-5) that

$$dY(t)/dt = Y_t - Y_{t-T} = Y_t \{1 - e^{-(m+n)T}\}$$

and

$$dL(t)/dt = nL(0) e^{nt} = L_t - L_{t-T} = L_t(1 - e^{-nT})$$

whence

$$L_t = nL(0) \frac{e^{nt}}{1 - e^{-nT}} \qquad (6D\text{-}7)$$

Using the production function, Eq. (6D-3), and substituting from Eqs. (6D-4) and (6D-7) one has

$$d Y(t)/dt = e^{m(1-\alpha)t} \{s Y(t)\}^{\alpha} \left\{ nL(0) \frac{e^{nt}}{1 - e^{-nT}} \right\}^{1-\alpha} \{1 - e^{-(m+n)T}\} \qquad (6D-8)$$

which may be simply integrated yielding a steady-state growth path for $Y(t)$ so long as the initial value, $Y(0)$, is appropriate. Thus,

$$Y(t) = Y(0) e^{(m+n)t} \quad \text{if} \quad Y(0) = nL(0)\{s^{\alpha}B/(m+n)\}^{1/(1-\alpha)} \qquad (6D-9)$$

where $B = \{1 - e^{-(m+n)T}\}/(1 - e^{-nT})^{(1-\alpha)}$, a constant for constant T.

That T is constant in a steady-state follows from the fact that $w(t)L_t/Y_t$ remains constant over time since $w(t)$ grows at the rate m, L_t grows at the rate n, and Y_t grows at the rate $m + n$. Hence,

$$T = m^{-1} \ln \{Y_t/w(t)L_t\} \qquad (6D-10)$$

is a constant. Moreover, the higher is the rate of technical progress, the shorter is the economic life of machines.

The fact that a steady-state growth path exists for the putty-clay vintage model says nothing concerning the stability of such a path. The question of stability cannot be answered from the basis of the differential equation, Eq. (6D-8), as has been possible from the similar differential equations of earlier models. The reason for this is that Eq. (6D-8) is derived from the assumption that the system is in steady-state equilibrium. It cannot be derived if the steady-state assumptions embodied in Eq. (6D-5) do not hold. Hence, whether or not an equilibrium path converges to a steady-state path through time is left an open question.

Between alternative steady-states with identical growth rates and different savings propensities, the economic life of capital goods will generally be shorter when the savings propensity is higher. But this need not always be the case, since it depends upon whether or not $w(t)$ is increased more than Y_t/L_t when the savings propensity is increased. The reason for this ambiguity is as follows. It is to be remembered that $w(t)$ is the average product of labor on machines of the oldest vintage (machines that are about to be scrapped) and not necessarily the marginal product of labor on new machines. The marginal product of labor on new machines is $\partial Y_t/\partial L_t = (1-\alpha)Y_t/L_t = (1-\alpha)w(t+T) = (1-\alpha) e^{mT}w(t)$ which is generally larger than $w(t)$ for T of any reasonable size. The trouble is that although the steady-state growth rate of $w(t)$ is determinate, it is not clear how $w(t)$ varies in response to changes in various parameters. The model is deficient as far as a theory of factor pricing is concerned.[25] However, if it is

25. Alternative hypotheses concerning factor pricing are studied in M. C. Kemp and P. C. Thanh, "On a Class of Growth Models," *Econometrica*, vol. 34, April 1966, pp. 257–282.

assumed that the relationship between the marginal product of labor on new machines and the average productivity of labor on oldest machines is a constant proportional one, then neither factor shares nor the economic lifetime (nor, for that matter, the weighted average age) of machines, T, is changed when there is a change in the savings propensity since $(1 - \alpha)\, e^{mT}$ is then a constant. If the elasticity of substitution between capital and labor is interpreted as the proportional responsiveness of Y_t/L_t to proportional changes in $w(t)$, rather than proportional changes in $\partial Y_t/\partial L_t$, then the above assumption implies an elasticity of substitution of unity. It may then be said that the economic lifetime (or the weighted average age) of capital goods will be longer or shorter with a higher savings propensity depending upon whether the elasticity of substitution (so defined) is greater than or less than unity.[26]

Finally, consider an economy which produces a single homogeneous output and which is initially in a steady-state equilibrium with a balanced age distribution of its capital stock. Suppose that this economy starts moving towards a higher net investment ratio (or a higher savings propensity, given savings–investment equilibrium at full employment). Then, if the economy is not deepening its capital stock, it must be reducing the economic lifetime (or the weighted average age) of its capital goods regardless as to the value of the elasticity of substitution, given that the labor supply conditions remain unchanged. During this process of modernizing the capital stock, the growth rates of output and of the average productivity of labor are higher than they were previously. But as there are limits to the extent to which the capital stock can be modernized, ultimately the rates of growth of output and labor productivity must fall back to their original levels. In other words, the growth rate of labor productivity cannot be sustained at a new higher level simply by modernizing the capital stock. Differences in the rate of modernization of the capital stock between two otherwise identical economies cannot by themselves produce perpetual differences in growth rates of labor productivity.

26. Compare R. C. O. Matthews, "The New View of Investment: A Comment," p. 164. See also C. J. Bliss, "On Putty-Clay," *Review of Economic Studies*, vol. 35, April 1968, pp. 105–132.

SEVEN

STRUCTURAL MODELS OF ECONOMIC GROWTH

A: TWO SECTORAL GROWTH MODELS

In the present section, the assumption that output is homogeneous is dropped. It is now assumed that there are two commodities, consumption goods and capital goods (or machines), which are produced on different production functions. Both production functions use machines and labor as inputs, but generally speaking in different proportions. This suggests that the idea of a capital intensity ordering of the two commodities may be important. The following definition of capital intensity will suffice at present. The consumption goods producing sector is more capital intensive than the machine producing sector if the equilibrium machine–labor ratio is higher in the production of consumption goods than in the production of machines. This definition implies the following: (a) if the consumption goods sector is capital intensive, the equilibrium factor share of capital in the production of consumption goods exceeds its share in the production of machines, and (b) if the consumption goods sector is capital intensive, then the relative price of machines will rise as the profit rate falls (or the wage rate rises). These statements are, of course, all reversed if the capital goods producing sector is capital intensive.

The analysis proceeds by assuming that the two underlying production functions are of the Leontief fixed coefficients variety, exhibiting constant returns to scale. The subscript 0 is used for variables applying to the consumption goods sector, and the subscript 1 is used for variables applying to the capital goods producing sector. Time subscripts are omitted for convenience. Let y_0 and y_1 be the outputs of consumption goods and capital goods, respectively, at time t. Let K be the capital stock at time t, measured simply as the number of machines. Then, continuous full employment of the capital stock requires

$$K = b_1 y_1 + b_0 y_0 \qquad (7A\text{-}1)$$

where b_1 is the machine input coefficient or capital–output ratio in the production of machines, and b_0 is the machine input coefficient or capital–output ratio in the production of consumption goods. Continuous full employment of labor requires

$$\bar{L} = c_1 y_1 + c_0 y_0 \tag{7A-2}$$

where c_1 is the labor input coefficient in the production of machines, c_0 is the labor input coefficient in the production of consumption goods, and $\bar{L}$ is the labor supply measured in efficiency units at time t.[1] It is assumed that $\bar{L}$ grows exponentially at the rate $m + n$, the natural rate of growth.

Let g be the growth rate of the capital stock at time t; g will depend upon the current output of capital goods and, given the assumption that machines do not depreciate, may be defined by

$$dK/dt = y_1 = gK \tag{7A-3}$$

Using Eq. (7A-3) to eliminate y_1 in (7A-1) and (7A-2), the quantity equations of the system may be reduced to

and
$$\begin{aligned} K &= b_1 g K + b_0 y_0 \\ \bar{L} &= c_1 g K + c_0 y_0 \end{aligned} \tag{7A-4}$$

In these two quantity equations there are three basic quantity variables, K, y_0, and $\bar{L}$. A necessary and sufficient condition for all three quantities to be always positive is that

$$1 - b_1 g > 0, \quad \text{or} \quad g < 1/b_1 \tag{7A-5}$$

This condition simply says that the growth rate of the capital stock cannot exceed the average productivity of machines in producing more machines (or the reciprocal of the capital–capital input–output coefficient). As will be seen later in this chapter, expression (7A-5) is the simplest possible variant of the Hawkins-Simon conditions.

Assuming that condition (7A-5) holds, one may eliminate y_0 between the two quantity equations given in Eq. (7A-4). Thus,

$$1/k = \bar{L}/K = \frac{c_1}{b_1}(gb_1) + \frac{c_0}{b_0}(1 - gb_1) \tag{7A-6}$$

where k is the overall capital to effective stock of labor ratio. Expression (7A-6) indicates that the overall labor–capital ratio is a convex linear combination or weighted average of the labor–capital ratios in the two sectors, the weights being gb_1 and $1 - gb_1$ for the machine producing and consumption goods producing

1. This can be done only if technological progress is of the Harrod-neutral form and it occurs in both sectors at the same rate, m. Complications that arise from different rates of technological progress in different sectors are discussed in Sec. A of chapter 9.

sectors, respectively. Notice that since the model requires that gb_1 be less than unity, the overall labor–capital ratio must always lie between the labor–capital ratios of the two sectors if outputs of both commodities are to be positive.

The way in which k changes with g may also be ascertained from Eq. (7A-6) by taking the first derivative, giving

$$b_0 \cdot \frac{d(1/k)}{dg} = c_1 b_0 - c_0 b_1 = \Delta \tag{7A-7}$$

where the sign of the derivative depends directly on the sign of the determinant, Δ. A positive Δ implies that the consumption goods sector is more capital intensive than the machine producing sector, and higher values of k are associated with lower values of g. A negative Δ implies that the machine producing sector is more capital intensive than the consumption goods sector, and higher values of k are associated with higher values of g. The reason for this is as follows. Full employment of both capital and labor implies that a higher capital–labor ratio, k, must be associated with a higher relative output of the capital intensive good. A higher weight must be given to this good in Eq. (7A-6), which depends directly on the full employment assumption. But the relative weights given to the two commodities in Eq. (7A-6) can only be changed by changing g. If the higher weight is required for the consumption good, $1 - gb_1$ must increase, and thus g must decrease. Hence, if consumption goods are capital intensive, g must decrease if k increases. On the other hand, if the higher weight is required for the capital good, gb_1 must increase, and thus g must increase. Hence, if capital goods (machines) are capital intensive, g must increase if k increases. It is to be noted that these conclusions depend directly upon the assumption of full employment of both factors of production.

Rather than eliminate y_0 between the two quantity equations given in (7A-4), one may alternatively eliminate K. Thus, one has

$$x = y_0/\bar{L} = \frac{1 - b_1 g}{c_0 + \Delta g}, \quad \text{where} \quad \Delta = c_1 b_0 - c_0 b_1 \tag{7A-8}$$

as before, and x is consumption output per unit of the effective stock of labor. It is easy to show that the derivative of x with respect to g is always negative, since

$$\frac{dx}{dg} = \frac{-c_1 b_0}{(c_0 + \Delta g)^2} \tag{7A-9}$$

It follows that consumption output per unit of the effective stock of labor (or per head, if there is no technical progress) falls when the growth rate of capital, g, rises.

The dual pricing equations to (7A-4) may be written as

$$p_1 = rp_1 b_1 + wc_1 \tag{7A-10}$$

and

$$p_0 = rp_1b_0 + wc_0$$

where p_1 and p_0 are the prices of the capital good and the consumption good respectively at time t, r is the rate of profit at time t, and w is the wage rate per efficiency unit of labor at time t.[2] Notice that $q = rp_1$ may be treated as the quasi-rent of the capital good at time t, since it has been assumed that capital goods do not wear out. The dual pricing equations may be normalized by selecting a numeraire. Here the consumption good is selected as numeraire, so that $p_0 = 1$. Then, the relative price of the capital good may be written as $p = p_1/p_0$. Notice that if both p and w are always to be positive, it is necessary and sufficient that

$$1 - rb_1 > 0, \quad \text{or} \quad r < 1/b_1 \tag{7A-11}$$

This condition is parallel to condition (7A-5). (It is again the simplest possible variant of the Hawkins-Simon conditions.) The condition simply says that the rate of profit cannot exceed the average productivity of machines in producing more machines (or the reciprocal of the capital–capital input–output coefficient).

Assuming that condition (7A-11) holds, one may eliminate w between the two price equations given in Eq. (7A-10). Thus,

$$1/p = \frac{b_0}{b_1}(rb_1) + \frac{c_0}{c_1}(1 - rb_1) \tag{7A-12}$$

This expression indicates that the relative price ratio of the two commodities is a convex linear combination or weighted average of the relative capital–input ratio and the relative labor–input ratio for the two sectors, the weights being rb_1 and $1 - rb_1$ for capital inputs and labor inputs, respectively. Notice that since the model requires that rb_1 be less than unity, the relative price ratio must always lie between the relative capital–input ratio and the relative labor–input ratio if all prices are to be positive. The parallelism of Eqs. (7A-12) and (7A-6) should be noted. Whereas Eq. (7A-6) depended upon the full employment assumption, Eq. (7A-12) depends upon the assumption that prices exactly cover costs, where costs are such that the reward for either factor is the same regardless of the sector in which it is used.

The way in which p changes with r may be ascertained from Eq. (7A-12) by taking the first derivative, giving

$$c_1 \frac{d(1/p)}{dr} = c_1b_0 - c_0b_1 = \Delta \tag{7A-13}$$

where the sign of the derivative depends directly on the sign of the determinant, Δ. A positive Δ implies that the consumption goods sector is more capital intensive than the machine producing sector, and the relative price of machines, p, falls as r

---

2. Technical progress, if it occurs, is assumed to take the Harrod-neutral form at the same rate in both sectors.

rises. A negative Δ implies that the machine producing sector is more capital intensive than the consumption goods sector, and p rises as r rises.

Rather than eliminate w between the two price equations given in (7A-10), one may alternatively eliminate p. Thus, the real wage rate per efficiency unit of labor may be expressed as

$$w = \frac{1 - b_1 r}{c_0 + \Delta r}, \quad \text{where} \quad \Delta = c_1 b_0 - c_0 b_1 \tag{7A-14}$$

as before. This is the equation for the factor-price curve or technique curve summarized by the set of coefficients, b_0, b_1, c_0, and c_1. Since it is currently being assumed that this is the only technique of production, Eq. (7A-14) may also be called the equation for the *factor-price frontier*.[3] It is easy to see from Eq. (7A-14) that w takes on its highest value, $1/c_0$, when r is zero, and that r takes on its highest value, $1/b_1$, when w is zero. Moreover, the derivative of w with respect to r is always negative, since

$$\frac{dw}{dr} = \frac{-c_1 b_0}{(c_0 + \Delta r)^2} \tag{7A-15}$$

It follows that the wage rate per unit of the effective stock of labor (or per head, if there is no technical progress) falls monotonically as the rate of profit, r, rises. The parallelism between Eq. (7A-14) and its derivative, Eq. (7A-15), on the one hand, and Eq. (7A-8) and its derivative, Eq. (7A-9), on the other hand, should be noted. Both the relationship between x and g and the relationship between w and r are quadratic, and the structures of these two quadratic relationships are identical.

Consider, now, the second derivative of the equation for the factor-price frontier, Eq. (7A-14), with respect to r:

$$\frac{d^2 w}{dr^2} = \frac{2 c_1 b_0 \Delta}{(c_0 + \Delta r)^3} \tag{7A-16}$$

which always takes the sign of Δ. It follows that $d(1/p)/dr$, $d^2 w/dr^2$, $d(1/k)/dg$, and $d^2 x/dg^2$ always take the *same* sign, the sign of $\Delta = c_1 b_0 - c_0 b_1$. If $\Delta > 0$, then the consumption good is more capital intensive than the capital good, $d^2 w/dr^2$ is positive, and the technique curve or factor-price frontier is inward bending or convex to the origin throughout the positive r, w quadrant. If $\Delta < 0$, then the capital good is more capital intensive than the consumption good, $d^2 w/dr^2$ is negative, and the technique curve or factor-price frontier is outward bending or concave to the origin throughout the positive r, w quadrant. Finally, if $\Delta = 0$, then

---

3. See Samuelson, "Parable and Realism in Capital Theory: The Surrogate Production Function," *Review of Economic Studies*, vol. 29, June 1962, pp. 193–206. See also Hicks, *Capital and Growth*, p. 150, where the terms wage-curve and wage-frontier are used in preference to the terms factor-price curve and factor-price frontier.

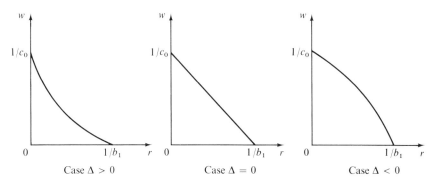

Figure 7A-1 Factor-price frontiers.

the two commodities have equal capital intensities, d^2w/dr^2 is zero, and the technique curve or factor-price frontier is linear. In this singular case, relative commodity prices do not change in response to changes in w and r, and the system may be unambiguously aggregated back into a one-sectoral model with fixed coefficients, and, therefore, with the twin Harrod-Domar problems of existence and stability. The three cases are illustrated in Fig. 7A-1.

So far, the primal quantity equations and the dual price equations of the two-sectoral growth model with fixed coefficients have been treated quite separately. The time has come to link them together. In order to do so, a savings equation is required. The flow equilibrium assumption that savings equal investment then completes the model, for it determines the relationship between the growth rate of the capital stock, g, and the rate of profit, r. Thus, one has

$$gpK = s_w w\overline{L} + s_r rpK \qquad (7A\text{-}17)$$

where gpK is investment in value terms, $w\overline{L}$ is the wage bill, rpK is total profits, and s_w and s_r are the propensities to save out of wages and profits, respectively. Since $k = K/\overline{L}$ and $w = p(1 - rb_1)/c_1$, expression (7A-17) reduces to

$$(s_r - s_w b_1/c_1 k)r = g - s_w/c_1 k \qquad (7A\text{-}18)$$

In the classical savings function case, $s_w = 0$, and Eq. (7A-18) reduces further to the simple expression

$$s_r r = g \qquad (7A\text{-}19)$$

Unfortunately, no similar simplification is available in the proportional savings function case.

The question that now arises is: does a steady-state growth path exist? Can g assume the constant value $m + n$ over time, where $m + n$ is the natural rate of growth? Since both $0 < r < 1/b_1$ and $0 < g < 1/b_1$ are necessary for the existence of an equilibrium with positive prices and quantities, in the classical savings function case it is evident that a steady-state equilibrium will exist provided that $m + n < s_r/b_1$, given $0 < s_r \leq 1$. In the proportional savings function case, where $s_w = s_r = s$, the existence of a steady-state equilibrium depends upon the degree of difference in capital intensity between the two sectors. Since $0 < r < 1/b_1$, expression (7A-18) implies that g is constrained to the range of values lying between s/b_1 and $s/c_1 k$. Since $1/k = gb_1(c_1/b_1) + (1 - gb_1)(c_0/b_0)$ from expression (7A-6), these limits may be rewritten as s/b_1 and $s/\{sb_1 + (1 - s)b_0 c_1/c_0\}$. Which of these two limits is bigger depends upon the relative capital intensity of the two sectors. A strictly positive steady-state exists if and only if

$$s/\{sb_1 + (1 - s)b_0 c_1/c_0\} < m + n < s/b_1 \quad \text{for} \quad \Delta > 0$$

and (7A-20)

$$s/b_1 < m + n < s/\{sb_1 + (1 - s)b_0 c_1/c_0\} \quad \text{for} \quad \Delta < 0$$

Finally, if there is no difference in capital intensity between the two sectors, so that $\Delta = 0$, then $b_0 c_1/c_0 = b_1$, and a steady-state growth path will exist if and only if $m + n = s/b_1$. The Harrod dilemma reappears.

Assuming that a steady-state solution does exist, is this solution stable? That is to say, does there exist a full employment, full capacity utilization path from arbitrary initial conditions to the steady-state solution? Can a disturbance of the steady-state path be corrected so that the system returns to a path on which the warranted and natural growth rates are equal, that is $g = m + n$? The answer to these questions depends upon the relative capital intensity of the two sectors.

From the definition of the growth rate of a ratio, one has

$$\frac{dk}{dt} = gk - (m + n)k \qquad (7A-21)$$

Since $k = b_0/(c_0 + \Delta g)$ from expression (7A-6), one may write Eq. (7A-21) as

$$\Delta \frac{dk}{dt} = b_0 - \{c_0 + (m + n)\}k$$

or (7A-22)

$$\Delta \frac{dk}{dt} = \{c_0 + \Delta(m + n)\}\{k^* - k\}$$

where $k^* = b_0/\{c_0 + \Delta(m + n)\}$ is the steady-state equilibrium value for the capital–labor ratio, k. Now for all steady-state growth rates satisfying $0 \leq m + n \leq 1/b_1$, $c_0 + \Delta(m + n)$ is positive, irrespective of the sign of Δ. It follows that dk/dt always takes the *same* sign as $k^* - k$ if $\Delta > 0$, which is the case when the consumption good sector is more capital intensive. On the other hand, dk/dt always takes the *opposite* sign to $k^* - k$ if $\Delta < 0$, and the capital goods sector is the more capital intensive. It follows that (a) so long as $k^* > k$, k must be rising if $\Delta > 0$, and falling if $\Delta < 0$, and (b) so long as $k^* < k$, k must be falling if $\Delta > 0$, and rising if $\Delta < 0$. Hence, k always moves towards k^* if the consumption goods sector is capital intensive, and always moves away from k^* if the capital goods sector is capital intensive. The steady-state growth path is stable if and only if the consumption goods producing sector is the more mechanized or capital intensive sector, and is unstable if and only if the capital goods producing sector is the more mechanized. This result is completely independent of savings considerations.

The intuitive reason for this result may be stated as follows. The full employment assumptions underlying Eq. (7A-6) or (7A-22) imply that if k is rising with t (capital is growing faster than labor), then the relative output of the capital intensive commodity must be increasing. If this commodity is the consumption goods, all is well, since a fall in g is implied. However, if the capital good is capital intensive, g must rise, increasing the growth rate of k. This leads to a continuous increase in g until it reaches the theoretical limit of $1/b_1$, at which point all output consists of machines, and the consumption goods industry is exterminated. After this point, the model ceases to be economically meaningful since the output of consumption goods would become negative. However, since it is the assumption of full employment that leads to this absurd result, it is much more likely that full employment, in this case of capital goods, should have been abandoned before g reaches $1/b_1$.

On the other hand, full employment also implies that if k is falling with t (capital is growing more slowly than labor), then the relative output of the capital intensive commodity must be falling. If this commodity is the consumption good, all is well, since a rise in g is implied. However, if the capital good is capital intensive, g must fall, decreasing the growth rate of k. This leads to a continuous decrease in g until it reaches the theoretical limit of zero, at which point all output consists of consumption goods, and the machine producing industry is exterminated. After this point, the model ceases to be economically meaningful since the output of machines would become negative. However, since again it is the assumption of full employment that leads to this absurd result, it is much more likely that full employment, in this case of labor, should have been abandoned before g reaches zero. In other words, instability really implies that there is no *full employment* (or equilibrium) path to the steady-state from any point not on a steady-state path. If the system is to converge to a steady-state path in the case $\Delta < 0$, then full employment of one or other factor must be abandoned.

Not only does the case where capital goods are capital intensive give rise to odd results concerning full employment paths, it also gives rise to some odd results when alternative steady-states are compared. It would be normal to suppose that a steady-state with a high wage rate, w, and a low profit rate, r, would also have a higher capital–labor ratio, k, and a higher level of consumption per head, x, than an alternative steady-state with low w and high r. While this expectation is fulfilled in the case $\Delta > 0$, whichever form of savings function is chosen, it is not fulfilled in the $\Delta < 0$ case. This may be illustrated as follows. (1) In the classical savings function case ($s_w = 0$, $0 < s_r \leq 1$), with $\Delta > 0$, higher rates of profit are associated with lower p (by Eq. 7A-13) and higher $g = m + n$ (by Eq. 7A-19). Higher g is associated with lower x (by Eq. 7A-9) and lower k (by Eq. 7A-7). Hence, x and k are both inversely associated with r. (2) In the classical savings function case with $\Delta < 0$, higher rates of profit are associated with higher p and higher $g = m + n$.

Higher g is associated with lower x and higher k. Hence, although x is well behaved in response to r, k is not. In fact, low rates of profit are associated with low capital–labor ratios. (3) In the proportional savings function case ($s_w = s_r = s, 0 < s < 1$), with $\Delta > 0$, higher rates of profit are associated with lower p and higher $g = m + n$ (by Eq. 7A-18). Higher g is associated with lower x and lower k. Hence, x and k are both inversely associated with r. (4) In the proportional savings function case with $\Delta < 0$, higher rates of profit are associated with higher p and lower $g = m + n$. Lower g is associated with higher x and lower k. Hence, although k is well behaved in response to r, x is not. In fact, low rates of profit are associated with low levels of consumption per head. Notice that in cases (1) and (3) where consumption goods are capital intensive, lower rates of profit are associated with higher capital–labor ratios and higher steady-state consumption per head. In cases (2) and (4), one or the other of the capital–labor ratio and the consumption per head ratio (but not both) behave perversely, the capital–labor ratio behaving perversely in the classical case and the consumption per head ratio behaving perversely in the proportional case.

The term "perversely" should, however, be taken with a grain of salt, simply because one's idea of "perverse" or "normal" is really based upon what would happen in a single sectoral model with a continuous production function.[4] The intuitive reason for this is as follows. For a single production function with first degree homogeneity (constant returns to scale), $-dw/dr = K/\bar{L}$, in competitive equilibrium. That is to say, in a single sectoral case with a continuous production function, the factor-price frontier has a slope whose absolute value is equal to $K/\bar{L}$. Since $K/\bar{L}$ must increase as w/r increases, the factor-price frontier for this single sectoral case must be convex to the origin or inward bending. Heuristically, therefore, in the two-sectoral case an inward bending factor-price frontier is required if the two-sectoral case is to behave "as if" it could be defined by a single continuous production function with the value of capital as the capital input at each point. The value of capital is here appropriate if g and r are approximately equal. Indeed, if they are equal, one has (from Eq. 7A-15)

$$-\frac{dw}{dr} = \frac{c_1}{c_0 + \Delta r} \cdot \frac{b_0}{c_0 + \Delta r} = p \cdot k, \quad \text{if} \quad g = r \tag{7A-23}$$

where pk is the value of capital to labor ratio. Both p and k increase as r falls if $\Delta > 0$, but p (and perhaps also k) falls as r falls if $\Delta < 0$. The case where the consumption goods sector is capital intensive and $\Delta > 0$ is associated with an inward bending frontier and behavior much like the single-sectoral neo-classical model. The case where capital goods are capital intensive and $\Delta < 0$ is associated with an outward bending frontier and behavior which is "perverse" from the point of view of a one-sectoral model.

---

4. This comparison is not wholly legitimate, however, since the single sectoral neo-classical model has a continuum of techniques, whereas "capital deepening" is not possible if there is no choice of technique.

Before concluding this section, a few comments are in order with regard to the question as to what happens to the two-sectoral growth model when certain assumptions are dropped. In particular, what are the consequences of introducing (a) depreciation of capital goods, and (b) variable production coefficients? Depreciation can be dealt with in short order. As long as depreciation is of the "radioactive or exponential decay" type, which is independent of age, nothing substantial is changed in the model. In particular, whether or not depreciation affects capital goods at a differential rate depending upon the sector in which they are used, it can have no effect on the capital intensity ordering of the two commodities. This ordering cannot be reversed by the introduction of depreciation. That is to say, the ordering still depends upon the sign of $\Delta = c_1 b_0 - c_0 b_1$. Notice, further, that (whether or not there is depreciation) the sign of Δ is independent of the rate of profit. Either the price of the capital good, p, rises with r over the *whole* length of the technique curve if machines are capital intensive, or p falls as r rises over the *whole* length of the technique curve if machines are labor intensive. Factor intensity orderings on a given technique curve are global, or unambiguous.

When there is more than one technique, but techniques are still of the programming or discrete variety, the factor-price frontier may be construed to be the outer envelope of all the individual technique or factor-price curves, one for each technique (or set of coefficients, b_1, b_0, c_1, and c_0). In this case, the factor-price frontier as a whole is likely to appear to be approximately convex to the origin, even if the individual technique curves are not. It will certainly be of this form if consumption goods are capital intensive on each technique. But even if they are not, the frontier as a whole will appear to be convex to the origin if the various techniques offer a wide range of substitution possibilities between capital and labor.

The introduction of a choice of technique may also be achieved by assuming that the underlying production functions are of the smooth neo-classical type. Certain anomalies may remain, however, in the case where capital goods are capital intensive. In particular, with a proportional savings function the steady-state solution need not be unique, and with a classical savings function momentary equilibrium need not be unique.[5] Moreover, with either type of savings function, the steady-state solution may not be stable if capital goods are capital intensive. Most of these anomalies may, however, be avoided if substitution elasticities are "reasonably" high. The Cobb-Douglas elasticity of unity is certainly over-sufficient in this regard.

When there is a choice of technique, the relative price of the capital good, p, will still move monotonically with r whenever $\Delta = c_1 b_0 - c_0 b_1$ is non-vanishing at every point on the factor-price frontier. That is to say, strict monotonicity and global capital intensity ordering requires that the determinant, Δ, be strictly of the same sign everywhere, that is for all techniques that make up some part of the factor-price frontier. This may not be the case. In particular, if the production

---

5. See F. H. Hahn and R. C. O. Matthews, "The Theory of Economic Growth: A Survey," *The Economic Journal*, vol. 74, December 1964, p. 820.

functions are of the constant elasticity of substitution type and substitution elasticities differ from one sector to the other, then the factor intensity ordering of the two commodities will reverse itself at some point. On the other hand, factor intensity reversal is impossible if the two sectors have the same substitution elasticities.

Finally, in the previous discussion of possible anomalies in comparative steady-state behavior when the Wicksell Effect is negative ($\Delta < 0$), one is reminded of the fact that comparative static (or dynamic) results are unlikely to be meaningful if the states that are compared are unstable. Indeed, this message is at the heart of Samuelson's "Correspondence Principle."[6] One is also reminded of the fact that it is difficult to believe that produced means of further production can be self-intensive; for how would they ever have been produced in the first place? It follows that the stable well-behaved case in which the Wicksell Effect is positive ($\Delta > 0$) is eminently the more sensible case to pursue.

B: A GENERAL CAPITAL-THEORETIC MODEL

As a direct extension of the two sectoral model, the present section outlines a general capital-theoretic model incorporating heterogeneous capital goods. Since the concept of capital as an augmentable and non-primary factor of production requires that capital goods be treated as both inputs and outputs of the production process, albeit at different points of time, the basic framework used is that of dynamic input–output analysis. Although the technological framework is necessarily specialized in so far as it is assumed that constant returns to scale prevail everywhere and that there are no joint products, at various times the Leontief fixed coefficients assumption of dynamic input–output analysis will be relaxed in favor of either a neo-classical technology based on Cobb-Douglas production functions or a linear activity analysis technology permitting a choice of technique. One will, of course, wish to say more at a later stage about the technological context of the model, but for the present fixed technical coefficients are assumed. Following the presentation of the model, two useful theorems are outlined and discussed in the third section of this chapter. These theorems are (a) the Debreu-Herstein or Frobenius theorem on non-negative square matrices, and (b) the non-substitution theorem. Finally, the last section this chapter uses these theorems in a preliminary analysis of the model.

The notation used in the construction of the model may be outlined in the following way. Time subscripts have been omitted for convenience. Throughout the analysis, a *strictly positive vector* implies a vector for which all components

---

6. See Samuelson, *Foundations of Economic Analysis,* p. 350. "Indeed, the *correspondence principle,* enunciating the relationship between the stability conditions of dynamics and the evaluation of displacements in comparative statics, provides the second great weapon in the arsenal of the economist interested in deriving definite, meaningful theorems."

are positive, and will be denoted by, for example, $v > 0$. A *semi-positive vector* implies a vector for which some, *but not all*, components may be zero, while the rest are positive, and will be denoted by, for example, $v \geq 0$. Any vector which may be allowed to have all of its components equal to zero, but for which some components may be positive may be denoted by, for example, $v \geqq 0$; and is called a *non-negative vector*. For the most part, we shall be concerned with semi-positive vectors.

Let $y \geq 0$ be an $n \times 1$ column vector of gross outputs of capital goods, with elements $y_j, j = 1, \ldots, n$.

Let $y_0 > 0$ be the scalar output of consumption goods.

Let $K \geq 0$ be an $n \times 1$ column vector of available capital stocks, with elements $K_i, i = 1, \ldots, n$.

Let $L > 0$ be the scalar supply of labor in efficiency units.

Let $q' \geq 0$ be a $1 \times n$ row vector of gross rental payments associated with each capital good, and with elements $q_i, i = 1, \ldots, n$.

Let $w > 0$ be the scalar wage rate per efficiency unit of labor.

Let $p' \geq 0$ be a $1 \times n$ row vector of capital goods output prices, with elements $p_j, j = 1, \ldots, n$.

Let $p_0 > 0$ be the scalar output price of consumption goods.

Let $B \geq 0$ be an $n \times n$ stock flow matrix of capital good input coefficients in the capital goods producing sectors, with elements $b_{ij}, i, j = 1, \ldots, n$.

Let $b_0 \geq 0$ be an $n \times 1$ column vector of capital good input coefficients in the consumption goods producing sector, with elements $b_{i0}, i = 1, \ldots, n$.

Let $c' \geq 0$ be a $1 \times n$ row vector of labor input coefficients in the capital goods producing sectors, with elements $c_j, j = 1, \ldots, n$.

Let $c_0 > 0$ be the scalar labor input coefficient in the consumption goods producing sector.

Let $\delta \geq 0$ be an $n \times n$ *diagonal* matrix of depreciation coefficients, where δ_i is the proportion of capital input i that is used up in production per unit period, with $\delta_i = 0$ for a permanent instrument i that does not depreciate at all, and $\delta_i = 1$ for an intermediate good that is wholly used up in production. Notice that this treatment of depreciation amounts to making no distinction, except through the depreciation matrix δ, between current material inputs and inputs of fixed capital. Fixed capital and circulating capital are only distinguished by their durability, expressed in δ.

Let R be an $n \times n$ *diagonal* matrix with net "own rates of interest," r_i, for each of the n capital goods along the principal diagonal and zeros elsewhere.

Let G be an $n \times n$ *diagonal* matrix with net growth rates, g_i, for each of the n capital stocks along the principal diagonal and zeros elsewhere.

Let D be the $n \times n$ *diagonal* matrix of differential operators, d_-/dt.

Let I be the $n \times n$ unit matrix, and i be the $n \times 1$ unit column vector.

From this notation the fundamental primal equations of the model may be constructed. In equilibrium, *after choosing the best technique* (if, indeed, there is any choice at all), there are the n capital balance equations and the single primary factor (labor) balance equation:

$$K_i = \sum_{j=1}^{n} b_{ij} y_j + b_{i0} y_0, \quad i = 1, \ldots, n$$

and $\qquad \bar{L} = \sum_{j=1}^{n} c_j y_j + c_0 y_0 \qquad\qquad$ (7B-1)

or $\qquad K = By + b_0 y_0 \quad$ and $\quad \bar{L} = c'y + c_0 y_0 \quad$ in matrix terms

There is also a set of n accumulation equations which define the net growth rates, g_j:

$$y_j = (g_j + \delta_j)K_j, \quad j = 1, \ldots, n$$

or $\qquad\qquad\qquad\qquad\qquad\qquad\qquad\qquad\qquad\qquad$ (7B-2)

$$y = (G + \delta)K \quad \text{in matrix terms}$$

Substituting the accumulation equations into the capital and labor balance equations yields the fundamental primal equations of the system, namely

$$K = B(G + \delta)K + b_0 y_0$$

and $\qquad\qquad\qquad\qquad\qquad\qquad\qquad\qquad\qquad\qquad$ (7B-3)

$$\bar{L} = c'(G + \delta)K + c_0 y_0$$

The primal quantity equations have now been outlined, but the dual pricing equations remain to be considered. In equilibrium, *after choosing the best technique*, there are the n price or cost equations for the flow outputs of capital goods and the single price or cost equation for the flow output of consumption goods:

$$p_j = \sum_{i=1}^{n} q_i b_{ij} + w c_j, \quad j = 1, \ldots, n$$

and $\qquad p_0 = \sum_{i=1}^{n} q_i b_{i0} + w c_0 \qquad\qquad$ (7B-4)

or $\qquad p' = q'B + wc' \quad$ and $\quad p_0 = q'b_0 + wc_0 \quad$ in matrix terms

There is also a set of n gross rental equations which define the net profit rates, r_i:

$$q_i = p_i(r_i + \delta_i), \quad i = 1, \ldots, n$$

or $\qquad\qquad\qquad\qquad\qquad\qquad\qquad\qquad\qquad\qquad$ (7B-5)

$$q' = p'(R + \delta) \quad \text{in matrix terms}$$

Substituting the gross rental equations into the capital good and consumption good pricing equations yields the fundamental dual equations of the system, namely

$$p' = p'(R + \delta)B + wc'$$

and $\qquad\qquad\qquad\qquad\qquad\qquad\qquad\qquad\qquad\qquad$ (7B-6)

$$p_0 = p'(R + \delta)b_0 + wc_0$$

So far, in the model outlined, the price equations have been shown to be dual to, but quite separate from, the quantity equations. A savings equation is required to link them. In the system as presented there is a fundamental accounting identity which may be obtained either by premultiplying the quantity Eqs. (7B-3) by $p'(R + \delta)$ and w respectively, and adding, or by postmultiplying the price Eqs. (7B-6) by $(G + \delta)K$ and y_0, respectively, and adding. This accounting identity may be written as

$$p'(R + \delta)K + w\overline{L} = p'(R + \delta)B(G + \delta)K + p'(R + \delta)b_0 y_0 + wc'(G + \delta)K$$

$$+ wc_0 y_0 = p'(G + \delta)K + p_0 y_0 \quad \text{(7B-7)}$$

Gross profits plus the wage bill equals gross investment plus consumption. Let savings equal the sum of savings out of labor income, $s_w w\overline{L}$, and savings out of profits, $s_r p'RK + p'\delta K$, assuming that all depreciation allowances are saved, where s_w is the propensity to save out of wages and s_r is the propensity to save out of net profits. Then setting gross savings equal to gross investment, there results:

$$s_w w\overline{L} + s_r p'RK + p'\delta K = p'(G + \delta)K$$

or

$$s_w w\overline{L} + s_r p'RK = p'GK \quad \text{(7B-8)}$$

since on the present formulation the depreciation term drops out from both sides of the equation. In the particular case in which there is no saving out of labor income so that the savings function is of the *classical* type, $s_w = 0$, and

$$s_r p'RK = p'GK \quad \text{(7B-9)}$$

Notice that in steady-state equilibrium when *all* rates of return are equal to a common value, r, and *all* rates of growth are also equal to a common value, g, both sides of this equation may be divided by $p'K$, the value of the capital stock, to yield $s_r r = g$. In general, of course, this reduction is not possible out of steady-state equilibrium. Nevertheless, it is always possible to *define* $p'RK/p'K$ to be the rate of profit and $p'GK/p'K$ to be the rate of growth of the capital stock so that in this sense (and in this sense alone) the growth rate of the capital stock is always proportional to the rate of profit when the savings function takes the classical form.

In order to proceed with the analysis of the system Eqs. (7B-3), (7B-6) and (7B-8) or (7B-9), it is necessary to make some further assumptions. On the quantity side of the model, it is assumed that the effective stock of labor, $\overline{L}$, grows at the steady-state rate $\mu \equiv m + n$, where m is the constant rate of Harrod-neutral technical progress occurring in *every* sector (including that producing consumption goods), and n is the growth rate of the labor force in natural units. Of course, the assumption of equal rates of technical progress in all sectors is extreme, and will be relaxed in Sec. A of chapter 9. Once again, if technical progress is occurring exponentially, it can only be handled simply (and, indeed, on present assumptions a steady-state can only exist) if it takes the Harrod-neutral form and occurs in all sectors, including the consumption goods sector, at the same rate. Indeed, everything that is true of a model without technical progress is true of a model in which technical progress is occurring at a constant Harrod-neutral rate, m, in every sector. All one need do is to measure labor in efficiency units rather than in natural units.

The primal quantity equations (7B-3) may now be expressed in capital–labor ratio form. Define $k = K/\bar{L}$ to be the vector of capital to the effective stock of labor ratios, and $x = y_0/\bar{L}$ to be consumption per efficiency unit of labor. Then, one may write the primal equations in the form

$$k = B(G + \delta)k + b_0 x$$

$$1 = c'(G + \delta)k + c_0 x \qquad (7B\text{-}10)$$

and $$Dk = \dot{k} = (G - \mu I)k$$

The last equation is simply definitional since it defines the growth rate of the ratio $k = K/\bar{L}$ to be the growth rate of K less the growth value of $\bar{L}$. Finally, one may eliminate the G operator and write the quantity equations in the form

and
$$k = B(\mu I + \delta)k + B\dot{k} + b_0 x$$
$$1 = c'(\mu I + \delta)k + c'\dot{k} + c_0 x \qquad (7B\text{-}11)$$

whence upon elimination of x across the two equations one has a set of n simultaneous linear differential equations in k, namely

$$\{B - c_0^{-1}b_0 c'\}\dot{k} = \{I - (B - c_0^{-1}b_0 c')(\mu I + \delta)\}k - c_0^{-1}b_0 \qquad (7B\text{-}12)$$

The detailed analysis of these equations is left for future sections.

On the price side of the model, it is assumed that the consumption good is the numeraire so that $p_0 = 1$. It is also assumed that the net rates of return, $r_i(t)$, for each of the n capital goods are interrelated through the following own rate of interest (or asset choice) equations

$$\frac{1}{p_i(t)}\frac{dp_i^e(t)}{dt} + r_i(t) = r(t), \quad \text{all} \quad i = 1,\ldots,n \qquad (7B\text{-}13)$$

where $r(t)$ is the common overall rate of return at time t, and $p_i(t)^{-1}\,dp_i^e(t)/dt$ is the expected proportional price change of capital good i at time t. These equations postulate that the net own rate of interest on capital good i plus the expected percentage capital gain from holding that capital good must be equal to a common rate of return for *all* capital goods. If, in addition, it is *assumed* that expectations are always realized so that the own rate of interest equations (7B-13) hold *ex post* as well as *ex ante*, then one may write the whole set of dual price equations (from Eq. 7B-6) in the form

$$p' = p'(R + \delta)B + wc'$$

$$1 = p'(R + \delta)b_0 + wc_0 \qquad (7\text{B-}14)$$

and
$$-Dp' = -\dot{p}' = p'(R - rI)$$

It cannot be stressed more strongly that the last set of equations in Eq. (7B-14) embodies the fundamental flow equilibrium assumption of *perfect foresight*, since the own rate of interest equilibrium condition is assumed to hold *ex post* as well as *ex ante*. Expected capital gains and actual capital gains are assumed to be equal. This perfect foresight assumption that expectations are always realized will be seriously questioned in the following chapter. Indeed, it will be argued that it makes no sense at all in the context of models with fixed coefficients, in which there is no possibility of asset choice if full employment of all inputs is to be maintained at all points of time.

On perfect foresight assumptions, however, one may eliminate R across Eqs. (7B-14) and write the price equations in the form

and
$$p' = p'(rI + \delta)B - \dot{p}'B + wc'$$
$$1 = p'(rI + \delta)b_0 - \dot{p}'b_0 + wc_0 \qquad (7\text{B-}15)$$

whence upon elimination of w across the two equations one has a set of n simultaneous linear differential equations in p', namely

$$-\dot{p}'\{B - c_0^{-1}b_0c'\} = p'\{I - (rI + \delta)(B - c_0^{-1}b_0c')\} - c_0^{-1}c' \qquad (7\text{B-}16)$$

The detailed behavior of these equations is also left for future sections.

The primal quantity equations and the dual price equations are, of course, linked by a savings equation. On the classical assumptions ($s_w = 0$, $0 < s_r \le 1$) underlying Eq. (7B-9), one may now rewrite this equation in the form

$$s_r(rp'k - \dot{p}'k) = \mu p'k + p'\dot{k} \qquad (7\text{B-}17)$$

which may be taken to determine the overall profit rate, r. If a steady-state exists with $\dot{p}' = 0$ and $\dot{k} = 0$, this expression reduces to the familiar $s_r r = \mu$, where $\mu \equiv m + n$, the steady-state growth rate of the system. For the complete model, Eqs. (7B-12), (7B-16), and (7B-17), two sets of initial conditions are required to set a process of capital accumulation in motion. These are (a) the initial stock positions or capital–labor ratios, and (b) the initial expectations of the proportional rates of change of the capital goods prices. Finally, the concern throughout the analysis of this model is with the viability of equilibrium dynamic paths on which (a) all capital goods and labor are fully employed at all points of time, and (b) prices are equal to costs at all points of time, where costs are such that the reward to each input is the same wherever that input is used. Whether or not such paths are viable, let alone sensible, we leave for the moment as an open question.

C: TWO USEFUL THEOREMS

Two important questions may be asked of any input–output system and its dual. First, under what conditions can positive, or at least semi-positive, final consumption demands (say $b_0 x$) and primary factor inputs (say wc') be associated *not only* with positive, or at least semi-positive, capital stocks k and prices p', *but also* with positive, or at least semi-positive, net outputs of capital goods, Gk, and net returns to capital inputs, $p'R$? That is to say, under what conditions does a meaningful and continuously viable solution to the system exist? Is the system "productive" or capable of generating a solution with semi-positive Gk and semi-positive $p'R$ at all points of time? Second, under what conditions can the input–output coefficients summarized in B, b_0, c', and c_0 be treated as constants? In discussing the first question, it will be assumed that the $(n + 1) \times (n + 1)$ matrix

$$\bar{B} = \begin{vmatrix} c_0 & c' \\ b_0 & B \end{vmatrix}$$ is in fact composed entirely of constants. This assumption is of no

consequence at this stage. For if there are alternative technique matrices (or alternative sets of B, b_0, c', and c_0 coefficients) that could be chosen at alternative factor prices, the conditions under which semi-positive $b_0 x$ and wc' are associated with semi-positive k, Gk, p', and $p'R$ must hold for any set of coefficients that is capable of generating a meaningful solution regardless as to how many such sets there are.

   With this in mind, consider solving the first equations of (7B-10) and (7B-14) for k and p', respectively, when Gk and $p'R$ are both zero vectors. That is to say, one is looking first to see whether even a zero net investment, zero net profit solution is possible. In addition, for simplicity, let it be assumed that all capital goods are intermediate goods, and hence all $\delta_i = 1$, $i = 1, \ldots, n$. On these assumptions, flow outputs (y) and stocks $(k\bar{L})$ of capital goods are indistinguishable, and the system reduces to the open static Leontief system

$$(I - B)k = b_0 x \quad \text{or} \quad (I - B)y = b_0 y_0, \quad \text{and} \quad p'(I - B) = wc' \quad (7\text{C-1})$$

In order that semi-positive $b_0 x = b_0 y_0 / L$ and wc' are *always* associated with semi-positive $k = y/L$ and p' it is required that the inverse matrix $(I - B)^{-1}$ not only exist but also be semi-positive. The conditions that are necessary and sufficient for this to be the case are known as the Hawkins-Simon conditions.[7]

   It will be useful to illustrate the importance of the Hawkins-Simon conditions in the case in which there are only two input commodities so that

$$(I - B) = \begin{bmatrix} 1 - b_{11} & -b_{12} \\ -b_{21} & 1 - b_{22} \end{bmatrix} \qquad (7\text{C-2})$$

where b_{ij}, $i = 1, 2, j = 1, 2$, represents the input–output coefficient for commodity i

---

   7. D. Hawkins and H. A. Simon, "Note: Some Conditions of Macro-economic Stability," *Econometrica*, vol. 17, July–October, 1949, pp. 245–248.

in the production of commodity j. Obviously, since inputs cannot be negative, all the b_{ij} must be non-negative. Moreover, in order that the system be "productive" or capable of yielding positive net outputs (to satisfy positive final demands) from positive gross outputs, or positive primary factor rewards from positive prices, it is necessary that both $1 - b_{11}$ and $1 - b_{22}$ be positive; for if they are not, then a commodity uses in a "direct" way at least one of itself to produce one more of itself and a positive net output of that commodity is impossible. It can also be shown, however, that "indirect" usage of commodity inputs must also be considered, where "indirect" usage occurs through the fact that if commodity one requires inputs of commodity two which itself requires inputs of commodity one, then commodity one requires indirect inputs of itself. Indeed, for the system to be "productive," every commodity must use either directly or indirectly less than one of itself to produce itself.

Equation (7C-2) implies that the attempt to produce one unit of commodity one generates a net output of commodity one of $1 - b_{11}$ units and a net output of commodity two of $-b_{21}$ units (that is, a net input of b_{21} units). It also implies that the attempt to produce one unit of commodity two generates a net output of commodity one of $-b_{12}$ units and a net output of commodity two of $1 - b_{22}$ units. The question is then: "When is it possible for a convex linear combination of these two activity column vectors to yield positive net outputs of both commodities?" The two vectors may be graphed as in Fig. 7C-1.

In Fig. 7C-1, the dotted line represents the locus of points generated by all convex linear combinations of the two activity vectors. Since the dotted line intersects the positive quadrant, the diagram illustrates the case in which the Hawkins-Simon conditions are satisfied. But in order for this to be the case (given $1 - b_{11} > 0$ and $1 - b_{22} > 0$), it is necessary and sufficient that the absolute slope of vector two exceed the absolute slope of vector one, namely,

$$\frac{1 - b_{22}}{b_{12}} > \frac{b_{21}}{1 - b_{11}}, \quad \text{or} \quad (1 - b_{11})(1 - b_{22}) - b_{12}b_{21} = \det(I - B) > 0 \quad (7\text{C-}3)$$

where $\det(I - B)$ is the determinant of $(I - B)$.

It follows that in the two by two case the Hawkins-Simon conditions may be expressed as

$$(1 - b_{11}) > 0, \quad \text{and} \quad (1 - b_{11})(1 - b_{22}) - b_{12}b_{21} > 0 \quad (7\text{C-}4)$$

which together imply $1 - b_{22} > 0$. Notice that since the inverse matrix, $(I - B)^{-1}$, may be expressed as

$$(I - B)^{-1} = \frac{1}{\det(I - B)} \begin{bmatrix} 1 - b_{22} & b_{12} \\ b_{21} & 1 - b_{11} \end{bmatrix} \quad (7\text{C-}5)$$

the conditions given in (7C-4) are both necessary and sufficient for $(I - B)$ to have a semi-positive inverse. Moreover, if B is indecomposable—that is, in this two by two case, if both b_{12} and b_{21} are positive—the inverse matrix is strictly

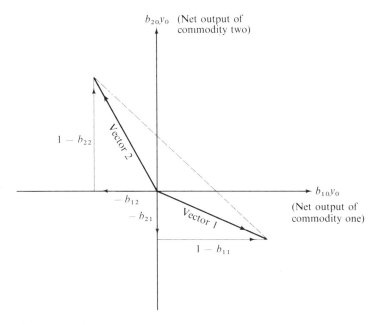

Figure 7C-1 The Hawkins-Simon conditions.

positive when Eq. (7C-4) holds. It has therefore been shown that positive outputs and prices are associated with positive final demands and primary factor inputs if and only if the Hawkins-Simon conditions expressed in Eq. (7C-4) hold.

Consider now the two solutions, λ_1 and λ_2, to the quadratic equation

$$\det (\lambda I - B) = (\lambda - b_{11})(\lambda - b_{22}) - b_{12}b_{21} = 0 \qquad (7C\text{-}6)$$

The two solutions to this quadratic equation are known as the *characteristic roots* of the matrix B. These roots may be written as

$$\lambda_1 = \frac{(b_{11} + b_{22}) + \sqrt{\{(b_{11} - b_{22})^2 + 4b_{12}b_{21}\}}}{2}$$

and

$$\lambda_2 = \frac{(b_{11} + b_{22}) - \sqrt{\{(b_{11} - b_{22})^2 + 4b_{12}b_{21}\}}}{2} \qquad (7C\text{-}7)$$

It is to be noted that since the discriminant (the term under the square root sign) is non-negative for non-negative inputs, both characteristic roots are real. Moreover, if B is indecomposable (b_{12} and b_{21} are both positive), the two characteristic roots cannot be equal, and in particular they cannot both be zero. Hence, since the sum of the two roots is $b_{11} + b_{22} \geq 0$, at least one of these roots must be positive. This is the larger root, λ_1. In the two by two case, therefore, if B is an indecomposable non-negative matrix, then there exists a unique dominant characteristic root of B, namely λ_1, which is real and positive.[8]

Now suppose that $\lambda_1 \geq 1$. Then, since

$$(\lambda_1 - b_{11})(\lambda_1 - b_{22}) - b_{12}b_{21} = 0,$$

one has either (7C-8)

$$(1 - b_{11})(1 - b_{22}) - b_{12}b_{21} \leq 0, \quad \text{or} \quad 1 - b_{11} \leq 0$$

and the Hawkins-Simon conditions cannot be satisfied. On the other hand, if $\lambda_1 < 1$ (which implies that $\lambda_2 < 1$ also), then

$$(1 - b_{11})(1 - b_{22}) - b_{12}b_{21} = \det(I - B) > 0, \quad \text{and} \quad (1 - b_{11}) > 0 \tag{7C-9}$$

since, obviously, $b_{11} \leq \lambda_1 < 1$. Hence, in the two by two case, the Hawkins-Simon conditions are satisfied if and only if the unique dominant characteristic root of the matrix B is less than unity.

The analysis has now reached the point where the Hawkins-Simon conditions can be generalized to the case where B is an $n \times n$ non-negative matrix. It is assumed that B is indecomposable; that is to say, B cannot be permuted into a block triangular matrix by suitable interchanges of both rows and columns. In this general case, the characteristic roots of B are given by the equation

$$\det(\lambda I - B) = 0 \tag{7C-10}$$

In this case, some of the characteristic roots may be complex (rather than real) numbers, occurring in conjugate complex pairs. The size of any complex root may be measured by its modulus or absolute value, which is always greater than its real part. If in the general case there exists a dominant root which is real and positive, all other roots must be smaller in modulus or absolute value than this root. Moreover, if there exists a dominant root which is real and positive but less than unity, all the roots must have modulus less than unity, and therefore must lie within the unit circle in the complex plane.

In the general case, the Hawkins-Simon conditions may be best expressed in terms of the Debreu-Herstein or Frobenius theorem.[9] This theorem may be stated as follows:

Theorem 7C-1: If B is an indecomposable primitive non-negative square matrix, then B has a unique dominant (largest in modulus) characteristic

8. The sign of the second root (λ_2) is positive if $b_{11}b_{22} - b_{12}b_{21} > 0$, zero if $b_{11}b_{22} - b_{12}b_{21} = 0$, and negative if $b_{11}b_{22} - b_{12}b_{21} < 0$. It therefore depends upon an input intensity comparison of the two sectors. In the decomposable case, λ_2 is positive and may be equal to λ_1 if $b_{11} = b_{22}$, so that the dominant characteristic root is not a single root. Indeed, in this exceptional case $\lambda_1 = \lambda_2 = b_{11} = b_{22}$. In the imprimitive or cyclic case, in which $b_{11} = b_{22} = 0$, the two roots are equal in magnitude and opposite in sign, so that the root with largest modulus or absolute value is again not unique. Indeed, in this exceptional case $\lambda_1 = \sqrt{(b_{12}b_{21})} = -\lambda_2$.

9. See G. Debreu and I. N. Herstein, "Non-negative Square Matrices," *Econometrica*, vol. 21, October, 1953, pp. 597–607.

root λ_1 which is real and positive. This root is known as the Frobenius root and is associated with a strictly positive eigenvector. (That is, $|\lambda_1 I - B| = 0$ and $(\lambda_1 I - B)z = 0$ for some $z > 0$.) If and only if this root is less than unity, then (a) $A = I - B$ has a dominant positive diagonal, that is there exists a set of positive measurement units expressed in a diagonal matrix E such that each of the diagonal elements of $A^* = I - B^* = E(I - B)E^{-1}$ exceeds the sum of the absolute values of all the other elements in the corresponding column,

$$a_{jj}^* > \sum_{i \neq j}^{n} |a_{ij}^*|, \quad \text{all} \quad j = 1, \ldots, n, \quad \text{or} \quad 1 > \sum_{i=1}^{n} e_i b_{ij} e_j^{-1}$$

so that $i'(I - EBE^{-1}) > 0$; (b) $A^{-1} = (I - B)^{-1}$ is a positive matrix, that is all of its elements are positive; (c) all the upper left hand corner n principal minors of $(I - B)$ are positive, so that

$$a_{11} > 0, \quad \begin{vmatrix} a_{11} & a_{12} \\ a_{21} & a_{22} \end{vmatrix} > 0, \ldots, \quad |A| = \begin{vmatrix} a_{11} & \cdots & a_{1n} \\ \vdots & & \vdots \\ a_{n1} & \cdots & a_{nn} \end{vmatrix} > 0$$

(these are the Hawkins-Simon conditions); and (d) $A = I - B$ is a *Leontief matrix*, and there exists a vector $y > 0$ such that $Ay = (I - B)y > 0$.[10]

Returning to the open static Leontief system (7C-1), one may now state the following. Strictly positive $b_0 y_0$ and wc' always imply strictly positive y and p' if and only if $(I - B)$ is a Leontief matrix, that is, if and only if the dominant characteristic root of B is less than unity so that all the characteristic roots lie within the unit circle. Moreover, as long as B is indecomposable and obeys the Hawkins-Simon conditions, even semi-positive $b_0 y_0$ and wc' always imply strictly positive y and p'. In the decomposable case, however, B may not have a *unique* dominant characteristic root since multiple occurrences of λ_1 are possible. In this case, Theorem 7C-1 must be weakened slightly to read that $\lambda_1 \geq 0$ is associated with a semi-positive eigenvector, $z \geq 0$, and with $(I - B)^{-1} \geq 0$ if and only if $\lambda_1 < 1$. Thus, in the decomposable case, if B obeys the Hawkins-Simon conditions (that is if all of its characteristic roots are less than unity in modulus), then semi-positive $b_0 y_0$ and wc' can only be said to imply semi-positive y and p'. Apart from this change, the theorem is unaltered in the decomposable case. Finally, in the imprimitive or cyclic case, the theorem is also unaltered except

---

10. The first part of these four parallel conditions is due to L. W. McKenzie, "Matrices with Dominant Diagonals and Economic Theory," pp. 47–62 in K. J. Arrow, S. Karlin, and P. Suppes (eds.), *Mathematical Methods in the Social Sciences*, Stanford, Stanford University Press, 1960. See also D. Gale and H. Nikaido, "The Jacobian Matrix and Global Univalence of Mappings," *Mathematische Annalen*, Band 159, Heft 2, 1965, pp. 81–93, and the useful summary in E. Burmeister and A. R. Dobell, *Mathematical Theories of Economic Growth*, London, Collier-Macmillan, 1970, pp. 437–440.

for the fact that there may be at least one other root equal in modulus to λ_1 (but with different real part or opposite sign).

Given indecomposability and the Hawkins-Simon conditions of clause (c) of Theorem 7C-1, the joint solution to expression (7C-1) may now be written as

$$k = (I - B)^{-1}b_0 x > 0, \quad \text{or} \quad y = (I - B)^{-1}b_0 y_0 > 0 \quad \text{for} \quad b_0 x = b_0 y_0 / \bar{L} \geq 0$$

and
$$p' = wc'(I - B)^{-1} > 0 \quad \text{for} \quad wc' \geq 0 \qquad (7C\text{-}11)$$

The question now arises, under what circumstances can the $(n + 1) \times (n + 1)$ matrix $\bar{B} = \begin{bmatrix} c_0 & c' \\ b_0 & B \end{bmatrix}$ be treated as a matrix of constants? That is to say, under what circumstances will a fixed set of coefficients, $\bar{B}$, always be chosen in competitive equilibrium even though the underlying technology allows the input–output coefficients to be variable?

In general, if there were more than one primary factor so that the vector wc' must be replaced by $w'C$ where w' is a $1 \times s$ row vector of primary factor prices and C is an $s \times n$ matrix of primary factor input coefficients, the components of the C matrix would depend directly upon the prices of the primary factors, w'. Moreover, the components of the B matrix would depend upon commodity prices, and, hence, ultimately upon the primary factor prices. (Similar statements apply to the input coefficients of the consumption goods producing sector.) However, as Samuelson has shown, given a normalization rule (such as $p_0 = 1$) a general equilibrium system of the type outlined has at most $s - 1$ degrees of freedom, where s is the number of scarce primary factors.[11] It follows that if there is only one primary factor as in the basic Leontief model (in which case $w'C = wc'$ is a row vector of unit labor costs, labor being the single primary factor), then there are no degrees of freedom and the system is completely determinate, up to a normalization rule. It is important to note, however, that this statement is not generally valid when the model is extended to include capital goods whose use is associated with the existence of a profit rate, r, which is allowed to be variable (as in the previous and following sections). For this introduces a further degree of freedom into the system and, with it, the likelihood that techniques will change when r changes.

Within the present open static Leontief framework, however, given the state of technology, the assumption of a single primary factor (coupled with the assumptions of constant returns to scale and no joint production) implies that one and only one set of input coefficients for the production of any commodity will be observed in competitive equilibrium no matter what is the pattern of final

11. P. A. Samuelson, "Prices of Factors and Goods in General Equilibrium," *Review of Economic Studies*, vol. 21, no. 54, 1953–54, pp. 18–20. Consequential upon the fact that a general equilibrium system (of the type described) with s scarce primary factors has at most $s - 1$ degrees of freedom is the fact that a two-factor general equilibrium system has at most one degree of freedom. Because of this, special results are derivable for models with two primary factors that are not extendable to models incorporating more than two primary factors.

demands[12] and the level of primary factor supply (with the trivial exception that in certain technologies two technique matrices could be tied for "best" and either one could be observed). To say this is to say that all relative prices remain fixed as long as no changes in the basic technology occur; the b_{ij}'s, $i = 1, \ldots, n$, $j = 0, 1, \ldots, n$, and c_j's, $j = 0, 1, \ldots, n$, act as if they were fixed technical constants, since with only one basic factor there is no possibility of factor substitution. Hence, given the price of the primary factor, w, all absolute prices would be completely determined. The economy has a unique constant cost transformation locus, which is a plane in $n + 1$ space. This is the essence of both Samuelson's Non-substitution Theorem[13] and the Ricardian Labor Theory of Value.

When there is only one primary factor, say labor, Samuelson's Non-substitution Theorem asserts that there exists a "best" technique matrix $\bar{B} = \begin{bmatrix} c_0 & c' \\ b_0 & B \end{bmatrix}$ — "best" because it maximizes the real wage rate in terms of *any* commodity (and especially the consumption good when there is only one such good) as numeraire — which will be observed regardless as to the specification of the pattern (or level) of final demands and as to the level of primary factor supply. This technique matrix will normally be unique, but ties for "best" are possible (and hence any convex linear combination of two basic techniques which are tied for "best" will also equally be "best").

The Non-substitution Theorem may now be expressed as follows:

Theorem 7C-2: Given a technology obeying the conditions of (a) constant returns to scale and (b) no joint products, if there is only a single primary factor (labor) then, at any given rate of profit (on a non-primary capital factor), there exists a technique matrix composed of pure activities (activities which are not convex linear combinations of other activities) which will minimize all prices in terms of the wage rate, or, rather, maximize real wages in terms of *any* commodity as numeraire. Given this preferred technique matrix, the prices of all commodities are fixed in terms of the wage rate and are hence independent of the pattern of final demands (and primary factor supply); the transformation locus facing the consumer is linear. This is the substance of the labor theory of value.

---

12. In our model, technically there is no "pattern" of final demands since we have assumed a single separate consumption good. This assumption has been made since disproportionate changes in the elements of the consumption bundle from one period to the next are incompatible with steady-state equilibrium. If technological progress is occurring, so that incomes per head are rising in steady-state equilibrium, it would therefore be required that all income elasticities of demand must be equal to unity (that is, the consumption indifference map of each "individual" must be homothetic with respect to rays through the origin). Because of these entanglements, it is useful to assume that there is simply a single separate consumption good.

13. See Samuelson, "Abstract of a Theorem Concerning Substitutability in Open Leontief Models," pp. 142–146 in T. C. Koopmans (ed.), *Activity Analysis of Production and Allocation,* New York, Wiley, 1951, and Arrow, "Alternative Proof of the Substitution Theorem for Leontief Models in the General Case," pp. 155–164 in the same volume.

It is to be noted that Theorem 7C-2 is specified in a way which will allow for the existence of capital goods and a rate of profit, so long as this profit rate is *fixed*. In other words, the non-substitution theorem may be extended into models of the type outlined in the previous section, models which have an additional, but non-primary, factor called capital, whose price is the rate of return, r, as long as this price is fixed. That is to say, a system with a fixed positive profit rate behaves, as far as its price relations are concerned, just like a zero profit system; the only difference is that the input–output coefficients are raised by the profit-ability factor.[14]

It is to be noted that the Leontief input–output model, Eq. (7C-1), does incorporate circulating capital goods in the form of current material inputs or intermediate goods; commodities are produced by means of inputs of other commodities. But it does not incorporate a profit rate. In the models to be analyzed, both fixed and circulating capital appear, as does the profit rate, r. Fixed and circulating capital are distinguished only by their durability, or the proportion of a given capital input i that is used up in the production of commodities j in a given period. Current material inputs or intermediate goods are wholly used up, whereas permanent instruments are not used up at all since, by definition, they do not depreciate. In general, however, both fixed capital goods and inventories of circulating capital goods are partly but not wholly used up in production in a given period, the former having smaller "depreciation coefficients" than the latter.

It is convenient to assume that the depreciation of any capital good i in all uses j is independent of the age of the capital good. This assumption is important. For depreciation must take this form if problems of "joint production" are to be avoided. Since the production of commodity j with fixed capital implies joint production in the sense that the production of commodity j also implies the production of older capital goods, fixed capital can be introduced into the model *and* Samuelson's non-substitution theorem can be used (given a fixed rate of return) if and only if the various end products of the model are not jointly produced, that is so long as old machines do not enter the consumption bundle as a distinct commodity. If depreciation is independent of age, this condition holds since a fixed proportion of the number of machines of any type "die" in any period and those remaining are not distinguishable from new machines in any way. Any force of mortality that is independent of age, such as the present assumption of exponential decay, will meet this condition and thus avoid the problems of "joint products."

If depreciation is *not* assumed to be independent of age, capital goods of different ages will yield different quasi-rents. It follows that in order for the own

14. See Samuelson, "A New Theorem of Nonsubstitution," p. 415, in H. Hegeland (ed.), *Money, Growth and Methodology, and Other Essays in Economics in Honor of Johan Akerman*, Lund, CWK Gleerup, 1961. See also D. Levhari, "A Nonsubstitution Theorem and Switching of Techniques," *Quarterly Journal of Economics*, vol. 79, February, 1965, pp. 98–105, and J. A. Mirrlees, "The Dynamic Nonsubstitution Theorem," *Review of Economic Studies*, vol. 36, January 1969, pp. 67–76.

rate of interest equilibrium condition to continue to hold the prices of capital goods of different ages must generally differ. In general, therefore, if depreciation is not independent of age, capital goods of different ages must be treated as different commodities. But if this is so, the production of any particular commodity with fixed capital equipment implies the production of older capital assets as well, and "joint production" cannot be avoided (with the consequent loss of the use of the non-substitution theorem at any given rate of profit).

The non-substitution theorem has therefore been shown to depend in a fixed capital model upon fairly special depreciation assumptions. As already noted, it also depends upon the assumption of a single primary factor and a fixed rate of profit. A variable profit rate introduces an extra degree of freedom into the system. Equally, so would a second primary factor. However, even if labor is the only primary factor and the rate of profit is fixed, the existence of international trade itself may introduce a further degree of freedom into the system if the trading country specializes and does not produce a specific capital good or intermediate product which is required as an input into further production. The reason for this is as follows. A "competing" import—that is, a commodity which is imported but also produced in the importing country—may simply turn the respective component of the final demand vector negative. That is to say, the final demand vector need not be semi-positive if there are imports (and exports) in the model. However, a "non-competing" import—that is, a commodity which is imported but not produced at home—cannot be treated simply as a negative component in the final demand column if it is used as a capital (or intermediate) input into further production. It must be incorporated through the introduction of an import input row in the technology matrix. It would therefore act as if it were a second primary factor of production. The system would then have to economize not only on the direct and indirect labor (indirect labor being capital) of one country, or, at a given profit rate, just on labor, but also on the direct and indirect labor of other countries. It would no longer act as if there were only one primary factor to be economized. The price system would have a further degree of freedom and the use of Samuelson's non-substitution theorem would be lost.[15]

Finally, our analysis of the non-substitution theorem has stressed the importance of the existence of only a single primary factor, labor. There is, of course, no difficulty in principle in the incorporation of inexhaustible (or renewable) land into the basic model as a secondary primary factor of production except in so far as it introduces another degree of freedom into the price system. For land earns a rental in the same way as capital goods so that the price of land, or its capitalized value, depends upon the rate of return. The introduction of land, however, does normally remove the possibility of a non-stationary steady-state unless technological progress is land augmenting. Indeed, in the present technological context, a steady-state is not generally possible unless all primary factors are growing at the same rate or, at least, unless their "effective stocks" are growing

15. Compare L. W. McKenzie, "Specialisation and Efficiency in World Production," *Review of Economic Studies,* vol. 21, no. 56, 1953–54, p. 179. See also Sec. B, chapter 9 of this book.

at the same rate. From this point of view, a steady-state can normally exist only if there is a single primary factor, say labor. Moreover, if labor is the only primary factor, and its effective stock is growing at the rate $\mu = m + n$, then a steady-state can only exist if it is possible for g to be equal to $m + n$ and the corresponding rate of return, r, to be feasible. It is to this question of existence that the following section turns.

D: PRELIMINARY ANALYSIS OF THE MODEL

Consider the general set of $n + 1$ primal or quantity equations, (7B-11). This set of equations assumes the single (equilibrium) technique summarized by the input coefficient matrix $\bar{B} = \begin{bmatrix} c_0 & c' \\ b_0 & B \end{bmatrix}$ and the depreciation matrix δ. For such a technique to be feasible, it must at least be practicable when $G = 0$ and $\dot{k} = (G - \mu I)k = -\mu k$. That is to say, there should exist a solution to the system with semi-positive capital stocks k and consumption allocations $b_0 x$ when $G = 0$. At zero growth rates,

$$k = B\delta k + b_0 x \quad \text{and} \quad 1 = c'\delta k + c_0 x \tag{7D-1}$$

(It should be noted that if all capital goods are intermediate goods, and hence $\delta = I$, this system reduces to the open static Leontief system of the previous section, that is $(I - B)k = b_0 x$ and $1 = c'k + c_0 x$.) Now $B\delta$ is a non-negative square matrix which is assumed (for convenience only) to be indecomposable. It must therefore have a unique dominant characteristic root which is real and positive. If this dominant root is less than unity, then $(I - B\delta)^{-1}$ is a positive matrix since its expansion, $I + B\delta + (B\delta)^2 + (B\delta)^3 + \cdots$, is convergent. If $(I - B\delta)^{-1}$ exists and is positive, then

$$k = (I - B\delta)^{-1}b_0 x \tag{7D-2}$$

is a solution which implies that positive capital–labor ratios, k, are associated with semi-positive consumption allocations per efficiency unit of labor, $b_0 x$.

Let all capital stocks grow at the same rate g, that is, let $G = gI$. Then as g increases from zero, the matrix which must remain positive if the technique is to remain feasible (or capable of associating positive capital–labor ratios, k, with semi-positive final consumption allocations, $b_0 x$) is $[I - (I - B\delta)^{-1}Bg]^{-1}$. This may be shown as follows. If $(I - B\delta)^{-1}$ is a positive matrix, then $(I - B\delta)^{-1}Bg$ is a positive matrix for $B \geq 0$ and $g > 0$. Moreover, it is indecomposable for B indecomposable. It will therefore have a unique dominant characteristic root which is real and positive. For any positive values of g at which this root is less than unity, the matrix $[I - (I - B\delta)^{-1}Bg]^{-1}$ will exist and be positive. For these values of g one may write

$$k = [I - (I - B\delta)^{-1}Bg]^{-1}[I - B\delta]^{-1}b_0 x \tag{7D-3}$$

or $$k = [I - B(gI + \delta)]^{-1}b_0 x$$

giving a solution which associates positive capital stocks with semi-positive final consumption allocations. It follows that there is a critical rate of growth given by the reciprocal of the dominant root of $(I - B\delta)^{-1}B$ which g cannot exceed if $b_0 x$ is to be at least non-negative.

This may be seen as follows. Let the dominant characteristic root (the Frobenius root) of $(I - B\delta)^{-1}B$ be λ_1. Then $\{I - (I - B\delta)^{-1}Bg\}$ has a dominant positive diagonal (and is hence a Leontief matrix) if and only if $g < 1/\lambda_1$. Positive capital stocks and semi-positive final consumption allocations will be associated if and only if g is less than the reciprocal of the dominant root of $(I - B\delta)^{-1}B$. It follows that $1/\lambda_1$ is the maximal balanced growth rate that the given technique is capable of producing. Moreover, in order for this growth rate to be possible, consumption per head must be zero. For in this case k is the Frobenius post-latent vector of $(I - B\delta)^{-1}B$, and a positive solution k implies $(I - B\delta)^{-1}b_0 x = 0$.

The steady-state growth rate is, of course, externally given by the natural rate of growth, $\mu \equiv m + n$. It follows that in order for the given technique to be consistent with the existence of a steady-state with positive consumption per head,[16] x, it is necessary for $\mu = g < 1/\lambda_1$, where λ_1 is the Frobenius root of $(I - B\delta)^{-1}B$. (It is not also sufficient, for the dual pricing system must also be considered.) Moreover, if a steady-state with positive consumption per head exists, then $\{I - (I - B\delta)^{-1}B\mu\}^{-1}$ exists and is positive, and one may use Eq. (7B-11) to write

$$\{c'(\mu I + \delta)[I - (I - B\delta)^{-1}B\mu]^{-1}[I - B\delta]^{-1}b_0 + c_0\}x = 1 \qquad (7D\text{-}4)$$

since in steady-state equilibrium $\dot{k} = 0$.

Now for all steady-state growth rates that are feasible, the bracketed *scalar* expression on the left hand side of Eq. (7D-4) is a strictly increasing function of μ. It rises monotonically with μ. It follows that x is a strictly monotonically declining function of μ. Given the technique, steady-state consumption per head (or per unit of the effective stock of labor) is a monotonically decreasing function of the steady-state growth rate $g = \mu$. For any given single technique that is feasible, there exists a monotonically decreasing "steady-state consumption curve" in the non-negative μ, x quadrant between the point where $\mu = g = 0$ and x is maximum, and the point where $\mu = g = 1/\lambda_1$ and x is zero. Of course, if alternative growth rates are associated with alternative rates of return, the technique may change as one moves across steady-states. Nevertheless, for *any* technique, θ, summarized in a set of coefficients $\bar{B}_\theta = \begin{bmatrix} c_{0\theta} & c'_\theta \\ b_{0\theta} & B_\theta \end{bmatrix}$ and (if depreciation rates vary across techniques) δ_θ, there exists (as long as the technique is feasible for some positive growth rates) a monotonically decreasing "steady-state consumption

---

16. Strictly speaking, x is consumption per efficiency unit of labor, but the present manner of speaking seems easier.

curve" in the non-negative μ, x quadrant running from a point of maximum consumption per head and $\mu = g = 0$ to a point of zero consumption per head and $\mu = g = 1/\lambda_{10}$, where λ_{10} is the Frobenius root of $(I - B_0\delta_0)^{-1}B_0$.

Consider, now, the general set of $n + 1$ dual or price equations, (7B-15). This set of equations also assumes the single (equilibrium) technique summarized by the input coefficient matrix $\bar{B} = \begin{bmatrix} c_0 & c' \\ b_0 & B \end{bmatrix}$ and the depreciation matrix δ. For such a technique to be feasible, it must at least be practicable when $R = 0$ and $-\dot{p}' = p'(R - rI) = -p'r$. That is to say, there should exist a solution to the system with semi-positive commodity prices p' and labor inputs wc' when $R = 0$. At zero profit rates,

$$p' = p'\delta B + wc' \quad \text{and} \quad 1 = p'\delta b_0 + wc_0 \tag{7D-5}$$

(It should again be noted that if all capital goods are intermediate goods, and hence $\delta = I$, this system reduces to the open static Leontief system of the previous section, that is $p'(I - B) = wc'$ and $1 = p'b_0 + wc_0$.) Now δB is a non-negative and (by assumption) indecomposable matrix. It must therefore have a unique dominant characteristic root which is real and positive. If this dominant root is less than unity, then $(I - \delta B)^{-1}$ is a positive matrix since its expansion, $I + \delta B + (\delta B)^2 + (\delta B)^3 + \cdots$, is convergent. If $(I - \delta B)^{-1}$ exists and is positive, then

$$p' = wc'[I - \delta B]^{-1} \tag{7D-6}$$

is a solution which implies that positive prices, p', are associated with semi-positive unit labor costs, wc'.

Let all capital goods earn the same profit rate, that is let $R = rI$. Then as r increases from zero, the matrix which must remain positive if the technique is to remain feasible (or capable of associating positive prices, p', with semi-positive unit labor costs, wc') is $[I - rB(I - \delta B)^{-1}]^{-1}$. This may be shown as follows. If $(I - \delta B)^{-1}$ is a positive matrix, then $rB(I - \delta B)^{-1}$ is a positive matrix for $B \geq 0$ and $r > 0$. Moreover, it is indecomposable for B indecomposable. It will therefore have a unique dominant characteristic root which is real and positive. For any positive values of r at which this root is less than unity, the matrix $[I - rB(I - \delta B)^{-1}]^{-1}$ will exist and be positive. For these values of r one may write

or
$$p' = wc'[I - \delta B]^{-1}[I - rB(I - \delta B)^{-1}]^{-1}$$
$$p' = wc'[I - (rI + \delta)B]^{-1} \tag{7D-7}$$

giving a solution which associates positive prices with semi-positive unit labor costs. It follows that there is a critical rate of return given by the reciprocal of the dominant root of $B(I - \delta B)^{-1}$ which r cannot exceed if wc' is to be at least non-negative.

This may be seen as follows. The characteristic roots of $B(I - \delta B)^{-1}$ are identical to the characteristic roots of $(I - B\delta)^{-1}B$. It follows that the dominant characteristic root (the Frobenius root) of $B(I - \delta B)^{-1}$ is λ_1. Then $[I - rB(I - \delta B)^{-1}]$ has a dominant positive diagonal (and is hence a Leontief matrix) if and only if $r < 1/\lambda_1$. Positive prices and semi-positive unit labor costs will be associated if and only if r is less than the reciprocal of the dominant root of $B(I - \delta B)^{-1}$. It follows that $1/\lambda_1$ is the maximal rate of return that the given technique is capable of sustaining. Moreover, in order for this rate of return to be possible the real wage rate must be zero. For in this case p' is the Frobenius pre-latent vector of $B(I - \delta B)^{-1}$, and a positive solution p' implies $wc'(I - \delta B)^{-1} = 0$.

It follows from this argument that in order for the given technique to be consistent with the existence of a steady-state with positive real wage rate,[17] w, it is necessary for $r < 1/\lambda_1$, where λ_1 is the Frobenius root of $B(I - \delta B)^{-1}$ and $(I - B\delta)^{-1}B$. This condition is not also sufficient because the other necessary condition $\mu = g < 1/\lambda_1$, obtained from the primal quantity equation system, must also be considered. In fact it may now be stated that it is necessary and sufficient for the given technique to be consistent with the existence of a steady-state that *both* $r < 1/\lambda_1$, *and* $\mu = g < 1/\lambda_1$ hold. Hence, a steady-state with positive consumption per head and positive real wage rate can exist if and only if $\max(\mu, r) < 1/\lambda_1$. The steady-state growth rate, μ, and profit rate, r, are of course linked together through the savings assumptions once these are specified. In particular, in the classical savings function case, $\mu = s_r r$ where $0 < s_r \leq 1$ is the propensity to save out of profits, from which it follows that $\mu \leq r$ and, thus, that $r < 1/\lambda_1$ is the binding constraint.

If a steady-state with positive real wage rate exists, then $[I \quad rB(I - \delta B)^{-1}]^{-1}$ exists and is positive, and one may use Eq. (7B-15) to write

$$w\{c_0 + c'[I - \delta B]^{-1}[I - rB(I - \delta B)^{-1}]^{-1}(rI + \delta)b_0\} = 1 \qquad (7D\text{-}8)$$

since in steady-state equilibrium $\dot{p}' = 0$. Now for all r such that $0 \leq r < 1/\lambda_1$, the bracketed scalar expression on the lefthand side of Eq. (7D-8) is a strictly increasing function of r. It follows that the real wage rate, w, is a strictly monotonically declining function of the rate of profit, r. Thus, for that range of r for which the technique is feasible there exists a factor-price curve or technique curve in the non-negative r, w quadrant which is strictly monotonically decreasing. The point on this factor-price curve where r is zero is the point where w is maximal, and the point where w is zero is the point where r is maximal, that is $r = 1/\lambda_1$.

Given the technique, it has been concluded that the real wage rate is a monotonically decreasing function of the rate of profit. It is important to show that this conclusion is still valid when techniques vary in response to changes in the rate of return. Indeed, for *any* technique, θ, summarized in a set of coefficients[18]

---

17. Strictly speaking, w is the real wage rate per efficiency unit of labor, but the present manner of speaking seems easier.

18. We assume that depreciation rates do not differ from technique to technique.

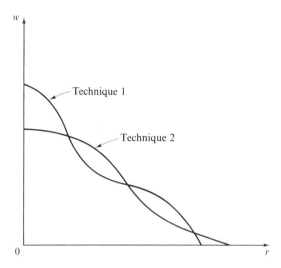

Figure 7D-1 Factor-price relationships.

$\bar{B}_\theta = \begin{bmatrix} c_{0\theta} & c'_\theta \\ b_{0\theta} & B_\theta \end{bmatrix}$, there exists (as long as the technique is feasible for some positive profit rates) a monotonically decreasing factor-price curve in the non-negative r, w quadrant running from a point where the real wage is maximal and $r = 0$ to a point where $w = 0$ and $r = 1/\lambda_{1\theta}$, where $\lambda_{1\theta}$ is the Frobenius root of $B_\theta(I - \delta B_\theta)^{-1}$. The outer envelope of the factor-price curves of all the (feasible) techniques taken together is called the "factor-price frontier." This outer frontier or envelope must be monotonically decreasing since it is made up of segments of the various factor-price curves, and these curves must all be monotonically decreasing. Figure 7D-1 shows the factor-price curves for two possible techniques. If they were the only two feasible techniques, then their outer frontier is the factor-price frontier.

From the fact that the real wage rate is a strictly monotonically decreasing function of the rate of profit in steady-state equilibrium it follows that, given r, w is uniquely determined (given the consumption good as numeraire), and *vice versa*. Hence, given either w or r, the whole steady-state price system is uniquely determined. In fact, once a numeraire is specified, there is only one degree of freedom in the system. It follows that if r is uniquely determined from $g = \mu$ in steady-state equilibrium through a savings function (which is easily seen to be the case for a classical savings function but not necessarily for other savings functions), the whole steady-state relative price system is uniquely determined.

Finally, if Harrod-neutral technical progress is occurring at a constant rate m *in every sector*, then the real wage rate per natural unit of labor grows at the exponential rate m in steady-state equilibrium. Every technique curve and, indeed, the whole factor-price frontier shifts vertically upwards through time at the constant proportional rate m at every point. This pivoting from the horizontal (or r) axis may be eliminated simply by measuring the real wage rate per efficiency unit of labor rather than per natural unit of labor on the vertical axis. With this change, the factor-price frontier remains stationary even though Harrod-neutral technical progress is occurring.

EIGHT

CAPITAL INTENSITIES, FORESIGHT, AND THE STABILITY ISSUE

A: CAPITAL AGGREGATION IN STRUCTURAL MODELS

In chapter 6, it was indicated that there are two distinct components to the problem of capital measurement. The first component is associated with disequilibrium. It has been discussed in some detail in chapter 6, and that discussion will not be repeated here. The second component is associated with coordinating measurements made at alternative equilibria. It is proposed to discuss this second component in detail in the present section. Equilibrium will therefore be assumed from the start. In particular, it will be assumed that all markets are cleared at competitive equilibrium prices; expectations are always correct, and there is no excess capacity or super-normal profits. The fundamental concern will be with the aggregation properties of the general capital-theoretic model outlined in chapter 7.

It is fairly obvious that if capital goods could always be aggregated into a single bundle (or even several distinct bundles) that in the context for which a capital aggregate is required always behaved in exactly the same way as would be expected of it if in fact it referred to the quantity of an individual homogeneous capital good, then there would be little need for concern about capital heterogeneity. The possibility of finding such a bundle (or bundles) depends heavily upon whether the bundle or aggregate is required to be appropriate only in the neighborhood (or at the margin) of a given equilibrium point, or whether it is required to be appropriate to all points within a system or model that are capable of being equilibrium points. An aggregate appropriate only in the neighborhood of a given equilibrium point will be said to be a *local* aggregate, whereas an aggregate with wider applicability will be said to be *global*. More precisely, if an aggregate can be found that is appropriate when the degrees of freedom on the motion of the variables of the model are limited only by the optimal conditions of production and exchange (so that relative prices correspond to marginal rates of substitution), then such an aggregate will be said to be *global*. The distinctíon between locally appropriate and globally appropriate aggregates is important. For it is normally the case that in competitive equilibrium *local* aggregates exist since the efficiency or dual prices of the system can be used as weights. The problem is that these weights will normally be different from one equilibrium position to the next, and therefore globally appropriate aggregates do not normally exist. There is, as usual, an index number problem.

The peculiarity of capital as a factor of production is that it is both an input and an output of the production process, albeit at different points of time. (It is, of course, the aggregation problem associated with this time aspect of production— the prospect of stock disequilibrium—from which the present discussion abstracts.) It follows from this that capital aggregation is largely a matter of aggregation over production processes, where aggregation is construed as the simultaneous aggregation of capital goods when they are designated both as inputs to various production functions (aggregation within processes) and as outputs of other production functions (aggregation across processes), so that aggregation is two directional. There is, of course, no reason to suppose that for arbitrary technologies capital aggregates appropriate to various different sectors exist. A great deal depends upon the shape of the underlying technology. In the first place, the assumption that all production processes are homogeneous of the first degree (that is, they exhibit constant returns scale) is a convenient one to make. It implies aggregates (where they exist) that are homogeneous of the first degree, and this is evidently a desirable property for any aggregate to possess. In the second place, the assumption that the substitution possibilities for any two inputs are more or less the same wherever these inputs are used is also convenient. Indeed, aggregation difficulties become acute whenever substitution possibilities differ from one production process to another.[1]

One particular case in which substitution possibilities between inputs are everywhere the same is the case in which all production coefficients are (or can be treated as if they are) fixed technical constants. Leontief's input–output system is therefore of interest in this regard. As indicated in the previous chapter, the static version of this system describes a circular flow in which all capital goods are intermediate goods that are produced and consumed instantaneously; therefore, no rate of return is included in the system. We shall, however, proceed directly to the aggregation properties of our general capital-theoretic model, for

---

1. The point is this, an industry may be defined by aggregating over all commodities that have similar substitution and distribution properties in their production functions; or, it may be defined by aggregating over all commodities which consuming sectors (which may be final consumers or other producers) treat as similar commodities insofar as their substitution and distribution properties *vis à vis* other commodities are similar. But an aggregate appropriate to both the production criterion and the consumption criterion may not exist. As Gorman has said, "The central difficulty about aggregation is that aggregates appropriate, for example, to the production sector, are normally meaningless in the consumption sector, and cannot, therefore, be used in complete models." (W. M. Gorman, "Capital Aggregation in Vintage Models," mimeographed paper, Oxford, 1965, p. 22.) This statement applies not only to the weighting system applied within any aggregate, but also to the choice of the set of commodities over which to aggregate.

which the open static Leontief system is a special sub-case.[2] These aggregation properties are studied on the basis of the assumption that the underlying technology is of the Leontief fixed coefficients variety; there is a single technique matrix of production coefficients which is appropriate to all feasible factor-price (w and r) configurations. Towards the end of this section, these aggregation properties are extended to the Cobb-Douglas case.

Consider, then, the question of aggregating the n capital goods producing sectors, $j = 1, \ldots, n$, of the system (repeated from Eqs. 7B-11 and 7B-15)

$$k = B(\mu I + \delta)k + B\dot{k} + b_0 x$$

and
$$1 = c'(\mu I + \delta)k + c'\dot{k} + c_0 x$$

$$p' = p'(rI + \delta)B - \dot{p}'B + wc' \qquad (8A\text{-}1)$$

$$1 = p'(rI + \delta)b_0 - \dot{p}'b_0 + wc_0$$

into a smaller set of N hybrid or aggregated sectors, $J = 1, \ldots, N$, where $N < n$. By implication, this implies aggregation of the n capital goods, $i = 1, \ldots, n$, themselves, into a smaller set of N capital aggregates, $I = 1, \ldots, N$. Let it be assumed that the rows and columns of the original matrices,

$$\bar{B} = \begin{bmatrix} c_0 & c' \\ b_0 & B \end{bmatrix}$$

and δ, are ordered in such a way that the first hybrid or aggregated sector refers to an aggregate over the first V_1 original sectors, the second hybrid or aggregated sector refers to an aggregate over the next V_2 original sectors, and so on, so that $\sum_{J=1}^{N} V_J = n$. Now define the aggregation matrix, S, whose dimensions are $N \times n$ and whose structure is

$$S = \begin{bmatrix} i_1', & 0, & 0, & 0 \\ 0, & i_2', & 0, & 0 \\ \cdot & & & \cdot \\ \cdot & & \diagdown & \cdot \\ \cdot & & & \cdot \\ 0, & 0, & 0, & i_N' \end{bmatrix} \qquad (8A\text{-}2)$$

where i_J', $J = 1, \ldots, N$, is a row vector of order V_J, $J = 1, \ldots, N$, whose elements are all unity. Define also the matrix P, which is an $n \times n$ diagonal matrix with the commodity prices, p_j, $j = 1, \ldots, n$, along the principal diagonal and zeros elsewhere. Hence, $p' = i_n'P$, where i_n' is an $l \times n$ row vector whose components are all unity.

---

2. Compare Y. Morimoto, "Aggregation Problems in Input–Output Analysis," unpublished D.Phil. dissertation, Oxford University, 1967.

Define u_j to be the output proportion (in value terms, of course) of the j-th original sector in the corresponding hybrid sector, J, in the *initial* or base period, period 0. Then

$$u_j = p_j(0)y_j(0)/\sum_{j \in J} p_j(0)y_j(0)$$

and

$$\sum_{j \in J} u_j = 1, \quad \text{all} \quad J = 1, \ldots, N$$

(8A-3)

The $n \times N$ matrix U may now be formed from the u_j's. It is of precisely the same form as the *transpose* of S but with the ones replaced by the u_j's. That is to say,

$$U = \begin{bmatrix} \bar{u}_1, & 0, & \ldots, & 0 \\ 0, & \bar{u}_2, & \ldots, & 0 \\ \cdot & & & \cdot \\ \cdot & & \diagdown & \cdot \\ \cdot & & & \cdot \\ 0, & 0, & \ldots, & \bar{u}_N \end{bmatrix}$$

(8A-4)

where $\bar{u}_J$, $J = 1, \ldots, N$, is a column vector of order V_J, $J = 1, \ldots, N$, whose elements are the weights u_j, $j \in J$. It can therefore be seen that S of order $N \times n$ and U of order $n \times N$ are conformable and, indeed, $SU = I_N$.

Now let it be assumed that *all* prices in the *initial*, or base, period are equal to unity. One may then construct the N Laspeyre's price index numbers, p_J^*, $J = 1, \ldots, N$, and the $N \times N$ aggregated input coefficients, b_{IJ}^*, $I = 1, \ldots, N$, $J = 1, \ldots, N$, from the expressions

$$P^* = SPU \quad \text{and} \quad B^* = SBU$$

(8A-5)

where P^* is the $N \times N$ diagonal matrix of price index numbers and B^* is the $N \times N$ aggregated technology matrix.[3] In addition, one may define the N price weighted capital aggregates, k_I^*, $I = 1, \ldots, N$, and the N aggregated final consumption allocations, $b_{I0}^* x$, $I = 1, \ldots, N$, by the expressions

$$k^* = P^{*-1}SPk \quad \text{and} \quad b_0^* x = P^{*-1}SPb_0 x$$

(8A-6)

respectively.

---

3. If one does not assume that all initial prices are equal to unity, one must write

$$P^*(t)P^*(0)^{-1} = SP(t)P(0)^{-1}U \quad \text{and} \quad P^*(0)B^*P^*(0)^{-1} = SP(0)BP(0)^{-1}U$$

This notation seems unnecessarily cumbersome for the problem at hand.

The basic capital balance equations of the original system (8A-1) may be written in the form

$$k = By/\overline{L} + b_0 x \qquad (8A\text{-}7)$$

where $y/\overline{L} = (\mu I + \delta)k + \dot{k}$ is the vector of normalized gross outputs of the n capital goods. Moreover, if B^{-1} exists, one may write

$$y/\overline{L} = B^{-1}(k - b_0 x) \qquad (8A\text{-}8)$$

In a parallel fashion to Eq. (8A-7) one may now write the basic capital balance equations of the aggregated system in the form

$$k^* = B^*(y^*/\overline{L}) + b_0^* x \qquad (8A\text{-}9)$$

where $y^*/\overline{L}$ is the vector of normalized gross outputs of the N hybrid or aggregated capital goods. Provided that B^{*-1} exists, one may write Eq. (8A-9) as

$$y^*/\overline{L} = B^{*-1}(k^* - b_0^* x) \qquad (8A\text{-}10)$$

It may now be asked under what conditions is it possible for both the aggregated system and the original system to yield identical predictions of gross hybrid outputs from a specified set of initial capital stocks and final consumption allocations. To answer this question, it is necessary to look at the difference between the "macro" gross output predictions derived from the aggregated system and the appropriately weighted sums of the "micro" gross output predictions derived from the original system. This difference may be defined to be the *aggregation bias*. The aggregation procedure underlying the system Eqs. (8A-9) or (8A-10) is said to be consistent if and only if the aggregation bias vanishes.

The aggregation bias may be written in normalized form as

$$(y^* - P^{*-1}SPy)/\overline{L} \qquad (8A\text{-}11)$$

where $y^*/\overline{L}$ is the $N \times 1$ column vector of hybrid gross outputs per efficiency unit of labor and $y/\overline{L}$ is the $n \times 1$ column vector of original gross outputs per efficiency unit of labor with $P^{*-1}SPy/\overline{L}$ being the appropriately weighted sum of these microvariables. Since it is evident from Eq. (8A-8) that

$$P^{*-1}SPy/\overline{L} = P^{*-1}SPB^{-1}(k - b_0 x) \qquad (8A\text{-}12)$$

the normalized aggregation bias may be written as

or
$$\begin{aligned}
(y^* - P^{*-1}SPy)/\overline{L} &= B^{*-1}(k^* - b_0^* x) - P^{*-1}SPB^{-1}(k - b_0 x) \\
(y^* - P^{*-1}SPy)/\overline{L} &= (B^{*-1}P^{*-1}SP - P^{*-1}SPB^{-1})(k - b_0 x)
\end{aligned} \qquad (8A\text{-}13)$$

using the definitions contained in expression (8A-6). The aggregation bias will therefore vanish for *any* feasible pattern of initial capital stocks, k, and consumption allocations, $b_0 x$, if and only if $B^{*-1} P^{*-1} SP - P^{*-1} SPB^{-1} = 0$, or

$$SPBP^{-1} = P^* B^* P^{*-1} S \tag{8A-14}$$

This condition can also be expressed as[4]

$$\sum_{i \in I} p_i b_{ij} p_j^{-1} = p_I^* b_{IJ} p_J^{*-1}, \quad \text{all} \quad j \in J \quad \text{and} \quad I, J = 1, \ldots, N \tag{8A-15}$$

In words, this condition means that within each hybrid sector J there must be N sets of price weighted column sums which are *identical* across the V_J original sectors which make up the J-th hybrid sector. That is to say, the coefficient matrix B must have "homogeneous input structure"; each original sector within the hybrid sector must use identical values of hybrid capital inputs from each hybrid sector per "dollar's worth" of original sector output. Looked at in terms of the hybrid sectors, the value share *hybrid* input coefficients of the original sectors which make up any given hybrid sector must be identical. Hence, the aggregation bias will vanish for any feasible pattern of initial capital stocks and consumption allocations if and only if there can be found N matrices of order $N \times V_J$ and *of unit rank*, of the form $P^* B^* P^{*-1} S$, which, together "fit" the $N \times n$ matrix $SPBP^{-1}$ perfectly, so that every element in the matrix $(SPBP^{-1} - P^* B^* P^{*-1} S)$ vanishes identically. The basic relationship between linear dependence and consistent aggregation is apparent.

It follows from the previous analysis that the aggregation bias in normalized gross output predictions always vanishes (and aggregation is said to be *globally consistent*) if and only if the coefficient matrix B has the property of "homogeneous input structure." However, if the "macro" prediction of the whole future course of the system is to be identical to the aggregated "micro" prediction, then *net* hybrid stock accumulations must also be identical for the two predictions. The *net* hybrid stock accumulation predicted from the "micro" system is $P^{*-1} SP(y/\bar{L} - \delta k) = P^{*-1} SP(\dot{k} + \mu k)$, whereas the *net* hybrid stock accumulation predicted from the "macro" system is $y^*/\bar{L} - \delta^* k^* = \dot{k}^* + \mu k^*$, where δ^* is the $N \times N$ diagonal matrix of depreciation coefficients for the "macro" system. Since $\mu k^* = \mu P^{*-1} SPk$ by definition, it follows immediately that $(y^* - P^{*-1} SPy)/\bar{L} = 0$ is associated with $\dot{k}^* = P^{*-1} SP\dot{k}$ if and only if $\delta^* k^* = P^{*-1} SP\delta k$. For this condition to hold for any feasible pattern of initial capital stocks, k, it is necessary and sufficient that

$$SP\delta P^{-1} = P^* \delta^* P^{*-1} S \tag{8A-16}$$

which is directly parallel to Eq. (8A-14). Since δ and δ^* are diagonal matrices, however, this condition reduces to

---

4. This condition was first formulated by Hatanaka. See M. Hatanaka, "Note on Consolidation within a Leontief system," *Econometrica*, vol. 20, April 1952, pp. 301–303. It says that $\Sigma_{i \in I} p_i b_{ij} p_j^{-1}$ should be independent of the sector $j \in J$ and of the weights u_j within the I, J hybrid sector for all $I, J = 1, \ldots, N$.

$$S\delta = \delta^*S \quad \text{or} \quad \delta_i = \delta_I^* \quad \text{for all} \quad i \in I, I = 1, \ldots, N \tag{8A-17}$$

Globally consistent aggregation also requires that the depreciation coefficients for all the capital goods, k_i, $i \in I$, which are aggregated into a single hybrid capital stock, k_I^*, *must be identical.* To aggregate capital goods with very different durabilities will ultimately lead to inconsistencies in prediction.

Finally, one should note that if there is no aggregation bias in *net* accumulation predictions from the "macro" system, then one may write

$$\dot{k}^* = P^{*-1}SP\dot{k} \tag{8A-18}$$

But it follows from the definition of k^*, namely $k^* = P^{*-1}SPk$, that by differentiation

$$\dot{P}^*k^* + P^*\dot{k}^* = S\dot{P}k + SP\dot{k} \tag{8A-19}$$

Substitution from Eq. (8A-18) into Eq. (8A-19) yields

$$(\dot{P}^*P^{*-1}SP - S\dot{P})k = 0 \tag{8A-20}$$

which holds for any pattern of initial capital stocks, k, if and only if

$$S\dot{P}P^{-1} = \dot{P}^*P^{*-1}S, \quad \text{or} \quad \dot{p}_i/p_i = \dot{p}_I^*/p_I^* \quad \text{all} \quad i \in I, \quad I = 1, \ldots, N \tag{8A-21}$$

The proportional rates of change in the prices of all the original capital goods which are aggregated into a given hybrid capital aggregate *must be identical.* The relative prices of these goods never change (and must never be expected to change), since they have equal hybrid "factor intensities." Indeed, all the individual capital goods producing sectors that are included in a given hybrid sector must have identical values for their hybrid input coefficients in terms of their own output prices as numeraires if aggregation is to be globally consistent.

It is worth looking at these propositions from the point of view of the dual capital goods pricing equations of expression (8A-1), which may be written in the form

$$(p' - wc')P^{-1} = p'(rI_n + \delta - P^{-1}\dot{P})BP^{-1} \tag{8A-22}$$

where $p'P^{-1}\dot{P} = i_n'\dot{P} = \dot{p}'$. Now if the complete set of conditions for globally consistent aggregation hold so that $SPBP^{-1} = P^*B^*P^{*-1}S$, $S\delta = \delta^*S$ and $S\dot{P}P^{-1} = \dot{P}^*P^{*-1}S$, then Eq. (8A-22) may be written as

$$\begin{aligned}
(p' - wc')P^{-1} &= p'(rI_n + \delta - P^{-1}\dot{P})BP^{-1} \\
&= i_N'SP(rI_n + \delta - P^{-1}\dot{P})BP^{-1} \\
&= i_N'(rI_N + \delta^* - P^{*-1}\dot{P}^*)SPBP^{-1} \\
&= i_N'(rI_N + \delta^* - P^{*-1}\dot{P}^*)P^*B^*P^{*-1}S \\
&= (p^{*\prime} - wc^{*\prime})P^{*-1}S
\end{aligned} \tag{8A-23}$$

where $wc^{*'}$ is the $1 \times N$ row vector of unit labor costs for the aggregated system. It is implied by Eq. (8A-23) that one may write

$$(p_j - wc_j)/p_j = \sum_{I=1}^{N} (r + \delta_I^* - \dot{p}_I^*/p_I^*)p_I^* b_{IJ}^* p_J^{*-1} \tag{8A-24}$$

$$= (p_J^* - wc_J^*)/p_J^*, \quad \text{all} \quad j \in J \quad \text{and} \quad J = 1, \ldots, N$$

Now this expression indicates that labor must be treated as one of the hybrid inputs if aggregation is to be globally consistent. Indeed, Eq. (8A-24) says that the value share of labor in a "dollar's worth" of output must be identical for each original sector that is aggregated into a given hybrid sector if aggregation is to be globally consistent, where "identical" is here interpreted as "a common linear function of r." For any feasible r, the relative price of *any* two commodities, i and j, which are both members of the hybrid sector J, never changes, since

or
$$(p_i - wc_i)/p_i = (p_j - wc_j)/p_j$$
$$p_i/c_i = p_j/c_j \quad \text{for all } i, \quad j \in J \tag{8A-25}$$

whatever r may be. It has therefore been shown that when hybrid inputs, including labor, are treated as factors of production, globally consistent aggregation requires that factor shares must be the same for all original sectors that are incorporated into a given hybrid sector.

So far, the conditions for consistent aggregation when no constraints (other then feasibility) are put on the possible patterns of capital stocks and final consumption allocations have been discussed. That is to say, the conditions that are necessary and sufficient for globally consistent aggregation have been derived and given in Eq. (8A-14) (with extensions in Eqs. 8A-17 and 8A-21). If, however the system is regularly progressive, so that individual capital stocks and final consumption allocations always move in proportion over the *whole* range of "micro" sectors and all relative prices remain constant, then the aggregation bias will vanish whether or not the conditions on the coefficient matrix, B, hold. This follows very simply from the fact that the weights, u_j, are constructed in such a way that there is no bias in the base period. That is, from Eq. (8A-3),

$$USP(0)y(0) = P(0)y(0) \quad \text{or} \quad USy(0) = y(0) \tag{8A-26}$$

where $y(0)$ is the gross output vector at time zero, and $P(0) = I_n$ (by assumption) is the diagonal matrix of prices at time zero. Pre-multiplying Eq. (8A-26) by SB yields[5]

$$SBUSy(0) = SBy(0), \quad \text{or} \quad B^*Sy(0) = SBy(0) \tag{8A-27}$$

---

5. With the initial prices restored, this expression reads

$$P^*(0)B^*P^*(0)^{-1}SP(0)y(0) = SP(0)BP(0)^{-1}USP(0)y(0) = SP(0)BP(0)^{-1}P(0)y(0).$$

since, by definition (see Eq. 8A-5), $B^* = SBU$. Now, if the capital stock vector and the final consumption allocation vector at time t are a simple scalar multiple $\bar{L}(t) = L(0) e^{\mu t}$ of their respective values at time 0, and *all relative prices remain constant,* then

$$y^*(t) = B^{*-1} \{ k^*(0) - b_0^* x(0) \} L(0) e^{\mu t}$$

$$= B^{*-1} S \{ k(0) - b_0 x(0) \} L(0) e^{\mu t}$$

$$= B^{*-1} \{ S B y(0) \} L(0) e^{\mu t} \qquad (8A\text{-}28)$$

$$= B^{*-1} \{ B^* S y(0) \} L(0) e^{\mu t}$$

$$= S y(t)$$

It is evident in this case that the aggregation bias $y^*(t) - Sy(t)$ always vanishes whether or not the fundamental condition on the coefficient matrix, B, holds. When prices are constant, this fundamental condition may be written as $SB = B^*S$ with appropriate choice of units; moreover it is apparent that in the general case with constant prices the equation $y^*(t) = B^{*-1} SBy(t)$ is consistent with zero aggregation bias, or $y^*(t) = Sy(t)$, if and only if $B^{*-1}SB = S$ or $SB = B^*S$.) It has therefore been shown that the aggregation bias always vanishes *locally,* that is for any capital stocks and commodity prices that are proportional to the base period stocks and prices. It might therefore be supposed that there may be combinations of conditions on the movement of stocks and prices and on the coefficient matrix under which the aggregation bias, or at least part of it, will vanish.

In summary, then, aggregation in both static and dynamic input–output analysis is a particular example of aggregation in linear systems. In such systems, the attempt is always made to find a matrix or a set of matrices of *unit rank* that fit a given matrix as well as possible. Perfect or globally consistent aggregation occurs when this fit is exact. For this to be the case, it is necessary and sufficient that the original matrix (in this case, $SPBP^{-1}$) can be partitioned into component matrices (in number equal to the set of matrices of unit rank—in this case the $N \times V_J$ matrices in $P^*B^*P^{*-1}S$ of which there are N) that are also of unit rank. Otherwise, it has to be hoped that certain variables (if they are not themselves part of the original matrix) move proportionally. This is the significance of the association between linear dependence among relationships and the possibility of collapsing or aggregating them unambiguously or consistently. The condition, $SPBP^{-1} = P^*B^*P^{*-1}S$, states that the value share of each kind of hybrid input (including, as has been shown, labor) must be the same for each microsector that is included in a given hybrid sector. Treating the hybrid inputs as factors of production, each microsector that is included in a given hybrid sector must generate identical (but not necessarily constant) factor shares if aggregation is to be globally consistent.

Before concluding this section, two extensions are in order. The first of these concerns the case in which the conditions for consistent aggregation hold over the *whole set* of production processes so that aggregation into a single aggregate capital goods producing sector is globally consistent. In this case, $S = i'_n$, where i'_n is a $1 \times n$ row vector of ones. Hence, from the fundamental aggregation condition, Eq. (8A-14), one has

$$p'B = b^*p' \quad \text{or} \quad p'(b^*I_n - B) = 0 \tag{8A-29}$$

where b^* is a *scalar*, which may be identified with the Frobenius root of the technology matrix B. Now p' is uniquely determined (up to a normalization rule) by Eq. (8A-29) and *relative* capital goods prices are independent of r. Thus, if aggregation into a single capital goods producing sector is globally consistent, then p' (and hence wc') is the Frobenius pre-latent vector of B. It remains to show the converse, namely if wc' is the Frobenius pre-latent vector of B, then aggregation into a single capital goods producing sector is globally consistent, provided of course that the other aggregation conditions hold (that is, $rI_n + \delta - P^{-1}\dot{P} = (r + \delta^* - p^{*-1}\dot{p}^*)I_n$, where $r + \delta^* - p^{*-1}\dot{p}^*$ is a *scalar*). Let λ_1 be the Frobenius root of B, and let wc' be the Frobenius pre-latent vector. Then, by definition, $wc'\{\lambda_1 I_n - B\} = 0$, and

$$
\begin{aligned}
p' &= wc'\{I - (rI_n + \delta - P^{-1}\dot{P})B\}^{-1} \\
&= wc'\{1 - (r + \delta^* - p^{*-1}\dot{p}^*)\lambda_1\}^{-1}
\end{aligned}
\tag{8A-30}
$$

Thus, p' is proportional to wc' with the coefficient of proportionality depending directly on r. Thus, aggregation into a single capital goods producing sector (and, consequently, aggregation of a collection of heterogeneous capital goods, whose depreciation rates and expected appreciation rates are common, into a single aggregate capital stock) is globally consistent *if and only if* wc' is the Frobenius pre-latent vector of B so that b^* can be identified with λ_1, the Frobenius root of B. In this case, there are no Wicksell effects among the prices of the various capital goods since their relative prices are constant, and the system collapses into the *two-sectoral* model of Sec. A of chapter 7. The complete set of dual pricing equations may then be written as

$$p' = p'(r + \delta^* - p^{*-1}\dot{p}^*)b^* + wc'$$

and

$$1 = p'(r + \delta^* - p^{*-1}\dot{p}^*)b_0 + wc_0 \tag{8A-31}$$

with $r + \delta^* - p^{*-1}\dot{p}^*$ redefined as the overall gross rate of return. Of course, the consumption goods producing sector must *also* have the same hybrid factor intensities as the aggregated capital goods producing sector if aggregation of outputs into a *one-sectoral* model of the Harrod-Domar variety is to be globally consistent, the factor-price curve is to be linear and no Wicksell effects are to occur at all. This will be so if and only if $b^* = \lambda_1$ is also the Frobenius root of the matrix b_0c'/c_0, or (since this matrix has rank one) $b^* = c'b_0/c_0$.

The second extension concerns the case in which the underlying input coefficients are derived from a set of Cobb-Douglas production functions with constant returns to scale. Since the Cobb-Douglas production function is a log-linear function (it is *separable* in logarithmic form), it might well be expected that some of the aggregation properties that were derived for the linear or fixed coefficient technology would be applicable to Cobb-Douglas technologies as well. The final part of this section explores this possibility and finds that there is, indeed, a direct correspondence between the aggregation properties of the two technologies.

For present purposes, the important property of Cobb-Douglas production functions is the fact that in competitive equilibrium, where factor prices correspond to marginal value products, one may write

$$P(rI_n + \delta - P^{-1}\dot{P}) = APB^{-1} \tag{8A-32}$$

where A is the $n \times n$ matrix of Cobb-Douglas input-output elasticities, a_{ij}, all $i, j = 1, \ldots, n$, for capital goods inputs into the capital goods producing sectors.[6] Consider, now, the matrix A^*, which corresponds to A, but which applies to the aggregated system. Define A^* implicitly by

$$P^*(rI_N + \delta^* - P^{*-1}\dot{P}^*) = A^*P^*B^{*-1} \tag{8A-33}$$

which is precisely parallel to Eq. (8A-31) for the original system. Now suppose that the complete set of conditions for globally consistent aggregation (Eqs. 8A-14, 8A-17, and 8A-21) hold. This set of conditions may be written as

$$SP(rI_n + \delta - P^{-1}\dot{P})BP^{-1} = (rI_N + \delta^* - P^{*-1}\dot{P}^*)P^*B^*P^{*-1}S \tag{8A-34}$$

Using Eqs. (8A-32) and (8A-33), it is immediately apparent that these aggregation conditions imply (and are implied by)

$$SA = A^*S \tag{8A-35}$$

which may be called the fundamental aggregation condition for Cobb-Douglas production functions. It has precisely the same interpretation as the earlier condition for globally consistent aggregation which applied to input-output coefficients, except that it applies to the elasticities of outputs with respect to factor inputs. It has no price weights because elasticities are unitless.

The condition, $SA = A^*S$, says that for all those original sectors that are aggregated into a given hybrid sector, the elasticities of output with respect to *hybrid inputs* (again including labor as a hybrid input)[7] must be the same

---

6. These conditions are effectively of the form

$$q_i = p_i(r + \delta_i - p_i^{-1}\dot{p}_i) = a_{ij}p_jy_j/K_{ij} = a_{ij}p_jb_{ij}^{-1}$$

where K_{ij} is the stock input of capital good type i required to produce one unit of flow output of type j. For greater detail, see Sec. D of this chapter.

7. Constant returns to scale implies $i_n'(I_n - A) = a_w'$ and $i_N'(I_N - A^*) = a_w^{*'}$, where a_w' and $a_w^{*'}$ are the original and hybrid sector labor input elasticity vectors, respectively. Thus, if $SA = A^*S$, then $i_N'SA = i_N'A^*S$; but $i_N'SA = i_n'A = i_n' - a_w'$, and $i_N'A^*S = (i_N' - a_w^{*'})S$. It follows immediately that a_w' must be equal to $a_w^{*'}S$, or $a_{wj} = a_{wJ}$, all $j \in J$.

if aggregation is to be globally consistent. Treating hybrid inputs as factors of production, factor shares must be the same. "Homogeneous input structure" in terms of the b_{ij}'s at all possible prices, P, is equivalent to homogeneous input structure in terms of the a_{ij}'s. Indeed, the relative price of any two commodities that may be consistently aggregated in a global sense is constant since the commodities have identical hybrid "factor intensities." It is evident, therefore, that the unitary elasticity of substitution of the Cobb-Douglas production function is an important property in relation to the possibility of consistent aggregation.

The possibility of consistent aggregation is considerably reduced when more general production functions are considered. Indeed, if any two production processes have different substitution elasticities, their hybrid factor shares cannot be identical at all feasible factor prices (including the rate of return). It is conjectured for a world of constant elasticity of substitution (CES) production functions that the necessary and sufficient conditions for globally consistent aggregation are (a) that the distribution parameters must obey the Cobb-Douglas elasticities condition, $SA = A^*S$, and (b) that the elasticities of substitution must be the same for all original sectors that are aggregated into a given hybrid sector. These are, of course, fairly formidable conditions, but it should be apparent that the more general are the production functions the more stringent become the aggregation conditions that apply to them. Perhaps more important, however, is the fact that aggregation where the consistency condition *does not hold* may result in certain anomalies with regard to the movement of aggregates with respect to other variables, and, in particular, with respect to the wage–rental (w/r) ratio. Some of these anomalies are analyzed in the following section, which discusses the question of choice of technique in alternative steady-state growth equilibria.

B: THE CHOICE OF TECHNIQUE

The basic dispute about capital theory between Samuelson and Solow at the Massachusetts Institute of Technology on the one hand and Mrs Robinson and Kaldor at Cambridge on the other hand (to mention only a few of the principal early contributors to the debate), which has continued for the last twenty years or so and which could be called, for a shorthand notation, "the Cambridge–Cambridge controversy,"[8] centres around the question whether or not long run capital and growth problems can be analyzed in terms of a production function, and, in particular, whether or not the rate of profit can in any way be associated with the marginal productivity of capital. The dispute has crystallized on three related issues. The first concerns the usefulness of equilibrium dynamic models

---

8. Compare G. C. Harcourt, *Some Cambridge Controversies in the Theory of Capital,* London, Cambridge University Press, 1972, M. Blaug, *The Cambridge Revolution, Success or Failure,* London, The Institute of Economic Affairs, 1974, and G. C. Harcourt, "The Cambridge Controversies: Old Ways and New Horizons—or Dead End?," *Oxford Economic Papers,* vol. 28, March, 1976, pp. 25–65.

to the study of economic growth and capital accumulation. This issue has been discussed to some extent in chapter 6 and will be taken up again later in this chapter. The second concerns aggregation. This has been discussed in some detail in the previous section. The third concerns the question whether or not a fall in the rate of profit relative to the wage rate is associated with the use of more capital intensive techniques. Insofar as the overall capital–labor ratio, $p'k$, is an index of this capital intensity, this question may be identified with the question whether or not there exists a monotonically increasing relation between the overall capital–labor ratio and the wage–rental (w/r) ratio. For if an increase in the wage–rental ratio does not lead to a greater capital intensity of technique it is impossible to characterize long run general equilibrium situations in terms of a neo-classical production function. It is this question that the present section analyzes. As might be expected, the answer depends upon the shape of the underlying technology.

The model in which this question of the choice of technique in steady-state growth equilibrium has recently been discussed in the literature is basically a linear programming version of the general capital-theoretic model that has been outlined in chapter 7. The central concept used in this discussion is the factor-price frontier, which in a linear programming technology is the outer envelope of the factor-price curves for the various possible underlying techniques. The programming technology in which the question of choice of stability is discussed is, of course, more general than the case in which the various techniques are derived from continuous production functions of either the Cobb-Douglas or CES variety. For these cases, there is a single curve relating w to r which is monotonically decreasing, rather than a frontier made up of segments of different "technique curves" as in the programming case. This is, however, simply a consequence of continuity.

To begin with, two techniques are compared with respect to their efficiency, and the idea of ordering technique matrices by capital intensity is introduced. A study is made of the associations between capital aggregation and capital intensity ordering of techniques. (It will be noted that to summarize the economy's production possibilities in terms of a single production function is simply an extreme of aggregation, the properties of which have been discussed in the previous section.) The phenomenon known as "reswitching" is then discussed, where "reswitching" refers to the possibility that a technique matrix which is the most efficient at some wage–rental ratio is also the most efficient at some other wage–rental ratio but is *not* the most efficient at some or all of those wage–rental ratios that lie between these two. It is suggested that reswitching (that is, the *return* of a technique to the factor-price frontier) is a special case of a more general phenomenon. This phenomenon is that it may not always be possible to order techniques by their roundaboutness or capital intensity in an unambiguous way, that is, independently of factor prices (w/r). In other words, it may not be possible to say that one technique is more capital intensive than another at all wage–rental ratios, and, hence, for each and every set of equilibrium commodity prices that could be used as weights for constructing an index number of the "quantity of capital" from the quantities of the individual capital goods. As a consequence, it is possible that over some ranges of factor prices (w/r) the ratio of an index number of the "quantity of capital" to the quantity of labor may not be a monotonic increasing function of the wage–rental ratio. A sufficiency condition for the absence of reswitching, and, indeed, for unambiguous or global ordering of techniques by capital intensity, is then derived for the general case. Finally, at the end of this section, the significance of "reswitching" for the choice of technique in growth equilibrium is discussed. It is noted that "reswitching" makes it difficult to place much reliance upon economic theories based upon the idea of strong or global capital intensity ordering of techniques. It does not, however, destroy the idea that the rate of return on an individual capital investment is intimately connected with the marginal productivity of such an investment.

As already noted, the factor-price frontier in the case of a linear programming technology is the outer envelope of a set of monotonically decreasing factor-price curves. Each of these curves is associated with a given technique of production, which may be summarized in a set of input-output coefficients,[9]

$$\bar{B} = \begin{bmatrix} c_0 & c' \\ b_0 & B \end{bmatrix}$$

Since the factor-price frontier is made up of segments of various monotonically decreasing functions, it also is monotonically decreasing. In the general linear programming technology there will of course be a whole set of techniques. Indeed, since there can be up to $n + 1$ commodities with v_i possible ways of producing any one commodity, there are $v_0 \times v_1 \times v_2 \times v_3 \times \cdots \times v_n = \Pi_{i=0}^{n} v_i$ possible combinations of pure activities and hence an equal number of distinct techniques. Some of these may, of course, be unfeasible; that is to say, they can produce nothing at non-negative factor prices. The factor-price curves of unfeasible techniques do not cross the non-negative r, w quadrant. Other techniques may be feasible but never used because at non-negative factor prices they are always dominated by some other techniques. That is to say, they are never chosen in competitive equilibrium because they do not, at any factor prices, form a segment of the factor-price frontier; their technique curves lie entirely under the outer envelope or frontier. The remaining θ^* techniques that do form a segment of the factor-price frontier may be defined as the collection of *relevant techniques*.

For any *relevant technique*, $\theta \in \theta^*$, there exists some range of non-negative factor prices for which all prices, p', would be strictly positive if this technique were chosen. Moreover, for any given relevant technique, $\theta \in \theta^*$, for all r such that $0 \le r < 1/\lambda_{1\theta}$, where $\lambda_{1\theta}$ is the Frobenius root of $B_\theta(I - \delta B_\theta)^{-1}$, the wage rate would be strictly positive if this technique were chosen. (The wage rate is, of course, zero if technique θ is chosen when $r = 1/\lambda_{1\theta}$.) As long as w is strictly positive, labor may be used as the numeraire and one may normalize by defining $\bar{p}' = w^{-1}p'$ and $\bar{p}_0 = 1/w$. Then, when a given relevant technique, $\theta \in \theta^*$, is used, one may

---

9. We assume that depreciation coefficients do not differ from technique to technique, for otherwise the specification of individual capital goods would differ among techniques.

write the complete dual price system in steady-state equilibrium with $\dot{p}' = 0$ in the form (from Eq. 8A-1)

$$[\bar{p}_0; \bar{p}'] = [\bar{p}_0; \bar{p}'] \begin{bmatrix} 1/\bar{p}_0 & 0 \\ 0 & rI_n + \delta \end{bmatrix} \begin{bmatrix} c_{00} & c'_\theta \\ b_{00} & B_\theta \end{bmatrix} \tag{8B-1}$$

from which it is evident that each $\bar{p}_j$, $j = 0, 1, \ldots, n$, is a monotonic increasing function of r. On a given technique, all prices in terms of the wage rate increase as r increases. (This simply implies that labor is the most labor intensive commodity!)

As r changes, of course, the technique of production may change as the system moves from a segment of the factor-price frontier where θ is most efficient to a segment where some other relevant technique is most efficient. One may therefore define a *switch point on the factor-price frontier* as a point on the frontier where two relevant techniques are *equally efficient* and their technique curves intersect. By *equally efficient* is meant that all commodities are produced at identical prices in terms of the wage rate on the two relevant techniques. In other words, the two relevant techniques (or set of pure activities) are tied for "best" and both share the property of maximizing real wages in terms of *any* commodity as numeraire. It is, therefore, a consequence of the non-substitution theorem that all the $\bar{p}_j$'s—or the wage rate and all the capital goods prices in terms of the consumption good as numeraire—are identical for two techniques at a point on the frontier where their technique curves intersect. (Of course, at any point on the factor-price frontier where two techniques composed of pure activities are equally efficient—that is, a switch point or a point where their technique curves intersect—any convex linear combination of them will also be equally efficient. At any other point on the factor-price frontier, only one technique, composed of pure activities, will be most efficient.)

It follows from the argument of the previous paragraphs that along the factor-price frontier every component of $[\bar{p}_0; \bar{p}']$ always increases as r increases, whether or not these increases in r imply a change in technique. Each $\bar{p}_j$, $j = 0, 1, \ldots, n$, is monotonically increasing with r along the factor-price frontier. In general, however, these prices will not all rise proportionally. Indeed, it has been shown in the previous section that *along a given technique curve* prices will only rise proportionally if the conditions for globally consistent aggregation hold over the whole set of production processes (including that producing consumption goods) so that these processes can be unambiguously aggregated into a single process. That is to say, relative prices never change along technique $\theta \in \theta^*$ if and only if c'_θ is the Frobenius pre-latent vector of B_θ so that $c'_\theta[b^*_\theta I_n - B_\theta] = 0$, *and* $c_{00} = c'_\theta b_{00}/b^*_\theta$, *and* $\delta = \delta^* I_n$ where δ^* is the common scalar depreciation coefficient for all capital goods. In this special case, the value share of labor per "dollar's worth" of output is identical for all commodities, and the factor-price curve for technique θ is *linear* rather than serpentine.

Now suppose that *every* relevant technique obeys the aggregation conditions so that every factor-price curve is linear rather than serpentine. Then relative prices do not change along the whole course of the factor-price frontier. This very special case implies four things. First, *any* two factor-price curves for relevant techniques can intersect each other *only once* in the non-negative r, w quadrant. Second, because they cross each other only once, the whole set of relevant technique curves can be unambiguously ordered by capital intensity. Third, the technique towards which the system moves when r falls is unambiguously more capital intensive than the one from which it moves. Indeed, at the constant relative prices, p', the overall capital–labor ratio, $p'k$, is always higher on the technique chosen at lower r. (Notice that the wage rate is *not* here used as numeraire.) Fourth, the economy acts in this case *as if* it could be defined completely in terms of a single unambiguous production function: Samuelson's surrogate.[10]

The reasoning behind all these statements is that for any technique, θ, for which the conditions for globally consistent aggregation into a single sector hold

$$-\left(\frac{\mathrm{d}w}{\mathrm{d}r}\right)_\theta = (p'k)_\theta = b_\theta^*/c_{0\theta} \tag{8B-2}$$

where b_θ^* is the Frobenius root of B_θ (compare Eq. 7A-23 when $c_\theta' b_{0\theta} - c_{0\theta} b_\theta^* = 0$).[11] If all relevant techniques obey the conditions for consistent aggregation into a single sector, then the technique to which one moves when r falls must have a higher b_θ^* and a lower $c_{0\theta}$ than the one from which one moves, since one must always move to a technique curve with larger *absolute* slope. (As in

---

10. See Samuelson, "Parable and Realism in Capital Theory: The Surrogate Production Function," *Review of Economic Studies,* vol. 29, June 1962, pp. 193–206.

11. As indicated in expression (7A-23), it is *always* possible to write

$$-\mathrm{d}w/\mathrm{d}r = p'k \quad \text{if} \quad g = r$$

whether or not the conditions for consistent aggregation hold. This follows by addition of the derivative equations

$$0 = \left\{\frac{\mathrm{d}p'}{\mathrm{d}r}(rI + \delta)b_0 + p'b_0 + \frac{\mathrm{d}w}{\mathrm{d}r}c_0\right\}x$$

and

$$\frac{\mathrm{d}p'}{\mathrm{d}r}(gI + \delta)k = \left\{\frac{\mathrm{d}p'}{\mathrm{d}r}(rI + \delta)B + p'B + \frac{\mathrm{d}w}{\mathrm{d}r}c'\right\}\{gI + \delta\}k$$

to obtain

$$-\frac{\mathrm{d}w}{\mathrm{d}r} = p'k + \frac{\mathrm{d}p'}{\mathrm{d}r}(r - g)k$$

Thus, in all cases in which $g = r$ (such as those with a strict classical savings function, $s_w = 0$ and $s_r = 1$), the technique to which one moves as r falls always has a higher capital–labor ratio than the one from which one moves, where the overall capital–labor ratios of the two techniques are evaluated at the steady-state prices that are appropriate to the switch point. On the other hand, in the special case where aggregation is globally consistent, $\mathrm{d}p'/\mathrm{d}r = 0$ and, once again, $-\mathrm{d}w/\mathrm{d}r = p'k$.

Fig. 7D-1, r is the abscissa and w is the ordinate.) Thus, the aggregation conditions imply that $p'k$ is necessarily higher for the technique chosen at lower r. The overall capital–labor ratio, $p'k$, is well behaved.

Apart from this extreme case where aggregation into a single sector is consistent on every relevant technique, relative prices may change as r varies along the factor-price frontier and individual technique curves may follow serpentine courses. The question then arises as to whether or not any sense can be made of the idea of the capital intensity ordering of techniques. For if technique curves are non-linear because of relative price movements in response to r (Wicksell effects), they may intersect more than once in the non-negative r, w quadrant and, hence, it may be possible for an individual technique to *return* to the frontier so that reswitching may occur. In such circumstances, techniques cannot be unambiguously or globally ordered as to capital intensity. It is, therefore, the existence of relative price movements in response to r (Wicksell effects), which occur when the conditions for consistent aggregation into a single sector do not hold, that gives rise to non-linear factor-price curves and therefore to the possibility that techniques cannot be globally ordered by capital intensity.

In order to illustrate these points, consider a pair of techniques, technique 1 and technique 2, which have a switch point on the factor-price frontier designated by the point r^*, w^* in Fig. 8B-1 and with corresponding prices $p^{*'}$. Suppose that a rise in the wage–rental ratio in the neighborhood of r^*, w^* is accompanied, as in Fig. 8B-1, by a movement from the use of technique 1 and to the use of technique 2. The monotonicity of the factor-price frontier indicates that when the wage–rental ratio rises, the factor-price curve of the new technique always has a larger absolute slope than that of the old technique. (Strictly, it must be assumed that both curves are smooth and that there is not a multiple intersection of the two technique curves at the point r^*, w^*.) Hence, it is known that in the neighbor-

Figure 8B-1 Factor-price relationships.

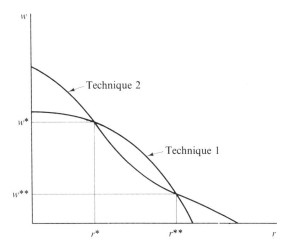

hood of the switch point between 1 and 2 it must be the case that

$$-\left(\frac{dw}{dr}\right)^*_{(2)} > -\left(\frac{dw}{dr}\right)^*_{(1)} \qquad (8B\text{-}3)$$

where the stars are inserted to indicate that the differentiation is evaluated at the point r^*, w^*.

Now it is known from the non-substitution theorem that *all* prices are identical whichever technique is used at the point r^*, w^*. However, at a profit rate marginally higher than r^*, technique 1 is superior to technique 2. That is to say, technique 1 can produce all commodities more cheaply than technique 2 in terms of the wage rate, w. If (a) $\{\bar{p}_0(r); \bar{p}'(r)\}_1$ and (b) $\{\bar{p}_0(r); \bar{p}'(r)\}_2$ are used to represent the prices (in terms of the wage rate) which would rule if, respectively, (a) technique 1 were chosen at any r, and (b) technique 2 were chosen at any r, then $\{\bar{p}_0(r); \bar{p}'(r)\}_1 < \{\bar{p}_0(r); \bar{p}'(r)\}_2$ for r marginally above r^*.[12] On the other hand, at a profit rate marginally lower than r^*, technique 2 is superior to technique 1. That is to say, technique 2 can produce all commodities more cheaply than technique 1 in terms of the wage rate, w. Hence, $\{\bar{p}_0(r); \bar{p}'(r)\}_1 > \{\bar{p}_0(r); \bar{p}'(r)\}_2$ for r marginally below r^*.

Since at r^*, $\{\bar{p}_0(r^*); \bar{p}'(r^*)\}_1 = \{\bar{p}_0(r^*); \bar{p}'(r^*)\}_2 = \{\bar{p}_0(r^*); \bar{p}'(r^*)\}$ it follows from the argument of the previous paragraph that all prices in terms of the wage rate must increase more rapidly on technique 2 than on technique 1 when the rate of profit increases in the neighborhood of r^*, w^*. Hence,

$$\frac{d}{dr}\{\bar{p}_0(r^*); \bar{p}'(r^*)\}_2 > \frac{d}{dr}\{\bar{p}_0(r^*); \bar{p}'(r^*)\}_1 \qquad (8B\text{-}4)$$

which may be taken to be a definition of *local* capital intensity ordering of two techniques. It says that technique 2 is more capital intensive than technique 1 in the neighborhood of r^*, w^*, for technique 2 is unambiguously more sensitive than technique 1 to changes in the rate of profit in the neighborhood of r^*, w^*. Notice that, on this definition or interpretation of capital intensity, a small increase in the wage–rental ratio in the neighborhood of r^*, w^* implies a movement towards a more capital intensive technique. Of course, the technique (technique 2) to which the system moves when the wage–rental ratio rises in a given neighborhood (in the neighborhood of r^*, w^*) may only be locally more capital intensive than the technique from which the system moves (technique 1). Indeed, the existence of the second switch point in Fig. 8B-1 shows that the capital intensity ordering in this example cannot be global (that is appropriate to all non-negative factor-price configurations). For suppose that this switch point (r^{**}, w^{**}) also lies on the factor-price frontier (as may always be done, for it can be assumed that techniques 1 and 2 are the only relevant techniques). Then, corresponding

---

12. The strong inequality ($<$ or $>$) applies if both technique matrices are assumed to be indecomposable; in the decomposable case it must be replaced by the weaker inequality ($\leq$ or $\geq$). This is also true for other similar expressions including (8B-4).

to r^{**}, w^{**} there exists a set of prices, $\{\bar{p}_0(r^{**}); \bar{p}'(r^{**})\}$, such that $\mathrm{d}\{\bar{p}_0(r^{**});$ $\bar{p}'(r^{**})\}/\mathrm{d}r_1 > \mathrm{d}\{\bar{p}_0(r^{**}); \bar{p}'(r^{**})\}/\mathrm{d}r_2$. In terms of these prices—that is, in the neighborhood of r^{**}, w^{**}—technique 1 is more capital intensive than technique 2.

If the prices r^{**}, w^{**} were used to construct an index number of the "quantity of capital" then it is probable that this index number would indicate a *fall* in the overall "capital"–labor ratio as w/r rises through the *original* switch point, r^*, w^*. On the other hand, if the prices of the original switch point, r^*, w^*, were used to construct an index number of the "quantity of capital" then it is again probable that this index number would indicate a *fall* in the overall "capital"–labor ratio as w/r rises through r^{**}, w^{**}. "Perverse" cases therefore arise because prices change and comparisons sometimes have to be made using inappropriate prices (as in an index number comparison). It is the existence of Wicksell effects which gives rise to the possibility of "perverse" behavior in the overall capital–labor ratio in response to the wage–rental ratio and to the possibility that techniques cannot be globally ordered by capital intensity.

Earlier in this section, the term reswitching has been used to refer to the phenomenon in which a technique that is best at a high rate of return ceases to be at a somewhat lower rate of return but, nevertheless, becomes best again at an even lower rate of return. Reswitching therefore occurs when a single technique forms two or more distinct (or separated) segments of the factor-price frontier; the technique "recurs" as best at different rates of return. If reswitching occurs, techniques cannot be unambiguously ordered as to their roundaboutness or capital intensity. But the absence of reswitching does not imply that unambiguous ordering is possible (except in an *"ex post"* sense), since, as will be shown, this ordering depends upon there being one and only one intersection in the non-negative factor-price quadrant between each and every pair of factor-price curves belonging to the collection of *relevant* techniques, θ^*, whether or not these intersections occur *on* the factor-price frontier (as distinct from *underneath* it).

In the remainder of this section, the derivation of a condition which is sufficient for there to be only a single intersection between the factor-price curves of any two relevant techniques in the non-negative factor-price quadrant will be outlined.[13] This sufficiency condition will be shown to imply that the two techniques can be ordered according to roundaboutness or capital intensity independently of factor prices. If this sufficiency condition holds for every pair of techniques belonging to θ^*, then the whole set of relevant techniques can be ordered as to their capital intensities independently of factor prices. In this case, the sufficiency condition implies that the ordering of the relevant techniques by maximum w is exactly the opposite of the ordering of the relevant techniques by maximum r. But the existence of such an inverse ordering does not imply that global capital intensity ordering is possible, except in an economy in which

---

13. The derivation is similar but not identical to that found in M. Bruno, E. Burmeister, and E. Sheshinski, "The Nature and Implications of the Reswitching of Techniques," *Quarterly Journal of Economics*, vol. 80, November, 1966, pp. 526–553.

there are only two capital goods. (It is to be noted that reswitching cannot occur in a two commodity model in which there is only one *capital* good which does not change its specification from technique to technique; that is to say, there must be at least two capital goods *prices* in order for reswitching to occur.)

At any point where two techniques are equally profitable or equally efficient, whether or not this point is on the factor-price frontier, it has been established that *all* prices would be the same whichever technique were operated. That is, ignoring all other techniques and therefore the fact that neither of the two techniques would *actually* be used at an intersection underneath the factor-price frontier, one may write (in terms of the wage rate as numeraire)

$$\{\bar{p}_0(r); \bar{p}'(r)\}_1 - \{\bar{p}_0(r); \bar{p}'(r)\}_2 = 0 \tag{8B-5}$$

for any r which is a "switch point r" for techniques 1 and 2. The question is, then, how many real positive roots or switch point r's are there to this set of $n + 1$ equations. Under what conditions is there one and only one real positive root (and, hence, only one intersection of the two techniques in the non-negative r, w quadrant)?

Suppose initially, that (at least) two switch points exist for techniques 1 and 2. Call these points r^*, w^* and r^{**}, w^{**} as in Fig. 8B-1, and let the associated price vectors be $\{\bar{p}_0(r^*); \bar{p}'(r^*)\}$ and $\{\bar{p}_0(r^{**}); \bar{p}'(r^{**})\}$, respectively. Then, ignoring all techniques other than technique 1 and technique 2, these techniques must satisfy *two* equations of the form (compare expression 8B-1)

$$[1; \bar{p}'(r^*)] \begin{bmatrix} 1 & 0 \\ 0 & (r^*I + \delta) \end{bmatrix} \begin{bmatrix} (c_{02} - c_{01}) & (c'_2 - c'_1) \\ (b_{02} - b_{01}) & (B_2 - B_1) \end{bmatrix} = [0, 0] \tag{8B-6}$$

with a similar equation holding at the second switch point. By subtracting the equations for the two separate switch points, one obtains the $n + 1$ equations

$$\{\bar{p}'(r^{**})[r^{**}I + \delta] - \bar{p}'(r^*)[r^*I + \delta]\}\{(b_{02} - b_{01}); (B_2 - B_1)\} = \{0, 0\} \tag{8B-7}$$

since the first (labor input) term in each equation vanishes.

Now it has already been shown that $\bar{p}'(r)$ is monotonically increasing in r, so that, given $r^{**} > r^*$, the first term in this expression is a strictly positive vector; that is, all n components of this $1 \times n$ row vector must be positive. There are then $n + 1$ column vectors in $\{(b_{02} - b_{01}); (B_2 - B_1)\}$ that are orthogonal to a positive vector. Several of these column vectors may be null vectors, possessing only zero elements. Indeed, switch points *on* the factor-price frontier will normally be between techniques that differ in only one activity or column. However, if the techniques are to be different, they must be different in at least one activity, and, therefore, at least one column of $\{(b_{02} - b_{01}); (B_2 - B_1)\}$ must have non-zero elements. Moreover, if Eq. (8B-7) is to be satisfied, every column of $\{(b_{02} - b_{01}); (B_2 - B_1)\}$ that has non-zero elements must have at least one positive element and at least one negative element. For any vector that is not a null vector and which is orthogonal to a positive vector *cannot* itself be one-signed. It follows that Eq. (8B-7) cannot hold if *any* single column vector in $\{(b_{02} - b_{01}); (B_2 - B_1)\}$ has one-signed elements. That is to say, if there exists a column vector in $\{(b_{02} - b_{01}); (B_2 - B_1)\}$ which is either semi-negative or semi-positive, then there cannot be more than one point in the non-negative factor-price quadrant at which the two techniques are equally profitable.

Suppose, then, that there exists a one-signed (semi-negative or semi-positive) column vector in $\{(b_{02} - b_{01}); (B_2 - B_1)\}$. Let this column vector be the *j*-th column $(b_{j2} - b_{j1})$. Then, Eq. (8B-7) does not hold and either the switch point r^{**}, w^{**} or the switch point r^*, w^* does not exist, or both do not exist. The possibility of no switch point in the non-negative r, w quadrant may be demonstrated as follows. If $(c_{j2} - c_{j1})$ is of the same sign as the elements of $(b_{j2} - b_{j1})$, then one technique is dominated by the other technique and there is no point in the non-negative r, w quadrant at which the two techniques can produce commodity *j* (and hence all commodities) equally cheaply. More particularly, if $(c_{j2} - c_{j1}) \geq 0$ and $(b_{j2} - b_{j1}) \geq 0$, then technique 2 is dominated, and if $(c_{j2} - c_{j1}) \leq 0$ and $(b_{j2} - b_{j1}) \leq 0$, then technique 1 is dominated.

It remains to consider the two cases in which neither technique need be dominated and yet there exists a one-signed vector in $\{(b_{02} - b_{01}); (B_2 - B_1)\}$. First, if $(b_{j2} - b_{j1}) \geq 0$ and $(c_{j2} - c_{j1}) < 0$, then technique 2 is more capital intensive than technique 1, and the single switch point (if it exists) is of the type r^*, w^* in Fig. 8B-1. Second, if $(b_{j2} - b_{j1}) \leq 0$ and $(c_{j2} - c_{j1}) > 0$, then technique 1 is more capital intensive than technique 2, and the single switch point (if it exists) is of the type r^{**}, w^{**} in Fig. 8B-1. Finally, if $\{(b_{02} - b_{01}); (B_2 - B_1)\}$ has one (or more) column(s) which is semi-positive, it cannot have another column which is semi-negative (and *vice versa*) if both techniques are to be relevant (or non-dominated) techniques. That is to say, it is impossible for relevant techniques that a switch between them lead to a substitution *away* from the use of *all* capital goods in the production of one commodity, and *towards* the use of *all* capital goods in the production of another commodity, for at a switch point *all* commodities are produced (locally) more capital intensively on one technique than on the other, by expression (8B-4).

The use of the phrases "all capital goods" and "capital intensity" in the previous paragraph should be noted. For, in economic terms, the importance of the existence of a semi-positive or a semi-negative vector is the implication that if there is a commodity (say the *j*-th) the production of which on one technique uses at *least* as much of *every* type of capital good (and more of some) as on the other technique, then one technique is unambiguously or globally more capital intensive than the other. Simply, *commodity j must be produced in an unambiguously more "real capital" intensive way on one technique than on other*. For, then, one technique is more "real capital" intensive than the other technique without regard to the non-negative commodity-price weights that are attached to the individual capital goods, and since commodity prices are simply a function of factor prices, the condition (of semi-negativity or semi-positivity) implies that the two techniques can be ordered by capital intensity independently of factor prices.

The analysis has proceeded to the point at which Bruno, Burmeister, and Sheshinski may be followed. For the whole set of relationships of Eq. (8B-7) may be reduced from $n + 1$ to one by post-multiplying them by any semi-positive column vector of gross outputs per efficiency unit of labor $\{x; y/\overline{L}\}$. One has, then, the following theorem (which appears in Bruno, Burmeister, and Sheshinski but is derived in a different way[14]) for two *relevant* techniques— that is, techniques which do at some factor-prices form a segment of the factor-price frontier.

Theorem 8B-1: If there exists a semi-positive vector $\{x; y/\overline{L}\}$ such that $\{(b_{02} - b_{01}); (B_2 - B_1)\}\{x; y/\overline{L}\}$ is either a semi-positive vector or a semi-negative vector, then there exists a single real positive root, $\bar{r}$, at which the two relevant techniques are equally productive, and the two techniques can then be ordered as to their capital intensity in a global fashion.

Notice that Theorem 8B-1 is satisfied if any single column of $\{(b_{02} - b_{01}); (B_2 - B_1)\}$ is a one-signed vector. But it can also be satisfied if no column is one-signed but positive and negative elements in different columns offset each other. For this to be the case, however, substitution has to go in opposite directions in different activities when the technique changes, which is perhaps an unlikely phenomenon. In particular, there cannot exist semi-positive $\{x; y/\overline{L}\}$'s such that Theorem 8B-1 holds and a change from one $\{x; y/\overline{L}\}$ to another changes $\{(b_{02} - b_{01}); (B_2 - B_1)\}\{x; y/\overline{L}\}$ from a semi-positive vector to a semi-negative vector (or *vice versa*). That is to say, since *composite* commodities constructed with fixed proportions of underlying commodities are also commodities, it is not possible for relevant techniques to have a switch point at which one composite commodity becomes produced more "real capital" intensively, and another composite commodity becomes produced less "real capital" intensively. For a switch point is a point at which *all* commodities are produced more capital intensively (locally, that is) on one technique than on the other.

It follows from the argument of the previous paragraph, that, if one semi-positive $\{x; y/\overline{L}\}$ satisfying Theorem 8B-1 exists, many do. Moreover, either $\{x; y/\overline{L}\}$'s exist such that $\{(b_{02} - b_{01}); (B_2 - B_1)\}\{x; y/\overline{L}\} \geq 0$, or $\{x; y/\overline{L}\}$'s exist such that $\{(b_{02} - b_{01}); (B_2 - B_1)\}\{x; y/\overline{L}\} \leq 0$, *or no such* $\{x; y/\overline{L}\}$'s *exist*. In particular, if $\{(b_{02} - b_{01}); (B_2 - B_1)\}$ has only one non-zero column so that the techniques differ in only one activity, and if the column has mixed positive and negative elements, then no semi-positive $\{x; y/\overline{L}\}$ satisfying Theorem 8B-1 can exist, and the possibility of more than one switch point cannot be ruled out.

---

14. See Bruno, Burmeister, and Sheshinski, *op. cit.,* p. 543. These authors have also shown that the number of switch points between any two techniques cannot exceed the number of distinct capital goods. Hence, reswitching is impossible if there is only one capital good. This should be obvious from Eq. (8B-7) since, in this case, $b_{02} - b_{01}$ and $B_2 - B_1$ are scalars, and hence are necessarily one signed.

Theorem 8B-1 has a corollary.

Corollary 8B-1: If for each and every pair of techniques, α and β, $\alpha \neq \beta$, in the collection of relevant techniques, θ^*, there exists a semi-positive $\{x; y/\overline{L}\}_{\alpha\beta}$ (which may be different in each case) such that $\{(b_{0\alpha} - b_{0\beta}); (B_\alpha - B_\beta)\}\{x; y/\overline{L}\}_{\alpha\beta}$ is either a semi-positive vector or a semi-negative vector, then every pair of relevant technique curves has one and only one intersection in the non-negative r, w quadrant, and the whole set of relevant techniques can be ordered as to their capital intensities in a global fashion.

Theorem 8B-1 and Corollary 8B-1 can be interpreted as saying that, if there exists a semi-positive vector $\{x; y/\overline{L}\}$ such that technique α uses at least as much of every capital good (and more of some) as technique β (or vice versa), then the two techniques can be ordered as to their "real capital" intensities—that is, independently of r—and, further, if all relevant techniques can be so ordered, then a fall in the rate of return will always imply a movement towards a more capital intensive technique; towards an increased usage of "real capital."

In the previous analysis, a sufficient condition for global capital intensity ordering of the set of relevant techniques has been derived. This sufficiency condition cannot be made necessary. Indeed, it is hard to see how necessary and sufficient conditions for there to be one and only one rate of return at which two techniques are equally efficient can be derived. This fact is not, however, fundamental to the argument. What is fundamental is that the corollary indicates in economically meaningful terms a set of conditions under which the whole set of relevant techniques can be ordered as to their roundaboutness or capital intensity, independently of factor prices. For, if these conditions hold, standard index number manipulations cannot lead to the capital-theoretic curiosum that a fall in the wage–rental ratio may be associated with a movement towards a technique with a higher overall "quantity of capital" to labor ratio.[15] If the conditions do not hold, however, it is only implied that this curiosum *may* arise, not that it *must* arise. This is, of course, just as well, for the corollary implies pretty formidable conditions.

Corollary 8B-1 is, of course, vastly over-sufficient for the absence of "reswitching" or the return of a technique to the factor-price frontier, since single intersections in the non-negative factor-price quadrant are not necessary for the absence of "reswitching" (as distinct from global capital intensity ordering). As previously indicated, switch points *on* the factor-price frontier will normally involve only one activity. That is to say, $\{(b_{02} - b_{01}); (B_2 - B_1)\}$ will normally have only one column with non-zero elements if techniques 1 and 2 have a switch point on the frontier. When there are many relevant techniques, the

---

15. The most appropriate index of the "quantity of capital" in the present context is a *chain index* whose price weights are chained at each successive switch point on the factor-price frontier. Compare D. G. Champernowne, "The Production Function and the Theory of Capital: A Comment," *Review of Economic Studies*, vol. 21, no. 55, 1953–1954, pp. 112–135.

actual phenomenon of the return of a technique to the factor-price frontier is fairly unlikely even if Corollary 8B-1 does not hold. It is not, however, simply "reswitching" that causes the problem of anomalous capital intensity ordering. It is the fact of multiple intersections between relevant technique curves *on or under* the frontier. For the existence of a *unique* intersection between two relevant technique curves implies that if technique 1 is capital intensive relative to technique 2 at their single intersection, there does not exist a set of prices for comparison which can make technique 2 capital intensive relative to technique 1. It is this fact that is important to the movement of an index number of the "quantity of capital" relative to the rate of interest. For quite apart from what happens along any given technique curve,[16] it is only when there exists a set of price weights (that could be used in an index number of the "quantity of capital") which "reverse" the ordering of two techniques that "perverse" behavior of the "quantity of capital" can occur when the system moves from one technique to another.

It is evident that the conditions which are sufficient for techniques to be unambiguously ordered as to capital intensity are fairly stringent. Why should one technique use at least as much of every capital good as another technique? Moreover, why should the specification of the various types of capital goods remain the same at several different factor-price configurations? There is no empirical justification for any of these things to be assumed in economic theory. There is, of course, a theoretical justification: it is often useful to be able to work in terms of an aggregative neo-classical production function.

Fundamentally, the whole debate concerning the choice of technique in steady-state growth equilibrium revolves around beliefs as to the operational significance of marginalism. The importance that one attributes to the possibility that techniques cannot be globally ordered by capital intensity depends very much on whether the conclusions that can be drawn from a piece of comparative analysis are required to be local or global conclusions, and therefore in part upon one's beliefs about the operational usefulness of marginal analysis. Solow, for example, is willing to suspend disbelief as to its operational usefulness;[17] Robinson apparently is not. For in the neighborhood of a given switch point between two techniques, that is, at the *margin* of switching, there is always a sense in which

16. These effects, from which we have abstracted in this section, are important. However, "perverse" behavior along a given technique curve will normally be associated with instability of the steady-state equilibria which are being compared.

17. See R. M. Solow, "The Interest Rate and Transition between Techniques," pp. 30–39 in C. H. Feinstein (editor), *Socialism, Capitalism and Economic Growth, Essays Presented to Maurice Dobb*, Cambridge, Cambridge University Press, 1967. On p. 38, Solow writes: "Both phenomena, 'recurrence' of technique and perverse behavior of consumption per head with the interest rate, point to a weakness in the 'neoclassical parable.' Evidently there are situations in which one can not speak safely of 'capital deepening' as the concomitant of both lower interest rate and higher steady-state consumption per head. But neither phenomenon, so far as I can see, subverts neoclassical capital theory in its full generality. They do suggest some further investigation of the microeconomics of the perverse cases."

one can say that a rise in the wage–rental (w/r) ratio leads to the choice of a more capital intensive technique. Moreover, at least for some savings relationships (for example, $s_w = 0$, $s_r = 1$), it is normally the case that at the switch point prices, a rise in w/r leads to a rise in the overall capital–labor ratio. It is also the case that the competitive rate of profit is an accurate measure of the social rate of return to saving.[18] On the other hand, if the capital intensities of two techniques have to be compared at points (incorporating price weights) that are more than infinitesimally removed from the actual point at which they are equally efficient (the switch point), then lack of global ordering may be problematic.

It is by no means clear that it is useful to ask whether or not techniques can be ordered by capital intensity independently of factor prices. Why are global orderings, as distinct from local orderings, required? The more the relevant range of profit rate variation is narrowed, the smaller becomes the number of relevant techniques, and the more likely it is that these techniques can be unambiguously ordered as to their capital intensities over the relevant range of profit rate variation. Be that as it may, what are the implications of the present analysis? In broad terms, its most significant implication is a warning that it should not be expected that general equilibrium analysis will generate many useful qualitative predictions unless the number of distinct sectors is severely constrained or unless the analysis is imbedded with highly restrictive and (probably) unrealistic assumptions. These assumptions seem to be required in order to generate unique determinate solutions to various systems of equations. This warning implies equally well to the question of the ranking of techniques by capital intensity and to the separate question of the ranking of commodities by capital intensity.

C: THE LEONTIEF DYNAMIC MODEL: DUAL INSTABILITY

In the previous sections of this chapter, systems incorporating heterogeneous capital goods have been discussed with regard to (a) the possibility of aggregation, and (b) the choice of technique in alternative steady-state equilibria. In the next two sections, the dynamic properties of particular systems incorporating heterogeneous capital goods will be discussed. The treatment will be confined to equilibrium dynamics; that is to say, it will be assumed that the system remains in flow equilibrium at each point of time. No mistakes are made since expectations of future competitive equilibrium prices are always correct. The basic model is, of course, that which was outlined in Sec. B of chapter 7.

18. *Ibid.,* p. 30: "In this discussion (the 'reswitching' debate), the rate of interest has generally been treated as a parameter, whose exogenous variation sweeps out alternative steady states. One consequence of this approach is that an important property of the interest rate has been overlooked: through all vicissitudes of 'normal' and 'perverse' cases, however the rate of interest is actually determined, so long as full employment and competitive pricing prevail, the rate of interest is an accurate measure of the social rate of return to saving."

One of the problems that arise in equilibrium dynamic systems incorporating heterogeneous capital goods is that if a regularly progressive or steady-state solution exists it may be characterized by relative instability. That is to say, the long run equilibrium or steady-state solution cannot, in general, be reached by following the dynamic equilibrium path originating from any set of initial conditions which are not exactly consistent with the steady-state. This problem has been stressed by Hahn, Jorgenson, and Burmeister, among others.[19] It should be noted that the problem is only one of the stability of steady-state equilibrium. That is to say, it is *not* being asked whether or not the dynamic equilibrium path is itself unstable, which is a question of disequilibrium dynamics. It is simply being asked whether or not the steady-state solution is the asymptotic growth path followed by any non-steady equilibrium dynamic path.

The question of the relative instability of steady-state equilibrium is discussed in two different technological contexts. In this section, it is assumed that the technology is a Leontief fixed coefficients one, whereas in Sec. D, the technology is assumed to be of the Cobb-Douglas form. Although more general technologies are omitted from this discussion, it should be clear that if stability problems arise in the context of these relatively uncomplicated technologies, it is unlikely that they can be avoided in more general technologies. In both cases, however, the question of the relative instability of the steady-state solution is also a question of the economic meaningfulness of the dynamic equilibrium path.

Consider the equilibrium dynamic system summarized in expressions (7B-12) and (7B-16) with associated (classical) savings function (7B-17). This system may be repeated here as

$$\{B - c_0^{-1} b_0 c'\}\dot{k} = \{I - (B - c_0^{-1} b_0 c')(\mu I + \delta)\}k - c_0^{-1} b_0$$

and

$$-\dot{p}'\{B - c_0^{-1} b_0 c'\} = p'\{I - (rI + \delta)(B - c_0^{-1} b_0 c')\} - c_0^{-1} c' \qquad (8C-1)$$

19. See F. H. Hahn, "Equilibrium Dynamics with Heterogeneous Capital Goods," *Quarterly Journal of Economics,* vol. 80, November, 1966, pp. 633–646, "On Warranted Growth Paths," *Review of Economic Studies,* vol. 35, April, 1968, pp. 175–184, and "Some Adjustment Problems," *Econometrica,* vol. 38, January, 1970, pp. 1–17. See D. W. Jorgenson, "A Dual Stability Theorem," *Econometrica,* vol. 28, October, 1960, pp. 892–899, "The Structure of Multi-Sector Dynamic Models," *International Economic Review,* vol. 2, September, 1961, pp. 276–293, and "Linear Models of Economic Growth," *International Economic Review,* Vol. 9, February, 1968, pp. 1–13. See E. Burmeister, R. Dobell, and K. Kuga, "A Note on the Global Stability of a Simple Growth Model with Many Capital Goods," *Quarterly Journal of Economics,* vol. 82, November, 1968, pp. 657–665, E. Burmeister, C. Caton, A. R. Dobell, and S. A. Ross, "The 'Saddle Point Property' and the Structure of Dynamic Heterogeneous Capital Good Models," *Econometrica,* vol. 41, January, 1973, pp. 79–95, and E. Burmeister and D. A. Graham, "Multi-Sector Economic Models with Continuous Adaptive Expectations," *Review of Economic Studies,* vol. 41, July, 1974, pp. 323–336. See also M. Kurz, "The General Instability of a Class of Competitive Growth Processes," *Review of Economic Studies,* vol. 35, April, 1968, pp. 155–174, M. Morishima, *Equilibrium, Stability, and Growth,* Oxford, Oxford University Press, 1964, and K. Shell and J. E. Stiglitz, "The Allocation of Investment in a Dynamic Economy," *Quarterly Journal of Economics,* vol. 81, November, 1967, pp. 592–609.

with

$$s_r\{rp'k - \dot{p}'k\} = \mu p'k + p'\dot{k}$$

On the usual assumptions (see Sec. D of chapter 7), there will exist a unique steady-state solution, k^*, with constant prices, $p^{*\prime}$, if and only if $\max(\mu, r^*) < 1/\lambda_1$, where μ and r^* are the steady-state growth rate and profit rate, respectively, and λ_1 is the Frobenius root of both $B(I - \delta B)^{-1}$ and $(I - B\delta)^{-1}B$. This solution depends upon the non-homogeneous parts of Eq. (8C-1) and may be written as

and

$$k^* = \{I - (B - c_0^{-1}b_0c')(\mu I + \delta)\}^{-1}b_0c_0^{-1}$$

where

$$p^{*\prime} = c_0^{-1}c'\{I - (r^*I + \delta)(B - c_0^{-1}b_0c')\}^{-1} \tag{8C-2}$$

$$r^* = \mu/s_r$$

which is obtained by setting $\dot{k} = 0$ and $\dot{p}' = 0$ in expression (8C-1). Under what conditions are these solutions stable? The answer to this question is that the primal stock balance system is stable if and only if all the n characteristic roots of the homogeneous part of the quantity system have negative real parts, whereas the dual pricing system is stable if and only if all the n characteristic roots of the homogeneous part of the price equations have negative real parts. To obtain the homogeneous parts of the two systems, let

so that

$$k(t) = k^* + \bar{k}e^{\alpha t} \quad \text{and} \quad p'(t) = p^{*\prime} + \bar{p}'e^{\beta t}$$

$$\dot{k}(t) = \alpha\{k(t) - k^*\} \quad \text{and} \quad \dot{p}'(t) = \beta\{p'(t) - p^{*\prime}\} \tag{8C-3}$$

Given the definitions of k^* and $p^{*\prime}$ in Eq. (8C-2), substitution of Eq. (8C-3) into Eq. (8C-1) yields

$$\{(B - c_0^{-1}b_0c')(\alpha I + \mu I + \delta) - I\}\{k(t) - k^*\} = 0$$

and

$$\tag{8C-4}$$

$$\{p'(t) - p^{*\prime}\}\{(-\beta I + r^*I + \delta)(B - c_0^{-1}b_0c') - I\} = p'\{r^* - r(t)\}(B - c_0^{-1}b_0c')$$

where $r^* - r(t)$ may be determined from the savings = investment relationship, namely $s_r\{rp'k - \dot{p}'k\} = s_r r^*p'k + p'\dot{k}$ if $s_r r^* = \mu$.

In order to proceed, the following assumptions are made. First, it is assumed that $\hat{B} \equiv -(B - c_0^{-1}b_0c')$ is non-singular so that $\hat{B}^{-1} \equiv -(B - c_0^{-1}b_0c')^{-1}$ exists. Second, it is assumed for the moment that the distinction between $r(t)$ and r^* can be ignored so that the right hand side of the second equation in Eq. (8C-4) *is also zero*. This second assumption generates a kind of local approximation in the neighborhood of steady-state equilibrium (where $r(t) = r^*$) to the set of dual pricing equations, and, since it is not wholly legitimate, the conclusions based upon it are not completely robust. It does not affect the global nature of the analysis of the set of primal quantity equations. Given these two assumptions, one may write Eq. (8C-4) in the form

and

$$\{(\alpha + \mu)I + \hat{B}^{-1}(I + \hat{B}\delta)\}\{k(t) - k^*\} = 0$$

$$\{p'(t) - p^{*'}\}\{(-\beta + r^*)I + (I + \delta\hat{B})\hat{B}^{-1}\} = 0$$

(8C-5)

It is evident from Eq. (8C-5) that the general solution to the primal equation system depends upon the characteristic roots of $-\{\mu I + \hat{B}^{-1}(I + \hat{B}\delta)\}$, while the solution to the dual equation system depends upon the characteristic roots of $+\{r^*I + (I + \delta\hat{B})\hat{B}^{-1}\}$. Since the characteristic roots of $\hat{B}^{-1}(I + \hat{B}\delta)$ and $(I + \delta\hat{B})\hat{B}^{-1}$ are identical, it is clear that $\alpha_i + \mu = -\beta_i + r^*$, all $i = 1, \ldots, n$. It follows that the solution to the dual equation system depends upon precisely the same set of characteristic roots as the solution to the primal equation system *except* that the real part of each root to the dual takes the *opposite* sign to the *sum* of $(\mu - r^*)$ *and* the real part of the corresponding root of the primal.

On the assumptions of the previous paragraph, the steady-state solution to the primal is globally stable if and only if all the characteristic roots of $-\hat{B}^{-1}(I + \hat{B}\delta)$ have real parts which are less than μ. A sufficient condition for this to be so is that $\mu I + \hat{B}^{-1}(I + \hat{B}\delta) = \{\mu I + \delta + (c_0^{-1}b_0c' - B)^{-1}\}$ have a dominant positive diagonal and non-positive off-diagonal elements. In this case $\mu I + \hat{B}^{-1}(I + \hat{B}\delta)$ is a *Leontief matrix,*[20] and $\{\mu I + \hat{B}^{-1}(I + \hat{B}\delta)\}^{-1} \geq 0$. Since all of the characteristic roots of a Leontief matrix have positive real parts,[21] it would then follow immediately that the real parts of all the α_i's, $i = 1, \ldots, n$, are negative and, hence, that the primal is globally stable. On the other hand, the steady-state solution to the dual is locally stable (in the neighborhood of $p' = p^{*'}$ and, more particularly, $r = r^*$) if and only if all the characteristic roots of $+(I + \delta\hat{B})\hat{B}^{-1}$ have real parts which are less than $-r^*$, which is the case if and only if all the characteristic roots of $-(I + \delta\hat{B})\hat{B}^{-1}$ have real parts which are greater than $+r^*$. It follows that the primal and the *dual* can both be stable (on present assumptions) if and only if *all* the characteristic roots of $\hat{B}^{-1}(I + \hat{B}\delta)$ and $(I + \delta\hat{B})\hat{B}^{-1}$ have real parts that are smaller than μ and larger than r^*. For most savings functions, this is very unlikely; for classical savings functions, where $\mu = s_r r^*$ and $\mu \leq r^*$, it is impossible.[22] It is therefore concluded that in most

---

20. Thus, $-\{(\mu I + \delta) + (c_0^{-1}b_0c' - B)^{-1}\}$ is a Metzler matrix (that is, a matrix with all of its off-diagonal elements non-negative and all of its diagonal elements strictly negative) *with* principal minors of each order j, for $j = 1, \ldots, n$, that take the sign of $(-1)^j$. All the characteristic roots of such a matrix have negative real parts. On this point, compare P. K. Newman, "Some Notes on Stability Conditions," *Review of Economic Studies*, vol. 27, October 1959, pp. 1–9.

21. If $A = I - B$ is a Leontief matrix, then $B = I - A$ has a dominant characteristic root which is real and positive but less than unity. Therefore, all the roots of $B = I - A$ lie within the unit circle and have real parts between -1 and $+1$. It follows that all the real parts of the roots of $A = I - B$ lie between 0 and $+2$, and are therefore all positive.

22. It is also impossible for all intertemporally efficient steady-states, since these must have $\mu \leq r^*$.

instances, if the primal is stable the dual will normally be unstable and *vice versa.*[23] This result is known as the dual instability property of the Leontief dynamic system. Hence, if the primal converges to the steady-state solution the dual normally cannot, and if the dual converges to the steady-state solution the primal normally cannot. Of course, there is in general no reason for either of these two parallel systems to converge to steady-state equilibrium; they may well both be unstable.

If either the dual system or the primal system is unstable, arbitrary semi-positive initial conditions will lead that system onto a path which cannot converge to the steady-state solution. Moreover, if the dual system is unstable the actual path followed will generate negative prices at some point of future time, while if the primal system is unstable the actual path followed will generate negative outputs (and associated stocks) at some point of future time.[24] In other words, unless the initial conditions are precisely appropriate and no perturbations occur, the Leontief dynamic system yields a time path for which, after some passage of time, either some prices or some outputs will no longer remain non-negative. But negative outputs or negative prices do not accord with common sense. It follows that dual instability and the economic meaningfulness of the dynamic equilibrium path are intimately associated.

Fundamentally, the problem of *dual instability* arises from the linearity of the system, from the fact that there are no direct links (apart from a savings

---

23. This proposition is strictly true only for a *closed* system in which μ and r^* (and thus the distinction between $r(t)$ and r^*) are irrelevant. Indeed, for closed systems Jorgenson has proved: "For systems of order greater than one, if the output system is globally relatively stable the price system is globally relatively unstable, and vice versa." See Jorgenson, "A Dual Stability Theorem," pp. 896.

24. This point may be illustrated very simply in the two capital good case, where for simplicity we ignore both (a) labor inputs and (b) the consumption goods producing sector, so that we are effectively dealing with a closed Leontief dynamic system of the form:

$$B\dot{k} = (I - B\delta)k, \quad \text{and} \quad -\dot{p}'B = p'(I - \delta B)$$

Since the roots of $(I - B\delta)^{-1}B$ are the real values λ_1 and λ_2 with $\lambda_1 > |\lambda_2|$, the two characteristic roots on which the motion of the primal system depends are $1/\lambda_1$ and $1/\lambda_2$. It follows that $1/\lambda_1$ is the larger root if and only if $\lambda_2 < 0$. This is the case if and only if $B^{-1}(I - B\delta)$ has non-negative off-diagonals and a negative diagonal (that is to say, it must be a Metzler matrix), for which it is necessary and sufficient that $\det(B) = b_{11}b_{22} - b_{12}b_{21} < 0$, *each capital good being intensive in the use of the other capital good.* In this case, the primal system converges to the eigenvector associated with $1/\lambda_1$, and $k_1/k_2 > 0$. However, if $\lambda_2 > 0$, then $B^{-1}(I - B\delta)$ has a positive diagonal and non-positive off-diagonals, giving $I - \lambda_2 B^{-1}(I - B\delta)$ as a semi-positive matrix. Hence, the corresponding eigenvector, which is the one approached, gives $k_1/k_2 < 0$. On the other hand, the two characteristic roots on which the motion of the dual system depends are $-1/\lambda_1$ and $-1/\lambda_2$. Since $\lambda_1 > |\lambda_2|$, it follows that $-1/\lambda_1$ is the larger root if and only if $\lambda_2 > 0$, or $\det(B) > 0$. In this case of *"self-intensive" production,* the dual system converges to the eigenvector associated with $-1/\lambda_1$, and $p_1/p_2 > 0$. However, if $\lambda_2 < 0$, then $-(I - \delta B)B^{-1}$ has a positive diagonal and non-positive off-diagonals, giving $I + \lambda_2(I - \delta B)B^{-1}$ as a semi-positive matrix. Hence, the corresponding eigenvector, which is the one approached, gives $p_1/p_2 < 0$.

relationship) between the primal and the dual. There is no way in which prices and quantities can be adjusted to each other so that movements in prices induce quantities to move in a way that leads to the steady-state, or so that movements in quantities induce prices to move in a way that leads to the steady-state. It is the lack of linkages between the primal variables and the dual variables that leads to dual instability, and this lack of linkages is endemic to the system's fixed technical coefficients.

It has already been shown that the steady-state solution to the primal is stable if and only if all the characteristic roots of $-\{\mu I + \hat{B}^{-1}(I + \hat{B}\delta)\} = -\{(\mu I + \delta) + (c_0^{-1}b_0c' - B)^{-1}\}$ have negative real parts. For this to be the case, it is sufficient that $+\{(\mu I + \delta) + (c_0^{-1}b_0c' - B)^{-1}\}$ be a Leontief matrix. If this is so, then from the steady-state primal equations and dual Eq. (8C-2) we may evaluate

$$-dk^*/d\mu = \{\mu I + \delta + (c_0^{-1}b_0c' - B)^{-1}\}^{-1}k^* > 0$$

and
$$-dp^*/dr^* = p^{*\prime}\{r^*I + \delta + (c_0^{-1}b_0c' - B)^{-1}\}^{-1} > 0$$

(8C-6)

for positive k^* and $p^{*\prime}$, since both inverse matrices are (at least) semi-positive, given $\mu \leq r^*$. The sufficient condition for the primal system to be stable generates comparative steady-state results that are always well behaved. That is to say, (a) an increase in the growth rate of the labor supply, which is necessarily associated with diminished steady-state consumption per head, is also associated with smaller steady-state capital–labor ratios, (b) an increase in the rate of return, which is necessarily associated with diminished steady-state real wage rate, is also associated with smaller steady-state capital goods prices, and (c) μ and r^* are (as usual) necessarily positively associated.

Investigating the conditions Eq. (8C-6) further, it is evident that $dk^*/d\mu$ and dp^*/dr^* are strictly negative vectors if $\{c_0^{-1}b_0c' - B\}k^*$ and $p^{*\prime}\{c_0^{-1}b_0c' - B\}$ are (at least) semi-positive vectors. There is then *a general tendency for the consumption goods producing sector to be the most capital intensive sector.* Thus, one way of ensuring well behaved steady-state comparisons *and* stability of the primal system is for relatively large outputs of specific capital goods *not* to require, both directly and indirectly, correspondingly large inputs of themselves, or, more specifically, for the consumption goods producing sector to be a relatively heavy user of produced inputs from other sectors. This must, of course, be the case if the production of consumption goods uses directly or indirectly more of every type of capital good relative to labor than the production of each type of capital good, a generalized capital intensity condition. Consumption goods will then genuinely appear to be the output of the "final stage" of production in the usual Austrian sense.

It follows from the reasoning of the previous two paragraphs that the prospect of deriving meaningful comparative steady-state theorems is directly related to the conditions for stability of the dynamic output system, an illustration of the correspondence principle. If, however, the primal system is unstable, there does not exist an accumulation path from arbitrary initial stocks to final steady-state stocks along which all stocks (including labor) are fully employed at all points of time. If technical input coefficients are fixed, it is essential to allow for inequalities in the stock balance relations,[25] thus permitting the system to choose at each point of time whether or not it is sensible to insist on the full employment of each particular input. It is the combination of (a) fixed technical input coefficients and (b) full employment of all inputs at all points of time that may often lead the primal equations of the uncoupled Leontief dynamic model to be unstable.

As to the dual system, whose stability appears to depend upon sectors being "own input intensive," and especially to the dual instability property of the Leontief dynamic model (that, in general, the two sides of the model cannot both be stable), it surely is based upon an inconsistent combination of assumptions. For with fixed coefficients, the net investment allocation is entirely determined from the full employment assumption underlying the primal equations. Given full employment there is no choice about this allocation. The primal system is "locked" into a particular allocation without regard to prices or price expectations. Indeed, because there is no choice, expectations are formally redundant in the determination of the net investment allocation. There is no room for asset choice equations at all, let alone asset choice equations involving the dubious assumption of "perfect foresight." It is therefore inconsistent to assume both full employment *and* perfect foresight in the fixed coefficient Leontief dynamic system, and it is this inconsistency which is responsible for the phenomenon of dual instability.

The basic reason for instability in the dual price system itself is the "perfect foresight" assumption that all expectations are realized. In other words, it is the assumption that the own rate of interest equilibrium condition holds *ex post* as well as *ex ante* which is suspect when instability occurs. Indeed, as we shall see, the "perfect foresight" assumption also tends to make unilaterally coupled systems of the Cobb-Douglas variety "go off the rails" as well as uncoupled systems, primarily because the asset choices dictated by the initial price expectations are the wrong ones to generate net investment allocations that could lead the system to the steady-state solution from its initial stock positions.

---

25. Compare Jorgenson, "Linear Models of Economic Growth," p. 8: "The basic problem appears to be that starting from arbitrary, non-negative initial output levels and prices we cannot guarantee that it will always be profitable to produce every commodity or to utilize all of the existing labor force and existing stocks of capital goods at every point of time in the future. Of course, this problem may be peculiar to systems with complete separation of output and price determination, as in the Leontief dynamic, input–output system or to systems with "unilateral coupling," that is, determination of prices in isolation from output levels, as in Morishima's generalizations of the dynamic, input–output system. . . . In models of capital accumulation equalities between supply and demand and between price and unit cost must be replaced by inequalities."

D: THE COBB-DOUGLAS DYNAMIC MODEL [26]

In the previous section, the Leontief dynamic model has been analyzed with regard to the question whether or not the dynamic equilibrium path from arbitrary initial conditions converges to a steady-state with constant prices. It appears that the steady-state solution for the primal and the dual cannot, in general, be reached simultaneously unless the initial conditions are precisely appropriate, that is, unless the system is in steady-state equilibrium initially. It was argued that the fixed technical coefficients of the Leontief dynamic model "lock" the system into a path which is bound to generate either negative activity levels or negative prices (or both) at some point of future time, from which point forward the system ceases to be economically meaningful.

In the present section, the assumption of fixed technical coefficients is dropped and choice is therefore reintroduced. The primal is made to depend upon the dual through the assumption that the underlying technology is of the Cobb-Douglas form. The dual does not, however, depend directly upon the primal so that the system may be characterized as a singly linked or unilaterally coupled system. Perfect foresight and dynamic equilibrium are assumed so that the path of the dual (and hence of the primal) depends upon capital gains that are expected *and* realized. It is shown that instability again arises, but not dual instability (in the sense that has been discussed in the previous section). Instability is then seen to be consequential upon the straightjacket of the system's equilibrium dynamic formulation, which depends crucially upon the perfect foresight assumption underlying the own rate of interest equilibrium condition.

The central problem with equilibrium dynamic models incorporating heterogeneous capital goods and allowing for a choice of technique is that these models are not closed unless price expectations are given. The course of the price system is causally indeterminate unless these expectations are specified. Furthermore, since these expectations may be treated as the independent variables in a set of $n - 1$ investment functions, where n is the number of distinct capital goods, the allocation of investment among the various capital goods is also indeterminate unless these expectations are specified. In a competitive market, the operation of the fundamental own rate of interest equilibrium condition, given as Eq. (7B-13), is required not only to determine the relative prices of the various types of capital goods but also to determine the relative quantities in which these capital goods are held. This equilibrium condition specifies that expected yields including capital gains should be equated for all capital goods. But it cannot be operative without the explicit introduction of expectations. It follows that unless the relative quantities in which capital goods are held are given exogenously, as is the case for a stationary or regularly progressive economy,

26. Certain portions of this section and the first section of chapter 9 appeared in my paper, "Multi-sectoral Growth and Technological Change," *Canadian Journal of Economics,* vol. 4, August 1971, pp. 299–313. I am indebted to the Canadian Journal of Economics and the University of Toronto Press for permission to quote these extracts herein.

they can only be determined by expectations, and hence, ultimately by the factors that generate these expectations.[27]

These points may be easily demonstrated in terms of the Cobb-Douglas technology. With an underlying technology of the Cobb-Douglas form the $n + 1$ production functions and factor balance relationships may be written in the form

$$\ln y_j(t) = a_{wj} \ln \xi_j(t) + a_{wj} \ln \bar{L}_j(t) + \sum_{i=1}^{n} a_{ij} \ln K_{ij}(t), \quad j = 0, 1, \dots, n$$

with

$$\bar{L}(t) = \sum_{j=0}^{n} \bar{L}_j(t) \quad \text{and} \quad K_i(t) = \sum_{j=0}^{n} K_{ij}(t), \quad i = 1, \dots, n \tag{8D-1}$$

where $y_j(t)$ is the output of commodity j at time t, $K_{ij}(t)$ is the input of class i capital goods in the production of commodity j at time t, with $K_i(t)$ being the fully employed stock of class i capital goods at time t, $\bar{L}_j(t)$ is the labor input in the production of commodity j at time t, with $\bar{L}(t)$ being the fully employed stock of labor at time t. The $a_{wj}, j = 0, 1, \dots, n$ and the $a_{ij}, i = 1, \dots, n, j = 0, 1, \dots, n$, represent labor and capital good input elasticities which obey the conditions $a_{wj} + \sum_{i=1}^{n} a_{ij} = 1$ for all $j = 0, 1, \dots, n$, indicating constant returns to scale, $\xi_j(t)$ is a shift parameter representing the differential level of Harrod-neutral technological development of sector j at time t,[28] and ln is the logarithmic operator. In competitive equilibrium, the marginal productivity conditions may be written as

$$w(t)\bar{L}_j(t) = a_{wj}p_j(t)y_j(t), \quad j = 0, 1, \dots, n$$

and

$$p_i(t)\{r_i(t) + \delta_i(t)\} K_{ij}(t) = a_{ij}p_j(t)y_j(t) \tag{8D-2}$$

$$i = 1, \dots, n, \quad j = 0, 1, \dots, n$$

or, in our earlier notation with time subscripts omitted for convenience,

$$\begin{bmatrix} w & 0 \\ 0 & P(R + \delta) \end{bmatrix} \begin{bmatrix} c_0 & c' \\ b_0 & B \end{bmatrix} = \begin{bmatrix} a_{w0} & a'_w \\ a_0 & A \end{bmatrix} \begin{bmatrix} p_0 & 0 \\ 0 & P \end{bmatrix} \tag{8D-3}$$

where

$$\begin{bmatrix} a_{w0} & a'_w \\ a_0 & A \end{bmatrix}$$

27. On this point, compare Hicks, *Capital and Growth*, p. 41, where he is discussing Adam Smith's model "Of the Accumulation of Capital, or of Productive and Unproductive Labour," *Wealth of Nations*, Cannan edition, London, Methuen, 1904, Book II, chapter 3.

28. This $\xi_j(t)$ notation is introduced for the convenience of the discussion of chapter 9; in this section it is largely ignored.

is the $(n + 1) \times (n + 1)$ matrix of Cobb-Douglas input elasticities with the first row referring to labor inputs and the first column to the consumption goods producing sector. Under these conditions to eliminate $\overline{L}_j(t)$ and $K_{ij}(t)$ in (a) the factor balance equations of expression (8D-1) and (b) the production functions themselves, one obtains the following set of primal and dual equations (in matrix notation)

$$w = a_{w0}x + a'_w(G + \delta)Pk$$

$$(R + \delta)Pk = a_0 x + A(G + \delta)Pk$$

$$0 = \ln V_0 + a_{w0}\{\ln w - \ln \xi_0\} + \{\ln p' + i'_n \ln(R + \delta)\}a_0 \quad (8\text{D-4})$$

and

$$\ln p' = \ln V' + a'_w\{(\ln w)I - \ln \xi\} + \{\ln p' + {}_ti'_n \ln(R + \delta)\}A$$

where we have used the conventions $y/\overline{L} = (G + \delta)k$, $y_0/\overline{L} = x$, and $p_0 = 1$, where $\ln \xi$ is an $n \times n$ diagonal matrix with the ξ_j's, $j = 1, \dots, n$, along the principal diagonal, and where $\ln V_0$ and $\ln V'$ contain constants of the form $\ln V_j = -(a_{wj} \ln a_{wj} + \sum_{i=1}^{n} a_{ij} \ln a_{ij})$, $j = 0, 1, \dots, n$.

To complete the system, one requires the set of n accumulation equations, the set of n own rate of interest equilibrium conditions embodying the "perfect foresight" assumption, and the savings–investment equation embodying the classical savings function, namely

$$\dot{k} = (G - \mu I)k, \quad -\dot{p}' = p'(R - rI) \quad \text{and} \quad s_r p'Rk = p'Gk \quad (8\text{D-5})$$

where μ is the growth rate of the labor supply and r is the overall profit rate. The complete set of Eqs. (8D-4) and (8D-5) constitute the formal Cobb-Douglas equivalents to Eqs. (7B-10), (7B-14), and (7B-17) of the Leontief dynamic system. For the Cobb-Douglas dynamic system, however, it should be obvious that the initial net investment allocation vector, $\dot{k}(0)$, cannot be determined from $k(0)$ until both $p'(0)$ and $\dot{p}'(0)$ are known; given the dual pricing equations, this requires one to postulate a set of initial price change expectations, $\dot{p}'(0)P(0)^{-1}$.[29]

The formal structure of the model has now been outlined. Some of its basic properties in the case in which there is no *differential* technological progress among sectors—which may be represented formally by the assumption that each and every $\xi_j(t)$, $j = 0, 1, \dots, n$, is equal to unity for all time t—can be described as follows. First, it can be shown[30] that a momentary equilibrium satisfying the Cobb-Douglas system (Eqs. 8D-4 and 8D-5) with positive prices and quan-

---

29. It turns out that only $n - 1$ initial price expectations are necessary. Indeed, if one were given n initial price expectations the system would be over-determined since the n-th initial price expectation may be derived from the other $n - 1$ via the savings–investment equilibrium condition. This is particularly evident in the one capital good case where no initial price expectations are necessary because there is no choice in the form that investment takes.

30. See F. H. Hahn, "Equilibrium Dynamics with Heterogeneous Capital Goods," pp. 638–640.

tities will exist for any given initial capital–labor ratios and any given initial price change expectations. Such an equilibrium may be represented by a point on an $n + 1$ dimensional factor-price frontier which relates the real wage rate, $w(t)$, to the net rates of return on each of the n types of capital goods, $r_i(t)$, $i = 1,\ldots,n$. This factor-price frontier has the form

$$\ln w = \{a_{w0} \ln \xi_0 - \ln V_0\} + \{a'_w \ln \xi - \ln V' - i'_n \ln (R + \delta)\}(I - A)^{-1}a_0 \quad \text{(8D-6)}$$

Notice that on the usual assumptions A is an indecomposable non-negative square matrix with all of its column sums less than unity (labor being required as an input in every productive sector). Thus, $I - A$ is a Leontief matrix so that $(I - A)^{-1}$ exists and is positive. It follows that the factor-price frontier defines $w(t) > 0$ as a continuous and differentiable function of $R(t)$ which is strictly monotonically decreasing in each of its arguments, $r_i(t)$, $i = 1,\ldots,n$. At any time t, this frontier specifies the maximal real wage rate that is achievable at each feasible configuration of net rates of return. Figure 8D-1 graphs the factor-price frontier for the case in which there are only two capital goods.

Second, momentary equilibrium need not be unique. Since non-uniqueness of momentary equilibrium at any point of time implies that the system may follow alternative trajectories from that time onwards so that the whole future path of the system is not unique, it is useful to specify a set of conditions which are sufficient for uniqueness. It is intuitively obvious that momentary equilibrium will be unique if the relative price, $p_i(t)$, $i = 1,\ldots,n$, of each and every capital good always increases as the wage rate, $w(t)$, increases, that is, if the consumption

Figure 8D-1 The factor-price frontier.

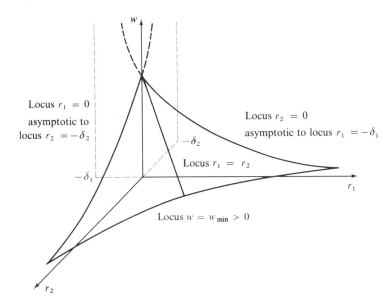

good is unambiguously the most capital intensive commodity, a generalized capital intensity condition. For in this case the relationships between $p(t)$ and $R(t)$, and thus between $k(t)$ and the net investment allocation vector $\dot{k}(t)$, are globally one for one. Substituting for $\ln w(t)$ from the consumption goods price equations into the capital goods pricing equations of (8D-5) and differentiating the resulting expression one has

$$\frac{dp'}{dw} P^{-1}(I + \hat{A}) + i'_n \frac{dR}{dw}(R + \delta)^{-1}\hat{A} = 0 \qquad (8\text{D-}7)$$

where $\hat{A} = a_{w0}^{-1} a_0 a'_w - A$. Now since it is known from the factor-price frontier that $w(t)$ is strictly monotonically decreasing in each $r_i(t)$, $i = 1,\ldots,n$, dR/dw is a diagonal matrix with strictly negative diagonal elements. It follows that dp'/dw will be strictly positive if $\hat{A}(I + \hat{A})^{-1}$ is a semi-positive matrix. Two alternative sufficiency conditions for this to be so are (a) that $I + \hat{A}^{-1}$ have a dominant positive diagonal and non-positive off-diagonal elements, thus being a Leontief matrix, and (b) that the production of the consumption good always uses at least as much of every capital good (and more of some) relative to labor as the production of every capital good uses, so that $\hat{A}$ is a semi-positive matrix. These two alternative sufficiency conditions are, of course, both pretty stringent, though both of them guarantee an unambiguously capital intensive consumption goods sector ($dp'/dw > 0$) and the uniqueness of momentary equilibrium.

Provided that a unique momentary equilibrium exists at every point of time along a warranted path of capital accumulation it is useful to consider the asymptotic properties of such a path. In particular, since it can easily be shown that in the absence of differential technological progress a unique steady-state solution with constant prices will exist, it may be asked whether or not a warranted path of capital accumulation from arbitrary initial conditions converges to a steady-state path asymptotically. That is to say, is a steady-state path with growth rate μ stable in the sense of equilibrium dynamics?

Now it has been shown by Hahn that the path traced out by the equilibrium dynamic system will diverge from the steady-state solution for a wide variety of initial conditions.[31] In general, therefore, the steady-state solution need not be stable. In particular, if dp'/dw is a strictly positive vector, the dual price system cannot be stable for non-zero initial price expectations, and the instability of the dual leads to instability of the primal. To illustrate the instability of the dual, from expression (8D-5) one has

$$-\{dp_i(t)/dw(t)\}\{dw(t)/dr_i(t)\}\{dr_i(t)/dt\} = -dp_i(t)/dt$$
$$= p_i(t)\{r_i(t) - r(t)\} \qquad (8\text{D-}8)$$

If $dp_i(t)/dw(t)$ is positive, while of necessity $dw(t)/dr_i(t)$ is negative, $dr_i(t)/dt$ must always take *the same sign* as $r_i(t) - r(t)$, all $i = 1,\ldots,n$, as long as $p_i(t)$ is positive.

31. *Ibid.*, pp. 642–644.

Hence, $r_i(t)$ will fall if it is less than $r(t)$ and rise if it exceeds $r(t)$. The continuation of such a process cannot lead all rates of return to converge on a common rate $r(t)$. It thus cannot lead to a constant price solution. Indeed, such a process may eventually lead to a situation in which some price(s) will become zero, at which point the dynamic equilibrium path ceases to be meaningful and the assumption of perfect foresight can no longer be maintained.[32]

On the other hand, if the system *is* allowed to remain on a constant price ray, then convergence to a steady-state must occur given the capital intensity condition that dp'/dw is strictly positive. For this same capital intensity condition also implies that dk/dx is strictly positive along any constant price ray.[33] But from expression (8D-5) one has

$$\{dk_i(t)/dx(t)\}\{dx(t)/dg_i(t)\}\{dg_i(t)/dt\} = dk_i(t)/dt$$
$$= k_i(t)\{g_i(t) - \mu\}$$

(8D-9)

Hence, if $dk_i(t)/dx(t)$ is positive, while of necessity along a constant price ray $dx(t)/dg_i(t)$ is negative, $dg_i(t)/dt$ must always take the *opposite sign* to $g_i(t) - \mu$, all $i = 1,\ldots,n$. Wherever $g_i(t)$ exceeds μ so that $k_i(t)$ is rising, $g_i(t)$ must fall towards μ, and wherever $g_i(t)$ falls short of μ so that $k_i(t)$ is falling, $g_i(t)$ must rise towards μ, for all $i = 1,\ldots,n$. The steady-state growth path of the output system on which all quantities grow at the rate μ must, in this case, be approached provided that prices can remain constant. Of course, if $r(t)$ must change in order that a steady-state be reached at $\mu = s_r r$, prices cannot remain constant.

The basic problem is that if the initial price expectations are given and assumed to be *realized* then there is nothing to ensure that these expectations, which (because of the perfect foresight assumption) govern the future course of the price system, are appropriately adjusted to the initial stocks in order for convergence to the steady-state solution to occur. Since it is the perfect foresight assumption that all expected capital gains become realized capital gains that is the cause of instability, this assumption might more appropriately be replaced by an assumption of zero foresight or static expectations whereby no capital gains or losses are expected.[34] Prices tomorrow are expected to be the same as prices today, and, if this expectation turns out to have been wrong, decision making units simply revise their expectations and expect the new prices to continue indefinitely. Expectations are then completely static or of unitary elasticity. If this alternative assumption is made, *anticipated* capital gains and losses are

---

32. See Shell and Stiglitz, "The Allocation of Investment in a Dynamic Economy," pp. 602–605, and the final section of this chapter.

33. This should be evident from the previous section of this chapter. Compare M. Bruno, "Fundamental Duality Relations in the Pure Theory of Capital and Growth," *Review of Economic Studies,* vol. 36, January 1969, pp. 50–52.

34. Of course, an adaptive expectations hypothesis would be most appropriate in this context, but to incorporate such an hypothesis would complicate the system seriously. See, for example, Burmeister and Graham, "Multi-sector Economic Models with Continuous Adaptive Expectations," pp. 323–336.

robbed of *any* causal significance in the economy. The own rate of interest equation is abandoned and all rates of return, $r_i(t)$, for $i = 1, \ldots, n$, are taken to be equal to the overall profit rate, $r(t)$, which is determined directly from the savings–investment condition, $g(t) = s_r r(t)$, where $g(t) = (p'Gk)/p'k$ may be defined to be overall growth rate of the capital stock. Prices move through time in an *ex post* manner in response to movements in $r(t)$, and hence, in response to the primal output system. On this assumption, both the primal and dual of the Cobb-Douglas dynamic system will normally be stable, converging to the unique steady-state solution dictated by the relation $\mu = s_r r$.[35] In particular, if dp'/dw is a strictly positive vector the whole Cobb-Douglas dynamic system must be stable on the zero foresight assumption.

Stability is also achieved if the assumption of perfect markets for old capital goods is replaced by the assumption that there are no markets for old capital goods so that the composition of investment depends only upon prospective rentals and not upon anticipated capital gains. In particular, if it is assumed that each type of capital good is owned by a group of firms whose rentals from ownership are either consumed or reinvested in the *same* type of capital good, then anticipated capital gains play no part at all in the allocation of investment. The direct positive association between expected capital gains and current outputs across the set of capital goods is replaced by a direct positive association between current rentals and current outputs across the set of capital goods, and the own rate of interest equilibrium conditions are replaced by a set of savings functions. Indeed, for a Cobb-Douglas model of this type, Burmeister, Dobell, and Kuga have shown that the steady-state solution is the asymptotic growth path followed by all dynamic equilibrium paths and is therefore globally stable.[36] Of course, the model is not particularly realistic since financial capital markets, on which ownership claims to collections of physical capital instruments are traded, may substitute for markets in the physical instruments themselves, thereby reintroducing the element of anticipated capital gains and losses. It is therefore evident that the assumption that expectations are completely static removes the speculative element in asset choice and therefore has effects which are similar to the assumption that capital markets are virtually non-existent. The analysis of technological progress in chapter 9 will proceed on the zero foresight or static expectations assumption rather than the alternative perfect foresight assumption with its associated instability problems.

E: SOME CONCLUDING REMARKS

According to Shell and Stiglitz (who have examined in detail the case in which all commodities are produced on the same Cobb-Douglas production function

35. It is possible to produce some counter-examples in those cases where factor intensities are perverse. See Hahn, "Some Adjustment Problems," pp. 14–15.

36. See Burmeister, Dobell, and Kuga, "A Note on the Global Stability of a Simple Model of Growth with Many Capital Goods," pp. 657–665.

so that $\hat{A}$ is a zero matrix), any path which does not converge to the steady-state solution will converge in finite time to a solution which implies a zero price for some capital good.[37] The possibility of a zero price is interesting since in the Cobb-Douglas case it implies that perfect foresight cannot be perpetually maintained on a path that does not lead to the steady-state solution. This can be shown as follows. Suppose that the dynamic equilibrium path of the Cobb-Douglas system would generate a zero price for a specific capital good in period T. Then, since rentals cannot be zero in the Cobb-Douglas case, a zero price for a capital good in period T would imply an infinite gross rate of return on that capital good. But the assumption that expectations are always realized implies that the possibility of an infinite gross rate of return in period T must have been anticipated in period T-1. This, in turn, implies a price for the capital good in period T-1 that takes this possibility into account and stops it from occurring. The price of the capital good in period T-1 is bid up so as to be high enough that the expected price change will not lead to a zero price in period T. But this "bidding up" of the price implies that the price of the capital good in period T-1 must be different from the price that was expected to rule in period T-1 when viewed from period T-2. In other words, any path that does not lead to the steady-state solution in the Cobb-Douglas dynamic model must eventually be inconsistent with the assumption of perfect foresight. Thus, it is not the strict positivity of the capital good price that can no longer be maintained, but rather the assumption of perfect foresight.

It is, therefore, possible to argue that the path followed by the Cobb-Douglas dynamic model on the postulate of short run or myopic perfect foresight from *given* initial stocks and *given* initial expectations is not a full dynamic equilibrium path; for there is nothing to ensure that the initial stocks are appropriate to the initial expectations, or *vice versa*. It may be that if they were constrained to be appropriate to each other the economy would follow a path that converges to the steady-state solution. By the same token, if initial expectations are appropriately adjusted to initial stocks the system would have a type of *double linkage*, and because of this it might be stable.

One way of ensuring that initial expectations are appropriately adjusted is to assume that the steady-state prices are known with certainty and are expected to rule after a finite period of time. Then expectations "all along the line" until the time when it is expected that the steady-state will be reached must be appropriately adjusted, and, in particular, initial expectations must be appropriately adjusted to a traverse that leads from the initial stock position to the steady-state. The path that would then be followed is equivalent to the intertemporally efficient path of an optimal capital accumulation program. Along an efficient path of capital accumulation the model is closed at each point of time by optimizing, rather than by postulating initial expectations as in the descriptive model, so that there is, therefore, no causal indeterminacy in prices. A "saddle point" solution is found to the primal and the dual systems simultaneously, and

37. Shell and Stiglitz, *op. cit.*, pp. 602–605.

the "tranversality conditions" (which imply that the own rate of interest equilibrium condition must hold at all points of time) determine the *appropriate* rates of change in capital goods prices.[38] As for the descriptive model, however, while convergence to the "saddle point" or steady-state solution may be achieved by making the economy behave as if it were optimizing over time, the fact that it does not necessarily behave in this manner, or, more specifically, that the initial price change expectations may be inappropriate, implies that it is the same "saddle point" property of long run competitive equilibrium that leads to instability.

It has therefore been argued that if the system acts as if the steady-state prices were known and expected to rule at some point in the future, it would behave in an intertemporally efficient way. The system would therefore aim for the steady-state prices. However, if initial expectations are not adjusted to initial stocks in a way that is appropriate to such "aiming," and if the system remains in dynamic equilibrium with short run (myopic) expectations being continuously realized, then the steady-state cannot be the asymptotic growth path of the equilibrium dynamic system. It follows that, at the very least, stability requires that initial price expectations must be appropriately adjusted to initial stock positions.

In summary, the question of the stability or instability of steady-state equilibrium depends upon both (a) the properties of the technology such as capital intensity conditions, and (b) the formation of price expectations. Equilibrium dynamic models with heterogeneous capital goods have instability properties that cast doubt upon the descriptive worth of models incorporating only a homogeneous capital substance, whether or not they have one, two, or more productive sectors. Indeed, in contrast to most capital-theoretic models with a single homogeneous capital substance, models with heterogeneous capital goods only asymptote to a steady-state solution if the system acts as if the steady-state price ray were known. That is to say, initial price expectations must be appropriate to a path of capital accumulation that leads from the initial capital stocks and initial prices towards the steady-state. However, there is no reason for arbitrary postulated expectations to have this property; the system is singly linked.

Although equilibrium dynamic systems with heterogeneous capital goods break down partly because their primal and dual relations are not coupled in *both* directions (apart from the savings relationship, the Leontief dynamic system is uncoupled, whereas the Cobb-Douglas dynamic system is unilaterally coupled), the major problem with them is their confinement to the straightjacket of their equilibria. Indeed, the main reason why the models that have been investigated herein break down is the assumption of dynamic equilibrium. For arbitrary but correct expectations lead to an arbitrary path of capital accumulation. If expectations were not constrained to be correct, let alone single valued for any one individual *and* across all individuals, the behavior of these models would be

---

38. Compare Samuelson, "Efficient Paths of Capital Accumulation in Terms of the Calculus of Variations," in Arrow, Karlin and Suppes, *op. cit.,* p. 82.

quite different. The exact realization of expected capital gains would not, in itself, virtually determine the whole course of the system. Without perfect foresight, the behavior of the dynamic system would still be analyzable in terms of mathematical models as long as the functions that explained how decision making units react to the unexpected could be kept simple enough. The simplest reaction or adjustment function, of course, postulates no adjustment at all. Indeed, it has already been indicated that if tomorrow's prices were always expected to be the same as today's prices, then both the primal and the dual would be stable (given reasonable substitutability and capital intensities that are not perverse)—that is, they would converge to steady-state equilibrium over time. Is, however, the assumption of static expectations any more legitimate than the assumption of perfect foresight? What happens if expectations are neither static nor constrained to be realized?

The introduction of the possibility of disequilibrium implies that the *ex post* equalization of yields from holding alternative capital assets must be abandoned. The fundamental own rate of interest equilibrium condition will continue to hold *ex ante* (as long as expectations remain single valued), but it will not necessarily hold *ex post* since expectations may be falsified..The consequential adjustments in both expectations and asset holding will generate a process of investment and disinvestment which will affect the relative outputs of the various productive sectors. Resource reallocation must occur. This resource reallocation is of fundamental importance to the process of economic growth. The speed at which institutions allow it to proceed governs the overall rate of economic growth in an actual economy. Since this resource reallocation is a process in which the primal system reacts to changes in the dual prices and the dual systems reacts to changes in the primal quantities, the study of the equilibrium behavior of doubly linked dynamic systems seems to be warranted. Some headway is made in this direction in later sections of this book. At the same time, the analysis takes a step towards reality.

NINE

TECHNOLOGICAL PROGRESS, TRADE, AND GROWTH

A : TECHNOLOGICAL PROGRESS AND CAPITAL TRANSMUTATION[1]

Although modern growth models stress that increases in labor productivity depend upon both capital accumulation and technological progress, recent multisectoral formulations of growth theory concentrate mainly on equilibrium paths of capital accumulation to the neglect of technological progress. This section outlines a method by which the impact of disembodied technological change on a multi-sectoral economy may be analyzed without excessive complication, even when this change is allowed to occur at different rates in different sectors. More precisely, differential technological progress of the Harrod-neutral form is introduced into the multisectoral Cobb-Douglas growth model of Sec. D of the previous chapter. The resulting changes in relative prices generate a process of investment and dis-investment, or capital transmutation, which alters the relative specification of the economy's capital stock vector.

Let it first be assumed that each $\xi_j(t)$, $j = 0, 1, \ldots, n$, is a continuous and differentiable function of time t with the properties

for
$$\xi_j(0) = 1, \quad \text{and} \quad \mathrm{d} \ln \xi_j(t)/\mathrm{d}t = \dot{\xi}_j(t)/\xi_j(t) \geq 0$$
$$t \geq 0, \quad \text{all} \quad j = 0, 1, \ldots, n \tag{9A-1}$$

Thus, the level of technology in each sector j is a positive non-decreasing function of time t, while the logarithmic derivative of this level at time t defines the rate of technological progress in sector j. The overall rate of (Harrod-neutral) technological progress in the economy at time t may be defined to be the rate of

---

1. As with Sec. D of chapter 8, certain portions of this section also appeared in my paper, "Multi-sectoral Growth and Technological Change," *Canadian Journal of Economics,* vol. 4, August 1971, pp. 299–313. I am indebted to the Canadian Journal of Economics and the University of Toronto Press for permission to quote these extracts herein.

growth of the real wage rate $w(t)$ that would occur if all rates of return $R(t)$ remained constant. This rate may be obtained from the equation of the factor-price frontier (Eq. 8D-6) which is repeated here as

$$\ln w = \{a_{w0} \ln \xi_0 - \ln V_0\} + \{a'_w \ln \xi - \ln V' - i'_n \ln (R + \delta)\}(I - A)^{-1}a_0 \quad (9A\text{-}2)$$

Thus, the overall rate of technological progress is

$$d \ln w(t)/dt = a_{w0} \, d \ln \xi_0(t)/dt + a'_w\{d \ln \xi(t)/dt\}(I - A)^{-1}a_0 \quad (9A\text{-}3)$$

Notice that this expression collapses to $d \ln w(t)/dt = d \ln \xi_0(t)/dt$ when there is a common Harrod-neutral rate of technological progress in every sector, including the consumption goods sector.[2]

The properties given in expression (9A-1) embody an assumption of "social memory." The stock of technological knowledge that is applied to production processes is assumed never to decline as time passes. It follows immediately that Harrod-neutral technological advances are global in nature, where a global improvement may be defined as one that shifts the factor-price frontier outwards over its whole range allowing a higher real wage rate at each given configuration of net rates of return. In terms of Fig. 8D-1, the factor-price frontier shifts upwards in the $w(t)$ direction at every feasible $r_1(t), r_2(t)$ combination. Although in more general technologies the exact form of the outward shift in the factor-price frontier will normally be fairly complicated, in the Cobb-Douglas case the factor-price frontier shifts outwards in the $w(t)$ direction *in a constant proportion* at every feasible $R(t)$ configuration. This is, however, simply a consequence of the log-separability of the Cobb-Douglas technology. In more general technologies, a constant proportional shift is not likely to occur except in the special case in which there is a common Harrod-neutral rate of technological progress in every sector at all points of time.

Consider, now, a situation in which all rates of return and capital stock growth rates remain constant (but are *not* necessarily equal). Such a situation may be defined as a "quasi-steady-state." The growth rate relationships of a "quasi-steady-state" may be obtained by differentiating the basic equations of the Cobb-Douglas dynamic system, Eq. (8D-4), with respect to time, holding G and R constant, to yield

$$d \ln w(t)/dt = a_{w0} \, d \ln \xi_0(t)/dt + a'_w\{d \ln \xi(t)/dt\}(I - A)^{-1}a_0$$

$$d \ln p'(t)/dt = i' \, d \ln w(t)/dt - a'_w\{d \ln \xi(t)/dt\}(I - A)^{-1}$$

$$d \ln k'(t)/dt = i' \, d \ln w(t)/dt - d \ln p'(t)/dt = a'_w\{d \ln \xi(t)/dt\}(I - A)^{-1}$$

and

$$d \ln x(t)/dt = d \ln w(t)/dt \quad (9A\text{-}4)$$

---

2. This follows from the assumption of constant returns to scale; that is to say

$$a'_w(I - A)^{-1}a_0 = i'a_0 = 1 - a_{w0}.$$

These "quasi-steady-state" relationships indicate that (a) the growth rate of the real wage rate, say θ where $\theta \equiv d \ln w(t)/dt$, is a weighted average of the rates of Harrod-neutral technological change in each sector, (b) the relative price of any particular capital good rises if the impact of rising wage rates more than offsets the direct and indirect cost reducing impact of technological change upon it, and falls if the opposite is true, (c) the *value* of the stock of every capital good contained in the vector Pk grows at the *same* rate θ, so that wherever an element of p' is rising the corresponding element of k is growing at a rate less than θ, and wherever an element of p' is falling the corresponding element of k is growing faster than θ, and (d) consumption per head and the real wage rate grow at the same rate, θ.

Except for the case in which technological change occurs only in the consumption goods producing sector ($d \ln \xi_0(t)/dt > 0$, $d \ln \xi(t)/dt = 0$) and the only effective change is a change in the numeraire, technological changes of the Harrod-neutral variety necessarily give rise to capital accumulation. Moreover, unless the pattern of technological change across productive sectors generates no substitution effects among the various capital goods, which could occur if there is no effect on their relative prices as in the case in which every $d \ln \xi_j(t)/dt$ is the *same* for every capital goods producing sector $j = 1, \ldots, n$,[3] the relative composition of the capital stock vector, k, must be changing. Since the proportions in which the various capital goods are held will normally be changing, capital reallocation may be said to occur along the process of adaptation to changes in technology.[4] Capital reallocation is thus a consequence of the substitution effects generated by uneven technical development across the various sectors of the economy. Fundamentally, therefore, we have identified one all important feature of technical improvements, namely, that through changes in relative prices technical improvements induce substitution effects which necessitate a process of capital transmutation and capital reallocation whereby the economy is adapted to the new technology. Capital is continuously being reinvested in more appropriate combinations of capital goods.

Although in the special Cobb-Douglas case there exists a "quasi-steady-state" (in which each element of the value capital stock vector, Pk, grows at a common rate, θ) even when technical improvements are unevenly spread across productive sectors, it should be evident from the preceding discussion that if technological progress is assumed to occur exponentially at a constant Harrod-neutral rate $m_j \geq 0$ in each sector so that $d \ln \xi_j(t) = m_j$, all $j = 0, 1, \ldots, n$, then a steady-state solution with constant prices cannot exist except in the very special case where the m_j's are identical for all $n + 1$ sectors. If, then, one is to study the effects of sectorally unbalanced Harrod-neutral technical progress while

---

3. It could also occur in an alternative technological context with fixed input coefficients.

4. Of course, the relative composition of the vector Pk remains unchanged, but this is a peculiarity associated with the Cobb-Douglas assumption of unitary substitution elasticities. With a more general technology, both k and Pk will ordinarily change their composition as technical improvements occur.

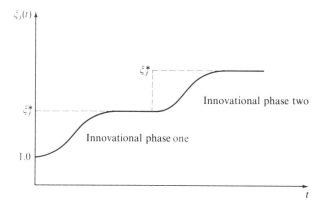

Figure 9A-1 A logistic functional form.

maintaining the rather useful notion of steady-state equilibrium, the somewhat unrealistic assumption that technical progress occurs exponentially must be abandoned.

Now there are certain continuous functional forms for technological progress which are compatible with at least the asymptotic existence of a steady-state solution. For example, if technological progress in each sector followed the logistic curve common to most diffusion processes, as illustrated (twice) in Fig. 9A-1, then an asymptotic steady-state would exist. Mathematically, this may be expressed by

$$\text{d} \ln \xi_j(t)/\text{d}t = \dot{\xi}_j(t)/\xi_j(t) = z_j\{\xi_j^* - \xi_j(t)\}/\xi_j^* \qquad j = 0, 1, \ldots, n$$

with solution   (9A-5)

$$\{\xi_j^* - \xi_j(t)\}/\xi_j(t) = \{[\xi_j^* - \xi_j(0)]/\xi_j(0)\}\, e^{-z_j t} \qquad j = 0, 1, \ldots, n$$

where the diffusion rate z_j is a positive constant and where $\xi_j^* \geq \xi_j(0) = 1$ is also a positive constant, or, more generally (as illustrated in Fig. 9A-1), a non-decreasing step function of time t. Moreover, there is some realism in this picture of sectoral technological progress as the following argument may suggest.

Suppose that it is asked whether a technical improvement is to be associated with (a) an invention, with (b) the first plan to utilize it or the innovation, with (c) the informational diffusion that ensues thereon in which others plan to utilize the invention or variations of it, or with (d) the process of capital transmutation that may be necessary to adapt the economy to the invention. By itself, an invention is not sufficient for a technical change, or a new combination of activities, to be introduced. Moreover, if mistakes can be made and reversed, neither is an innovation, for a reasonable degree of permanence for the new combination of activities may be assumed. On the other hand, if mistakes cannot be made (perfect foresight), innovation will be quickly followed by informational diffusion and the two will always be closely associated. It follows that (a) invention,

(b) innovation, and (c) informational diffusion can all be treated as component parts of the notion of a technical improvement.

Informational diffusion is, of course, a time consuming process. The effect of any particular improvement in a given productive sector is felt gradually as the number of production plants incorporating it expands. The number of production plants introducing the improvement at any particular point of time is, however, likely to follow some fairly regular distribution. Indeed, since it is largely a question of communication, informational diffusion must surely occur in the same sort of way as the spread of any communicable disease through a population. It is this feature which justifies the logistic functional form for each $\xi_j(t)$, though, of course, a further logistic form may follow at a later date as the productive sector responds to a second improvement—a possibility which obviously cannot be ruled out.

Whether or not an improvement must be embodied in new forms of capital goods its implementation will generally require a change in the specification of the economy's capital stock vector, that is some time consuming process of investment and disinvestment or capital transmutation, which may, of course, occur simultaneously with the process of informational diffusion. The difference between embodied and disembodied progress is simply whether or not the investment part of the process of capital transmutation is connected with the introduction of capital goods whose stock has always been held previously in zero quantities. (From the point of view of analysis this difference is, unfortunately, not so simple.) However, in either case, much the same sort of capital transmutation occurs along any non-steady dynamic equilibrium path, whether or not technical progress takes place. It can therefore be argued that in economic terms a technical improvement or a general shift in the state of technical knowledge must be indelibly associated with all three of (a) invention, (b) innovation, and (c) informational diffusion, but that (d) capital transmutation is a distinct but related process whether or not technical progress takes an embodied form.

One of the consequences of the above argument is that it suggests the following analytically convenient simplification.[5] Consider an economy in which innovations occur discontinuously as suggested by the ξ_j^* step functions. Suppose, moreover, that the gap between one innovational phase and the next is so long that the economy fully adjusts to one innovational phase before the next one is upon it. The economy is in an initial steady-state equilibrium at time $t = 0$ before the innovation occurs. A single isolated innovation occurs between time $t = 0$ and time $t = 0 + \varepsilon$, but a new steady-state equilibrium is attained before the subsequent innovation occurs. There is, in effect, only a single "once and for all" step in each step function ξ_j^*, $j = 0, 1, \ldots, n$, a step which occurs between time $t = 0$ and time $t = 0 + \varepsilon$ in all sectors, though it does not necessarily affect labor efficiency in all sectors proportionately.

The assumption of a classical savings function implies that the steady-state rate of profit, r, is uniquely determined by the constant natural rate of growth,

---

5. A similar simplification is made in Hicks, *Capital and Growth*, chapter 24, pp. 293–306.

μ, via the savings–investment relation, $\mu = s_r r$. Hence, if a new steady-state is to be approached after the single discrete innovation occurs, the rate of profit, $r(t)$, must eventually return to its initial steady-state value, r. This implies that the real wage rate must be higher in the new steady-state than in the old. However, in order that a new steady-state will eventually be reached, it must be assumed that the system is stable. One convenient way of ensuring that this is so is to assume (a) that expectations are completely static, and (b) that dp'/dw is a strictly positive vector. The first of these two assumptions implies that $r_i(t) = r(t)$, all $i = 1, \ldots, n$, so that all motion along the factor-price frontier, given $\xi_0(t)$ and $\xi(t)$, is in the single two-dimensional $r(t)$, $w(t)$ plane. The second of these two assumptions implies both uniqueness and stability in the zero foresight or static expectations case, with the consumption good being unambiguously the most capital intensive commodity.[6]

Now suppose for the moment that the process of informational diffusion occurs very quickly relative to the process of capital transmutation. Suppose, indeed, that informational diffusion is virtually instantaneous so that $z_j \to \infty$, all $j = 0, 1, \ldots, n$, and $\xi_j(0 + \varepsilon) \to \xi_j^*$. Then the two-dimensional factor-price frontier must shift outwards to the right between time $t = 0$ and time $t = 0 + \varepsilon$ as illustrated in Fig. 9A-2. This shift increases both the rate of profit $r(t)$ and the real wage rate $w(t)$ from the initial steady-state point on the old factor-price frontier, say r_1, w_1 in Fig. 9A-2, to a point such as r_2, w_2 on the new factor-price frontier. The motion from α to β represents this initial shift in factor prices. It therefore represents the effect of the informational diffusion associated with the technological change. But the economy cannot remain at the point r_2, w_2 since (given the assumptions made earlier) it must proceed to the new steady-state equilibrium point which is given as the point r_1, w_3 in Fig. 9A-2. Thus, the motion from β to γ along the new factor-price frontier represents the ensuing time consuming process of capital transmutation whereby the economy adapts its capital stock position to the technological improvement.

More realistically, however, if informational diffusion is allowed to take time, the shift in the factor-price frontier occurs gradually through time so that the complete motion from α to γ follows a path such as the dotted arc in Fig. 9A-2, thus smoothing out the kink at β. Nevertheless, it is still possible to keep the effects of informational diffusion conceptually separate from those of capital transmutation in any single innovational phase. The question remains, therefore, what happens to prices and quantities in this combined process of informational diffusion and capital transmutation? The answer to this question depends upon the analysis of equations of the form given in expression (9A-4).[7]

The main lessons to be learned are (a) that the traverse towards the new steady-state is associated with a *temporary* increase in both the rate of profit and the overall growth rate of the capital stock, (b) that the traverse is associated with a gradual but *permanent* increase in both the real wage rate and consumption

6. See Sec. D of the previous chapter.
7. For more detail, see Scarfe, "Multi-sectoral Growth and Technological Change," pp. 310–312.

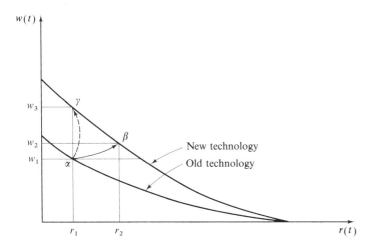

Figure 9A-2 Factor prices and technological change.

per head, (c) that eventually both the rate of profit and the capital stock growth rate must settle back to their initial values, and (d) that capital transmutation as well as accumulation will have occurred along the traverse in response to induced changes in relative prices.[8] The resulting trajectory is illustrated by the dotted arc from α to γ in Fig. 9A-2.

In summary, this section has been concerned with the introduction of technological progress into a multisectoral model of economic growth. The process of economic growth may be regarded as a process in which the real wage rate increases over time, where the real wage rate may be measured when there are many consumption goods in terms of some index number of consumption goods prices, such as a Divisia index. However, the process of economic growth is not simply a process of "capital deepening" or accumulation "along the production function" with a declining rate of profit. Fundamentally, capital accumulation occurs in response to increases in the rate of profit that are generated by technological improvements. Since improvements tend to increase the rate of return and accumulation tends to decrease it, a rising rate of return might be observed on average over a period of time in which the effects of technological improvements outstrip the effects of capital accumulation, while a falling rate of return might

8. These conclusions are similar to those of Hicks, *Capital and Growth*, pp. 300–304: "Every technical improvement implies a loss of capital: *capital being measured in terms of the consumption that has to be foregone in order that the productive power that is embodied in the physical instrument should be replaced* ... the rate of profit on new investment is raised, while the profit that is earned on past investment may be lowered. On our present formulation it is the profit on new investment which is *the* rate of profit; it is the value of the previously invested capital that must be marked down, when (as will often be the case) it is unable to earn an equal rate of profit on its historical cost.... The economy that is being analysed is always in a state of transition, losing 'capital' by improvements, and offsetting that loss by accumulation."

be observed on average over a period of time in which the effects of technological improvements are outstripped by the effects of capital accumulation. In a monetary economy, the first of these phases might be associated with inflationary periods and the second with deflationary periods or, given sticky money wages and prices, with Keynesian unemployment of both men and machines. In any case, insofar as the effects of technological improvements in increasing the rate of return are not spread randomly through time but are to some degree bunched, the process of growth may in fact follow a cyclical path, growth and cycles thus being intimately related.[9]

Finally, the "overall rate of economic growth" in an economy depends very strongly on its ability to introduce technological improvements, and on the responsiveness of capital accumulation to these technological improvements. It is not possible for the real wage rate in an economy to rise very rapidly unless both technological improvements and capital accumulation are occurring at a "reasonable pace." For without technological improvements, the rate of return and the pace of accumulation would fall, while without capital accumulation technological improvements of the Harrod-neutral type would simply tend to increase the rate of return. It follows that a very rapid increase in the real wage rate requires both the ability to introduce technological improvements and the ability to invest the resources required to transfer the initial effects of technological improvements on the rate of return into resultant effects on the real wage rate. Of course, whether or not technological progress is embodied in new forms of capital goods, it does not really fall as manna from heaven. Such progress can only be made by a process of investment: of experimentation, of toil, and of waiting.

B: TRADE, SPECIALIZATION, AND GROWTH[10]

In the previous section, we investigated the impact of sectorally different rates of technological progress on a multisectoral Cobb-Douglas model of economic growth. It was shown that even when technological change takes a once and for all form leading to a new steady-state (with the level of technology applied in each sector being allowed to follow a logistic functional form in common with

9. Compare J. A. Schumpeter, *The Theory of Economic Development*, New York, Oxford University Press, 1961.

10. Related references to this section include: H. Oniki and H. Uzawa, "Patterns of Trade and Investment in a Dynamic Model of International Trade," *Review of Economic Studies*, vol. 32, January 1965, pp. 15–38, P. A. Samuelson, "Equalization by Trade of the Interest Rate along with the Real Wage," pp. 32–52 in R. E. Caves (ed.), *Trade, Growth, and the Balance of Payments*, Amsterdam, North-Holland, 1965, R. E. Baldwin, "The Role of Capital-Goods Trade in the Theory of International Trade," *American Economic Review*, vol. 56, September 1966, pp. 841–848, J. E. Stiglitz, "Factor Price Equalization in a Dynamic Economy," *Journal of Political Economy*, vol. 78, May/June 1970, pp. 456–488, and A. V. Deardorff, "The Gains from Trade in and out of Steady-State Growth," *Oxford Economic Papers*, vol. 25, July 1973, pp. 173–191.

many diffusion processes), the steady-state configurations of capital stocks, relative prices, real wages, and consumption per head are altered from their previous values. The transition to a new steady-state involves a process of capital re-allocation which transfers the initial increase in the rate of return into a resultant increase in the real wage rate. In the remaining sections of this chapter, a similar model is opened up to international trade in order to explore the interactions between capital accumulation and comparative advantage in a world of techno-logical change. The basic features of the model are (a) that sectoral production functions are different among trading economies, but are allowed to shift through time, and (b) that capital goods are heterogeneous commodities, but are not necessarily all tradeable. More specifically, sectoral production functions are allowed to differ between countries in a Harrod-neutral or labor augmenting fashion; through time, however, these differences are allowed to increase or decrease, thereby introducing the phenomena of technological divergence and technological convergence. Also more specifically, physical capital is treated as a non-primary, non-homogeneous, and augmentable factor of production rather than as a primary, homogeneous, and non-augmentable factor of production as in traditional models of international trade.

The purpose of this section is to explore in an introductory way some of the consequences of opening up a multisectoral growth model to international trade. Three problems spring to mind immediately. The first of these concerns the tradeability of capital goods, the second concerns the omission of land as a second primary factor, and the third concerns the prospect of complete specializa-tion. These problems will be discussed briefly in turn.

In most models of international trade, labor is assumed to be internationally immobile; in keeping with this assumption, it would be quite reasonable to assume that existing stocks of capital goods are not tradeable once investment in them by a given country has occurred. Only those capital goods which are newly produced at time t could then be traded internationally at time t. Under this assumption, gross investment in *each* type of capital good by each country would be non-negative at all points of time. In order for this to be so, however, it is necessary to ensure that a country's net exports of each type of capital good cannot exceed its current output of that good. Unfortunately, this assumption cannot be incorporated directly into an open economy version of the model we have been discussing, since there are no reasonable criteria that could be introduced to ensure that this must be the case in momentary equilibrium.[11] The reason for this is that in order to avoid problems arising from joint production (and, in particular, the consequential loss of the non-substitution theorem), depreciation has been assumed to follow the pattern of "exponential decay," a force of mortality

11. Of course, it is possible to rig up savings assumptions (such as those suggested by Burmeister, Dobell, and Kuga, *op. cit.*, pp. 657–665) which force this result because there are no markets for old capital goods. But these savings assumptions will also be incompatible with the existence of capital markets in general, and with the international mobility of financial capital in particular. On this point, see Secs. D and E of the previous chapter.

which is independent of age. Since this assumption implies that new and old capital goods are indistinguishable (as long as technical progress is not embodied in new forms of capital goods), it is impossible to confine trade to newly produced capital goods.

Too much significance should not, however, be attached to this problem. In the first place, not all types of capital goods need be tradeable, whether new or old; non-tradeable "buildings" may be distinguished from tradeable "machines." In the second place, as long as the various economies save more than they invest abroad, overall gross investment in each economy must be non-negative even if it is not non-negative in every type of capital good; in particular, this will be the case if all economies save and no international capital flows occur. Finally, in *steady-state* equilibrium (if such an equilibrium exists) this problem does not arise since, if all capital stocks grow in proportion, gross investment in each type of capital good must be positive.

The model which is being opened up to international trade incorporates the Ricardian assumption of a single primary factor of production, labor. All aspects of land and geography are omitted from the determination of comparative advantages. Of course, a trading world without geography is not particularly plausible. This is especially so if it is assumed that the various trading economies have identical underlying technologies; for it is possible to conceive of geographical differences being simulated by technological differences. As Samuelson has pointed out for trading models with a single primary factor and a collection of non-primary or capital inputs whose usage is associated with a common rate of return, "When I push the Heckscher-Ohlin axioms all the way, we come full circle back to a *uniform* Ricardian world. To break the circle and return to the real world, which does involve geography, we must, as Bertil Ohlin long ago insisted, study the uneven endowment of primary factors that does characterize the only globe we yet know."[12] Alternatively, for trade in manufactured goods at least, one may drop the crucial uniformity axiom of the Heckscher-Ohlin model and allow trade to depend upon Ricardian technological differences rather than Heckscher-Ohlinian capital–labor ratios.

---

12. Samuelson, "Equalization by Trade of the Interest Rate along with the Real Wage," p. 52. See also E. F. Heckscher, "The Effect of Foreign Trade on the Distribution of Income," pp. 272–300 in H. S. Ellis and L. A. Metzler (eds.), *Readings in the Theory of International Trade*, London, Allen and Unwin, 1950, B. Ohlin, *Interregional and International Trade*, Cambridge, Harvard University Press, 1933, and J. Viner, *Studies in the Theory of International Trade*, New York, Harper, 1937, p. 503, footnote 3: "I venture the guess, moreover, that the relative abundance of natural resources as compared to all other factors taken together has been in the past and continues to be to-day, a much more important element of determining the nature of international specialisation than the relative abundance of capital as compared to labour." But this still leaves open the question as to the determination of the pattern of trade in manufactured products, and, as Hicks has suggested, "the comparative advantages of industrialised countries have a complex origin, and are not to be reduced into any very simple terms. Though the attempt to express them in terms of capital–labour ratios has not been *proved* to be a failure, it does not look like being a great success." J. R. Hicks, *International Trade: The Long View*, Cairo, National Bank of Egypt, 1963, p. 13.

The inclusion of land as a second primary factor would lead to important modifications of the analysis. In particular, it would reduce the possibility (which will become apparent) of equilibrium solutions implying either no trade or complete specialization. The possibility of complete specialization has some important implications for both (a) the relationship between $w(t)$ and $r(t)$, and (b) the choice of technique. In a closed or non-specialized economy with a given state of technology, the real wage rate, $w(t)$, is a strictly monotonically decreasing function of the rate of profit, $r(t)$.[13] This functional relationship, which cannot shift unless there is an underlying shift in the state of technology, is known as the factor-price frontier. Moreover, since the system has precisely one degree of freedom remaining after the specification of a numeraire, all relative prices are uniquely determined once the rate of profit, $r(t)$, is given. Indeed, for a closed or non-specialized economy with a given rate of profit, equilibrium prices including the real wage rate cannot change unless the underlying state of technology changes. Thus, as long as $r(t)$ remains constant there can be no substitution effects and the technique of production chosen in equilibrium cannot change. This result, which depends upon the four assumptions of (a) constant returns to scale, (b) no joint production, (c) a single primary factor, and (d) a fixed rate of profit, is known as the dynamic non-substitution theorem.[14]

The factor-price frontier is, of course, constructed on the assumption that all the cost functions are binding as equations and, as long as they remain so, its position cannot shift. It follows that if an economy does not specialize in trading equilibrium it must remain on its no-trade factor-price frontier (though, of course, the impact of trade will normally induce a movement along this frontier). When complete specialization occurs and a particular cost function becomes an inequality (with price less than unit cost), some combinations of $w(t)$ and $r(t)$ to the north-east of the no-trade (and non-specialized) factor-price frontier become attainable. At a given rate of profit, the economy is able to operate at a higher real wage rate than would be possible without trade and specialization. However, the actual point to the north-east of the no-trade factor-price frontier at which the economy operates is not, in general, uniquely determined by the domestic rate of profit. The reason for this is that there is no reason for the price of the "non-competing" import to be uniquely determined by the domestic rate of profit. The appearance of this price in the dual equations introduces an extra degree of freedom into them. Indeed, for each type of non-competing import, an extra degree of freedom will normally be added to the dual equations in a similar fashion. The factor-price frontier no longer remains a simple two-dimensional relationship between the wage rate and the rate of profit.

From the point of view of the non-substitution theorem, however, it is important to distinguish the effect of complete specialization away from the numeraire consumption good from the effect of complete specialization away

---

13. It should be remembered that we are proceeding on the zero foresight assumption that no capital gains and losses are anticipated, and $R(t) = r(t)I_n$.

14. For more detail, see chapter 7, Sec. C.

from a particular capital good. For although the occurrence of non-competing imports of the numeraire consumption good will increase the real wage rate at any given rate of profit, it cannot affect the *relative* prices of productive inputs or the choice of technique. In terms of the consumption good as numeraire, the prices of all capital goods simply rise in the same proportion as the real wage rate. Given $r(t)$, the non-substitution theorem is unaffected by this change. However, suppose that the economy imports all of its current requirements for gross investment purposes of a particular capital good. This capital good is then a non-competing import and, in effect, its capital balance equation will normally act as if it were a balance equation for a *second primary factor*, an input which is not produced within the economy in question. Although this capital good will have to earn the same rate of profit as domestically produced capital goods, the rental that it earns will depend upon its price. This price constitutes an additional influence on the choice of technique since, in general, it is not uniquely determined by the domestic rate of profit. Indeed, in order for this to occur it would be necessary for there to be a unique one for one relationship between the domestic profit rate and foreign profit rates so that, given the domestic rate of profit, the price of the non-competing capital good import is uniquely determined. It is, however, precisely such a relationship that specialization and lack of factor-price equalization rules out. Thus, a specialized economy importing non-competing capital goods no longer acts as if labor were the only primary factor of production. The non-substitution theorem loses its general validity and $w(t)$ is no longer uniquely determined by $r(t)$, though, generally speaking, in the *complete* trading system it will still be uniquely determined.

Direct relationships between foreign and domestic profit rates can, however, be reinstated by allowing for the international mobility of financial capital in response to differences in rates of return, finance generally moving from the country with the lower profit rate to the country with the higher profit rate. It is useful to constrain the responsiveness of foreign lending and borrowing to differential rates of return in such a way that net investment is always non-negative in any economy. So constrained, net foreign investment is never so large as to result in the running down of the value of the economy's capital stock. Within these bounds, it may be assumed that there are no transfer problems associated with international capital mobility; the balance of trade accommodates itself to the financial flows that occur on both the capital account and the debt service account. Finally, in so far as trade is unable to equalize rates of return among the trading economies the remaining differentials will tend to be partially (but not necessarily wholly) eliminated by the process of international capital mobility. This mobility is, however, a totally distinct phenomenon from the international exchange of physical capital goods. In the following discussion (and until Sec. D of this chapter), we abstract from international capital mobility in order to concentrate on patterns of trade and growth in a dynamic framework.

In the remainder of this section, patterns of trade and growth are discussed in a two country context. It is assumed that the two economies, alpha (α) and beta (β), have identical underlying technologies, the standard Heckscher-Ohlinian assumption. This brief preliminary excursion serves as a stepping stone to the more extensive discussion, in the following section, of trade and growth when the two economies have different underlying technologies, the standard Ricardian assumption. In both sections, it will often be useful to make the simplifying assumption that there are only two capital goods, "buildings" (commodity 2) which are assumed to be non-tradeable, and "machines" (commodity 1) which, along with consumption goods (commodity 0) are assumed to be tradeable. In this "machines-buildings" model, it will always be assumed that there is an unambiguous capital intensity ordering of commodities, with consumption goods being the most capital intensive commodity (the relative capital intensity ordering of the two capital goods being rather inessential in the following analysis). A sufficient condition for this to be so is that the production of the consumption good always use at least as much of both capital goods (and more of some) relative to labor as the production of both capital goods uses, so that the 2×2 matrix of Cobb-Douglas input elasticity differences, $\hat{A} = a_{w0}^{-1} a_0 a_w' - A$, is a semi-positive matrix.[15]

Before proceeding to examine trade patterns in a world of similar technologies, it will be useful to categorize certain types of steady-state solutions. We begin by ruling out one class of steady-state, a *degenerate* one, by the assumption of identical labor force growth rates in alpha and beta. For, if the effective labor force growth rates differ, the only "steady-state" that can possibly exist is a degenerate one in which the economy with the higher growth rate becomes so large relative to the slower growing economy that this latter economy becomes completely dominated and insignificant in the two-country world. The faster growing economy approaches its closed steady-state solution and dictates the terms of trade, while the slower growing economy is likely to become completely specialized. This assumption does not, of course, imply that alpha and beta have equal overall growth rates out of steady-state equilibrium.

Among the remaining *non-degenerate* cases, there are basically two types, which may be denoted as (a) Ricardian steady-states in which rates of profit would be equal even if no trade were occurring, and (b) Wicksellian steady-states, or steady-states in which rates of profit would not be equal if no trade were occurring. An important question that arises in the context of Wicksellian steady-states is, therefore, whether or not trade is able to equalize rates of profit. In the classical savings function case (where all savings come from profits), where these two classes of non-degenerate steady-states dichotomize according to whether alpha and beta have (a) the same, or (b) different, savings propensities, it will be shown that trade cannot equalize profit rates in Wicksellian steady-state equilibrium. It is to be noted, however, that this conclusion does not necessarily hold in the alternative proportional savings function case.

If both economies have the same technology and the same effective labor force growth rate, then the characterization of the trading aspects of steady-state equilibrium depends only upon the savings assumptions. If the two economies have identical savings propensities (of either type), in steady-state equilibrium

---

15. On this point compare Sec. D of chapter 8.

they must be *uniform* economies which differ only in absolute size. In particular, they will have identical prices and individual capital good to labor ratios, from which it follows that they must have identical overall capital–labor ratios, $p'_\alpha k_\alpha$ and $p'_\beta k_\beta$. There will be no incentive for trade to occur in this Ricardian steady-state.

If the two economies have different classical savings propensities, in the ensuing Wicksellian steady-state equilibrium the rate of profit must differ from one economy to the other. Factor-price equalization is precluded, and (given an unambiguous capital intensity ordering of any two tradeable commodities) at least one of the two economies must specialize in steady-state equilibrium. Indeed, the two economies cannot commonly produce any pair of tradeable commodities whose relative price moves strictly monotonically with the rate of profit. As Samuelson has shown; "Now suppose that there are uniform differences in factor intensity, so that for some two goods that are simultaneously produced in both countries—say goods 1 and $2-p_1(r)/p_2(r) = p_{12}(r)$ is a monotone strictly increasing (or decreasing) function of r. *Then, the interest rate will be equalised by positive trade in those goods alone.*"[16] By the same token, if profit rates cannot be equalized by trade, any two tradeable goods whose relative price is a strictly monotonic function of the rate of profit cannot be simultaneously produced in both economies.

The reason why profit rates cannot be equalized is very simple. Since by assumption $g_\alpha = \mu = g_\beta$ in steady-state equilibrium, and since $g_\alpha = s_{r\alpha} r_\alpha$ and $g_\beta = s_{r\beta} r_\beta$, the assumption that $s_{r\alpha} \neq s_{r\beta}$ implies that r_α cannot be equal to r_β. Indeed, if the rate of profit is fixed by the effective labor force growth rate in steady-state equilibrium, then by the non-substitution theorem the steady-state transformation frontier is *linear* and shifts outwards in a parallel fashion with t, given a positive growth rate. A closed economy is normally at one point on this transformation frontier, the precise point depending upon the savings propensity. (As growth occurs and the transformation function shifts outwards in parallel fashion, this point moves out on a ray through the origin.) But when trade occurs between two economies with different classical savings functions, in steady-state equilibrium at least one economy must be specialized, for they have linear transformation functions with *different* slopes. A proper steady-state in which neither economy is specialized is impossible, for factor prices cannot be equalized. The only possible steady-state is a specialized or quasi-separable one.

The pattern of trade in a quasi-separable steady-state equilibrium depends upon Heckscher-Ohlinian considerations. That is to say, the economy with the higher (classical) savings propensity and the lower rate of profit exports the capital intensive commodity, namely consumption goods. Moreover, since at least one economy must specialize, the economy which exports the capital intensive commodity must also have (a) the higher machine–labor ratio, (b) the higher buildings–labor ratio, and (c) the higher relative price of buildings. Unambiguously, therefore,

---

16. Samuelson, "Equalisation by Trade of the Interest Rate along with the Real Wage," p. 49.

the economy with the higher savings propensity will have the higher aggregate capital–labor ratio, $p'k$. Thus, in this case, the standard Heckscher-Ohlinian conclusion that the economy with the higher capital–labor ratio will export the capital intensive commodity is borne out. This conclusion does not necessarily carry over to cases in which the consumption good is not unambiguously the most capital intensive commodity.

Having summarized the steady-state properties of the "machines-buildings" model, the analysis now turns to the trading properties of non-steady paths of trade and growth starting from an initial momentary equilibrium in which economy alpha has higher initial machine–labor and buildings–labor ratios than economy beta. Suppose, first, that the two economies have identical savings functions of either the classical or the proportional type. Then, since there can be no demand bias, economy alpha will export the capital intensive commodity, namely the consumption good. Provided that neither economy specializes in momentary equilibrium, factor prices, $w(t)$ and $r(t)$, will be equalized; in consequence, the price of the non-tradeable buildings will also be equalized. Whether or not factor prices are equalized, however, economy alpha will have the higher overall capital–labor ratio $(p'_\alpha k_\alpha > p'_\beta k_\beta)$, and Heckscher-Ohlinian conclusions again emerge. Of course, we have ruled out numerous perverse cases by our capital intensity and initial endowment assumptions.

Given our assumptions, it has now been established that (a) if savings functions differ, in steady-state equilibrium the economy with the higher overall capital–labor ratio will export the capital intensive commodity, and (b) if savings functions are the same, in an initial momentary equilibrium the economy with the higher overall capital–labor ratio will export the capital intensive commodity. What happens in an initial momentary equilibrium when savings propensities are allowed to differ? The answer to this question depends upon the interaction of the differences in initial endowment ratios and the difference in savings propensities. The basic rule is that if the savings propensity difference (the demand bias) and the differences in initial endowment ratios when taken separately predict the same pattern of trade, the trade pattern is determinate. Otherwise, that is when the separate effects go in opposite directions, it is not. This, of course, reflects the usual Heckscher-Ohlinian possibility that a country with a demand bias towards the commodity which uses intensively its relatively abundant factor may in fact import this commodity. In the present context, it leads to the possibility that trade reversal will occur along a dynamic path of trade and accumulation.

Along a dynamic path of trade and accumulation that leads to the steady-state solution, the overall growth rates of the capital stock in both economies will be continuously changing. It is apparent, however, that the process of trade in capital goods ("machines") in itself alters the path of capital accumulation from that which would be followed by either economy if it were closed. As time passes, transformation frontiers are continuously being altered by the joint process of trade and growth. Capital accumulation and comparative advantage are thus seen to be interdependent elements in the complete dynamic process.

C: TECHNOLOGICAL DIFFERENCES AND TRADE PATTERNS

In the present section, the pattern of international trade between economies whose underlying technologies are different is studied. As before, it is assumed that there are two countries, alpha (α) and beta (β). Technological differences between economy alpha and economy beta are assumed to take the Harrod-neutral form, but these differences are not normally assumed to affect all sectors proportionately. Indeed, if between the two economies there were a common Harrod-neutral technological difference across *all* productive sectors at time t, then technological differences would have no effect whatsoever on trade patterns. Given unambiguous capital intensity orderings and no offsetting demand effects, if trade occurred it would simply follow the Heckscher-Ohlin theorem. Simply, technological differences at any time t must have an effect on relative prices if they are to have an effect on the pattern of trade.

Let it be assumed that economy alpha and economy beta are initially in steady-state equilibrium at time t. The technology used by economy alpha is such that $\xi_{j\alpha}(t) = 1$, all $j = 0, 1, \ldots, n$, whereas the technology used by economy beta is such that at least some of the $\xi_{j\beta}(t)$'s, $j = 0, 1, \ldots, n$, differ from unity. This formulation allows the alpha technology to be used as a standard of reference to which the beta technology may be directly compared. Indeed, the size of the initial *technological gap* between beta and alpha in the production of commodity j at time t may be defined by $\ln \xi_{j\beta}(t) - \ln \xi_{j\alpha}(t) = \ln \xi_{j\beta}(t)$ for $j = 0, 1, \ldots, n$, which may be either positive or negative. In the present section, it is assumed that no differential technological changes take place at all so that $\xi_{j\alpha}(t)$ and $\xi_{j\beta}(t)$, all $j = 0, 1, \ldots, n$ remain constant at all points of time. The effects of technological differences are simply of concern herein.

Consider, then, an initial steady-state equilibrium in which economy alpha and economy beta have identical natural rates of growth. This assumption insures that the steady-state equilibrium will be a non-degenerate one in the sense used in the previous section. Given this assumption, which eliminates degenerate cases, the remaining non-degenerate steady-state solutions may be divided into two basic classes depending upon whether the rate of profit in economy beta, r_β, would be (a) the same as, or (b) different from, the rate of profit in economy alpha, r_α, if both economies were closed. These two basic classes of steady-states may be denoted by the following terminology: (a) steady-states in which rates of profit would be equal even if no trade were occurring, or in which $r_\alpha = r_\beta$, may be called Ricardian steady-states, and (b) steady-states in which rates of profit would not be equal if no trade were occurring, or in which $r_\alpha \neq r_\beta$, may be called Wicksellian steady-states.

In the classical savings function case, these two classes of non-degenerate steady-states dichotomize according to whether alpha and beta have (a) the same or (b) different savings propensities (out of profits). In the proportional savings function case, the relationship between savings propensities (out of "income") and the classification of steady-states is not quite so simple. More specifically, since the spectrum of relative prices will normally differ between alpha and beta if they are taken to be closed economies, it is unlikely that their rates of profit will be the same even if their proportional savings propensities are identical. It follows that the Ricardian steady-state case, *par excellence,* is the classical savings function case when the two economies have the same classical savings propensities. For in this case steady-state equilibrium implies that r_α and r_β are not only constant but also equal for all $t \geq 0$, regardless as to whether alpha and beta are open or closed.

Of the two classes of non-degenerate steady-states, the Ricardian class is much more easily analyzed with respect to trade patterns than is the Wicksellian class. The reason for this is that in the Wicksellian steady-state Ricardian elements in the determination of trade patterns are confounded with Heckscher-Ohlinian elements, whereas in the Ricardian steady-state for the most part they are not. Consequently, in this section, patterns of trade generated by the Ricardian class of steady-state solution will be analyzed prior to the consideration of those generated by the Wicksellian class of steady-state. In discussing the Ricardian class of steady-state, it will be assumed that the two economies have the same classical savings propensities.

As long as all commodities are tradeable, trade patterns in a Ricardian steady-state depend directly on the configuration of Harrod-neutral technological differences embodied in $\ln \xi_{j\beta}(t)$, $j = 0, 1, \ldots, n$. That is to say, it will normally be the case that the two economies will specialize in the production of commodities in which they have a relative efficiency advantage in the Harrod-neutral sense. If the set of commodities, $j = 0, 1, \ldots, n$, all tradeable, are ranked according to the corresponding efficiency parameters of economy beta, $\xi_{j\beta}(t)$, $j = 0, 1, \ldots, n$, then economy beta will be observed to export a spectrum of products for which the corresponding $\xi_{j\beta}(t)$ parameters are relatively large, and to import a spectrum of products for which the corresponding $\xi_{j\beta}(t)$ parameters are relatively small, the exact dividing line between the spectrum of beta's exportables and the spectrum of beta's importables depending upon "reciprocal demands" and balance of payments considerations. Hence, if all commodities are tradeable, each of economy beta's exports will have a larger $\xi_{j\beta}(t)$ than each of its imports.

It is implied by the assertions of the previous paragraph that standard Ricardian conclusions apply to trade patterns when the trading economies have identical (pre-trade and post-trade) profit rates but technologies that differ in a Harrod-neutral way. In particular, it should be noted that if trade occurs at least one of the two economies must specialize, thus achieving a higher real wage rate (in terms of the consumption good as numeraire) at its steady-state profit rate than would be possible if the economy remained closed. On the other hand, in the special case where the Harrod-neutral technological differences between economy alpha and economy beta affect all sectors proportionately, so that $\ln \xi_{j\beta}(t) = m$, all $j = 0, 1, \ldots, n$, where m is a simple scalar, there will be no incentive for trade at all. In this special case, all relative commodity prices are equal in the two economies without trade occurring. Of course, the more advanced economy

(economy beta if $m > 0$, and economy alpha if $m < 0$) will have the higher real wage rate.[17]

In the "machines–buildings" model, an additional feature is added in the form of a non-tradeable capital good. "Buildings" (commodity two) are assumed to be non-tradeable. In consequence, the price of buildings will generally differ between the two economies and this difference in the price of a capital good input may have an effect on the pattern of trade. Indeed, whenever a non-tradeable capital good is produced at a different relative level of efficiency in the Harrod-neutral sense in the two economies, there is likely to be an effect on trade patterns.

Consider, then, the case in which $\xi_{0\beta}(t) = \xi_{1\beta}(t) = 1$ and $\xi_{2\beta}(t) \neq 1$. In particular, let $\xi_{2\beta}(t) > 1$ so that economy beta has a Harrod-neutral technological advantage in the production of buildings and a lower relative price of buildings in terms of the consumption good as numeraire. Then, economy beta will export the consumption good and import machines if for both economies at the given steady-state profit rate the buildings/labor input coefficient ratio in the production of consumption goods exceeds the buildings/labor input coefficient ratio in the production of machines. On the other hand, with $\xi_{2\beta}(t) < 1$, so that economy beta has a Harrod-neutral technological disadvantage in the production . of buildings and a higher relative price of buildings, economy beta will export machines and import consumption goods if the buildings/labor ratio in the production of consumption goods exceeds the buildings/labor ratio in the production of machines.

In more general cases of the "machines–buildings" model in Ricardian steady-state equilibrium, however, $\xi_{0\beta}(t) \neq \xi_{1\beta}(t)$. There are then two pieces to consider in the determination of the pattern of comparative advantages and trade. For the indirect effect on trade patterns through $\xi_{2\beta}(t)$ may either reinforce or counteract the direct effect through $\xi_{0\beta}(t)$ and $\xi_{1\beta}(t)$. For example, suppose that $\xi_{0\beta}(t) > \xi_{1\beta}(t) > \xi_{2\beta}(t)$. Then, the direct effect suggests that beta should export the consumption good and import machines. The indirect effect suggests that (a) beta should export the consumption good if machines are "building intensive" relative to consumption goods (that is, if machines have a higher buildings/labor input coefficient ratio than consumption goods), and that (b) beta should export machines if consumption goods are "building intensive" relative to machines. If (a) is the case, then beta will export the consumption good, since the direct and indirect effects reinforce one another. On the other hand, if (b) is the case, then the pattern of trade is ambiguous, since the direct and indirect effects offset or counteract each other. Indeed, it is even possible for there to be no incentive for trade at all.

---

17. In terms of a two sectoral model with a single homogeneous capital good, for example, the following may be said of the Ricardian steady-state case. Economy beta will export the consumption good (commodity 0) and import the capital good (commodity 1) if $\xi_{0\beta}(t) > \xi_{1\beta}(t)$. It will export the capital good and import the consumption good if $\xi_{0\beta}(t) < \xi_{1\beta}(t)$. In both these cases, either alpha or beta or both must be specialized, but if one economy does not specialize it receives no gains from trade. Finally, no trade will take place if $\xi_{0\beta}(t) = \xi_{1\beta}(t)$.

In Ricardian steady-state equilibrium, the rate of profit is identical in the two economies. In general, however, the wage rate (in terms of the consumption good as numeraire) will not be identical in alpha and beta. It is worth while at this point to consider the effects of trade on the real wage rate in a Ricardian steady-state. The first point to be noted is that if a country does not specialize it must remain on its no-trade or non-specialized factor-price frontier at the point determined by its steady-state profit rate. For such a country, there is no change in the real wage rate from a closed or non-trading situation to an open or trading situation, and there are no gains from trade. In order to achieve a higher real wage rate at its steady-state profit rate, a country must specialize. The fact that trade and specialization allow an economy to attain certain points to the north-east of its no-trade factor-price frontier in a similar manner to technological progress (including, as we shall see, technological convergence or borrowing) indicates the vital importance of international trade as a substitute for expensive domestic production in a world of Ricardian technological differences. The second point to be noted is that, whereas the pattern of trade in Ricardian steady-state equilibrium is determined by the relative sizes of the $\xi_{j\beta}(t)$'s, the level of the real wage rate in economy beta relative to economy alpha is determined by the absolute sizes of the $\xi_{j\beta}(t)$'s in relation to unity (given $\xi_{j\alpha}(t) = 1$, all $j = 0, 1, \ldots, n$), in conjunction with the pattern of specialization. It follows that in certain circumstances trade and specialization act as a substitute for technological borrowing; what appears to be a technological gap for a closed economy ceases to be relevant for an open economy which specializes *away from* a commodity in which it possesses a comparative (and absolute) disadvantage. Of course, in the "machines–buildings" model a technological disadvantage in the production of the non-tradeable "buildings" cannot be circumvented simply by trade and specialization.

The determination of the pattern of trade in the Ricardian class of steady-state equilibria has now been discussed in some detail. The effect of technological differences and associated patterns of trade and specialization on relative real wage rates has also been explored. Attention is now turned to the determination of the pattern of trade in the Wicksellian class of steady-state equilibria. In the Wicksellian case, it is assumed that pre-trade profit rates would differ from alpha to beta. One situation in which this is so is the case in which the two economies have the same natural rates of growth but different savings propensities of the classical type. In this case, pre-trade and post-trade profit rates are the same in a given economy. It is, therefore, impossible for trade to equalize profit rates in alpha and beta. On the other hand, the Wicksellian case can also arise with proportional savings functions. In this case, it is possible, but by no means likely, that trade will equalize profit rates in alpha and beta.

In Wicksellian steady-states, one has two features to contend with in the determination of the pattern of trade, first the Harrod-neutral technological differences (including differences in the production of non-tradeable capital goods) generating Ricardian trading patterns, and, second, the capital intensity differences from commodity to commodity generating Heckscher-Ohlinian trading patterns.

These two features may either reinforce or counteract each other in the determination of the pattern of specialization and trade. It might therefore be expected that certain cases give unambiguous predictions of the direction of trade, while others (the majority) do not.

In the "machines–buildings" model, the determination of the pattern of trade in Wicksellian steady-state equilibrium requires that the Heckscher-Ohlinian effect must be considered in conjunction with the combination of (a) the direct Ricardian effect working through $\ln \xi_{0\beta}(t)$ and $\ln \xi_{1\beta}(t)$, or the technological differences in the production of tradeable consumption goods and machines, and (b) the indirect Ricardian effect working through $\ln \xi_{2\beta}(t)$, or the technological difference in the production of non-tradeable buildings. In the ensuing analysis of this model, it should be remembered that the sufficiency condition for the consumption good to be the most capital intensive commodity implies that the production of the consumption good requires at least as high a buildings/labor input coefficient ratio as the production of machines.

Suppose, then, that without trade economy beta would have the higher profit rate. Then, the Heckscher-Ohlinian effect suggests that beta should export the labor intensive tradeable, namely machines, and import consumption goods. This can be reinforced by the direct Ricardian effect if $\xi_{0\beta}(t) < \xi_{1\beta}(t)$. It can also be reinforced by the indirect Ricardian effect if $\xi_{2\beta}(t) < \xi_{0\beta}(t)$. However, the Heckscher-Ohlinian effect is offset by the direct Ricardian effect if $\xi_{0\beta}(t) > \xi_{1\beta}(t)$, as well as by the indirect Ricardian effect if $\xi_{2\beta}(t) > \xi_{0\beta}(t)$. On the other hand, suppose that without trade economy beta would have the lower profit rate. Then, the Heckscher-Ohlinian effect suggests that beta should export the capital intensive tradeable, namely consumption goods, and import machines. This can be reinforced by the direct Ricardian effect if $\xi_{0\beta}(t) > \xi_{1\beta}(t)$. It can also be reinforced by the indirect Ricardian effect if $\xi_{2\beta}(t) > \xi_{0\beta}(t)$. However, the Heckscher-Ohlinian effect is offset by the direct Ricardian effect if $\xi_{0\beta}(t) < \xi_{1\beta}(t)$, as well as by the indirect Ricardian effect if $\xi_{2\beta}(t) < \xi_{0\beta}(t)$. It is, therefore, fairly apparent that in the majority of cases, and in most of those not considered in detail herein, the pattern of trade will be ambiguous.

Finally, if trade occurs in Wicksellian steady-state equilibrium, specialization by at least one economy will generally be implied. At least one economy will generally be able to attain a point to the north-east of its no trade and non-specialized factor-price frontier. It is, however, extremely unlikely that both profit rate equalization and equalization of real wage rates will occur through trade. Insofar as profit rates remain unequal in trading equilibrium, there will be an incentive for international financial capital flows to occur.

In summary, it may be said that if (a) Ricardian technological differences do not vary much from sector to sector, and (b) pre-trade profit rates differ considerably, then the Heckscher-Ohlinian effects will tend to be dominant. On the other hand, if Ricardian technological differences vary substantially from sector to sector, and (b) pre-trade profit rates do not differ very markedly, then the Ricardian effects (direct and indirect) will tend to be dominant. Indeed, the following possibility may be considered. Suppose that trade cannot by itself equalize profit rates (as in a non-degenerate steady-state in which alpha and beta have different classical savings propensities). In this case, financial capital flows in response to existing profit rate differentials may occur. Trade is, of course, required in order to effect the real transfer of resources which is called for by these financial capital flows. If capital flows tend to reduce profit rate differentials between countries, then trade may be said to facilitate partial profit rate equalization indirectly, even though its direct effect may not be to do so. If this trade is based primarily on Ricardian technological differences, then through its effect of facilitating capital mobility and partial profit rate equalization it may be said to reduce further the importance of the Heckscher-Ohlinian component in the explanation of trade patterns in manufactured products. In any case, international trade in a world of Ricardian technological differences will not normally equalize either the real wage rate or the rate of return on capital investment across the set of trading economies. A tendency towards equalization of the real wage rate and the rate of return generally requires the joint occurrence of both (a) technological convergence, and (b) international capital mobility.

D: THE PROCESS OF TECHNOLOGICAL CONVERGENCE

In the previous section, trade patterns have been discussed in the case in which the trading economies have different but stationary technologies. In this section technological progress is reintroduced and particular attention is paid to the notion of technological convergence. It will be seen that technological improvements generally have a tendency to alter the pattern of comparative advantages not only through their immediate direct effects on relative prices but also through their induced effects on the pattern of capital accumulation. In consequence, the pattern of trade, and probably the volume of trade as well, will undergo some alterations as technological improvements occur. Comparative advantage is neither a simple nor a stationary phenomenon. Its underlying multisectoral foundations are both complex and gradually changing.

In general terms, technological convergence may be said to occur whenever the underlying technology of a "less advanced economy" becomes more similar to that of a "more advanced economy" through a process of technological diffusion. The factor-price frontier of the "less advanced economy" moves closer to the factor-price frontier of the "more advanced economy" as time passes. The purpose of this section is to study the implications of technological convergence in more detail. That it is a potentially important process is illustrated by reference to some "stylized facts" related to patterns of trade and growth in the postwar period.

Recent empirical research related to (a) the explanation of observed differences in postwar growth rates among advanced Western economies, and (b) the explanation of observed changes in the pattern of international trade among advanced Western economies in the postwar period, seems to suggest the following broad generalization, namely, that it is difficult, if not impossible, to explain either the differences in growth rates or the changes in trade patterns if one starts from the supposition that, sector by sector, these economies employ the same average levels of technological know-how at any given point of time. When the production function in any given productive sector is defined in terms of the *average degree* of application of technological knowledge to production processes within the sector, this production function will generally be observed to differ from one economy to another. But these differences in sectoral production functions (or technological leads and lags) among advanced Western economies do not remain unchanged through time. Indeed, the effects generated by intertemporal changes in these sectoral differences are, in combination, largely responsible for the observed differences in overall rates of economic growth and for the observed changes in broad trading patterns.

This broad generalization suggests that the comparative advantage positions underlying the international exchange of manufactured products cannot be explained adequately by the capital–labor ratio version of the Heckscher-Ohlin theorem. This observation is supported not only by much of the literature surrounding the well known Leontief scarce factor paradox but also by the fact that it is patently misleading to treat physical capital as a primary, homogeneous, and non-augmentable factor of production. Fundamentally, the comparative advantage positions underlying the exchange of manufactured products are largely *acquired* through the combined processes of technological change and capital accumulation. These processes are at the same time responsible for the determination of overall rates of economic growth. Moreover, just as comparative advantage positions can be acquired they can also be lost as the application of technological knowledge becomes more widely diffused among trading economies. While an original innovation may lead to a short term or medium term technological advantage, the ensuing diffusion process tends to reduce this advantage. Such a diffusion process may be called *technological convergence*.

The process of technological convergence involves the diffusion of the usage of "best-practice techniques"[18] across the various producers of a particular commodity, in whichever countries these producers are located. This diffusion process normally implies some degree of "anti-import bias"[19] in the pattern of productivity improvements introduced by countries which are, on the whole, importers of new techniques of production, and makes it progressively more difficult for a country which is largely an exporter of new productive techniques to continue exporting relatively large quantities of commodities in the production of which it initially possesses a comparative cost advantage.

The reason for this is as follows. Consider a world of m industrialized countries, with each country possessing n broad productive sectors. These sectors

18. The term "best practice techniques" is borrowed from W. E. G. Salter, *Productivity and Technical Change*, Cambridge, Cambridge University Press, 1960.

19. For a useful summary of the literature on "anti-import biased" productivity improvements see Gerald M. Meier, *International Trade and Development*, New York, Harper and Row, 1963, chapters 2 and 3.

each embody some degree of aggregation not only across commodity outputs but also across "best-practice" through "worst-practice" techniques. The *average degree* of application of technological knowledge to production processes within any particular sector will, however, generally differ from one country to the next. It is convenient to assume that these differences in production functions take a simple Harrod-neutral, labor augmenting, or Ricardian form. In such a world, trade patterns are largely determined by the configuration of Ricardian differences in labor efficiency parameters across the corresponding production functions in the various countries.

While trade patterns depend upon the configuration of Ricardian differences in sectoral labor efficiency parameters, *changes* in trade patterns depend upon the intertemporal *shifts* in these parameters. If these shifts were simply taken to be exogenous, there would be little more to be said. However, while the intertemporal shifts in the labor efficiency of the "best practice" technique used in the m country-specific sectors in a given industrial class may be taken to be exogenous, the intertemporal shifts in the labor efficiency of the actual techniques used may not be. Let $\xi_j^*(t)$, $j = 1,\ldots,n$, represent the labor efficiency parameter of the "best practice" technique for the m sectors in industrial class j, and let it be taken to be exogenous. Let $\xi_{ij}(t)$, $i = 1,\ldots,m$, $j = 1,\ldots,n$, represent the labor efficiency parameter of the actual average technique for sector j in country i. Let it then be supposed that the differential growth rate of each labor efficiency parameter is proportional to the technological gap behind the "best-practice" technique used in the given industrial class, when this gap is itself measured as a proportion. Thus, one may write

$$\text{d} \ln \xi_{ij}(t)/\text{d}t - \text{d} \ln \xi_j^*(t)/\text{d}t = z_{ij}\{\xi_j^*(t) - \xi_{ij}(t)\}/\xi_j^*(t) \quad i = 1,\ldots,m, \quad j = 1,\ldots,n$$

with solution

$$\{\xi_j^*(t) - \xi_{ij}(t)\}/\xi_{ij}(t) = \{[\xi_j^*(0) - \xi_{ij}(0)]/\xi_{ij}(0)\}\ e^{-z_{ij}t} \tag{9D-1}$$

where z_{ij} is the response proportion or diffusion rate for sector j in country i. It is implied by this equation that technological diffusion follows a logistic functional form.[20]

For lack of direct evidence to the contrary, let it be assumed that z_{ij} is equal to the product $z_i z_j$ with z_i being the "country specific" component of z_{ij} and z_j being the "sector-specific" component of z_{ij}. Thus, there are no "comparative advantages" in diffusion rates, z_{ij}. The ratios of the z_{ij}'s across the $i = 1,\ldots,m$ countries for any pair of sectors are identical, implying also that the ratios of the z_{ij}'s across the $j = 1,\ldots,n$ sectors for any pair of countries are identical. If this were in fact the case, the logistic functional form would imply that technological diffusion always has a tendency to be biased against imports since labor efficiency would grow relatively fastest in the relatively least advanced sector of an economy

---

20. The rationale behind the assumption that technological diffusion follows a logistic functional form is discussed in Sec. A of this chapter. In that section, we assumed that d $\ln \xi_j^*(t)/\text{d}t = 0$ in every sector; for present purposes this seems unnecessarily restrictive.

adapting to "best-practice" techniques. Moreover, if the z_{ij}'s are not very different from country to country, this diffusion process would imply technological convergence. Thus, as a central proposition, one may suppose that technological convergence makes it progressively more difficult for countries to continue exporting relatively large quantities of manufactured commodities in those industrial classes in which they initially possess a comparative advantage. Just as the comparative advantage positions underlying the exchange of manufactured products are largely *acquired* through the combined processes of technological change and capital accumulation, they can also be lost as the application of technological knowledge becomes more widely diffused among trading economies.

In addition to this, it has been shown in Sec. A of this chapter that an economy adapting to labor augmenting technological improvements experiences not only a higher capital stock growth rate but also a higher rate of profit than an economy in which no such improvements are occurring, given that the economies have similar savings functions. Indeed, it is the higher rate of profit which induces the capital accumulation necessary to transfer the initial effects of technological change on the rate of profit into resultant effects on the real wage rate. On the same reasoning, economies growing rapidly through the reduction of an existing productivity gap will experience higher rates of profit and higher rates of capital accumulation than a slower growing economy with a higher level of productivity. If long term direct foreign investment responds to relative profit rates, capital will flow from a slower growing more advanced economy to faster growing less advanced economies, this flow tending to equalize profit rates among the countries under consideration.

The logic of our discussion so far suggests that the process of technological convergence or "catching up" is capable of explaining in large part not only the observed differences in postwar growth rates among advanced Western economies but also the observed changes in the pattern of international trade among advanced Western economies in the postwar period. The fact is that if there exists a productivity gap between Europe and the United States that is at least partly explicable by the degree of application of knowledge to economic processes, then by borrowing existing technologies from the United States the growth rate of European labor productivity can be sustained for some period of time at a higher level than the growth rate of US labor productivity. This difference in growth rates is enhanced if the relative rates of capital accumulation are such that European capital–labor ratios rise towards US capital–labor ratios, a fact that is statistically confirmed in the postwar period for several European countries, particularly those that have experienced the fastest growth rates in labor productivity. The ability to close at least that part of an initial labor productivity gap that is not explained by natural resources and geography facilitates a higher relative growth rate of labor productivity in Europe. Moreover, as has previously been argued, it also facilitates a convergence in broadly defined comparative cost positions (implying as it does a somewhat "anti-import biased" pattern of productivity improvements in countries which are, on the whole, importers of new technologies), and induces a flow of long term direct foreign investment to these same countries from the technological leader, namely the United States. The connections between technological convergence, capital mobility, and the considerable swing in the payments fortunes of the United States of America in the postwar period are discussed briefly in chapter 13 of this book.[21]

In summary, the interactions of capital accumulation and comparative advantage are inseparably intertwined with the processes of technological change. As far as international trade in manufactured goods is concerned, if quantities of productive factors grow at different rates—and particularly if capital, with its diversity of form and function, its varying and dated embodied techniques, and its versatility as both a complement to and a substitute for other productive factors, continues to grow—then no long run statement of comparative costs seems possible at all. We are left with the inferences that are possible from the fact of natural resource positions, and those that are possible from the fact and inheritance of history, but little else despite Heckscher, Ohlin, and Samuelson and all the other perpetuators of general equilibrium analysis. Until more is known of the empirical intricacies affecting the changing pattern of technological leads and lags across productive sectors in various trading countries, one cannot really hope to develop a complete and appropriate theory of capital accumulation and comparative advantage.

21. Some empirical support for the hypothesis that broad patterns of production costs and commodity consumption have been converging in the postwar period can be found, for example, in E. F. Denison, *Why Growth Rates Differ*, Washington, Brookings, 1967, especially pp. 235–261. As incomes expanded in Europe in the postwar period, increased consumption was concentrated on commodities such as automobiles and consumers' durables because of the high income elasticities associated with these commodities. However, these commodities were also those that sold at relatively high prices (in comparison with the United States) in the immediate postwar period. The increase in demand for them ushered in the use of new methods of mass production which were available in the United States and only needed to be borrowed by Europe when incomes and demand started to rise.

THE INFLATION PROBLEM

TEN

THE PRICE LEVEL:
A POST-KEYNESIAN SYNTHESIS

A: AGGREGATE SUPPLY AND DEMAND

The fix-price dynamic models and the equilibrium dynamic models presented in Parts One and Two of this book have one fundamental feature in common. In both cases, neither demand nor the composition of demand has a direct impact on prices. Fix-price models ignore the repercussions of demand fluctuations on prices; they therefore make greatest sense in a world in which money wage rates are roughly constant, though, as we shall see, even here there are difficulties. In these models, prices are usually taken to be exogenous and the price-quantity nexus is *uncoupled*. When there is no choice of technique, equilibrium dynamic models also possess an uncoupled price-quantity nexus; quantities do not appear as arguments in the price equations because constant returns to scale are all pervading, and prices do not appear as arguments in the quantity equations because the possibility of choosing among alternative techniques of production is assumed not to exist. Most equilibrium dynamic models are, however, *unilaterally coupled*, since prices appear directly in the quantity equations through the choice of productive techniques. On the other hand, quantities do not appear directly in the price equations because of the assumption of constant returns to scale. Indeed, in these models the only way in which quantity movements can affect prices is indirectly through savings considerations and variations in the rate of profit. Of course, since the assumption of constant returns to scale (when coupled with a given technology, no joint products, a single primary factor — labor — and a constant rate of profit) gives rise to the non-substitution theorem, both prices and technical input-output coefficients will remain unchanged if the rate of profit is constant. In consequence, unilaterally coupled systems behave much like uncoupled systems whenever the non-substitution theorem holds.

If one is concerned with the construction of macrodynamic systems which are capable not only of providing an analysis of the proper role of prices in a dynamic economy but also of modelling the process of inflation, neither fix-price nor equilibrium dynamic models are appropriate or adequate for the task.

It is necessary to go back to the drawing board and build a new dynamic in which demand does have a direct impact on prices. From this reconstruction emerges a variety of flex-price dynamics which is *bilaterally coupled* in the sense that quantities appear as arguments of the price equations and prices appear as arguments of the quantity equations.

The purpose of Part Three of this book is to build up a number of bilaterally coupled flex-price systems step by step, borrowing wherever necessary from the analysis of the previous chapters. Before proceeding with explicitly dynamic formulations, however, the first two sections of this chapter summarize the familiar *static* post-Keynesian model of the price level in an open economy under both fixed and flexible exchange rates (with passing reference to the closed economy case). This summary is intended to serve as a background against which the explicitly dynamic formulations of the following chapters may be studied. It also allows us to address two basic questions. First, to what extent can any small open economy be insulated from foreign inflationary pressures by exchange rate appreciation? Second, to the extent that such insulation is possible, in what circumstances would such a strategy be desirable? The discussion of these two basic questions will carry us well into the analytical sections of the final three chapters to this book. The answers to them will be seen to depend upon both (a) "terms of trade effects," or (more broadly) which commodity prices are inflating and at what rates, and (b) "transmission mechanisms" or (more broadly) how labor, commodity, money, and exchange markets are supposed to work.

To fix ideas, let us begin by exploring the equilibrium properties of a *short run* model of the post-Keynesian or neo-classical synthesis variety in which these four markets are included. The variables are

Endogenous

y = aggregate domestic output in real terms
r = domestic nominal interest rate
P = price of aggregate domestic output
z = relative price or "terms of trade" variable

either

M = nominal money supply (fixed exchange rate model only)

or

π = exchange rate, given as the foreign price of domestic currency, (flexible exchange rate model only)
B/P = overall balance of payments surplus in real terms
L = level of employment
W = nominal wage rate

Exogenous

y_f = aggregate foreign output in real terms
r_f = foreign nominal interest rate

P_f = price of foreign produced commodities

g = government expenditure in real terms

γ = "cost push" shift parameter on supply side of labor market

either

M = nominal money supply (flexible exchange rate model only)

or

π = exchange rate (fixed exchange rate model only).

In order to proceed with the derivation of the aggregate supply relationship, we begin by postulating the existence of a simple aggregate neo-classical production function of the form

$$y = f(L) \quad \text{with} \quad f_L > 0 \quad \text{and} \quad f_{LL} < 0 \tag{10A-1}$$

associated with which is a demand side money wage rate of the form $W = P \cdot f_L$ (the value marginal product of labor). The supply side money wage rate may be written as $W = G\{P \cdot h(z), L, \gamma\}$, the partial derivatives of which are all assumed to be non-negative. The labor market equilibrium condition may therefore be written as

$$P \cdot f_L = W = G\{P \cdot h(z), L, \gamma\} \tag{10A-2}$$

Within this relationship, the expression $P \cdot h(z)$ requires further explanation. $P \cdot h(z)$ refers to the "price of domestic absorption" or the *consumer price index*. It is constructed in the following way. Let $z \equiv P_f/\pi P$ be the price of foreign produced commodities relative to the price of domestic output when both prices are expressed in terms of a similar currency, and let the function $h(z)$ be homogeneous of degree $1 - a$ in z, where $0 < a \leq 1$ is the weight of *domestic output prices* in the consumer price index. Thus,

$$P \cdot h(z) = (P_f/\pi)^{1-a} P^a \quad \text{and} \quad h(z) = (P_f/\pi P)^{1-a} \quad \text{with} \quad z = P_f/\pi P \tag{10A-3}$$

The consumer price index is therefore a (geometrically) weighted average of foreign prices expressed in domestic currency and the price of domestic output. $P \cdot h(z)$ increases relative to P whenever the terms of trade deteriorate ($z = P_f/\pi P$ increases), whereas $P \cdot h(z)$ decreases relative to P whenever the terms of trade improve ($z = P_f/\pi P$ decreases). Thus, the *prices affecting the two sides of the labor market are different and vary in relationship to each other whenever the terms of trade variable, z, changes.* Firms producing final goods and services are interested in the price of domestic output, whereas households supplying labor services are interested in the consumer price index.

Implicit in the labor market equilibrium condition is the economy's aggregate supply curve. This curve is an upward sloping (and possibly vertical) relationship in y, P space, as illustrated by the solid line(s) in Fig. 10A-1. Its slope may be obtained by totally differentiating the labor market equilibrium condition,

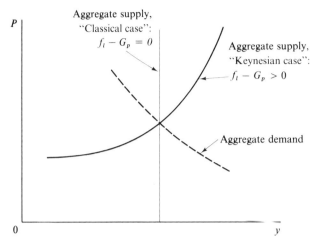

Figure 10A-1 Aggregate supply and demand curves.

and using the differential version of the production function, $dy = f_L\,dL$, to replace dL by $f_L^{-1}\,dy$. Thus, one has ·

$$f_L^{-1}(Pf_{LL} - G_L)dy + (f_L - G_P)dP - G_h h_z\,dz = G_y\,dy$$

where $\qquad\qquad\qquad\qquad\qquad\qquad\qquad\qquad\qquad\qquad$ (10A-4)

$$f_L > 0, \quad f_{LL} < 0, \quad G_P \geq 0, \quad G_h \geq 0, \quad G_L > 0, \quad G_y > 0 \quad \text{and} \quad h_z > 0$$

If both dz and dy are zero, it follows quite clearly that

$$dy/dP = -(f_L - G_P)f_L/(Pf_{LL} - G_L) \geq 0$$

since $f_L^{-1}(Pf_{LL} - G_L)$ is definitely negative and $f_L - G_P$ is at least zero, as we shall explain.

The size of $f_L - G_P$ depends upon the degree of money illusion on the supply side of the labor market, as measured by the elasticity of W with respect to the consumer price index, $Ph(z)$. If z is constant, this elasticity has the simple form $\varepsilon_W \equiv G_P \cdot P/W$. Thus, one may write $f_L - G_P = (1 - \varepsilon_W)W/P$. With either complete money illusion ($\varepsilon_W = 0$) or partial money illusion ($0 < \varepsilon_W < 1$), it is evident that $f_L - G_P > 0$, whereas with no money illusion ($\varepsilon_W = 1$) one has $f_L - G_P = 0$. It follows that if there exists any money illusion on the supply side of the labor market, the aggregate supply schedule is upward sloping. It is vertical only in the case in which no money illusion exists. In the following analysis, all those labor market cases in which the aggregate supply schedule is upward sloping are labelled "Keynesian,"[1] while the case of a vertical aggregate supply schedule is labelled "classical." Finally, it should be clear from expression (10A-4) that an increase (decrease) in either z or y will shift the aggregate supply

---

1. The "Keynesian" label can also include the case of rigid money wage rates.

curve to the left (right) so that lower (higher) levels of real domestic output are associated with given domestic output prices.

On the demand side of the model, the commodity market equilibrium condition may be written in real terms as

$$y = c\{\hat{y} - t(\hat{y})\} + i(r) + g + x(z, y_f) - zm(z, y) \tag{10A 5}$$

where (a) consumption $c\{\hat{y} - t(\hat{y})\}$ is an increasing function of disposable income, $\hat{y} - t(\hat{y})$, with marginal propensity to consume, $0 < c < 1$, (b) disposable income is the difference between national income $\hat{y}$ and tax revenue $t(\hat{y})$, with marginal propensity to tax $0 < t < 1$, (c) real national income $\hat{y} \equiv y/h(z)$ is equal to the market value of domestic output, Py, *divided by* the price of domestic absorption $Ph(z)$ so that the fundamental accounting identity is $Py \equiv Ph(z) \cdot y/h(z)$, (d) investment $i(r)$ is a decreasing function of the rate of interest so that $i_r < 0$, (e) government expenditure, g, is exogenous, (f) the quantity of exports, x, is positively related to both z and y_f so that $x_z > 0$, $x_{yf} > 0$, and (g) the quantity of imports, m, *whose value in terms of real domestic output is $z \cdot m$*, is negatively related to z and positively related to y, so that $m_z < 0$ and $m_y > 0$. Two assumptions are made about the relative sizes of parameters. First, it is assumed that the denominator of the traditional multiplier, $1 - c(1 - t) + zm_y$, is positive. Thus, if real domestic income increases by one dollar, induced consumption expenditure rises by less than one dollar since there are positive net leakages from the circular flow of income and expenditure. Second, it is assumed (for the moment) that the Marshall-Lerner condition is satisfied, namely that $x_z - zm_z - m$ is positive.[2] Thus, the trade balance in real terms, $x(z, y_f) - z \cdot m(z, y)$, improves whenever foreign produced commodities become relatively more expensive (that is, whenever z increases).

The money market equilibrium condition may be written as

$$M = Pl(y, r) \quad \text{with} \quad l_y > 0, \quad l_r < 0 \tag{10A-6}$$

The demand for real balances, $l(y, r)$, is equal to the supply of nominal balances, M, divided by the price of domestic output, P. Although $M = Ph(z)l\{y/h(z), r\}$ might be considered to be a more appropriate version of the money market equilibrium condition, it is evident that the two versions are equivalent if the real income elasticity of the demand for money is equal to unity. It is not difficult to show that the elimination of the rate of interest across Eqs. (10A-5) and (10A-6) yields a downward sloping (and possibly vertical) relationship in y, P space called the aggregate demand schedule, as illustrated by the broken curve in Fig. 10A-1. This curve shifts to the right (left) whenever g or y_f increase (decrease). This curve will also shift to the right (left) whenever the nominal money supply increases (decreases), provided that one is not in a liquidity trap situation with $l_r = -\infty$ or a completely interest inelastic investment situation

---

2. It is easy to see that $x_z - zm_z - m > 0$ is the Marshall-Lerner condition since $(z/x)x_z = |\eta_x|$, and $-(z/m)m_z = |\eta_m|$, where η_x and η_m are the foreign demand elasticity for exports and the domestic demand elasticity for imports, respectively. Thus, $x_z - zm_z - m = |\eta_x|x/z + \{|\eta_m| - 1\}m = m\{|\eta_x| + |\eta_m| - 1\} > 0$ if trade is initially balanced with $zm = x$. On this point, compare footnote 12 (chapter 3).

with $i_r = 0$; in both these latter cases, the aggregate demand schedule is vertical. Finally, given the Marshall-Lerner elasticity condition, it may also shift to the right (left) whenever domestic production becomes relatively more (less) competitive, that is whenever z increases (decreases); however, this effect may be partly, wholly, or more than offset by the effect of changes in z on the level of real consumption. Thus, the direct impact of the relative price variable on the aggregate demand schedule is unclear. However, it will be assumed for the moment that the offsetting consumption effects are small enough to leave $x_z - zm_z - m + c(1 - t)\hat{y}_h h_z > 0$ where $\hat{y}_h < 0$ and $h_z > 0$, so that the aggregate demand schedule shifts to the right (left) when z increases (decreases). This may be called the *extended* Marshall-Lerner condition.

Finally, the balance of payments or exchange market equation may be written as

$$B/P = x(z, y_f) - zm(z, y) + F(r, r_f) = 0 \qquad (10A\text{-}7)$$

where $x(z, y_f) - zm(z, y)$ is the trade balance in real terms as before, again (for the moment) with $x_z - zm_z - m > 0$, and where $F(r, r_f)$ is the real capital inflow function, with $F_r > 0$ and $F_{r_f} < 0$. Under flexible exchange rates, equilibrium ($B/P = 0$) is brought about by movements in π, whereas under fixed exchange rates it is assumed that reserve changes are *not* sterilized and the money supply adjusts in the usual Humean fashion to keep the balance of payments in equilibrium (see chapter 3, Sec. A). For example, if B were temporarily positive, M would expand, and if B were temporarily negative, M would contract. Thus, we are looking at the situation *after* the Humean adjustment process has worked itself out.

B: FIXED AND FLEXIBLE EXCHANGE RATES AGAIN

The comparative statics analysis of the model outlined in the previous section proceeds as follows. We begin with the *fixed* exchange rate case in which the money supply, M, is an endogenous variable and the exchange rate, π, is exogenous. Totally differentiating the model under *fixed* exchange rate assumptions, one obtains (after eliminating L, W, and B/P)

Labor	$(Pf_{LL} - G_L)/f_L$	0	$f_L - G_P$	$-G_h h_z$	0
Commodity	$-\{1 - c(1 - t) + zm_y\}$	i_r	0	$x_z - zm_z - m$ $+ c(1 - t)\hat{y}_h h_z$	0
Money	Pl_y	Pl_r	M/P	0	-1
Definition	0	0	z/P	1	0
Foreign exchange	$-zm_y$	F_r	0	$x_z - zm_z - m$	0

$$\begin{bmatrix} dy \\ dr \\ dP \\ dz \\ dM \end{bmatrix} = \begin{bmatrix} 0 & 0 & 0 & 0 & G_\gamma & 0 \\ -x_{y_f} & 0 & 0 & -1 & 0 & 0 \\ 0 & 0 & 0 & 0 & 0 & 0 \\ 0 & 0 & z/P_f & 0 & 0 & -z/\pi \\ -x_{y_f} & -F_{r_f} & 0 & 0 & 0 & 0 \end{bmatrix} \begin{bmatrix} dy_f \\ dr_f \\ dP_f \\ dg \\ d\gamma \\ d\pi \end{bmatrix} \qquad \text{(10B-1)}$$

Given the extended Marshall-Lerner condition, the determinant of the 5×5 matrix on the lefthand side is *negative*, and the sign pattern of *total* derivatives is

	dy_f	dr_f	dP_f K	dP_f C	dg	$d\gamma$	$d\pi$ K	$d\pi$ C
dy	+	−	+	0	+	−	−	0
dr	−	+	−	0	+	+	+	0
dP	+	−	+	+	+	+	−	−
dz	−	+	+	0	−	−	−	0
dM	+	−	+	+	?	?	−	−

$$\text{(10B-2)}$$

where K stands for the "Keynesian" case with some degree of money illusion in the labor market and $f_L - G_P > 0$, and C stands for the "classical" case with no money illusion in the labor market and $f_L - G_P = 0$. It is possible to sign certain ambiguous cases (marked "?" in expression 10B-2) if stronger assumptions are made. In particular, dM/dg and $dM/d\gamma$ are both *negative* if the BF curve is steeper than the LM curve, and *positive* if the reverse is true (that is, if capital flows are very interest elastic).

In the *classical* case, the 3×3 upper lefthand corner matrix of the *closed economy* model in y, r, and P becomes triangular, and the system decomposes in such a way that changes in y are determined in the labor market, changes in r are determined in the commodity market (given the predetermined changes in y), and changes in P are determined in the money market (given the predetermined changes in y and r). Of course, the *Keynesian* closed economy model does not decompose in this way, though other decompositions can be obtained if $i_r = 0$, $l_r = -\infty$, or $l_r = 0$. Indeed, in the interest inelastic investment ($i_r = 0$) and liquidity trap ($l_r = -\infty$) cases, changes in y are determined in the commodity market, changes in r (if they occur) are determined in the money market (given, if necessary, the predetermined changes in y), and changes in P are determined in the labor market (given, once again, the predetermined changes in y).

Finally, in the "monetarist" or quantity theory case ($l_r = 0$), changes in y and P are jointly determined in the money and labor markets, and changes in r are determined in the commodity market (given the predetermined changes in y and P); whereas in the basic "fix-price" case with constant labour productivity ($f_{LL} = 0$) and exogenous money wage rate ($G_L = 0$), changes in y and r are jointly determined in the commodity and money markets, and changes in P are determined exogenously in the labour market.

In the *flexible* exchange rate case, the money supply, M, is an exogenous variable and the exchange rate, π, is endogenous. Totally differentiating the model under *flexible* exchange rate assumptions, one obtains (again after eliminating L, W, and B/P)

$$
\begin{array}{l}
\text{Labor} \\
\text{Commodity} \\
\\
\text{Money} \\
\text{Definition} \\
\text{Foreign} \\
\text{exchange}
\end{array}
\begin{bmatrix}
(Pf_{LL} - G_L)/f_L & 0 & f_L - G_P & -G_h h_z & 0 \\
-\{1 - c(1-t) + zm_y\} & i_r & 0 & \begin{matrix} x_z - zm_z - m \\ + c(1-t)\hat{y}_h h_z \end{matrix} & 0 \\
Pl_y & Pl_r & M/P & 0 & 0 \\
0 & 0 & z/P & 1 & z/\pi \\
-zm_y & F_r & 0 & x_z - zm_z - m & 0
\end{bmatrix}
$$

$$
\begin{bmatrix} dy \\ dr \\ dP \\ dz \\ d\pi \end{bmatrix}
=
\begin{bmatrix}
0 & 0 & 0 & 0 & G_y & 0 \\
-x_{y_f} & 0 & 0 & -1 & 0 & 0 \\
0 & 0 & 0 & 0 & 0 & 1 \\
0 & 0 & z/P_f & 0 & 0 & 0 \\
-x_{y_f} & -F_{r_f} & 0 & 0 & 0 & 0
\end{bmatrix}
\begin{bmatrix} dy_f \\ dr_f \\ dP_f \\ dg \\ d\gamma \\ dM \end{bmatrix}
\qquad \text{(10B-3)}
$$

Notice that this system is the same as the previous fixed exchange rate system *with the exceptions* that (a) the last columns of the lefthand side and righthand side matrices have been multiplied by minus one and interchanged and, correspondingly, (b) the last elements of the lefthand side and righthand side vectors (dM and $d\pi$) have also been interchanged. The only difference is, therefore, the choice between M and π as endogenous variables.

Once again, given the extended Marshall-Lerner condition, the determinant of the 5×5 matrix on the lefthand side is *negative*, and the sign pattern of *total* derivatives is

	dy_f	dr_f		dP_f	dg		$d\gamma$	dM	
		K	C		K	C		K	C
dy	$+$	$?$	$-$	0	$+$	$+$	$-$	$+$	0
dr	$-$	$+$	$+$	0	$+$	$+$	$+$	$-$	0
dP	$?$	$+$	$+$	0	$?$	$?$	$+$	$+$	$+$
dz	$-$	$+$	$+$	0	$?$	$-$	$-$	$+$	0
$d\pi$	$+$	$-$	$-$	$+$	$?$	$?$	$?$	$-$	$-$

$$(10B-4)$$

As before, K and C stand for "Keynesian" and "classical" labor market cases, respectively. Moreover, $d\pi/dg$ and $d\pi/d\gamma$ are both negative (positive) if the BF curve is steeper (less steep) than the LM curve. It also can be shown that $dP/dg > 0$ if BF is steeper than LM in the classical case.

Comparing the two cases, it is clear that there are some difficulties in signing the price level effects of various exogenous shocks in the flexible exchange rate case. It is also clear that the effects on M from the first five shocks in the fixed exchange rate case are the same as the effects on π in the flexible exchange rate case and, moreover, that the effects of a currency *appreciation* in the fixed exchange rate case are the same as the effects of a monetary *contraction* in the flexible exchange rate case.

Turning briefly to the effects of a pure foreign price shock (an increase in P_f *not* coupled with a simultaneous movement in y_f or r_f), it is clear that in the fixed exchange rate case three basic transmission mechanisms will be at work: (a) demand-pull linkages or substitution effects, (b) cost-push linkages or cost of living effects, and (c) monetary linkages or balance of payments effects. Through these three linkages, foreign inflation is fully transmitted to the domestic economy provided that there is no residual money illusion in the labor market; the transmission is, however, incomplete if residual money illusion exists. The transmission process is associated with an inflationary expansion, though (presumably after some adjustment lags) the expansion component is fully reversed in the classical case. On the other hand, with a flexible exchange rate, the whole impact of the foreign inflation is taken on the exchange rate and full insulation occurs.

These strong conclusions are analyzed in much greater detail in the following chapters. It will be seen that they require qualification in a more realistic world in which (for example) (a) the economy is a price taker with respect to some of its exports in addition to its imports, (b) the foreign price shock is impure, with y_f and r_f moving simultaneously with P_f, (c) there are a variety of dynamic adjustment lags in both the private economy and the public policy reaction functions, (d) there are non-market transmission mechanisms of an institutional and expectational form, which may perhaps be associated with the existence of exchange rate expectations that are inelastic in the short run, and (e) P_f is a vector with different rates of inflation for different components (when compared with domestic sectoral rates of productivity increase), etc.

Much of the remainder of this book is concerned with these problems. The most interesting conclusions that emerge from this further study are: (a) that foreign inflation can produce inflationary recession in the domestic economy, and (b) that exchange rate flexibility may not provide full insulation from imported inflation.[3] The main reasons for the first conclusion are that the substitution or demand-pull effects (working through export demand) may be subject to significant lags in comparison to the cost-push effects (working through import prices), and that there may be a significant deterioration in the terms of trade implied in the component by component variability of the P_f vector. In either case, the balance of trade does not improve, or (more narrowly) the Marshall-Lerner condition may fail in the short run. In these circumstances, there is at best zero pressure towards appreciation of the domestic currency; indeed, if in this situation inelastic exchange rate expectations do not stabilize the foreign exchange market, monetary contraction may be necessary to prevent currency depreciation. The main reasons for the second conclusion are that (even if the Marshall-Lerner condition is satisfied) exchange rate expectations may be inelastic in the short run so that (without deliberate monetary contraction) the exchange rate appreciates too slowly to be of much help in insulating the economy from foreign price inflation, and that an inflation that is unevenly distributed across tradeable commodities may be coupled with institutional asymmetries in particular labor markets. Both of these reasons have the implication that complete insulation may involve a decrease in employment in the short run, or alternatively that the maintenance of aggregate employment in the face of an acceleration in world price inflation may involve the acceptance of the fact that some part of the acceleration will be imported.

Despite these problems, for small open economies it is especially important to note that the management of the exchange rate is interdependent with monetary and fiscal policies; indeed, these policies are the primary instruments through which the exchange rate may be appropriately managed. To maintain a fixed exchange rate in the face of fluctuations in the rate of world price inflation is to keep the big lever tied behind one's back and, thus, to make it exceedingly difficult to stabilize the economy. For, on the one hand, monetary policy ceases to be an internal stabilizing device when it is tied to the maintenance of a rigid exchange rate, while, on the other hand, fiscal policy may be constrained by the unwillingness or inability of the authorities to withstand large scale changes in the public debt.

C: THE DEMAND FOR MONEY AND THE INFLATIONARY PROCESS[4]

The following two chapters will analyze the problem of inflation in some detail without always paying explicit attention to the way in which movements in the

3. These two conclusions, of course, are not new and have been substantiated for the Canadian economy by some unpublished simulation results based upon RDX2, the Bank of Canada quarterly econometric model. These results have been reported in Scarfe, "Inflation and the Exchange Rate," unpublished monograph, Ottawa, Bank of Canada Research Department, 1974.

4. The fundamental model discussed in this section bears a family resemblance to that outlined

volume of money that is outstanding fit into the picture. This is not because the quantity of money is unimportant to the inflation problem; on the contrary, it is of paramount importance as the catalytic agent through which inflationary impulses are transmitted through the various sectors of the economy. The purpose of this section is to pay more formal attention to the explicitly monetary aspects of the inflation problem. In this discussion, which takes place in the context of a closed economy, the money supply and its rate of growth are taken to be exogenously determined. This may be inappropriate, of course, because of the link between the nominal stock of money and governmental borrowing requirements. This link is important, however, since there can be no doubt that the monetization of excessive government expenditure is a fundamental element in the drift towards higher rates of price inflation in many Western industrial economies. A substantial reduction in the growth rate of government expenditures is a necessary ingredient in any program designed to stabilize the rate of inflation.

The demand for real cash balances may be assumed to be homogeneous of degree zero in money income (Y) and prices (P). It may also be assumed to be an increasing function of the level of real national income $(y = Y/P)$, and a decreasing function of both the nominal interest rate (r) and the expected rate of price inflation $(p*)$.[5] The reason for including both r and $p*$ as separate variables is to incorporate the opportunity costs of holding money. These opportunity costs take the form of both (a) the interest that may be earned by holding longer term debt instruments (fixed interest securities) and (b) the capital gains that may be obtained by holding one's wealth in the form of real capital assets (or ownership claims to these assets). Thus, in equilibrium, when the demand for and supply of real balances are equal, one may write

$$M = P \cdot l(y, r, p*) \quad \text{with} \quad l_y > 0, \quad l_r < 0 \quad \text{and} \quad l_{p*} < 0 \qquad (10C\text{-}1)$$

where l_y, l_r, and l_{p*} are the partial derivatives of the demand function for real balances, $l(y, r, p*)$, with respect to real income, the nominal interest rate, and the expected rate of price inflation, respectively.

The fact that the demand for real cash balances is a decreasing function of the expected rate of inflation provides a potential source if instability to a monetary economy. Its counterpart in a complete model of portfolio selection is that the demand function for real capital assets is an increasing function of the expected rate of inflation (as suggested by the long run equilibrium dynamic models of chapters 7 and 8, and by the Marshallian flex price model that will be discussed in Sec. C of chapter 11). The higher is the expected rate of inflation, the greater is the incentive for wealth holders to substitute real capital assets for both money and bonds in their portfolios, thereby increasing the actual rate

in Scarfe, "A Model of the Inflation Cycle in a Small Open Economy," *Oxford Economic Papers,* vol. 25, July, 1973, pp. 192–203. I am indebted to Oxford University Press, the publisher of the Oxford Economic Papers, for permission to reproduce herein a few short excerpts from this paper.

5. Of course, a "permanent income" concept as a proxy for real wealth may well be a more appropriate explanatory variable than real national income.

of inflation. In consequence, if p^* adjusts to the actual rate of price inflation, $p \equiv P^{-1} \, dP/dt$, via an adaptive expectations mechanism such as $dp^*/dt = \lambda(p - p^*)$ where $\lambda > 0$ is the speed of response, then the resulting positive feedback mechanism may be strong enough to generate an unstable system. This is most likely to be the case if the speed of response of the adaptive expectations mechanism is large, and especially if there is myopic perfect foresight ($\lambda \to \infty$ and $p^* \to p$). Of course, such an unstable path leading towards hyper-inflation will normally require a continuous increase in the rate of monetary expansion; and it could eventually be broken if the rate of monetary expansion is substantially reduced, though the costs of doing so will normally include a lengthy period of inflationary recession if not outright depression.

The logic of the previous paragraph suggests that one may write the commodity market equilibrium condition in the form

$$y = z(y, r, p^*) \quad \text{with} \quad 0 < z_y < 1, \quad z_r < 0 \quad \text{and} \quad z_{p^*} > 0 \qquad \text{(10C-2)}$$

where z_y, z_r, and z_{p^*} are the partial derivatives of the aggregate demand function, $z(y, r, p^*)$, with respect to real income (or output), the nominal interest rate, and the expected rate of price inflation, respectively. Although it may be customary to define $r - p^*$ to be the real rate of interest, and to let aggregate demand be inversely related to this variable, this seems unnecessarily restrictive in the current analytical framework. Of course, it could easily be imposed by letting $-z_r = z_{p^*}$.

In order to explore the dynamic behavior of the system, and particularly the question of stability, it is necessary to complete the model by postulating a price change relationship. The relationship chosen has the form of a simple Phillips curve or trade-off function. Thus,

$$p = \phi(y) + \theta p^* \quad \text{with} \quad \phi_y > 0 \quad \text{and} \quad 0 \le \theta \le 1 \qquad \text{(10C-3)}$$

This equation says that the rate of price inflation is an increasing function of the level of domestic output, as a proxy for the "utilization rate" or the level of resource utilization; but the position of this trade-off function shifts (but not necessarily in a one for one manner) whenever the expected rate of inflation changes. The theoretical foundations of equations of this form are explored in depth in chapter 12 of this book. Two comments should be made about Eq. (10C-3). The first is that it really represents a simple proxy for the labor market equation. The second is that, as a labor market equation, it relates the proportional *rate of change* of prices, rather than the *level* of prices, to the level of real output. This change in specification from the model of the previous sections is of fundamental importance to the comparative behavior of the system.

The general model to be analyzed, therefore, consists of the five basic equations

$$p = \phi(y) + \theta p^*$$

$$y = z(y, r, p^*)$$

and

$$M = P \cdot l(y, r, p^*)$$

where

$$dp^*/dt = \lambda(p - p^*)$$

and

$$P^{-1} dP/dt \equiv p$$

(10C-4)

It is not difficult to see that the equilibrium position of this model has the property that $p = m$ where $m \equiv M^{-1} dM/dt$, since in equilibrium $l(y, r, p^*)$ is constant. Thus, the equilibrium rate of price inflation is equal to the rate of monetary expansion, which is herein assumed to be given exogenously.[6] Moreover, in equilibrium, price expectations are realized so that $p^* = p$, from which it follows that $\phi(y) = (1 - \theta)p$. This relationship may be called the steady-state trade-off function. One additional feature of equilibrium follows from these facts, namely that the equilibrium level of real national income (and the corresponding utilization rate) is determined from the equation $\phi(y) = (1 - \theta)m$. The equilibrium level of real national income is directly dependent upon the *growth rate* of the nominal money supply, except in the case with $\theta = 1$ where there exists a natural rate of utilization given by the value of y which satisfies the equation $\phi(y) = 0$. An in depth discussion of the natural rate of utilization concept can be found in chapter 12, Secs. A and B.

The disequilibrium behavior of the model in the neighborhood of its equilibrium position, as well as the question of the local stability of this solution, may be explored by linearizing the model around its equilibrium position. Letting $y(t) = \bar{y} + \hat{y} e^{\rho t}$, $r(t) = \bar{r} + \hat{r} e^{\rho t}$, $p(t) = \bar{p} + \hat{p} e^{\rho t}$ and $p^*(t) = \bar{p}^* + \hat{p}^* e^{\rho t}$, where $\bar{y}$, $\bar{r}$, $\bar{p}$, and $\bar{p}^*$ are the equilibrium levels of the four basic variables, one may linearize the system of Eqs. (10C-4) around the equilibrium solution to obtain the fundamental matrix equation:[7]

$$
\begin{array}{l}
\text{Labor} \\
\text{Commodity} \\
\text{Money} \\
\text{Adaptive expectations}
\end{array}
\begin{bmatrix}
-\phi_y & 0 & 1 & -\theta \\
-(1 - z_y) & z_r & 0 & z_{p^*} \\
\rho l_y & \rho l_r & M/P & \rho l_{p^*} \\
0 & 0 & -\lambda & \rho + \lambda
\end{bmatrix}
\begin{bmatrix}
\hat{y} \\
\hat{r} \\
\hat{p} \\
\hat{p}^*
\end{bmatrix}
=
\begin{bmatrix}
0 \\
0 \\
0 \\
0
\end{bmatrix}
\quad (10C-5)
$$

The main trick required in the derivation of this matrix equation is to use the differential version of Eq. (10C-1), namely

$$\frac{M}{P}(m - p) = l_y Dy + l_r Dr + l_{p^*} Dp^*$$

(10C-6)

6. Of course, the short run framework that is assumed herein has a zero equilibrium growth rate of real output. To incorporate the possibility of real output growth would complicate the analysis unnecessarily.

7. The formal structural similarity between the left hand side 4×4 matrix and the upper left hand corner 4×4 matrices contained in the left hand side 5×5 matrices of expressions (10B-1) and (10B-3) should be noted.

or

$$\frac{M}{P}(m - \bar{p} - \hat{p}\, e^{\rho t}) = \rho l_y \hat{y}\, e^{\rho t} + \rho l_r \hat{r}\, e^{\rho t} + \rho l_{p^*} \hat{p}^*\, e^{\rho t}$$

where $\bar{p} = m$. All partial derivatives as well as the level of real balances, M/P, are taken to be evaluated in the neighborhood of the equilibrium position. Evaluating the determinant of the 4×4 matrix on the lefthand side of expression (10C-5) and setting it equal to zero, one obtains the quadratic characteristic equation of the system, namely

$$a\rho^2 + [(1 - \theta)\lambda a + \lambda b + c]\rho + \lambda c = 0$$

where

$$a = -\{z_r l_y + (1 - z_y)l_r\} > 0$$

$$b = \phi_y(z_{p^*} l_r - z_r l_{p^*}) < 0 \tag{10C-7}$$

and

$$c = -\phi_y z_r M/P > 0$$

Since a and λc are both positive, the two characteristic roots both have negative real parts (and thus the equilibrium solution is stable) if and only if $(1 - \theta)\lambda a + \lambda b + c$ is also positive. This is most likely to be the case the smaller are θ, λ, and $-b$. Notice, in particular, that instability can only occur if a higher expected rate of inflation generates strong incentives for wealth holders to substitute real capital assets for both money and bonds in their portfolios, thereby increasing the actual rate of price inflation and, with it, the expected rate of inflation. That is to say, the positive feedback loop operating through $b = \phi_y(z_{p^*} l_r - z_r l_{p^*}) < 0$ is the only cause of potential instability in the model.[8]

Whether or not the system is stable, it may well be characterized by cyclical oscillations in the neighborhood of equilibrium. The phase diagram, Fig. 10C-1, is designed to illustrate this possibility. Figure 10C-1 is constructed from the following pair of differential equations[9]

$$\begin{bmatrix} Dy \\ Dp \end{bmatrix} = \begin{bmatrix} a\phi_y & 0 \\ -\phi_y & 1 \end{bmatrix}^{-1} \begin{bmatrix} c & -\theta^{-1}\lambda b \\ 0 & \lambda \end{bmatrix} \begin{bmatrix} m - p \\ \phi(y) - (1 - \theta)p \end{bmatrix} \tag{10C-8}$$

8. If $\lambda \to \infty$ and $\theta = 1$, the second order differential equation system collapses to an *unstable* first order system with single characteristic root $\rho = -c/b > 0$, since the expected and actual rates of inflation are always equal and $\phi(y) = 0$, whereas if $\lambda = 0$ it becomes a *stable* first order system with single characteristic root $\rho = -c/a < 0$, since the expected rate of inflation is constant. Of course, if $\lambda = 0$ and $\phi_y = 0$, the system corresponds to the traditional static Hicks-Hansen *IS–LM* model without the Phillips curve.

9. These equations are obtained as follows. First, from the adaptive expectations hypothesis combined with the trade-off relationship one may write both

(a) $Dp = (D + \lambda)\phi(y) - \lambda(1 - \theta)p = \phi_y Dy + \lambda[\phi(y) - (1 - \theta)p]$,

and

(b) $Dp^* = \theta^{-1}\lambda[\phi(y) - (1 - \theta)p]$.

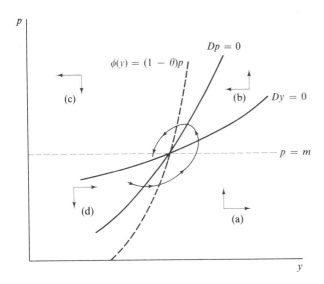

Figure 10C-1 Phase diagram for a simple inflation model.

The relationship between these equations and the phase diagram may be explained in the following way. First, the equilibrium locus $p = m$ is given by the horizontal broken line in the phase diagram, whereas the equilibrium locus $\phi(y) = (1 - \theta)p$ is the steeply sloping broken line in the phase diagram. This latter locus is the steady-state trade-off locus and it is steeper than the family of short run trade-off functions traced out as p^* shifts, from which it is derived, namely $p = \phi(y) + \theta p^*$. Indeed, if $\theta = 1$, the steady-state trade-off locus is vertical, indicating the existence of a natural rate of utilization. Second, expression (10C-8) indicates that both Dy and Dp are *positive* weighted averages of the two deviations from equilibrium, namely $m - p$ and $\phi(y) - (1 - \theta)p$. If both of these deviations are positive (negative), it is clear that both Dy and Dp must be positive (negative). On the other hand, there also exist combinations of positive (negative) values of $m - p$ and negative (positive) values of $\phi(y) - (1 - \theta)p$ for which $Dy = 0$, and similarly

---

Substituting the second of these equations into the differential versions of both the commodity market and money market equilibrium conditions, one obtains

(c) $Dy = z_y Dy + z_r Dr + z_{p^*} \theta^{-1} \lambda [\phi(y) - (1 - \theta)p]$,

and

(d) $(m - p)M/P = l_y Dy + l_r Dr + l_{p^*} \theta^{-1} \lambda [\phi(y) - (1 - \theta)p]$.

Eliminating Dr across these equations yields

(e) $a\phi_y Dy = c(m - p) - \theta^{-1} \lambda b [\phi(y) - (1 - \theta)p]$,

given the definitions of a, b, and c contained in expression (10C-7). Equations (e) and (a) are easily recognized as Eqs. (10C-8) given in the text. Finally, it is not difficult to derive the characteristic equation, (10C-7), directly from equations (e) and (a), or Eq. (10C-8).

for which $Dp = 0$. Thus, both the singular curves $Dy = 0$ and $Dp = 0$ are upward sloping relationships which lie between the equilibrium loci $p = m$ and $\phi(y) = (1 - \theta)p$. In addition, the *relative* weight attached to the deviation $\phi(y) - (1 - \theta)p$ in the $Dp = 0$ locus *exceeds* that attached to this deviation in the $Dy = 0$ locus. In consequence, the $Dp = 0$ locus must be *steeper* than the $Dy = 0$ locus as illustrated in Fig. 10C-1. Finally, it should be implicitly clear from the above reasoning that the phase arrows in Fig. 10C-1 have been correctly drawn.

Four phases are identified in Fig. 10C-1. Phase (a) is one of inflationary expansion in which both y and p are rising. Phase (b) is one of inflationary recession in which y is falling but p continues to rise. Phase (c) is one of deflationary recession in which both y and p are falling, and phase (d) is one of deflationary expansion in which y is rising but p continues to fall. It is evident that when these four phases are put together into a single story, cyclical oscillations are likely to occur. These oscillations are illustrated by the counter-clockwise spiral in Fig. 10C-1 around the stationary equilibrium point, $p = m$ and $\phi(y) = (1 - \theta)p$. They may be said to characterize an *inflation cycle*. Of course, oscillations are not inevitable; but there is a strong probability that an oscillatory solution will occur. Finally, the cyclical fluctuations may be either stable or unstable depending upon the strength of the impact of inflationary expectations on asset choices, as measured by the relative size of the coefficient $-b$.

In an inflation cycle, peaks and troughs in the rate of inflation lag behind peaks and troughs in the utilization rate by one cyclical phase. In addition, it is not difficult to see that peaks and troughs in the rate of interest lag behind peaks and troughs in *both* y and p. This may be seen from the following equation,

$$a\phi_y Dr = \left(\frac{1 - z_y}{z_r}\right) c(m - p) + \theta^{-1}\lambda h[\phi(y) - (1 - \theta)p]$$

where

$$h = \phi_y\{z_{p^*}l_y + (1 - z_y)l_{p^*}\} \gtrless 0$$

(10C-9)

which may be easily derived by eliminating Dy across equations (c) and (d) of footnote 9. Since $(1 - z_y)/z_r < 0$ it is clear that Dr must be positive as the system crosses the upper portion of the steady-state trade-off locus, that is when $p > m$ and $\phi(y) = (1 - \theta)p$, whereas Dr must be negative as the system crosses the lower portion of the steady-state trade-off locus, that is when $p < m$ and $\phi(y) = (1 - \theta)p$. It is therefore evident that peaks and troughs in the cyclical movement of the rate of interest (r) must occur after peaks and troughs in the cyclical movements of both the rate of inflation (p) and the level of real output (y).

In the previous analysis, the rate of growth of the money supply, $m \equiv M^{-1}\,dM/dt$, has been treated as an exogenous constant. Variations in m, however, will upset the course of the cyclical story. Quite obviously, an increase (decrease) in m will shift the equilibrium locus $p = m$ upwards (downwards), thus generating a higher (lower) equilibrium inflation rate and, except in the natural rate case with $\theta = 1$, a higher (lower) equilibrium real output level. Moreover, cyclical movements in m will generate cyclical responses to these exogenously imposed oscillations.

Comparing alternative equilibrium positions with different growth rates of the money supply, one has already established that

$$d\bar{p}/dm = d\bar{p}^*/dm = 1 \quad \text{and} \quad \phi_y \, d\bar{y}/dm = \phi_y \, d\bar{y}/d\bar{p} = 1 - \theta \geq 0 \text{ (10C-10)}$$

It remains to consider the way in which the nominal interest rate ($\bar{r}$) and the equilibrium level of real balances ($\overline{M/P}$) vary with m. Differentiating the commodity market and money market equilibrium conditions with respect to m, and using expression (10C-10), one obtains

$$\frac{d\bar{r}}{dm} = \left(\frac{1 - z_y}{z_r}\right)\left(\frac{1 - \theta}{\phi_y}\right) - \frac{z_{p^*}}{z_r} \gtrless 0$$

and

$$(\overline{M/P})^{-1} \, d(\overline{M/P})/dm = \frac{(1 - \theta)a + b}{c} \gtrless 0$$

(10C-11)

where $a = -\{z_r l_y + (1 - z_y)l_r\} > 0$, $b = \phi_y(z_{p^*}l_r - z_r l_{p^*}) < 0$, and $c = -\phi_y z_r(\overline{M/P}) > 0$ as defined in expression (10C-7). Although the signs of $d\bar{r}/dm$ and $d(\overline{M/P})/dm$ are ambiguous, it is evident that as θ increases towards unity $d\bar{r}/dm$ must necessarily become positive, while $d(\overline{M/P})/dm$ must necessarily become negative. It is therefore not only possible but very probable that a permanent increase in the rate of monetary expansion will eventually lead to a *higher* nominal interest rate and a *lower* level of real balances, despite the fact that the initial impact of such an increase will normally be to lower the nominal interest rate and raise the level of real balances. In particular, in the natural rate case with $\theta = 1$, these conclusions necessarily follow.[10] The reason for both conclusions, of course, is the higher expected inflation rate that is thereby generated.

In summary, this section has explored the dynamic behavior of a simple model of the inflationary process. This behavior suggests the likelihood of an inflation cycle in which the normal expansionary phase is followed by a phase of inflationary recession, and the normal recessionary phase is followed by a phase of deflationary expansion. If this cyclical momentum is to be avoided in such an economy, it is essential that movements in the growth rate of the money supply be controlled in such a way as to force the economy onto a trajectory leading to a *feasible*[11] target pair y^T, p^T, and thereafter to maintain m at a constant level. One way in which this might be done is to choose a time path for m which *minimizes* the intertemporal quadratic loss function,

$$L = \int_0^\infty e^{-\gamma t}\{\alpha(t)[y(t) - y^T]^2 + \beta(t)[p(t) - p^T]^2\} \, dt \qquad (10C-12)$$

10. If it is additionally assumed that r and p^* enter the aggregate demand function, $z(y, r, p^*)$, in the form of the real interest rate, $r - p^*$, so that $-z_r = z_{p^*}$, then $d\bar{r}/dm = 1$ and $d(\overline{M/P})/dm = l_r + l_{p^*} < 0$ in the $\theta = 1$ case.

11. Unless it is possible to shift the steady-state trade-off locus, $\phi(y) = (1 - \theta)p$, a target pair can only be *feasible* if it lies on this locus; that is to say, the target pair, y^T, p^T, must satisfy $\phi(y^T) = (1 - \theta)p^T$.

where $\alpha(t) > 0$ and $\beta(t) > 0$ are a pair of weighting functions and $\gamma \geq 0$ is simply a discount factor,[12] *subject to* the pair of differential equations given in expression (10C-8) above. We shall not pursue this problem at this time.

Two fundamental conclusions follow from this brief analysis. First, although a rapid increase in the money supply is a necessary condition for the continuation of high rates of inflation, there may be serious problems involved in getting the growth rate of the money supply under control. This is especially the case when large and continuing fiscal deficits (perhaps related to the goal of full employment) are responsible for the rapid monetary expansion in the first place. Second, stable domestic price expectations, coupled with a low elasticity of substitution between money and real goods as alternative means of holding one's wealth, are the cornerstone of Keynesian liquidity preference theory.[13] Once the experience of rapid inflation has undermined the stability of these expectations, it may be exceedingly difficult to restore stability to our monetary affairs.

D: SOME INTERPRETATIVE REMARKS

The crisis in Keynesian economics[14] is associated with the failure of models of the post-Keynesian or neo-classical synthesis variety (as illustrated in Secs. A and B of this chapter) to come to grips with the problem of inflation, and in particular with the persistence of inflation in the face of widespread under-utilization of labor (and other) resources. This phenomenon of inflationary recession cannot easily be explained within the context of a model in which involuntary unemployment normally requires downwards rigidity in money wage rates and in which upwards wage flexibility normally requires an expanding labor market, except by attributing it entirely to exogenous cost-push forces.

---

12. For simplicity, of course, one may wish to assume that $\alpha(t)$ and $\beta(t)$ are constant for all time t, and that the discount factor γ is zero. In addition, it may be relevant to assume that $\beta(t) = 0$, or in other words that only output deviations are relevant.

13. Keynesian liquidity preference theory should not be identified with the theory of portfolio selection. Whereas this latter theory deals with a *single* choice among alternative investment portfolios, a choice that takes place at a particular point of time under conditions in which the decision maker's expectations concerning the future "state of nature" that will occur are uncertain, Keynesian liquidity preference theory is concerned with a *sequence* of interdependent choices, a sequence in which the degree of flexibility permitted with respect to the choices that must necessarily be postponed until the future depends upon the choices among alternative ways of holding one's wealth that are made today. The holding of money (and certain types of monetary assets) can provide this flexibility as long as the future value of money in terms of real goods and services is fairly predictable. In order to capture liquidity preference in this sense, it is necessary for an economic model to involve essential spot transactions at every point of time; such a model economy is usually said to be an essential sequence economy. On these points, see F. M. Hahn, "On the Foundations of Monetary Theory," pp. 230–242, in J. M. Parkin and A. R. Nobay (eds.), *Essays in Modern Economics*, London, Longman, 1973, and J. R. Hicks, *The Crisis in Keynesian Economics*, chapter 2. It seems much too early, however, to survey the literature on essential sequence economies.

14. It is well known that J. R. Hicks recently published a book under this title. See Hicks, *The Crisis in Keynesian Economics*.

Models of the post-Keynesian or neo-classical synthesis variety are therefore vulnerable to attack. One such attack comes from the so-called "monetarist school," the main proponent of which is Friedman.[15] A model which captures the principal elements of the monetarist position was presented in the previous section, though it too is deficient since it attributes inflation entirely to an exogenously determined growth rate of the nominal money stock. It should be noted, however, that the fundamental changes that occurred between Secs. A and B of this chapter, on the one hand, and Sec. C on the other, were of two kinds: first, the introduction of inflationary expectations and, second, the structural change in the labor market equation. The rate of inflation rather than the price level is associated positively with the level of real output (or the utilization rate), though to the monetarists, who generally assume that $\theta = 1$ and therefore that there exists a natural rate of utilization, it is only *unanticipated* inflation, $p - p^*$, which is positively associated with the level of real output through the $\phi(y)$ function. This corresponds to the "classical" labor market case of the neo-classical synthesis model.

These two fundamental changes are directly related to a growing literature on the "microfoundations" of macroeconomic reasoning.[16] Chapter 12 of this book develops some of the main themes of this literature as they apply to the labor market. In particular, it is concerned with the theoretical foundations of the Phillips curve trade-off function and with the determinants of the rate of change in money wage rates in both closed and open economies. Chapter 13 explores the application of these (and other) themes to an explanation of some of the "stylized" facts of recent inflationary experience.

The microfoundations literature also has its place in commodity market analysis. The following chapter is concerned with some of these developments. In particular, it presents two distinct bilaterally coupled flex-price dynamic systems, which are labelled Keynesian and Marshallian, respectively. In the course of this presentation, we shall suggest that it is difficult to make sense of the economics of Keynes[17] without introducing markets which are imperfectly competitive, at least in the short run. We shall also suggest that the process of price inflation is quite different in Keynesian and Marshallian markets, as well as emphasize some essential differences in the form that market signals take. It will be seen, however, that both of these models represent a sort of halfway house in which prices are not fully flexible since (for the most part) money wage rates are assumed to be given exogenously. This limitation, of course, is one of the principal motivations for the further analytical developments of the final two chapters of this book.

15. See, for example, M. Friedman, *The Optimal Quantity of Money and Other Essays,* London, Macmillan, 1969.

16. See, for example, E. S. Phelps (ed.), *Microeconomic Foundations of Employment and Inflation Theory,* New York, Norton, 1972.

17. Compare A. Leijonhufvud, *On Keynesian Economics and the Economics of Keynes,* New York, Oxford University Press, 1968.

ELEVEN

KEYNES, MARSHALL, AND THE PROCESS OF PRICE INFLATION

A: PRODUCTION AND PRICES

In recent years, much has been written on the microfoundations of macroeconomic reasoning and on the question of "what Keynes really said." Not least of these contributions has been that of Leijonhufvud,[1] for whom the crucial difference between Marshall and Keynes lies in the inversion of the ranking of price and quantity adjustment velocities. More recently, Hicks[2] has suggested that the familiar multiplier process needs to be reworked to allow for the existence of both "fix-price" (Keynesian) and "flex-price" (Marshallian) commodity markets. Chapter 11 may be interpreted as an attempt to formalize these revisionist ideas in terms of explicit macrodynamic models. This formalization no doubt does more justification to Hicks' ideas than to those of Leijonhufvud, since only slight attention is paid to the differences between notional and effective demands.

In this chapter, both the Keynesian and the Marshallian market mechanisms are given explicit mathematical formalizations in an n-sectoral context. Both market mechanisms are seen to involve the simultaneous determination of prices, outputs, quantities sold, and inventory stocks, and show how these four variables interact in an essentially dynamic process. Even though in an actual economy one market form may be quantitatively more important than the other, any complete story of the inflationary process must ordinarily involve a consideration of both kinds of markets simultaneously, since the time sequence of the cyclical movements of the basic variables differs between the two adjustment processes. In Keynesian markets, producers have some short run discretion over their prices and the effect of demand changes works through the inventory-sales nexus to generate output shifts and thence (in conjunction with cost changes) price changes; in Marshallian markets, producers are price takers and the effect of

1. See Leijonhufvud, *On Keynesian Economics and the Economics of Keynes.*
2. See Hicks, *The Crisis in Keynesian Economics,* chapter 1.

demand changes works through the stockholding function of active traders to generate price shifts and thence (in conjunction with cost changes) output changes. Of course, in a multisectoral context some of the cost components in Keynesian sectors may themselves behave in a Marshallian manner and *vice versa*.

Consider an economy[3] in which there are n commodities produced non-jointly on a set of n linearly homogeneous production functions. To facilitate the analysis, these production functions are taken to be of the familiar Cobb-Douglas form; similar but more complicated analyses would follow from the assumption of some more general form for the production functions. Each productive sector $j = 1,\ldots,n$ requires inputs of fixed capital and labor as well as intermediate inputs (or inputs of circulating capital goods) purchased from other sectors. Thus, one may write:

with
$$\ln q_j = \ln N_j + a_j \ln K_j + c_j(\ln L_j + \ln \xi_j) + \sum_{i=1}^{n} b_{ij} \ln M_{ij}$$

$$a_j + c_j + \sum_{i=1}^{n} b_{ij} = 1 \quad \text{and} \quad j = 1,\ldots,n$$

(11A-1)

where q_j is the output of sector j, N_j is a constant, K_j is fixed capital input into sector j, L_j is labor input into sector j, ξ_j represents the level of Harrod-neutral technological development in sector j, M_{ij} is intermediate input of type i into sector j, a_j, c_j, and b_{ij} are the capital, labor, and i-th intermediate input elasticities, respectively, for sector j, and ln is the natural logarithmic operator.

Assuming that both labor and intermediate inputs are used up to the point at which their value marginal products are equal to their prices, the short run marginal conditions may be written as:

$$p_i M_{ij} = b_{ij} p_j q_j \quad \text{all} \quad i,j = 1,\ldots,n \quad \text{and} \quad w_j L_j = c_j p_j q_j, \quad j = 1,\ldots,n \quad (11A-2)$$

where p_j is the price of commodity j and w_j is the wage rate in sector j. Substituting these marginal conditions back into the production functions one obtains:

$$(1 - a_j) \ln p_j = \ln V_j + a_j(\ln q_j - \ln K_j) + c_j(\ln w_j - \ln \xi_j) + \sum_{i=1}^{n} (\ln p_i)b_{ij}$$

$$j = 1,\ldots,n \qquad (11A-3)$$

with $\ln V_j = -(\ln N_j + c_j \ln c_j + \sum_{i=1}^{n} b_{ij} \ln b_{ij})$, a constant for all $j = 1,\ldots,n$. Sectoral prices are explained by the capacity utilization ratio q_j/K_j, normal unit labor costs w_j/ξ_j, and a geometrically weighted input price index J_j with

3. The remaining portion of this section basically appeared in my Prices and Incomes Commission monograph. See Scarfe, *Price Determination and the Process of Inflation in Canada*, Ottawa, Information Canada, 1972, chapter 1, pp. 2–4. This extract is reproduced by permission of the Minister of Supply and Services, Canada.

$\ln J_j = \sum_{i=1}^{n} (\ln p_i) b_{ij}$, the form of the functional relationship being log-linear.[4] In the short run, demand fluctuations will have a direct effect on prices through changes in the ratio of output to capacity, even though there are constant returns to scale in the long run.

This may be shown by completing the model in the following way. Assuming for the moment that commodities used are equal to commodities produced, one also has a set of commodity balance equations of the form:

$$q_i = e_i = \sum_{j=1}^{n} M_{ij} + f_i, \quad i = 1,\ldots,n \qquad (11\text{A-}4)$$

where e_i is the quantity of commodity i that is purchased (or sold), $\sum_{j=1}^{n} M_{ij}$ is the total intermediate usage of commodity i, and f_i is the total final demand for commodity i. Substituting the marginal conditions into these commodity balance equations, one obtains:

$$p_i q_i = p_i e_i = \sum_{j=1}^{n} b_{ij} p_j q_j + p_i f_i, \quad i = 1,\ldots,n \qquad (11\text{A-}5)$$

Thus, Eqs. (11A-5) and (11A-3) together constitute the primal commodity balance (or expenditure) functions and the dual cost (or price) relationships of a complete Cobb-Douglas model of the production structure of an economy in short run competitive equilibrium. Notice, however, that quantities enter the price equations and prices enter the quantity equations, so that the complete system is bilaterally coupled.

Although expressions (11A-3) and (11A-5) are consistent with marginal cost pricing behavior, they need not be interpreted in this manner. For they are also consistent with "normal cost" pricing behavior, where price is given by a normal mark-up on average variable costs, and where either average variable costs or the mark-up factors themselves are positively related to the ratio of output to capacity (or the utilization ratio). Thus, increases in prime costs tend to be passed on in terms of higher prices except when there is a simultaneous downward shift in the demand function leading to a fall in output relative to capacity. This interpretation still allows for varying profit margins over the business cycle as the ratio of fixed to variable costs changes.

---

4. Even if one had started with a more general production function, it would be possible to show that the dual cost function may be written in the form:

$$d \ln p = (k - 1) d \ln q + \sum_{i=1}^{n} \alpha_i \, d \ln p_i$$

where p is the product price, q is the volume of output, the α_i's are a set of non-negative weights attached to the input prices p_i and $1/k$ is the degree of homogeneity of the production function. (In our case, the degree of homogeneity in the short run is $1/k = 1 - a$, so that $k - 1 = a/(1 - a)$.) It follows that the Cobb-Douglas cost function given in Eq. (11A-3) is the first order linear approximation to a more general cost function.

It can be shown readily that the only changes introduced by non-competitive market behavior are associated with the introduction of mark-up and/or elasticity terms into the sectoral cost and demand functions outlined in expressions (11A-3) and (11A-5). But it is difficult if not impossible in an econometric exercise to separate these terms from the other underlying structural parameters of the model. As indicated, therefore, the cost and demand functions are compatible with various market forms. Indeed, they are robust with respect to the mechanism by which inflationary impulses are transmitted through the economy, but they cannot say much about the importance of "market power" in the inflation transmission process. It should be noted, however, that any price equation which is based upon production costs is in fact a "reduced form" equation resulting from the collapsing of a unit cost function into a behavioral relationship between price and unit cost. Unfortunately, there does not seem to be any satisfactory way of separating these two components of the price determination mechanism.

B: PRICE FORMATION IN A KEYNESIAN PROCESS

The system of equations as portrayed so far is an equilibrium system, whose comparative static behavior has been analyzed elsewhere.[5] The dynamics of the system depend upon the way in which its out of equilibrium behavior is specified. This section presents a dynamic framework with a distinctly Keynesian flavor. In this presentation, the post-Keynesian assumption of given money wage rates is maintained. Moreover, the model is short run in the sense that fixed capital stocks (or output capacities) in each industrial sector are held constant, although inventories of circulating capital goods are not. Given these two assumptions, one is effectively asking the question: "What happens to prices in a Keynesian cumulative process?" The Keynesian aspects of this process are illuminated in Sec. C of this chapter by comparison with an alternative Marshallian formulation of the dynamic framework.[6]

In the first place, expression (11A-3) may be considered to explain equilibrium or "desired" prices, towards which actual prices adjust only with a lagged response. In the second place, output may not be equal to quantity sold so that repercussions on inventory stocks must be considered. Using matrix notation, one may write

$$\ln p^* = (I - A)^{-1}\{\ln v + A(\ln q - \ln k) + C(\ln w - \ln \xi) + B' \ln p\} \quad (11\text{B-1})$$

and

$$D \ln p = \gamma(\ln p^* - \ln p) \quad (11\text{B-2})$$

where $p = Pi$, p^*, q, k, w, ξ, and v are $n \times 1$ column vectors of actual prices, desired or target prices, outputs, capital stocks or capacities, wage rates, Harrod-neutral technological levels, and constants, respectively, with the corresponding capital letters referring to the corresponding $n \times n$ diagonal matrices, and with ln representing the natural logarithmic operator; I and i are the $n \times n$ identity matrix and the $n \times 1$ unit vector, respectively; A, C, γ, and D are $n \times n$ diagonal matrices of capital input coefficients (a_j), labor input coefficients (c_j), price adjustment coefficients, and differential operators, respectively, and B is the $n \times n$ matrix of input-output value-share coefficients (b_{ij}), with B' being its transpose. The assumption of constant returns to scale (in the long run) implies that $(I - A - C - B')i = 0$. Thus, in each sector, $j = 1, \ldots, n$, actual prices (ln p_j) adjust (via an exponentially distributed lag function with speed of response γ_j) towards desired prices (ln p_j^*), where desired prices are a log-linear function of the capacity utilization ratio, normal unit labor costs, and the sectorally specific price index for materials inputs.

On the quantity side of the model, it is possible to develop a stock adjustment model along the following lines, using the exact logic of the original stock adjustment model of chapter 1. Let

$$e = P^{-1}BPq + f \tag{11B-3}$$

$$Ds = q - e \tag{11B-4}$$

$$q - e^* = \mu(s^* - s) \tag{11B-5}$$

$$s^* = H(e^*, r) \tag{11B-6}$$

and

$$De^* = \lambda(e - e^*) \tag{11B-7}$$

where q, e, e^*, s, s^*, and f are $n \times 1$ column vectors of sectoral outputs, quantities sold, expected sales, actual stocks, desired stocks, and final demands, respectively; P, λ, μ, and D are $n \times n$ diagonal matrices of sectoral prices, expectational adjustment coefficients, stock adjustment coefficients, and differential operators, respectively; B is the $n \times n$ matrix of input-output value-share coefficients for materials inputs, and H is a general functional notation with r being the rate of interest, though for the most part it will be assumed in this section that r is constant and that Eq. (11B-6) may be written as $s^* = He^*$ where H is an $n \times n$ diagonal matrix of desired inventory–sales ratios. Notice in Eq. (11B-3) that q, e, and f all refer to quantities; their value counterparts may be written as Pq, Pe, and Pf, respectively.

It should be evident that the set of quantity equations, Eqs. (11B-3) to (11B-7), has identical structure to the original one sectoral inventory adjustment model discussed in chapter 1. In particular, Eq. (11B-3) indicates that actual sales (e) are positively related to both final demands (f) and actual outputs (q) via the nexus of intermediate demands $P^{-1}BPq$, a nexus which itself depends upon relative prices. Equation (11B-4) indicates that the change in stocks (Ds) equals the difference between output (q) and sales (e). This difference $(q - e)$

may be interpreted as the sum of planned inventory accumulation $(q - e^*)$ and unplanned inventory accumulation $(e^* - e)$. Planned inventory accumulation $(q - e^*)$ is proportional to the difference between desired and actual stocks $(s^* - s)$, as indicated by Eq. (11B-5). Desired stocks (s^*) are positively related to expected sales (e^*) and negatively related to the rate of interest (r) as indicated by Eq. (11B-6). Finally, Eq. (11B-7) indicates that sales expectations (e^*) adapt through time to the levels attained by actual sales (e). Of course, if in sector i inventories cannot be held because of the nature of that sector's output, then the i-th component of Eq. (11B-4) becomes $ds_i/dt = q_i - e_i = 0$; output and quantity sold are then simply identified with each other. In this service sector case, however, blatant disequilibrium consequences may arise.

The remainder of this section provides a reasonably formal analysis of the model outlined in Eqs. (11B-1) to (11B-7) above. If it is assumed that r is constant and that $s^* = He^*$ where H is an $n \times n$ diagonal matrix of desired inventory-sales ratios, then the seven equations may be easily reduced to four by eliminating e^*, s^*, and p^* to obtain:

$$e = P^{-1}BPq + f$$
$$Ds = q - e$$
$$Dq = \lambda\mu(He - s) - (\lambda + \mu)(q - e)$$
(11B-8)

and

$$(D + \gamma) \ln p = \gamma\{I - A\}^{-1}\{\ln v + A(\ln q - \ln k) + C(\ln w - \ln \xi) + B' \ln p\}$$

The first three of these equations exactly parallel in n sectors the single sectoral system given in expression (1B-4) above. Indeed, when $n = 1$, $P^{-1}BP$ is a scalar which operates exactly like the marginal propensity to consume.

The equation system (11B-8) is a system of $4n$ equations in $4n$ endogenous variables, the prices (p), outputs (q), quantities sold (e), and inventory stocks (s) for each of the n industrial sectors. The variables which are temporarily taken to be predetermined or exogenous include the sectoral capital stocks or capacities (k), wage rates (w), technological levels (ξ), and final demands $(f$ or $Pf)$. Later, towards the end of Sec. D of this chapter, the consequences of making sectoral capacities and wage rates also endogenous will be briefly discussed.

Of the $4n$ equations, $3n$ are differential equations; all but the expenditure equations contain a linear term in the differential operator D. (More realistically, if one allowed for lags on the demand side, the expenditure equations would also include the operator D.) The main technical problem in solving the system of dynamic equations explicitly is the fact that the quantity side of the model is linear in expenditures while the price side of the model is log-linear. In general, however, there will exist a unique equilibrium solution to the system of equations,[7]

---

7. It should be evident from the Frobenius theorem that $I - P^{-1}BP$ is a Leontief matrix, that is it has a dominant positive diagonal and non-positive off-diagonal elements. Since a matrix

and $3n$ characteristic roots (ρ) to the linearized version of the system. Letting $\bar{e}$, $\bar{s}$, $\bar{q}$, and $\bar{p}$ represent the equilibrium values of the endogenous variables, one may write

$$\bar{e} = \{I - \bar{P}^{-1}B\bar{P}\}^{-1}f$$

$$\bar{s} = H\{I - \bar{P}^{-1}B\bar{P}\}^{-1}f$$

$$\bar{q} = \{I - \bar{P}^{-1}B\bar{P}\}^{-1}f \tag{11B-9}$$

and

$$\ln \bar{p} = \{I - A - B'\}^{-1}\{\ln v + A(\ln \bar{q} - \ln k) + C(\ln w - \ln \xi)\}$$

Letting $e = \bar{e} + \hat{e}\exp \rho t$, $s = \bar{s} + \hat{s}\exp \rho t$, $q = \bar{q} + \hat{q}\exp \rho t$, and $p = \bar{p} + \hat{p}\exp \rho t$, one may linearize the system (11B-8) around its equilibrium solution Eq. (11B-9) to obtain the matrix equation:

$$\begin{bmatrix} \bar{P} & 0 & -B\bar{P} & \bar{E} - B\bar{Q} - F \\ I & \rho I & -I & 0 \\ -(\lambda + \mu + \lambda\mu H) & \lambda\mu & \rho I + \lambda + \mu & 0 \\ 0 & 0 & -\gamma A\bar{Q}^{-1} & \{(I - A)(\rho I + \gamma) - \gamma B'\}\bar{P}^{-1} \end{bmatrix} \begin{bmatrix} \hat{e} \\ \hat{s} \\ \hat{q} \\ \hat{p} \end{bmatrix} = \begin{bmatrix} 0 \\ 0 \\ 0 \\ 0 \end{bmatrix}$$

$$\tag{11B-10}$$

The $3n$ characteristic roots (ρ) may be obtained, in principle, by setting the determinant of the $4n \times 4n$ matrix on the lefthand side equal to zero.[8] If and

is said to have a dominant positive diagonal if and only if there exists some set of positive measurement units or rescaling of rows and columns such that each of its diagonal elements exceeds the sum of the absolute values of all the other elements in the corresponding column, it is clear that $I - P^{-1}BP = P^{-1}(I - B)P$ is a Leontief matrix if and only if B is a non-negative square matrix whose column sums are all less than unity so that $\sum_{i=1}^{n} b_{ij} < 1$, all $j = 1,\ldots,n$. If labor and fixed capital are required inputs into every productive sector, these inequalities are automatically satisfied as a consequence of the assumption of constant returns to scale. Finally, it is a property of Leontief matrices that their inverses exist and have all elements non-negative. Thus, $(I - P^{-1}BP)^{-1} \geq 0$, and the corresponding equilibrium levels exist, given $f \geq 0$. A similar argument holds for $(I - A - B')$, which is also a Leontief matrix as long as labor is a required input into every productive sector. On these points, compare chapter 7, especially Theorem 7C-1.

8. Of course, when $n = 1$ and $P^{-1}BP = B$ is a scalar that operates exactly like the marginal propensity to consume, the system decomposes into a quantity system with a price equation tacked on the end, provided that f as opposed to Pf is taken to be exogenous. The obvious reason for this is that $\bar{E} - B\bar{Q} - F = 0$ in the one sectoral case and so there is no feedback from prices onto quantities. In this case, the characteristic equation for the quantity system is

$$\rho^2 + \{(\lambda + \mu)(I - P^{-1}BP) - \lambda\mu H P^{-1}BP\}\rho + \lambda\mu\{I - P^{-1}BP\} = 0$$

which is formally equivalent to expression (1D-2). The obvious stability condition for the resulting inventory cycle is $(\lambda + \mu)(I - P^{-1}BP) > \lambda\mu H P^{-1}BP$, as discussed in Sec. D of chapter 1. Notice, however, that if the true exogenous variable is Pf and not f the appropriate decomposition would be between *values* (Pq's) and prices, rather than between quantities and prices. Of course, if the rate of interest is endogenous and the demand for money is specified in terms of real balances, this decomposition is not, in general, possible.

only if all these characteristic roots have negative real parts, the complete system will be stable.

In order to see how the system of equations functions, it is instructive to work through the response of this model economy to an increase in final demand in one sector, say sector i. Starting from an initial equilibrium position, then, let it be assumed that f_i increases. The immediate repercussion from this shock is an increase in the volume of sales from sector $i(e_i)$. This increase in the volume of sales and the consequential fall in the level of inventories (s_i) both lead to a rise in the volume of output (q_i). The increased pressure of output demand on capacity then leads to an increase in the price of commodity i.

These initial repercussions are not the end of the story, however. Not only will the inventory adjustment model tend to generate a cyclical response to the initial shock, but also the ensuing price adjustments will feed back into the quantity equations in such a way as to dampen the ultimate quantitative impact in sector i. Although the detailed mechanics of these continuing repercussions in a multisectoral economy are rather complicated to trace out, it is likely that, starting from an initial equilibrium solution, the process set in motion by the initial final demand shock will converge to a new equilibrium solution, though the process of convergence will probably be characterized by damped cyclical oscillations. In the new equilibrium, there will be a general tendency for both prices and quantities to be higher than in the initial equilibrium that prevailed before the expansionary shock occurred. The effects of the initial shock will tend to be diffused to other sectors.

The reasons for supposing that convergence will occur are associated with the fact that for any particular sector taken in isolation the inventory adjustment mechanism will be damped because the positive multiplier–accelerator feedback from sectoral output to sectoral sales through the appropriate diagonal element of the matrix B will be small. For the model as a whole, of course, the complete positive feedback through the multiplier–accelerator mechanism will depend upon the sizes of all the coefficients in the matrix B (and indirectly A) as well as the various adjustment coefficients or speeds of response. Nevertheless, even if there are reasons for instability in the complete inventory adjustment process when prices are simply taken to be parameters, these causes of instability will be kept in check by the negative feedback on quantities which occurs through the substitution effects inevitably created in the commodity balance demand equations when prices are allowed to respond to the pressure of demand on sectoral output capacities.

The model just described illustrates the importance of input substitution to the stability of economic systems. Input substitution is important to stability because it greatly increases the responsiveness of the system to the price mechanism. Nevertheless, the relative speeds with which producers respond to particular disequilibria remain of the greatest importance to stability. Most especially, for this model, the smaller are the speeds of response in the inventory adjustment mechanism (μ especially, but also λ) relative to the speeds of response in the price adjustment mechanism (γ), the more likely will it be that the equilibrium position is stable.[9]

C: KEYNESIAN AND MARSHALLIAN MARKET ADJUSTMENT PROCESSES

So far, the discussion has centered upon a basically Keynesian model. The reasons why the model has been labelled Keynesian go beyond the short run assumptions that money wage rates and sectoral output capacities are roughly fixed. More fundamentally, the Keynesian nature of the model is directly reflected in its structure. This fact may be brought out more clearly by comparing the structure of the present Keynesian model with the structure of an alternative Marshallian formulation of the system.[10]

The alternative Marshallian system has the following structure:

$$\ln q^* - \ln k = A^{-1}\{(I - A)\ln p - C(\ln w - \ln \xi) - B' \ln p - \ln v\} \quad \text{(11C-1)}$$

$$D \ln q = \gamma(\ln q^* - \ln q) \quad \text{(11C-2)}$$

$$e = P^{-1}BPq + f \quad \text{(11C-3)}$$

$$Ds = q - e \quad \text{(11C-4)}$$

$$\theta = \mu S^{-1}(s^* - s) \quad \text{(11C-5)}$$

$$s^* = H(\theta^*, r) \quad \text{(11C-6)}$$

and

$$D\theta^* = \lambda(\theta - \theta^*) \quad \text{(11C-7)}$$

where q^*, $\theta \equiv P^{-1}Dp$, and θ^* are $n \times 1$ column vectors of desired or target outputs, actual proportional rates of price change, and expected proportional rates of price change, respectively, and the rest of the variables have interpretations similar to the Keynesian model discussed in the previous section of this chapter. The seven equations (11C-1) to (11C-7) exactly parallel the seven equations (11B-1) to (11B-7) of the earlier model.

Several preliminary points of comparison between system (11C-1) to (11C-7) and system (11B-1) to (11B-7) should be noted. First, Eqs. (11C-3) and (11C-4) are identical to Eqs. (11B-3) and (11B-4). Second, the relevant expectations are

---

9. On the points raised in this paragraph compare F. H. Hahn, "The Stability of Growth Equilibrium," especially p. 224. Notice that the dampening effect of price repercussions in the present model is very similar to the dampening effect of interest rate repercussions in simple multiplier–accelerator models of the type discussed in chapter 2 of this book.

10. In Chapter One of *The Crisis in Keynesian Economics,* Hicks uses the term "fix-price" to refer to commodity markets which are herein called Keynesian and the term "flex-price" to refer to commodity markets which are herein called Marshallian. Since prices may be variable in both kinds of commodity markets, the terminology used herein seems preferable. However, on this point compare footnote 6 of this chapter.

the price change expectations of traders or middlemen who hold inventory stocks (Eq. 11C-7) rather than the sales expectations of firms that produce flow outputs (Eq. 11B-7). Third, it is these price change expectations (Eq. 11C-6) rather than sales expectations (Eq. 11B-6) that have a positive impact on corresponding desired stocks (with the rate of interest, r, having a negative impact in both cases).[11] Fourth, it is prices (Eq. 11C-5) that change rather than quantity outputs (Eq. 11B-5) when desired and actual inventory stocks are different. Fifth, it is quantity outputs which adjust to the discrepancy between actual (demand) prices and flow production costs (or supply prices), thus accounting for the Marshallian character of the model (Eqs. 11C-1 and 11C-2), rather than prices which adjust to output–capacity ratios and unit labor and materials costs (Eqs. 11B-1 and 11B-2). Notice that Eq. (11C-1) can be derived by substituting the marginal conditions for labor and intermediate inputs back into the original production functions exactly as illustrated earlier for Eq. (11B-1). Of course, the dynamic interpretation is different, which is the main point.[12]

Although the equilibrium properties of these two models are very similar, their basic institutional structures and their dynamic behavior are quite distinct. In the Keynesian model, prices are determined or set by producers in a manner which reflects both the demand situation and their production costs. In the short run, the existence of adjustment costs provides individual producers with some discretionary power in their pricing decisions. The pricing equations (11B-1) and (11B-2) try to capture the effects of this short run discretion by allowing for the lagged response of actual prices to desired prices. Trading at "false prices" is therefore allowed, and individual producers hold stocks of own produced commodities to accommodate this. Output rates are first adjusted to the level of effective demand as determined by the multiplier process, and only later are prices adjusted in accordance with movements in the ratio of output to capacity. "Sectoral prices therefore tend to reflect scarcities that have already come into being; they do not normally foreshadow or signal approaching future scarcities in a way that aids the planning of production. Movements in these prices serve the allocative function of reducing existing scarcities rather than the signalling function of preventing future scarcities from arising."[13] As we shall see, this is not so in the basic Marshallian model.

In contrast to the Keynesian model where prices depend directly upon conditions in the flow or production nexus, in the Marshallian model prices are directly determined by conditions in the stock or inventory nexus. The stocks that are held, and the price change expectations on which stockholding is based, belong to active commodity traders. These traders are not to be confused with the individual producers of flow outputs, who are basically price takers in the

---

11. In this case, the H-function will not generally be of a diagonal form since active traders and speculators will normally hold stocks of several commodities.

12. Compare Leijonhufvud, *On Keynesian Economics and the Economics of Keynes.*

13. Scarfe, *Price Determination and the Process of Inflation in Canada,* p. 40. This quotation has been reproduced by permission of the Minister of Supply and Services, Canada.

Marshallian model. In response to an expansion in demand which leads to an initial decline in existing stocks, it is prices (and eventually price expectations) which first move upwards in order to clear the market. Output rates only increase in response to the signals provided by the fact that market (demand) prices exceed supply prices (or marginal costs).

In the Marshallian model, cyclical behavior is again likely to occur. Once again, input substitution is important to the stability of the cyclical process. However, for this model, the smaller are the speeds of response in the price adjustment mechanism (μ especially, but also λ) relative to the speeds of response in the output adjustment mechanism (γ), the more likely will it be that the equilibrium position is stable. Of course, a strong positive feedback between actual price changes, expected future price changes, and desired stocks will lead to cyclical instability if it is not offset by the negative feedback between price changes and actual stocks (via both output and quantities sold).

It is, however, crucially important to note that whereas in the Keynesian model cyclical movements in q tend to lead cyclical movements in p and s, in the Marshallian model cyclical movements in p tend to lead cyclical movements in q and s.[14] The central idea behind the Keynesian model is the assumption that the cost function is the basic relationship that determines the direction of price movements in a disequilibrium situation while the demand function is the fundamental relationship that determines the direction of output movements. Oscillations in price-quantity space occur in a *counter-clockwise* direction. Cyclical peaks (troughs) in output rates tend to precede cyclical peaks (troughs) in prices by approximately one cyclical phase.

In the Marshallian model, all of this is reversed. The demand function becomes the singular curve which determines the direction of price movements while the cost function becomes the singular curve which determines the direction of output movements. In this case, oscillations in price-quantity space occur in a *clockwise* direction, as in the simple cobweb model. Cyclical peaks (troughs) in prices tend to precede cyclical peaks (troughs) in output rates by approximately one cyclical phase. The Keynesian (K) and Marshallian (M) reactions to an initial increase in demand from dd to d'd' along a given cost or supply function ss are illustrated in Fig. 11C-1. Of course, in the complete story inventory stocks will be moving as well as prices and output rates.

It may well be argued that the Marshallian course of events with prices leading output rates is a much less realistic view of the way in which the majority of product (and factor) markets work in industrialized societies than is the Keynesian course of events with output rates leading prices. Although historically there has been a general tendency for the Keynesian adjustment process to become increasingly dominant as industrial development occurs, in any actual industrial economy some commodity markets (the majority) will tend to operate in Keynesian fashion, while others (the minority) will tend to operate in a Marshallian fashion. Apart from asset markets, including the housing market,

---

14. On this point, see *ibid.*, chapter 2, pp. 13–22.

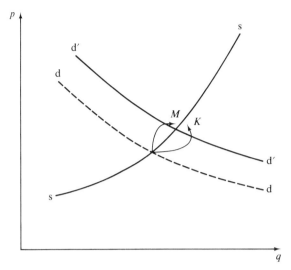

Figure 11C-1 Keynesian and Marshallian adjustment processes.

the leading examples of Marshallian commodity markets are those for primary products with fairly long gestation periods. Indeed, for many primary commodities, there exist well organized international spot and forward markets where prices are determined by the actions of active traders and speculators. Most markets for secondary manufactures are, however, of the Keynesian variety. Apart from the absence of stocks, markets for services fit into the Keynesian category as well.

One reason why most large scale econometric models have experienced difficulties in simulating (let alone in forecasting) the inflationary outburst of 1972–74, relates to the fact that they treat virtually all markets as being Keynesian, thus neglecting the important minority of markets—notably those for primary commodities including foodstuffs and for financial and real assets including housing—whose behavior is Marshallian in nature. If we are to construct macro-economic models which are capable of explaining the acceleration of inflation in the 1972–74 period, it is essential that Marshallian markets be appropriately modelled as such. For it is these markets in which monetary expansion can have a direct effect on prices through the portfolio choices of traders and speculators which transcend both real and monetary assets.[15]

15. Although harvest failures and petroleum cartels can produce important cost push shocks to the economic system, the inflationary forces which emerged in 1972 were spread across too wide a range of primary commodities and real properties for these to have been the sole causes. Indeed, it will be argued in chapter 13 that the huge increase in the world money supply associated with the attempt by numerous countries to avoid appreciation of their currencies relative to the US dollar in 1971–72 had a direct effect on prices. This effect appeared first in Marshallian commodity markets. Only later did the inflationary impulse get transmitted into markets for industrial products and final manufactures, as well as into organized labor markets, all of which tend to operate in a Keynesian fashion.

In conclusion, it is clear from the foregoing discussion that the form which market signals take is distinctly different in the two market forms. In Keynesian markets, the signals received by producers are quantitative in nature whereas in Marshallian markets they are price signals. Prices play an allocative or rationing role in both market forms, but a signalling function in only one of them. Moreover, Keynesian markets are incompatible with a situation in which all producers are price-takers. On this interpretation, the so-called Keynesian revolution encompasses significant changes in microeconomic as well as macroeconomic analysis.

D: TRANSMISSION MECHANISMS AND IMPORTED INFLATION

In this chapter, our discussion of the way in which domestic prices are determined has so far ignored international influences. The time has come to remedy this defect, and to expand the discussion (which began in chapter 10) of the mechanisms by which inflationary impulses are transmitted from one country to another.[16] This discussion of the inflation transmission process is continued into the final two chapters of this book.

In each sector of an economy in which markets are organized in a Keynesian fashion, output prices are largely determined by (a) the pressure of demand for sectoral output on sectoral output capacity, (b) the cost of labor per unit of output that would be experienced at the normal (or trend) level of labor productivity, and (c) the average price paid for inputs of goods and services that are purchased from other sectors or from abroad and used up in the process of production. In conjunction, output demands in each sector are largely determined by (a) the price of sectoral output relative to the prices of substitute commodities, including those produced abroad, (b) the overall levels of broad categories of functional final demands such as consumption, investment, government expenditure, and exports, and (c) demands arising from sectors which purchase the output of the sector in question for use as a productive input. Thus, it is apparent that within a Keynesian economy, the intersectoral trans-

16. Discussion of the mechanisms by which inflationary impulses are transmitted from one country to another is not new; indeed, it probably dates back at least to David Hume. However, in the modern era the literature on imported inflation probably originates from the problems created by the undervaluation of the Deutschemark for the management of German monetary policy around 1960. The contributions of F. A. Lutz to the analysis of these problems are particularly informative. See, for example, F. A. Lutz, *International Payments and Monetary Policy in the World Today*, Wicksell Lectures 1961, Stockholm, Almqvist and Wiksell, 1961. More recently, several explicitly mathematical models of the response of an open economy to imported inflation have been constructed. See, for example, B. L. Scarfe, "A Model of the Inflation Cycle in a Small Open Economy," Y. Shinkai, "A Model of Imported Inflation," *Journal of Political Economy*, vol. 81, July/August, 1973, pp. 962–971, and S. J. Turnovsky and A. Kaspura, "An Analysis of Imported Inflation in a Short-run Macroeconomic Model," *Canadian Journal of Economics*, vol. 7, August, 1974, pp. 355–380.

mission of demand-pull effects works through a "backward linkage" network of intermediate demand flows, while the intersectoral transmission of cost-push effects works through a "forward linkage" network of intermediate input prices.

Much the same sort of "backward linkage" and "forward linkage" mechanisms are at work in the transmission of inflationary impulses across international boundaries. The main difference is that foreign prices must be converted into domestic prices via the use of the exchange rate, which for the moment is assumed to be fixed. Demand pull effects occur whenever foreign inflation leads to an increase in the demand for domestic exports or import competing products by making their foreign substitutes temporarily more expensive. This expansion in demand increases the price of domestically produced commodities, thereby tending to stabilize the relative price of foreign and domestically produced commodities. In addition, the expansion in demand for domestic output reduces unemployment which increases the rate of money wage inflation, with ultimate effects on domestic price inflation. Cost-push effects occur directly through the domestic pricing equations when the prices of imported commodities that enter either further production or the domestic consumption bundle rise. In addition, the resulting increase in the cost of living gives rise to higher wage demands, which again feed back into the domestic pricing process.

One of the crucial aspects of the Keynesian demand-pull and cost-push linkages that have just been summarized is that they depend directly upon international transactions that naturally flow through the foreign exchange market. In principle, therefore, they are capable of being regulated by movements in the foreign exchange rate. They are, however, not the only exchange market linkages in operation. Indeed, precisely because they operate through the foreign exchange market, they give rise to monetary linkages.

The effects of foreign inflation tend to move the trade balance of an open economy with a fixed exchange rate into surplus (though as we shall see later there are some exceptions to this). Moreover, the increased profitability of the export and import competing sectors may also give rise to an inflow of long term direct capital investment. Furthermore, since the foreign inflation may have been generated by excessive monetary expansion, interest rate differentials may induce an inflow of short term portfolio capital; this would also be the case if an appreciation of the domestic currency was expected to occur.

In combination, all these inflows of foreign exchange will ultimately induce an increase in the domestic money supply if the exchange rate remains fixed, and this addition to domestic liquidity will propel the economy in an inflationary direction. Thus, direct monetary linkages will be in operation simultaneously with the demand-pull and cost-push linkages. These monetary linkages result from the fact that, with interest elastic capital flows, it is difficult, if not impossible, to continue sterilizing the inflows of foreign exchange that are generated by the foreign inflationary pressures.

Given that commodity markets are organized in a Keynesian fashion, the demand-pull and cost-push transmission mechanisms may be formalized in the following way. First, the sectorally specific price indexes for materials input prices, $B' \ln p$, may be split into two components, a set of domestically produced materials price indexes and a set of foreign produced materials indexes, given of course the short run marginal conditions for both sets of materials inputs. These two sets of price indexes may be written as, respectively, $B'_h \ln p$ and $B'_m \ln p_m$, where p is the $n \times 1$ column vector of sectoral output prices as before, p_m is an $n \times 1$ column vector of import prices expressed in terms of domestic currency, and B'_h and B'_m are the transposes of $n \times n$ matrices of input-output value-share coefficients for domestically produced materials inputs and foreign produced materials inputs, respectively.[17] Thus, the equation for desired or target prices (Eq. 11B-1) may be rewritten as

$$\ln p^* = (I - A)^{-1}\{\ln v + A(\ln q - \ln k) + C(\ln w - \ln \xi) + B'_h \ln p + B'_m \ln p_m\}$$

$$(11D\text{-}1)$$

Second, the expenditure equations (11B-3) may be augmented and rewritten as

$$e = P^{-1}B_h Pq + f_h + x$$

and

$$(11D\text{-}2)$$

$$m = P_m^{-1}B_m Pq + f_m \qquad (11D\text{-}3)$$

where x, m, f_h, and f_m are $n \times 1$ column vectors of export quantities, import quantities, and final domestic demands for home produced goods and foreign produced goods, respectively. (Re-exports of imported commodities are ignored.) Of course, Eqs. (11D-2) and (11D-3) may be value-aggregated to obtain

$$Pe + P_m m = (B_h + B_m)Pq + (Pf_h + P_m f_m) + Px \qquad (11D\text{-}4)$$

This equation states that total expenditure on domestic production and imports for each commodity group equals the sum of intermediate purchases, final domestic purchases, and exports, all in value terms. Moreover, the overall trade balance in domestic currency may be written as

$$\text{Trade balance} = i'(Px - P_m m) = p'x - p'_m m \qquad (11D\text{-}5)$$

where p' and p'_m are the $1 \times n$ row vectors of domestic prices and import prices obtained by transposing p and p_m, respectively. One should note, however, that Eqs. (11D-2) and (11D-3) cannot be quantity-aggregated unless $p = p_m$.

In order to see how the basic Keynesian system of equations functions, it is instructive to work through the response of this model economy to a foreign inflationary shock. Consider the approximations

$$p_m = \pi^{-1}p_w \qquad (11D\text{-}6)$$

---

17. The assumption of constant returns to scale must now be rewritten as $(I - A - C - B'_h - B'_m)i = 0$.

and

$$x = \pi^{-1} P^{-1} B_x P_w q_w + f_x \tag{11D-7}$$

where q_w is a $n \times 1$ column vector of world outputs, p_w is an $n \times 1$ column vector of world prices expressed in terms of foreign currency, with P_w being the $n \times n$ diagonal matrix corresponding to p_w, f_x is an $n \times 1$ column vector of exogenous exports, B_x is an $n \times n$ input-output value-share matrix for materials inputs from the domestic economy to the rest of the world, and π is the (scalar) price of domestic currency in terms of foreign exchange, or the exchange rate. It follows from these approximations that, unless the exchange rate is allowed to appreciate, an increase in world prices (p_w) will imply an initial increase in both export quantities (x) and import prices (p_m).

Suppose, then, that an external inflationary shock induces an initial increase in both export quantities (x) and import prices (p_m). The first repercussion from this is evident from expressions (11D-2), (11D-3), and (11D-5). The volume of sales (e) increases and, in association, there is an expansion in the overall trade balance. The increase in the volume of sales and the consequential fall in the level of inventories via Eq. (11B-4) both lead to a rise in the volume of output via Eqs. (11B-5) to (11B-7). The increased pressure of output demand on capacity leads to an increase in domestic prices via expressions (11D-1) and (11B-2), thereby illustrating the demand-pull transmission mechanism. In addition, of course, the rise in import prices leads directly to an increase in domestic prices via expressions (11D-1) and (11B-2), thus illustrating the cost-push transmission mechanism.

These initial repercussions are not the end of the story, however. Not only will the inventory adjustment model tend to generate a cyclical response to the initial shock, but also the price adjustments occurring through Eqs. (11D-1) and (11B-2) will feed back into the quantity Eqs. (11D-2) and (11D-3) in such a way as to dampen the ultimate quantitative impact. Given that these continuing repercussions are stable, the system will eventually converge to a new equilibrium solution in which there will be a general tendency for both prices and quantities to be higher than in the initial equilibrium that prevailed before the foreign inflationary shock occurred. However, in the model outlined so far, domestic prices *do not* rise proportionately to foreign prices and the transmission of the foreign inflationary shock is incomplete.[18] Of course, important components of the total inflation transmission process have been held in abeyance via the assumed exogeneity of wage rates (w) and capacities (k), via the neglected implications of the improvement in the trade balance for the domestic money supply, and via the fact that some commodity markets will behave in a Marshallian fashion.

The transmission mechanisms outlined in the previous paragraphs assume that foreign commodities and domestically produced commodities are not perfect substitutes for each other, and that there exists an explicit downward sloping

---

18. For a rigorous discussion of these points in a parallel case, see Scarfe, *Price Determination and the Process of Inflation in Canada*, pp. 5–6. Also see chapter 10, Sec. B, of this book.

demand curve for the output of each domestic industrial sector. For those commodity groups in which the domestic economy is entirely a price taker, however,
the inflation transmission process is short-circuited; unit wage and materials
costs then only serve to determine the volume of output, but not the final price
for these commodities. Indeed, for domestic purposes these commodity groups
may be treated in a Marshallian manner.

In each sector of an open economy in which markets are organized in a
Marshallian manner, the equations for desired or target outputs (Eq. 11C-1)
should be rewritten as

$$\ln q^* - \ln k = A^{-1}\{(I - A)\ln p - C(\ln w - \ln \xi) - B'_h \ln p - B'_m \ln p_m - \ln v\}$$

(11D-8)

and the corresponding expenditure Eqs. (11C-3) may now be rewritten in quantity
aggregated form as

$$e + m = P^{-1}(B_h + B_m)Pq + f + x \qquad (11\text{D-9})$$

since

$$p = p_m \qquad (11\text{D-10})$$

for Marshallian sectors. In general, since the commodities produced by these price
taking sectors will either be exported or imported but not both, at least one of
x_i and m_i will be zero. Indeed, Eq. (11D-9) may be taken to *determine* the level
of net exports, $x - m$, *plus* the change in domestically held stocks, $Ds - q - c$,
since output (q) is determined elsewhere (that is, by Eqs. 11D-8 and 11C-2, given
11D-10). Of course, for these Marshallian commodities stockholding will generally
be the function of traders who operate in the international sphere, so that the
relevant stocks from the point of view of world market prices are global stocks
rather than those which happen to be either domestically held or, for that
matter, the result of domestic production.

Although this Marshallian specification does not seem to be appropriate,
at least in the short run, to the process of price-quantity determination in the
majority of productive sectors in open industrial economies, it is important to
remember that a significant minority of commodity markets will operate in this
fashion.[19] Moreover, since it is evident that for the price taking open economy
with a fixed exchange rate the transmission of foreign inflation is necessarily

19. The oligopolistic case of "entry-limit pricing" in which there is a kinked domestic demand
function whose upper segment is horizontal at a price corresponding to the world price when
expressed in domestic currency also behaves in a similar manner, *except that* domestic output is
unresponsive to changes in the relationship between this price and unit wage and materials costs
within a range whose limits are inversely related to the absolute elasticity of the downward sloping
lower segment of the domestic demand function. This exception has obvious importance when one
comes to consider parallel situations in the labor market, since if output and employment can get
stuck in this way underemployment equilibrium may easily result. On this point, compare T. Negishi,
"Existence of an Under-Employment Equilibrium," unpublished mimeograph, 1975.

complete, it is important to note that cost-push linkages from Marshallian price taking sectors into Keynesian industrial (price making) sectors will enhance the degree to which foreign inflationary impulses are transmitted to the domestic economy, even before consideration is given to wage rate and capacity adjustments and to monetary repercussions.

The two fundamental difficulties of incorporating wage rate and capacity adjustments into the analysis are (a) the problem of specifying a set of investment functions that are not only consistent with pricing behavior but also can feed easily into final demands, and (b) the problem of specifying the supply side of sectoral labor markets. (The demand side of sectoral labor markets is much easier to specify, though the marginal conditions for labor inputs should not be assumed to hold instantaneously at all points of time; quite evidently, sectoral employment tends to adjust to sectoral output with a lagged response leading to cyclical variations in measured labor productivity.) That is to say, the model requires an appropriate specification of the way in which the interdependent factor demands embodied in employment and investment functions feed back through factor pricing into the spectrum of functional final demands and, thence, sectoral demands.

The implications of adjustments in sectoral capacities (k) need not detain us here except to note that, if they occur, these longer run adjustments will work through the final domestic demand vector (f, or f_h and f_m) and add to the cyclical propensities of the model.[20] Of course, in addition to this initial positive demand effect through f, increases in sectoral capacities have a subsequent negative effect on prices through the capacity utilization ratio ($\ln q - \ln k$) in the Keynesian model. The implications of adjustments in sectoral wage rates (w) are much more crucial, however. Although these adjustments may in part reflect sectorally specific employment effects, to a greater extent they reflect the combined impact of the initial overall employment growth and the increase in consumer prices that are generated by the external inflationary shock.[21] The consequential rise in unit labor costs will put further upward pressure on domestic prices, and will lead to a

20. One way in which these adjustments may be handled is outlined in Scarfe, *Price Determination and the Process of Inflation in Canada*, pp. 7–8. In the approach outlined therein, the rate of physical capital accumulation by sector is taken to depend positively upon the rate of profit in that sector and negatively on the national rate of interest, where the rate of profit is a monotonically increasing function of both the output–capacity ratio and the rate of productivity improvement $((d \ln \xi_j(t)/dt)$, and the national rate of interest is determined simultaneously with national income, given monetary and fiscal policy, in a standard Keynesian way (though an allowance must be made for the impact of inflationary expectations). It is then necessary to provide an appropriate transformation to get from the value of investment expenditure by sector to the value of investment expenditure by commodity group. The dual of such a transformation must be applied to establish a relationship between changes in commodity prices and changes in the unit value of each sector's capital stock.

21. "Although the previous analysis suggests that prices respond to the pressure of demand on capacity and to normal unit labour costs there are reasons for believing that normal unit labour costs are themselves responsive to demand pressure. This responsiveness results not only from the fact that output demands give rise to employment demands which affect the going wage rates of

reduction in the eventual impact on domestic quantities. Indeed, if the absolute value of the longer run elasticity of labor supply with respect to consumer prices is equal to the longer run elasticity of labor supply with respect to money wage rates, then wage bargains which may be struck in *money* terms in the short run are ultimately bargains for *real* wages.[22] If this is so, then there is no longer run money illusion in the operation of labor markets, and the apparent existence of money illusion in the short run is simply the combined result of expectational and institutional lags.[23] On the assumption that this is so, two conclusions follow. First, the ultimate impact on domestic output and employment must, in an over-all sense, net out to zero. Second, the ultimate impact on domestic prices must be to bring them fully into alignment with foreign prices. Thus, it is evident that the longer run maintenance of the initial competitive advantage created by the foreign inflationary shock ultimately depends upon the existence of *money illusion* in the operation of labor markets as reflected in money wage rates that either do not adjust or adjust only partially in response to an increase in the cost of living.[24]

The tendency for the initial output and employment effects of the foreign inflationary shock to be eradicated through time is enhanced if the monetary repercussions of the improvement in the trade balance are incorporated as well.[25] The increase in foreign exchange earnings must lead to an increase in the domestic money supply unless the Central Bank simultaneously sells treasury bills or government bonds on the open market in order to sterilize the inflow of foreign exchange. In this context, however, sterilization necessarily allows upwards pressure on domestic interest rates to occur, which leads to an induced capital inflow. This additional inflow makes the problem of preventing an increase in the domestic money supply much more difficult. Indeed, if foreign and domestic monetary assets are close substitutes for each other, and capital flows are highly interest elastic, then the domestic money supply cannot be prevented from increasing. In the short run, the pressure towards monetary expansion can be moderated by running a stringent fiscal policy, but in the longer run the authorities will inevitably be forced to allow the domestic money supply to adapt to external

---

particular employee groups but also from the fact that changes in the prices of final consumption goods and services tend to affect going wage rates. However, the resulting variations in wage rates at the sectoral level appear to be more dependent upon variations in over-all demand conditions than upon variations in sectorally-specific demand conditions. This may reflect the fact that sectorally-specific demand conditions are usually a poor proxy for occupationally-specific demand conditions." *Ibid.*, p. 51. (This quotation has been reproduced by permission of the Minister of Supply and Services, Canada.) Of course, there will generally be an important minority of sectors in which sectorally specific demand conditions *do* influence wage rates.

22. This corresponds to the classical labor market case of chapter 10, Secs. A and B.

23. On this point see chapter 12 of this book.

24. For a rigorous proof of this proposition in a parallel case, see Scarfe, *Price Determination and the Process of Inflation in Canada*, pp. 6–7, especially footnote 3. See also chapter 10, Sec. B, of this book.

25. For a mathematical treatment of these monetary repercussions in a two commodity model with exogenous domestic output, see Shinkai, *op. cit.*, pp. 962–971.

conditions. The final outcome will be a higher price level supported by larger foreign exchange reserves and a larger stock of money, though the process leading to this outcome may well have seen a temporary expansion in output and employment followed by a cyclical retrenchment. Equilibrium prices eventually reassert themselves, though quantitative repercussions are observed on route.

The speed with which equilibrium prices are re-established is influenced by the openness of the economy and by the institutional setting in which prices and wages are determined. The more open is the economy to foreign trade and capital flows, and the faster is the response of domestic wage rates to variations in the underlying price and employment situation, the smaller will be the potential for maintaining a balance of payments surplus and domestic prices that are below prevailing world prices.

The discussion so far has assumed that the foreign inflationary shock is of a "once and for all" nature leading to new equilibrium price levels, rather than, more realistically, a continuous upward movement in each of the n foreign prices (p_w) at a pace which differs not only from commodity to commodity but also from one moment of time to the next. The lags involved in the response of the domestic economy to this more realistic view of foreign inflation will be such that output and employment effects will be observed continuously along the process through which domestic prices are brought into alignment with foreign prices, and domestic inflation rates into line with foreign inflation rates. These lags constitute one of the main reasons why, for example, short run price movements in the Canadian economy do not correspond very closely to their American counterparts even in periods when the exchange rate remains unchanged. They also help to explain why a chronic balance of payments surplus, such as experienced by Germany during most of the period 1966–1973, could persist for so long without correction. Nevertheless, "A country which tries to prevent inflation at home while inflation is going on abroad cannot succeed in the longer run unless it is willing to alter its foreign exchange rate. So long as the rate is kept fixed the Central Bank is bound to lose control over the money supply, and therefore over the level of total spending."[26]

In summary, this section has established the proposition that the three interdependent categories of exchange market transmission mechanisms, namely demand-pull linkages, cost-push linkages, and monetary linkages, are sufficient by themselves to make it difficult, if not impossible, to prevent domestic inflation rates from adapting to foreign inflation rates if the exchange rate remains unchanged. As long as short run money illusion in the labor markets does not persist in the longer run, full adaptation must eventually occur, though the numerous lags involved in the process take time to work themselves out. It follows from this that a rational anti-inflationary stabilization policy for any small open economy requires, *as a necessary ingredient*, a willingness to allow the domestic currency to appreciate whenever foreign inflation rates are accelerating to levels which are incompatible with the norms established for the rate

26. Lutz, *op. cit.*, p. 37.

of domestic price inflation. Whether or not such appreciation would also be sufficient to insulate the economy from accelerating world price inflation is discussed in the following section.

E: IMPORTED INFLATION AND INSULATION STRATEGY

The three kinds of exchange market linkages need not be the only transmission mechanisms that can occur. In addition, there may well be non-market mechanisms, mechanisms which *do not* depend directly upon international transactions flowing through the foreign exchange market. These non-market mechanisms are of two basic types, namely institutional linkages and expectational linkages. Institutional linkages transmit inflation via direct wage emulation within the international union structure and via direct price setting within the structures of multinational corporations. Expectational linkages transmit inflation through the fact that the increased socio-economic interchange among countries in a jet age world of ever-improving transportation and communications networks renders it more and more likely that individuals and organizations form their expectations of commodity price movements from the same basic "news" that the media provide. Since it is only the combined effects of the international linkages which work through the foreign exchange market that can, on average, be offset by exchange rate appreciation, it is essential that some attempt be made to assess the relative importance of the exchange market and non-market mechanisms.

From a more fundamental point of view, however, the apparent existence of non-market linkages may well simply reflect the possibility that exchange rate expectations are inelastic in the short run, as discussed in Sec. D of chapter 3. This may be illustrated, for example, by considering the Canadian case. It is fairly well known that in the short run the Canadian selling prices of many tradeable commodities do not respond to small scale changes in the foreign exchange rate.[27] One reason for this[28] is that in normal circumstances firms have inelastic exchange rate expectations, pricing their products in Canada in relation to similar products available in the United States on the basis of their view of the "normal" exchange rate. The main consequence of this phenomenon, where it occurs, is that small scale changes in the foreign exchange rate will *not* serve to create deviations between foreign price movements and domestic price movements unless these changes are *expected* to be permanent and firms change their view of the "normal" exchange rate.

---

27. See, for example, R. M. Dunn, "Flexible Exchange Rates and Oligopoly Pricing: A Study of Canadian Markets," *Journal of Political Economy,* vol. 78, January/February, 1970, pp. 140–151.

28. Another possible reason is that published selling prices do not accurately reflect the true prices at which transactions are actually occurring; rather, they reflect list prices that only respond to the average prices at which transactions are occurring after some short time lag. On this view, the failure of Canadian selling prices to respond in the short run to small scale changes in the foreign exchange rate is a statistical illusion rather than a real phenomenon.

It follows from this that the approximations given as Eqs. (11D-6) and (11D-7) require some revision. Whenever the actual exchange rate, π, appears in these expressions it should be replaced by the expected or "normal" exchange rate, π^*. On the assumption that observations of the actual exchange rate lead firms to adapt their view of the "normal" exchange rate, one may let $\pi^* = (D + \delta)^{-1}\delta\pi$, with $\delta > 0$, as implied by expression (3D-1). The main consequence of this revision is to introduce a time lag into the response of our model economy to changes in the actual exchange rate. In econometric studies of the short run behavior of sectoral prices in the Canadian economy, for example, this time lag often shows up in the fact that statistical estimates of the elasticities attached to US price variables (as proxies for p_w) are significantly larger than statistical estimates of the elasticities attached to the price of US dollars (as a proxy for π^{-1}). This fact is often interpreted as an indication of the strength of non-market transmission mechanisms, presumably working through direct price linkages within multinational firms. However, it may result from a simple mis-specification of dynamic adjustment lags. The mis-specification involves the imposition of the constraint that the time profile of the lagged response of particular Canadian prices to movements in US prices be the same as the time profile of their lagged response to the price of US dollars. The inference that long run elasticities differ simply because short run elasticities differ is not valid if, in fact, the lag patterns are dissimilar.

There are, one suspects, good reasons for dissimilarities between these two lag patterns. Individual firms are likely to be very familiar with monitoring and interpreting the movements in the narrow range of microeconomic prices with which they are crucially concerned. Through trade associations and other institutional linkages they are quickly able to take a view about the direction in which these prices, whether they are domestic or foreign, are likely to move. This is less so with the exchange rate, which is determined by macroeconomic interactions which are only remotely connected with the discretionary pricing decisions that an individual firm has to make in the short run.

It follows from the argument of the previous paragraphs that, in the short run, for example, variations in Canadian prices may reflect variations in US prices without regard to the possibility that the exchange rate may also be changing. (This is also likely to be true for asset prices, particularly stock market prices, though more for psychological than for institutional reasons.) A similar argument can be applied to the short run discretionary behavior of individual trade unions, who may bargain for approximate wage parity with their American counterparts without regard to the possibility of exchange rate movements. These linkages all depend upon the expectation that the US dollar exchange rate will remain roughly constant through time.[29]

In summary, it has been argued by way of example that the apparent existence of non-market transmission mechanisms may well reflect exchange rate expectations that are generally inelastic in the short run. When foreign inflation rates

29. On this point, see footnote 18 (chapter 3).

are accelerating, the inelasticity of exchange rate expectations makes it more difficult to stabilize the economy. Indeed, effective insulation of the domestic economy from an acceleration in world price inflation requires that the monetary and fiscal authorities make credible their determination to offset the effects on the domestic economy of cyclical bursts of price inflation in other economies by implementing whenever necessary policies which are restrictive enough to induce rational decision making units to revise their view of the "normal" or expected exchange rate smoothly in an upward direction.

Such policies are unlikely to be without cost in terms of employment, especially if the expansionary trade balance effects that would otherwise occur are slow to develop because substitution elasticities are low in the short run. Indeed, if the lags involved in the demand-pull transmission mechanism are long in relationship to the lags involved in the cost-push and monetary transmission mechanisms, it is quite likely that the cost-push linkages may dominate the demand-pull linkages in the short run, particularly when these latter are offset by the negative response of domestic demand to interest rates that gradually rise in response to the change in inflationary expectations thereby generated. In consequence, the initial response of the economy to a foreign inflationary shock may well be a phase of inflationary recession.

In these circumstances, the exchange rate will not move automatically since the positive trade balance effects do not occur immediately, and the restrictive monetary and fiscal policies that are thereby necessary to generate an appreciation in both π and π^* may well reduce the inflation but only (though gradually) at the expense of worsening the recession. If, without any alteration in the reaction functions of the monetary and fiscal authorities, the exchange rate is likely to respond fairly slowly at first to an acceleration in the rate of world price inflation, the effectiveness of an insulating strategy must depend crucially upon the determination of the authorities to implement such a strategy and carry through with it. Given the slow responsiveness of the exchange rate, it is also obvious that the effectiveness of an insulating strategy will be enhanced if some way can be found to reduce the recognition and implementation lags involved in the formulation of aggregate economic policy. The moral is, of course, that the exchange rate should be made to appreciate in the expansionary phase that normally will have preceded the phase of inflationary recession. Indeed, as will be indicated in the following chapter, the avoidance of inflationary recession requires the avoidance of the excessive expansion that will have led to it in the first place.

Finally, attention has been directed more recently to the possibility of introducing two-price systems to insulate the domestic consumers of commodities that are also exported from increases in world commodity prices. Under these systems, the prices charged to domestic consumers would somehow be kept at a lower level than the corresponding world prices. Quite apart from the fact that two-price systems are impractical, except in the case of homogeneous commodities, such as crude petroleum, with few close substitutes in the short run and with domestic production concentrated in the hands of a few large corporations, and would lead to serious distortions if an attempt was made to apply them over a wide range of commodities, it is obvious that a higher external value of the domestic currency can provide the same kind of insulation, to the domestic prices of real assets as well as to the domestic prices of consumable products, though the insulation so provided is constrained to be the same across all commodities. This qualification is important, of course, because it is difficult to overemphasize the point that during an inflation the prices of various tradeable commodities will be changing at rates that are not only highly volatile but also differ considerably from commodity to commodity. It follows from this phenomenon that an appreciation of the exchange rate can only be used to offset the *average* rate of price increase in foreign currencies for these tradeable commodities. The problems that arise from this constraint if market responses are asymmetric are discussed at length in chapter 12 of this book.

TWELVE

REAL WAGES, UTILIZATION, AND INFLATION

A: TRADE-OFF FUNCTIONS AND THE NATURAL RATE OF UTILIZATION

Most contemporary models of the inflationary process have imbedded within them an inflation–unemployment trade-off locus or Phillips curve. For present purposes, this relationship may be written in the following way,

$$w = \phi(z, Dz) + w^*, \quad \phi'_z > 0, \quad \phi'_{Dz} > 0 \tag{12A-1}$$

where w is the actual proportional rate of increase in money wage rates at time t, w^* is the expected or "going" rate of increase in money wage rates at time t, z is a measure of the degree of tightness in the labor market at time t, herein referred to as the "utilization rate," and $D \equiv d_-/dt$ is the differential operator, as before.[1,2]

The utilization rate, z, is defined to be the ratio $z = (1 - u)/(1 - v)$, where u is the unemployment rate and v is the vacancy rate. Thus, the utilization rate is positively related to the vacancy rate and negatively related to the unemployment rate. If the sum of employment, E, and vacancies, V, is used to measure the quantity of labor that is demanded (L_d), then $1 - v$ is the ratio of employment to the quantity of labor demanded since, by definition, $v = V/(E + V)$. Similarly, if the sum of employment, E, and unemployment, U, is used to measure the quantity

---

1. It should be observed that the notation which has been used (in a vector sense) for *levels* of variables in chapter 11 will normally be used for *proportional rates of change* of these same variables in the present chapter.

2. Given the derivative conditions, the expression $w = \phi(z, Dz) + w^*$ may also be written as $Dz = G(z, w - w^*), G'_z < 0, G'_{w-w^*} > 0$. This alternative expression is thoroughly explored in the "search theory" model of Mortenson. In this model, for any given level of utilization the change in the utilization rate will be higher the larger is the excess of w over w^* since the aggregate rate of acceptance of job offers then necessarily increases. See D. T. Mortenson, "A Theory of Wage and Employment Dynamics," pp. 167–211 in E. S. Phelps (ed.), *Microeconomic Foundations of Employment and Inflation Theory.*

of labor that is supplied (L_s), then $1 - u$ is the ratio of employment to the quantity of labor supplied since, by definition, $u = U/(E + U)$. It follows immediately that the utilization rate, $z = (1 - u)/(1 - v)$, may be taken to be a measure of the ratio L_d/L_s, that is, the quantity of labor demanded divided by the quantity of labor supplied.

Despite the fact that from a more rigorous point of view the degree of labor market tightness will depend in a non-linear way on a variety of labor market statistics such as vacancy rates, participation rates, and quit rates as well as the overall unemployment rate, most empirical studies of the Phillips curve trade-off relationship simply use the overall unemployment rate as a proxy for the degree of labor market tightness. In the present chapter, however, attention is concentrated on the utilization rate rather than the unemployment rate *per se*. This shift in emphasis from more traditional discussions has been motivated by two facts. First, the utilization rate is a more attractive theoretical concept than the unemployment rate; second, the measured unemployment rate is an unreliable statistical estimate of the overall degree of labor market tightness. Of course, it is also likely that $z = (1 - u)/(1 - v)$ only measures L_d/L_s in an approximate manner, as will be illustrated in the latter sections of this chapter.

Equation (12A-1) asserts that the actual rate of change in money wage rates, w, is equal to the sum of $\phi(z, Dz)$ and the expected or "going" rate of change in money wage rates, w^*, where $\phi(z, Dz)$ is a positive function of both the utilization rate and the change in the utilization rate.[3] Both high utilization rates and high rates of change of the utilization rate are conducive to a more rapid expansion of money wage rates. The reason for specifying that the actual rate of change in money wage rates is equal to the sum of $\phi(z, Dz)$ and w^* is to allow for the effects of "wage-wage" linkages in the labor markets in addition to the combined impact of demand pressure and (as we shall see) cost of living pressure on wage bargains. These "wage-wage" linkages are the consequence of (a) competitive bidding by potential and actual employers, (b) emulation effects, and (c) the attempt by trade unions to maintain or re-establish differentials among various occupational groups. In the present formulation, they are crudely proxied by the inclusion of the term w^*, while the combined impact of demand pressure and cost of living pressure is captured by $\phi(z, Dz)$. Later sections of this chapter attempt to justify this assertion.

Assuming that the expected or "going" rate of wage increase adapts to the actual rate of wage increase via an exponentially distributed lag function, one may write

$$Dw^* = \beta(w - w^*) \tag{12A-2}$$

---

3. Of course, there may well also be institutional rigidities inherent in the behavior of actual labor markets. If these rigidities are crudely represented by an exponentially distributed lag function with speed of response $\mu > 0$, then one may rewrite Eq. (12A-1) as

$$w = \frac{\mu}{D + \mu}\{\phi(z, Dz) + w^*\}$$

This possibility indicates one of the reasons why Eq. (12A-1) has not been written in the alternative form given in the previous footnote.

where $\beta > 0$ is the speed of response of the adaptive expectations mechanism. Thus, past settlements continue to affect present settlements through their effect on perceptions of the "going" rate of wage increase. The resulting expectational lag operates in addition to the institutional lag that was mentioned in footnote 3 of this chapter.

Combining expressions (12A-1) and (12A-2), one obtains

$$w = \phi(z, Dz) + \frac{\beta}{D + \beta} w \qquad (12A\text{-}3)$$

as the final specification of our Phillips curve relationship. This relationship may be solved for w in terms of $\phi(z, Dz)$ yielding the expression[4]

$$w(t) = w(0) + \phi\{z(t), Dz(t)\} - \phi\{z(0), Dz(0)\} + \beta \int_0^t \phi\{z(\tau), Dz(\tau)\} \, d\tau \qquad (12A\text{-}4)$$

It is implied by this equation that over a complete cyclical movement the rate of change in money wage rates will return to its initial value if and only if the average value of $\phi(z, Dz)$ over the cycle is zero. More formally, since the definition of a complete cyclical movement implies the condition $\phi[z(t), Dz(t)] = \phi[z(0), Dz(0)]$, it is evident that $w(t) = w(0)$ if and only if $\int_0^t \phi[z(\tau), Dz(\tau)] \, d\tau = 0$, given $\beta \neq 0$ of course. This illustrates the central importance of the term $\int_0^t \phi[z(\tau), Dz(\tau)] \, d\tau$.

Expression (12A-3) (or equivalently, 12A-4) collapses to the simpler expression

$$\phi[z, Dz] = 0 \qquad (12A\text{-}5)$$

once the expectational (and institutional) lags have been allowed to work themselves out. Stationarity in the rate of change in money wage rates can be maintained through time if and only if the equation $\phi[z, Dz] = 0$ is maintained through time. Thus, expression (12A-5) may be called the "labor market equilibrium condition."

It should be noticed that the labor market equilibrium condition is consistent with any rate of increase in money wage rates. By itself, it does not determine what w is. Indeed, it is implied by expression (12A-4) (or, more exactly, by the adaptive expectations mechanism) that w will depend upon the whole past history of deviations from labor market equilibrium. In particular, w will tend to increase

---

4. If the institutional lag of footnote 3 of this chapter is incorporated as well, this expression must be rewritten as

$$w(t) = w(0) + \frac{1}{\mu + \beta} \{1 - e^{-(\mu + \beta)t}\} \frac{dw(0)}{dt} + \frac{\mu}{\mu + \beta} \int_0^t (\mu + \beta) e^{(\mu + \beta)(\tau - t)}$$

$$\times \left[\phi\{z(\tau), Dz(\tau)\} + \beta \int_0^t \phi\{z(\tau), Dz(\tau)\} \, d\tau \right] d\tau$$

where $w(0)$ and $dw(0)/dt$ are arbitrary initial conditions.

over any period of time during which on the average $\phi(z, Dz)$ is positive, while it will tend to decrease over any period of time during which on average $\phi(z, Dz)$ is negative (though there may well be some asymmetries involved). Moreover, positive values of $\phi[z, Dz]$ will generally be associated with high and rising levels of economic activity while negative values of $\phi[z, Dz]$ will generally be associated with recessionary periods.

Once the necessarily convergent changes in utilization that are compatible with expression (12A-5) have been allowed to work themselves out, it is evident that there will be one and only one level of the utilization rate which is consistent with the continued maintenance of labor market equilibrium, namely the unique solution to $\phi(z, 0) = 0$. This level may be called *the natural rate of utilization*. It should be clear from the foregoing analysis that the actual rate of utilization cannot be maintained above the natural rate of utilization for any lengthy period of time without generating an acceleration in the rate of change in money wage rates. There is, then, no long run or permanent trade-off between higher levels of the utilization rate and higher but steady rates of wage inflation. Long run stability in the rate of change in money wage rates implies that the only true trade-off relation is between the level of utilization today and the level of utilization tomorrow.[5] It is, however, crucial for the existence of the natural rate of utilization that the coefficient attached to the w^* term in the original Phillips curve specification be precisely equal to unity; if this coefficient is less than unity, there will still exist a long run trade-off relation.[6]

The existence of a natural rate of utilization should not be taken to imply that there exists a "natural rate of unemployment"[7] which is immutable to man-power policies and other similar measures. As long as these policies are designed to improve the dissemination of relevant labor market information and increase the efficiency of job search activity, then they may be able to reduce both the unemployment rate, u, and the vacancy rate, v, simultaneously, while leaving the utilization rate unchanged. On the other hand, policies which have the effect of reducing the private costs of job search activity, such as more generous un-employment insurance benefits, may simultaneously increase both u and v (though they may still be socially desirable, of course). With this qualification, however, the existence of a natural rate of utilization will tend to imply the existence of a

5. For expansion on these ideas, see for example E. S. Phelps, "Money Wage Dynamics and Labour Market Equilibrium," pp. 124–166 in E. S. Phelps (ed.), *Microeconomic Foundations of Employment and Inflation Theory*, and M. Friedman, "The Role of Monetary Policy," pp. 95–110 in M. Friedman, *The Optimal Quantity of Money and Other Essays*.

6. See, for example, Scarfe, "On the Economic Implications of a Short-Term Wages Freeze," Appendix C, pp. 80–83 of *Price Determination and the Process of Inflation in Canada*, and Scarfe, "A Model of the Inflation Cycle in a Small Open Economy," pp. 192–203. See also chapter 10, Sec. C, of this book.

7. "The 'natural rate of unemployment,' in other words, is the level that would be ground out by the Walrasian system of general equilibrium equations, provided there is imbedded in them the actual structural characteristics of the labour and commodity markets, including market imperfections, stochastic variability in demands and supplies, the costs of gathering information about job vacancies and labour availabilities, the costs of mobility, and so on." Friedman, *op. cit.*, p. 102.

natural rate of unemployment given that labor market institutions remain unchanged.

B: TRADE-OFF FUNCTIONS AND INFLATION CYCLES

There are several other ways in which government policies may affect the Phillips curve relationship. The most fundamental of these is obvious. Macroeconomic policies directed towards the management of the volume of aggregate demand will influence both the utilization rate and its rate of change. These policies therefore affect the value assumed by $\phi(z, Dz)$ at each moment of time, and ultimately affect the rate of change in money wage rates. It is important to note, however, that policies designed to have an expansionary impact on the utilization rate will normally lead to an increase in prices relative to wage rates per efficiency unit of labor while policies of a contractionary nature have the reverse effect.[8] Thus, a cyclical expansion in z will generally be associated with a fall in the product wage rate (equals real wage rate in a one-commodity closed economy) per efficiency unit of labor. This fall may be larger or smaller depending upon the underlying parameters involved, particularly the elasticities of demand for and supply of labor. It follows that there exists a short run trade-off between higher utilization rates and higher product (real) wage rates per efficiency unit of labor. The position on this trade-off curve at which the economy finds itself at any moment of time affects the way in which money wage rates will evolve through time. High utilization rates and low real wage rates per efficiency unit of labor tend to generate an increase in the rate of change in money wage rates, while low utilization rates and high real wage rates per efficiency unit of labor tend to generate a decrease in the rate of change in money wage rates, though again there may be some asymmetries involved. It is this inverse short run association between utilization rates and product (real) wage rates per efficiency unit of labor that allows us to associate $\phi(z, Dz)$ with both demand pressure and cost of living pressure on wage bargains.

All of these ideas may be formalized in the following way. Let

$$z = \Omega(c, w - p^* - \xi, r - p^*), \quad \Omega'_c < 0, \quad \Omega'_{w-p^*-\xi} < 0, \quad \Omega'_{r-p^*} < 0 \quad \text{(12B-1)}$$

and

$$c^{-1}Dc = w - p - \xi \quad \text{(12B-2)}$$

where c is the product (real) wage rate per efficiency unit of labor, $r - p^*$ is the real rate of interest as given by the money rate of interest (r) minus the expected rate of increase in final goods prices (p^*), and $p + \xi$ is the actual rate of increase

8. The empirical evidence on this point is not overwhelming, though it is unlikely that the reverse possibility occurs.

in final goods prices (p) plus the rate of improvement in labor efficiency (ξ).[9] Equation (12B-2) is simply definitional and implies that the proportional rate of change in the product (real) wage rate per efficiency unit of labor is equal to the rate of increase in money wage rates less the rate of improvement in labor efficiency less the rate of increase in final product prices. Equation (12B-1), however, requires to be rationalized in the following way. Each firm in the economy is assumed to choose a wage and employment policy which maximizes the present discounted value of the firm, subject to the constraint that there are costs involved in the adjustment of the size of the firm's labor force. Indeed, because of imperfect information and search costs, each firm is a dynamic monopsonist in the sense that it must raise its own wage rate relative to that offered by other firms in order to increase the net flow of workers to it. The resulting problem of intertemporal choice may be solved to generate a time path for labor utilization by each firm. Along this time path, actual utilization is a decreasing function of the product wage rate, the rate of change of the product wage rate that is expected by the (temporarily) wage setting firm, and the real rate of interest. Aggregation over all the firms in the economy yields Eq. (12B-1). In the aggregate, of course, labor force utilization may not increase (decrease) instantaneously in response to a fall (rise) in c, $w - p^* - \xi$, or $r - p^*$ if there are institutional lags involved in the adjustment of the overall utilization rate.[10]

If r, p^*, p, and ξ are for the moment taken to be exogenously determined, the four Eqs. (12A1-2) and (12B1-2) constitute a complete model of the dynamic behavior of both the rate of change of money wage rates and the utilization rate. In general, given $p^* = p$ for the sake of consistency, this model will possess a unique stationary solution (when all the D's are zero) of the form:

$$\phi(\bar{z},0) = 0, \quad \bar{w}^* = \bar{w}, \quad \bar{z} = \Omega[\bar{c},0,r - p^*], \quad \text{and} \quad \bar{w} = p + \xi \quad (12\text{B-}3)$$

Thus, the stationary equilibrium solution implies that the actual and expected rates of change of money wage rates are both equal to $p + \xi$, that the level of utilization is at its natural rate, and that (given this level of utilization) the product (real) wage rate per efficiency unit of labor is a monotonically decreasing function

---

9. Again the change in notation from levels in chapter 11 to proportional rates of change in the present chapter should be observed.

10. If these institutional lags can be represented by an exponentially distributed lag function with speed of response $\alpha > 0$, then Eq. (12B-1) may be rewritten as

$$z = \frac{\alpha}{D + \alpha} \Omega(c, w - p^* - \xi, r - p^*)$$

This possibility indicates one of the reasons why Eq. (12B-1) has not been solved for $w - p^* - \xi$ in terms of the other variables giving

$$w - p^* - \xi = H(z, c, r - p^*), \quad H_z' < 0, \quad H_c' < 0, \quad H_{r-p^*}' < 0$$

This alternative expression is implicitly used by Mortenson, *op. cit.*, pp. 167–211. For a more detailed discussion of all the various points raised in this paragraph, the interested reader should consult Mortenson's paper.

of the real rate of interest $(r - p^*)$, a functional relationship which is akin to the factor–price frontiers that were discussed in Part Two of this book. Given the state of the demand side of the labor market, the higher is the natural rate of utilization the lower is the equilibrium product (real) wage rate associated with a given real rate of interest.

In order to study its dynamic properties, the system of equations may be linearized around its stationary equilibrium point. Letting $w = \bar{w} + \hat{w}\,e^{\rho t}$ and similarly for the other variables, one obtains the matrix expression

$$\begin{bmatrix} 1 & -1 & -(\phi'_z + \phi'_{Dz}\rho) & 0 \\ -\beta & \rho + \beta & 0 & 0 \\ -\Omega'_w & 0 & 1 & -\Omega'_c \\ -\bar{c} & 0 & 0 & \rho \end{bmatrix} \begin{bmatrix} \hat{w} \\ \hat{w}^* \\ \hat{z} \\ \hat{c} \end{bmatrix} = \begin{bmatrix} 0 \\ 0 \\ 0 \\ 0 \end{bmatrix} \qquad (12B\text{-}4)$$

where the various partial derivatives are all evaluated at the stationary equilibrium solution. The 4×4 determinant on the left hand side may be evaluated and equated to zero to yield the cubic characteristic equation,

$$\rho^2 - (\Omega'_w\rho + \bar{c}\Omega'_c)(\phi'_{Dz}\rho + \phi'_z)(\rho + \beta) = 0 \qquad (12B\text{-}5)$$

It is not difficult to show that all three characteristic roots to this equation have negative real parts, from which it follows immediately that the system is locally stable. First, all of the coefficients k_i, $i = 0, \ldots, 3$, are necessarily positive, given $\bar{c} > 0$ of course. Second, the condition $k_1 k_2 > k_0 k_3$ is also satisfied since (a) there would obviously be three real negative roots if the term ρ^2 were ignored and (b) the reinstatement of this term simply adds unity to k_2 thus reinforcing the satisfaction of the $k_1 k_2 > k_0 k_3$ inequality. Hence, the Routh-Hurwitz conditions are necessarily satisfied, and the system is stable in the neighborhood of the stationary equilibrium point.[11]

---

11. This conclusion must be modified if the institutional lags in the adjustment of w to $\phi(z, Dz) + w^*$ and the adjustment of z to $\Omega(c, w - p^* - \xi, r - p^*)$ that were mentioned in footnotes 3 and 10 of this chapter are reintroduced. In this case the characteristic equation becomes the quartic:

$$\rho^2(\rho + \alpha)(\rho + \mu + \beta) - \alpha\mu(\Omega'_w\rho + \bar{c}\Omega'_c)(\phi'_{Dz}\rho + \phi'_z)(\rho + \beta) = 0$$

It is not difficult to show that there cannot be any real non-negative characteristic roots to this equation, though there may well be conjugate complex roots with non-negative real parts. Thus, this enlarged system may be unstable, but if it is it will be cyclically unstable. Indeed, cyclical instability is likely to occur unless the speed of response (α) in the utilization adjustment mechanism is large relative to the speed of response (β) of the expectational adjustment mechanism. This may be seen by considering the case in which ϕ'_{Dz} and Ω'_w both approach zero, in which case the Routh-Hurwitz conditions reduce to the inequality

$$(\mu + \alpha + \beta)(\mu\alpha - \mu\beta - \beta^2) > -\mu\alpha\bar{c}\Omega'_c\phi'_z$$

Since the resulting system will be stable if and only if this inequality is satisfied, it is obvious that stability requires α to be large relative to β. Of course, this is guaranteed in the case discussed in the text, where α and μ both approach infinity. On the points raised in this footnote, compare Scarfe, "A Model of the Inflation Cycle in a Small Open Economy," pp. 196–7. For a statement of the Routh-Hurwitz conditions in the quartic case see footnote 9 (chapter 3).

Suppose, now, that our model economy is initially in equilibrium at the natural rate of utilization. An expansionary monetary shock[12] then occurs which temporarily lowers the real rate of interest (so that $r - p^*$ falls) and increases the actual rate of product price inflation (so that $p + \xi$ rises). In consequence, there is a temporary fall in the product (real) wage rate (c). The resulting expansion in aggregate demand in turn creates a positive gap between the actual and the natural rates of utilization since z must begin to rise, and a cumulative process of wage inflation is underway. As long as $r - p^*$ and $p + \xi$ are taken to be exogenous, this process is self-limiting, though it may well be characterized by damped cyclical oscillations. This oscillatory feature is a consequence of the positive and negative feedback combination inherent in the derivative conditions ϕ'_z, $\phi'_{Dz} > 0$ and Ω'_c, $\Omega'_w < 0$. One has, therefore, a model in which utilization responses are the means by which the rate of change in money wage rates adjusts to establish a target product (real) wage rate per efficiency unit of labor.

In general, of course, neither $r - p^*$ nor $p + \xi$ can be taken to be exogenous since an increase (decrease) in w will normally feed back to generate an increase (decrease) in p and ultimately p^* as well if price expectations are adaptive. It is, therefore, necessary to couple this model of the wage adjustment process with a simple model of the pricing process. If this were done for a one sectoral closed economy (in which in the long run p adjusts to $w - \xi$ with a coefficient that is precisely unity), one would be led to a Wicksellian analysis of a cumulative inflationary process.[13] The pricing and savings–investment equations would together determine *the natural rate of interest,* which in a world of pure competition and certainty may be identified with the rate of profit.[14] Only if the real rate of interest ($r - p^*$) is kept at a level equal to this natural rate of interest can the rate of inflation be prevented from changing.

In the Wicksellian cumulative process, the story begins from an expansionary monetary shock which disturbs an initial equilibrium situation by lowering the real rate of interest relative to the natural rate of interest, thus generating a *negative gap* between the real and natural rates of interest. Aggregate demand begins to expand, thus opening up a *positive gap* between the actual and natural rates of utilization. The resulting cumulative process of price and wage inflation has two crucial features. The first of these is the "duality" between the negative interest rate gap and the positive utilization gap. An actual utilization rate which is higher than the natural rate of utilization is associated with a real interest rate which is lower than the natural rate of interest. The second of these is that, roughly speaking, the acceleration of inflation cannot cease until the actual rate of utilization and the real rate of interest converge on the natural rate of utilization

---

12. By an expansionary monetary shock, we mean a sustained once and for all increase in the rate of growth of the money supply as illustrated in chapter 10, Sec. C, of this book.

13. See K. Wicksell, *Interest and Prices,* London, Macmillan, 1936 (*Geldzins und Guterpreise,* 1898). See also J. L. Stein, *Money and Capacity Growth,* New York, Columbia University Press, 1971.

14. On this point, see Part Two of this book, especially chapter 5. Of course, a natural rate of interest or rate of profit emerges from more general capital-theoretic models as well.

and the natural rate of interest, respectively, once again.[15] Since the expected rate of price inflation (p^*) will have adjusted upwards in the meantime, this necessarily implies a considerable increase in the money rate of interest (r). Of course, an even larger increase in r is required if the rate of inflation is to be brought down again. The associated movements in the actual utilization rate explain "What happens to quantities in a Wicksellian cumulative process?"[16]

In the Wicksellian story of the cumulative inflationary process, the natural rate of utilization and the natural rate of interest play similar and interdependent roles; moreover, as we shall see, they are functionally related to the same economic variables (especially the natural rate of economic growth). This interdependence draws our attention to the fact that the problem of inflation is seriously intertwined with questions of income distribution. Other things being equal, the shape and position of the $\phi(z, Dz)$ and $\Omega(c, w - p^* - \xi, r - p^*)$ functions reflect the degree to which there is disagreement over income shares among the various occupational groups in the economy (and, as we shall see, how economic resources are to be distributed among present and future generations). The inflationary consequences of this disagreement can only be held in check by allowing for a sufficient degree of slack in the economy, via the maintenance of sufficiently high real rates of interest. We shall return to this theme later in this chapter and again in chapter 13 of this book.

C: THE IMPORTANCE OF ASYMMETRICAL RESPONSES

Given the core model presented in the two previous sections, it is possible to produce a variety of models of the inflation cycle. All of these models have the following two features in common. First, there is a positive "Phillips curve" trade-off relationship explaining w in terms of z. Second, there is a negative "labor cost" feedback relationship explaining z in terms of w and other variables. Different models may be generated by specifying these other variables in alternative ways.

One such variant is provided by the case of a small open economy[17] in which the domestic rate of price inflation, p, may be approximated by an equation of the form

$$p = a(w - \xi) + (1 - a)(p_w - \pi) \tag{12C-1}$$

---

15. The approximation involved in this statement results from the pattern of lags involved, especially the expectational adjustment lag. For expansion on this point see Scarfe, "On the Economic Implications of a Short-Term Wages Freeze," pp. 80–83, which discusses a simpler formulation of the Phillips curve relation expressed in terms of discrete time periods.

16. Compare Hicks, *Critical Essays in Monetary Theory*, p. 205.

17. See Scarfe, "A Model of the Inflation Cycle in a Small Open Economy," pp. 192–203. I am indebted to Oxford University Press for permission to quote a few short extracts from this paper in the present section.

where $w - \xi$ is the rate of increase (w) in money wage rates less the rate of growth (ξ) in labor efficiency, $p_w - \pi$ is the rate of increase (p_w) in foreign prices less the rate of appreciation (π) of the domestic currency, and the positive weights a and $1 - a$ are the value shares of domestic and foreign inputs into the domestic pricing process, respectively. Substituting for p from this equation into Eq. (12B-2) yields

$$c^{-1}Dc = (1 - a)(w - \xi - p_w + \pi) \qquad (12C-2)$$

Once the various lag processes have been allowed to work themselves out and c remains stationary, this expression collapses to the equality $w = p_w - \pi + \xi$. Thus, in the long run, the rate of change in money wage rates must be equal to the rate of foreign price inflation plus the rate of improvement in labor efficiency minus the rate of appreciation of the domestic currency.

In the short run, however, if a foreign inflationary shock which disturbs an initial equilibrium situation is not offset by an appreciating domestic currency, then c must initially fall leading to higher values of z and, therefore, w as well. These higher values of w in turn feed back to produce an eventual expansion in c and so forth. The outcome of this process depends not only upon the time path of the basic exogenous variable, $p_w - \pi + \xi$, but also upon the exact configuration of characteristic roots generated by Eq. (12B-5) or its counterpart when institutional lags are incorporated as in footnote 11 of this chapter.[18] However, even in the stable case discussed in the previous section where these institutional lags are ignored, a cyclical convergence to equilibrium is likely to occur.

In the open economy model just described, the main variables through which government stabilization policies can operate are the rate of appreciation (π) of the domestic currency and the real rate of interest ($r - p^*$), where (for both simplicity and consistency) the expected rate of domestic price inflation (p^*) may be assumed to be equal to $p_w - \pi$.[19] Given the rate of world price inflation (p_w), the levels assumed by π and $r - p^*$ will depend upon the stance of domestic monetary and fiscal policies, though the extent to which $r - p^*$ can be controlled domestically will be inversely related to the interest elasticity of international capital flows.[20] In particular, the level assumed by π will depend upon the extent to which the fiscal deficit is financed by new money creation, that is upon the volume of monetarily financed fiscal transfers. The larger is this volume, the more likely is

18. Strictly speaking, if for both simplicity and consistency p^* is assumed to be equal to $p_w - \pi$, every term containing $\bar{c}$ in these characteristic equations should be multiplied by $1 - a$; but this does not affect either the behavior or the stability properties of the corresponding models.

19. No doubt it would be more appropriate to let the expected rate of domestic price inflation be determined in the usual adaptive manner. However, this would unduly complicate the analysis since the real rate of interest ($r - p^*$) could no longer be taken to be exogenously determined. Nevertheless, on the basis of the analysis of Sec. C of chapter 10, one may conjecture that a potential source of instability is consequently being neglected.

20. Of course, a stock adjustment or portfolio balance approach to international capital movements should really be used, given the sort of middle range time horizons one is contemplating herein.

currency depreciation (a negative value of π), while the smaller is this volume the more likely is appreciation (a positive value of π). Irrespective of the combinations of monetary and fiscal policies needed to generate particular values of π, however, it is clear that the basic objective of stabilizing the domestic rate of inflation cannot be achieved in the face of fluctuations in the rate of world price inflation unless π is allowed to fluctuate in an offsetting manner. For otherwise $\phi(z, Dz)$ cannot be kept close to its zero equilibrium value, with ultimate consequences for the rate of change in money wage rates.

The purpose of the remainder of this section is to explore the implications of asymmetrical market responses for an insulating strategy. The types of asymmetries explored herein are associated with downwards rigidities and non-linearities in behavioral responses. Since these asymmetries give rise to aggregation biases when aggregation takes a simple linear form, they are of special importance when insulation strategy is viewed in a multimarket context.

In a one-commodity world, the rate of world price inflation is a simple one-dimensional entity. Fluctuations in this single entity can be offset by variations in the rate of appreciation of the domestic currency, given the greater desirability of a stable domestic inflation rate than a stable foreign exchange rate. For example, if the target rate of inflation in $w - \xi$ is four percent per annum, then, as a rule of thumb, π should be allowed to vary between zero and three percent in response to fluctuations in p_w between four and seven percent.

In a multicommodity world, the rate of world price inflation is a multi-dimensional entity. Variations in the rate of appreciation of the domestic currency can only be used to offset fluctuations in the average rate of price increase in foreign currencies for the gamut of tradeable commodities. Exchange rate changes cannot be used to offset the particular price changes experienced by each separate tradeable commodity. It follows from this that exchange rate changes cannot be expected to insulate an economy from fluctuations in individual markets generated by microeconomic events occurring elsewhere in the world. This fact has certain important implications if market responses are asymmetric.

It is instructive to begin by considering an example in which there are two tradeable commodities, each of which has equal weight in an appropriate domestic inflation indicator. The world market prices of these two commodities are initially inflating at six and four percent, respectively. The rates of increase in labor efficiency in the domestic production of the two commodities are two and four percent, respectively. Thus, $p_w + \xi$ initially takes the same value of eight percent for both commodities. Labor market equilibrium prevails with constant values of the utilization rate, z, and the product (real) wage rate per efficiency unit of labor, c. Thus, if the exchange rate remains unchanged, money wage rates will be escalating at eight percent per annum.

Suppose, now, that the rate of inflation in the world market price of the first commodity accelerates to ten percent per annum. Notice that $p_w + \xi$ now differs between the two commodities, so that unless factor incomes can be made to grow at different rates in the domestic production of the two commodities there can be no microeconomic equilibrium. Resources must begin to shift from the production of commodity two towards the production of commodity one. This shift is inevitable and does not depend upon the response of the foreign exchange rate.

Without exchange rate appreciation, $\phi(z, Dz)$ will start to increase and an acceleration in the rate of change in money wage rates will eventually occur. This acceleration will be associated with a relative inflation of factor incomes in the production of commodity one, a relative inflation which induces the required shift of resources from commodity two to commodity one to occur. In principle, however, the increase in $\phi(z, Dz)$ and the ensuing acceleration in wage inflation could be prevented from occurring by an appreciation of the exchange rate at two percent per annum, provided that there are no asymmetries involved. This appreciation will be associated with a relative disinflation of factor incomes in the production of commodity two, thereby again inducing the required shift in resources to occur.

In either case, the factor inputs released from the production of commodity two may not be absorbed readily in the production of commodity one, particularly if factor intensities are different and factor mobility is slow. This is especially likely to be the case if the production of the two commodities is centered in different regions. However, if there are downwards rigidities in the rate of change of factor incomes in the production of commodity two, the transition via the importation of inflation and no appreciation may be faster and less painful than the transition via insulation and exchange rate appreciation. Indeed, with downwards rigidities, an appreciation greater than the increase in the average rate of world price inflation (in this case two percent) may be required for complete insulation, as defined by no change in w, while an appreciation less than the increase in the average rate of world price inflation may be required to maintain aggregate employment, as defined by no change in $1 - u = z(1 - v)$, given that the increase in world price inflation is unevenly distributed across tradeable commodities. Thus, in this example, the existence of downwards rigidities implies that, in the short run, an appreciation of the exchange rate at two percent per annum in response to a two percent increase in the average rate of world price inflation will lead to a small downwards drift in $1 - u = z(1 - v)$ coupled with a small upwards drift in w.

Before leaving this section, some additional investigation of the causes and consequences of asymmetries and downwards rigidities seems to be warranted. It has already been suggested that the response of the rate of change in money wage rates to demand-pull and cost-push pressures in the labor market, as measured by $\phi(z, Dz)$ is strongly lagged, first because of institutional lags in the form of long contracts and secondly because of expectational lags reflecting the slow adaptation of w^* to w. Once the rate of increase in money wage rates has been augmented through the combination of demand-pull and cost-push pressures contained in $\phi(z, Dz)$, however, it may be difficult if not impossible to get this higher rate of increase out of the system without severe and prolonged unemployment. It follows from this that while demand-pull pressures in the product market are normally responsible for an acceleration in the pace of price inflation, the inevitable upwards readjustment in the rate of change in money wage rates leads to cost-push pressures in the product market that tend to perpetuate the new higher rate of price inflation once it is established.

Associated with this phenomenon is an inherent non-linearity in the ϕ-function, which may be represented by the condition $\phi''_z > 0$ and $\phi''_{Dz} \geq 0$. Given such a non-linearity, it must be the case that

$$\int_0^t \phi[z(\tau), Dz(\tau)] \, d\tau \geq \phi\left[\int_0^t z(\tau) \, d\tau, \int_0^t Dz(\tau) \, d\tau\right] \qquad (12C\text{-}3)$$

with equality if and only if $z(\tau)$ is constant at all points of time in the interval from 0 to t. Since it is implied by the logic of the Phillips curve specification outlined in Sec. A of this chapter (and especially by expression 12A-4) that long run stability in the rate of change of money wage rates requires the integral $\int_0^t \phi[z(\tau), Dz(\tau)] \, d\tau$ to vanish, it is clear from expression (12C-3) that the optimal policy for long run stability in w is to keep the economy in labor market equilibrium at the natural rate of utilization (and the natural rate of interest) so that $\phi(z, Dz) = 0$ at all points of time. For if $\phi(z, Dz)$ is allowed to fluctuate over time, long run stability in w implies that, on average, the actual rate of utilization must fall short of the natural rate of utilization. Fluctuations in $\phi(z, Dz)$ are, therefore, seen to be inefficient and their inefficiency increases with their amplitude.[21]

It should be noticed that it is the appearance of the expected or "going" rate of wage increase with a unitary coefficient in the basic Phillips curve specification which leads to the conclusion that long run stability in w requires the integral $\int_0^t \phi[z(\tau), Dz(\tau)] \, d\tau$ to vanish. The inclusion of w^* reflects the fact that labor contracts are negotiated discretely, allowing leapfrogging of wage claims to occur; the system does not behave as if there were "one big union." No trade union negotiator can accept much less than the "going" rate of wage increase without militant objections from the rank and file. In addition, there may also be asymmetries in the formation of wage expectations, such that the past maximal value of w, w_m, enters the expectations function as an argument. If this is so, then Eq. (12A-2) must be reformulated as

$$(D + \beta)w^* = \beta[bw + (1 - b)w_m], \quad 0 < b < 1 \qquad (12C\text{-}4)$$

---

21. See also Scarfe, "On the Economic Implications of a Short-Term Wages Freeze," pp. 80–83, and "A Model of the Inflation Cycle in a Small Open Economy," p. 203. As noted by S. F. Kaliski and D. C. Smith, "Inflation, Unemployment and Incomes Policy," *Canadian Journal of Economics,* vol. 6, November 1973, p. 587: "It is also clear that these results, although based on 'natural rate' assumptions, do not yield simple natural rate results. 1. As we have just seen, there is no unique average rate of unemployment that is compatible with *any* average rate of inflation. 2. In order to avoid a positive trend in inflation rates over time, one will need to keep the average rate of un-employment at some level higher than the steady state natural rate. How much higher it will have to be depends both upon the amplitude of the cycle and, most damagingly for natural rate theory, upon the shape (degree of convexity) of the short-term unstable Phillips curve."

thus introducing a "ratchet effect" into the system. Finally, the lag parameters themselves, namely β, μ, and α, may be increasing functions of z, so that the speed of response of the system is faster on the upside than on the downside.

Whatever combination of reasons leads to asymmetries and downwards rigidities, the fact remains that they exist. Since accelerating inflation leads to serious distributional repercussions it cannot be tolerated for long. Stabilization of the inflation rate must be an important social goal. Given asymmetric responses, the costs involved in reducing the rate of inflation are enormous. It is, therefore, essential that the inflation rate be prevented from rising. The only way in which this can be done is to prevent a long series of positive values for $\phi(z, Dz)$ from accumulating, and this cannot be achieved in an environment of accelerating world inflation rates unless the exchange rate is allowed to appreciate. Thus, the fundamental rationale for an insulating strategy is to reduce the instability of the economy, and thereby avoid some of the social costs of instability. These costs involve not only lower average utilization rates and lost output through industrial unrest, but also changes in the distribution of income and wealth which are likely to be perverse.

D : A REVISED VERSION OF THE MODEL

To summarize, the existence of downwards rigidities leads directly to the conclusion that complete insulation of the economy from an acceleration in the rate of world price inflation may involve an increase in unemployment in the short run, the magnitude of this increase depending upon the dispersion of $p_w + \xi$ across tradeable commodities.[22] Alternatively, to maintain aggregate employment in the face of an acceleration in world price inflation may involve the acceptance of the fact that some part of the acceleration will be imported. This is especially the case in a situation in which the acceleration in world price inflation involves a significant worsening of the terms of international trade. In such circumstances, it is crucial to understand that the prices affecting the two sides of the labor market differ. That is to say, the consumer price index (which affects the supply side) and the price of final domestic output (which affects the demand side) part company, and the real and product wage rates per efficiency unit of labor diverge.

In normal circumstances, when the prices affecting both sides of the labor market are roughly the same, $\phi(z, Dz)$ is an adequate proxy for the combined impact of both demand pressure and cost of living pressure on wage bargains. The reason for this is the fact that the utilization rate (z) is an inverse function of the product *and real* wage rate per efficiency unit of labor (c), as given by

---

22. Notice that $p_w + \xi$ can vary widely across commodities in the short run depending upon fluctuations in the pressure of world demand on available supplies (and, in some instances, upon changes in the degree of monopoly power). In the long run, however, the existence of these variations implies that the relative rates of improvement in labor efficiency for pairs of commodities must *differ* from country to country, as described, for example, in chapter 9, Sec. D, of this book.

expression (12B-1). It follows that if there are no dramatic changes in the relationship between the consumer price index and the price of final domestic output the indirect measure of excess demand (c^{-1}) and the direct measure of excess demand (z) need not both appear in the equation explaining the rate of change in money wage rates since that would represent double counting.

It is precisely in the case of significant changes in the terms of trade when this argument does not apply; $z = (1 - u)/(1 - v)$ is no longer an adequate representation of the L_d/L_s ratio, and $\phi(z, Dz)$ fails to capture the effects of cost of living pressure on wage bargains. Indeed, in these circumstances, the basic trade-off relation, $w = \phi(z, Dz) + w^*$, given in expression (12A-1) should be replaced by the expression

$$w = \phi(c/h, Dz) + w^*, \quad \text{with} \quad \phi'_{c/h} < 0, \quad \text{and} \quad \phi'_{Dz} > 0 \qquad (12D\text{-}1)$$

where c is the product wage rate per efficiency unit of labor as before, and where h is the ratio of the consumer price index to the price of final domestic output. Thus, c/h is the *real* wage rate per efficiency unit of labor. This revised formulation of the determination of the rate of change of money wage rates is strongly supported by the available empirical evidence.[23] Given Dz and w^*, it suggests that the normal response to a fall (rise) in the real wage rate per efficiency unit of labor is an increase (decrease) in the rate of change in money wage rates.[24]

It is not difficult to show that the linearized version of the revised model consisting of Eqs. (12D-1), (12A-2), (12B-1), and (12B-2) has the cubic characteristic equation

$$\rho^2 - \{\bar{c}\phi'_{c/h} + (\Omega'_w\rho + \bar{c}\Omega'_c)\phi'_{Dz}\rho\}(\rho + \beta) = 0 \qquad (12D\text{-}2)$$

given that h is taken to be an exogenous variable. As with Eq. (12B-5), the Routh-Hurwitz conditions are again satisfied and the revised model is, therefore, stable. The equilibrium properties of the revised model imply a negative relationship between the equilibrium (or natural) rate of utilization and the real rate of interest, given the equilibrium product and real wage rates per efficiency unit of labor. The higher is the equilibrium product wage rate per efficiency unit of labor, the lower is the equilibrium utilization rate associated with a given real rate of interest. Thus, the equilibrium decomposition of the revised model differs from that of the original model.

As before (see expression 12C-1), one may take the rate of change in the price of domestic output to be given by

$$p = a(w - \xi) + (1 - a)(p_w - \pi) \qquad (12D\text{-}3)$$

23. See, for example, the wage equations of RDX2, the quarterly econometric model constructed by the Research Department of the Bank of Canada. (J. F. Helliwell *et al., The Equations of RDX2 Revised and Estimated to 4Q 1970,* Bank of Canada, 1974, p. 113.) See also J. G. Cragg, "Structural Aspects of Price Inflation," unpublished mimeograph, 1976.

24. On this point, compare Hicks, *The Crisis in Keynesian Economics,* chapter 3.

where p_w is now the world rate of inflation for the economy's exportables. One may also assume that the rate of change in the consumer price index is given by

$$p_{cpi} = a(w - \xi) + (1 - a)(p_m - \pi) \tag{12D-4}$$

where p_m is the world rate of inflation in the economy's importables. (As a convenient empirical approximation the same weights are used for both price index numbers.) Thus,

$$h^{-1} \, dh/dt = p_{cpi} - p = (1 - a)(p_m - p_w) \tag{12D-5}$$

It follows that h decreases if the terms of trade are improving ($p_m < p_w$), and h increases if the terms of trade are deteriorating ($p_m > p_w$).[25]

Since import prices enter the consumer price index with a positive weight and since export prices enter with a positive weight into the price of final domestic output, an adverse movement in the terms of trade must increase h. *It follows that $\phi(c/h, Dz)$ must rise unless z is simultaneously allowed to fall.* It is, therefore, immediately evident that an imported inflation which is associated with a serious adverse movement in the terms of international trade must inevitably lead to inflationary recession. For, in this case, the distributional problem of sharing the *real* burden of adjustment provides additional fuel to the inflationary fires, which can be kept in check only if the utilization rate is allowed to fall and the unemployment rate to rise. This is the fate of many economies, and especially that of the United Kingdom, in the wake of the worldwide food shortage and the cartelization of world petroleum production that occurred in 1973.

It should not be inferred from this conclusion and the associated reformulation of the ϕ-function that the attempt to insulate the economy from an acceleration in world price inflation by maintaining $\phi(c/h, Dz)$ close to zero is not worth the effort. Although downwards rigidities make it more difficult to insulate the economy from an acceleration in world price inflation which is unevenly distributed across tradeable commodities and, in particular, one that is associated with a serious adverse movement in the terms of trade, these same downwards rigidities provide a most forceful argument in favor of preventing $\phi(c/h, Dz)$ from moving too far from its zero equilibrium value through the implementation of an insulating strategy. In the present case, however, any insulating strategy will necessarily be associated with a fall in the utilization rate. Sooner or later, adjustment via recession is unavoidable.

E: INFLATION, UTILIZATION, AND THE DISTRIBUTION OF INCOME

Since the problem of inflation is seriously intertwined with distributional questions, a cost benefit framework for policy analysis which is devoid of value judgements

---

25. In the open economy model, every term containing $\bar{c}$ in the characteristic Eq. (12D-2) must be multiplied by $1 - a$, given the assumption that $p^* = p_w - \pi$ as before. This affects neither the behavior nor the stability properties of the model, however.

about the distribution of income and wealth is a logical impossibility. The value judgements that will be stated explicitly here are already implicit in the formal models presented in the previous sections of this chapter. First, it is desirable to maximize the utilization rate, z, subject to the condition that there is no tendency for wage inflation to accelerate or decelerate. It follows that it is desirable to reduce the amplitude of cyclical fluctuations in the economy and to maintain the economy close to labor market equilibrium as defined either by the condition $\phi(z, Dz) = 0$, or by the condition $\phi(c/h, Dz) = 0$, depending upon which model is empirically more relevant.[26] Stability is therefore seen to be a desirable policy goal. Second, it is desirable to maximize the real wage rate per efficiency unit of labor. The natural rate of interest, however, provides a constraint on this goal. It follows from these two value judgements that the creation of rewarding employment opportunities is regarded as a desirable policy goal, provided that the expectations of those already holding useful jobs are not thereby falsified through the generation of an unanticipated acceleration of inflation which undermines the real value of their remuneration from employment. The costs of accelerating inflation must be weighed against the benefits gained from employment creation.

What are some of these costs? In a general sense, these costs are all associated with greater uncertainty about future rates of inflation. This increased uncertainty reduces the willingness of decision making units to enter into long term contracts with fixed transactions values at finite points of time in the future. These contracts may be for the services of land, labor, or capital in the form of rents, wages, and interest, or they may be for specific deliveries of particular commodities in various future time periods.

In the particular case of labor services, however, it should now be obvious that accelerating inflation generates an increase in industrial unrest. In many cases, numerous man-days of employment and associated output are lost, both directly and indirectly, when an old contract based on expectations that have since been falsified by accelerating inflation expires. Often, these losses commence before that date, either through wildcat strikes or through low worker morale. A fair day's work requires a fair day's pay.

Output gained from higher utilization rates must be charged with output lost through greater industrial unrest if the higher utilization rates lead to accelerating inflation. Indeed, all the extra energy that needs to be expended to avoid falling behind in a world of accelerating inflation and increasing uncertainty about future rates of inflation must be counted as costs to be set against the temporary gain in the form of higher levels of resource utilization. For this expenditure of energy is ultimately self-defeating for the aggregate of all decision making units.

The benefits in the form of higher levels of resource utilization that accrue from a series of positive values of $\phi(z, Dz)$ are generated before most of the costs

---

26. For simplicity, in the remainder of this chapter we shall use the $\phi(z, Dz)$ notation rather than the $\phi(c/h, Dz)$ notation of our alternative model. This is not meant to imply that the alternative model is less relevant than the original model.

appear. Thus, a sufficiently myopic outlook coupled with a suitably high subjective discount rate may make it worthwhile to pursue permissive demand management policies in the short run, even though it is known that this will lead to accelerating inflation in the longer run. The pigeons may come home to roost only after the next election.[27] However, if accelerating inflation involves significant costs, and if the responsiveness of individual markets involves asymmetries which render it difficult if not impossible to reduce the rate of inflation once it has become established, then it would seem to require an inordinately high discount rate to make such permissive policies worthwhile. It is perhaps an encouraging sign that the voting public soon learns about the game, and may eventually force our political leaders to take a longer run perspective with respect to the management of aggregate demand.

It should not be implied by the foregoing discussion that there is much to be gained by deliberately designing policies that generate a series of negative values of $\phi(z, Dz)$. On the contrary, it is simply implied that $\phi(z, Dz)$ should be maintained as close to zero as possible in order to stabilize the inflation rate. The reason for recommending this as a desirable policy goal is precisely *to reduce the recurrent need to create excessive unemployment* that arises whenever the rate of inflation is allowed to accelerate out of hand. For there are few policies which are more inefficient than the attempt to reduce the rate of inflation via the creation of excessive unemployment, except perhaps to impose wage and price controls with the same purpose in mind.[28]

It used to be said that inflation is the consequence of the incompatibility of full employment with free collective bargaining. In order to suppress inflation one must either sacrifice full employment, presumably by monetary and fiscal restraint, or sacrifice free collective bargaining, presumably by replacing it with some form of prices and incomes policy. Both of these avenues have distributional consequences. Their common vulnerability to political pressures suggests that neither can be successful in suppressing inflation in the long run. More fundamentally, however, inflation is the consequence of excessive demand pressure in relation to the ability of labor markets to clear themselves efficiently. Although the institution of collective bargaining may influence relative wage rates, it is unclear at this time whether the existence of collective bargaining increases or

---

27. On this point compare W. D. Nordhaus, "The Political Business Cycle," *Review of Economic Studies,* vol. 42, April, 1975, pp. 169–190. In particular, Nordhaus indicates on p. 185 that: "The highly simplified model of macro-economic policy outlined above has two important predictions: (I) that the politically determined policy choice will have lower unemployment and higher inflation than is optimal and (II) that the optimal policy will lead to a political business cycle, with unemployment and deflation in early years followed by an inflationary boom as elections approach. Proposition I is not easily tested, but we can look for evidence of II."

28. On this point, see Scarfe, "On the Economic Implications of a Short-Term Wages Freeze," pp. 80–83, and Kaliski and Smith, *op. cit.,* pp. 587–590. See also J. Tobin, "Monetary Policy in 1974 and Beyond," *Brookings Papers on Economic Activity,* Washington, Brookings 1974, pp. 219–232, especially Fig. 3, p. 230.

decreases the efficiency of the operation of labor markets. Nevertheless, it is difficult to imagine a satisfactory solution to the inflation problem that does not entail effective changes in labor legislation that recognize the increasing integration and interdependence of the specialized production processes of modern industrial societies.

It is, however, a hard fact of life that in an economy as geographically and culturally diverse as Canada, for example, whose comparative advantages lie in highly capital intensive industrial processes, the average unemployment rates that are consistent with labor market equilibrium are inordinately high. The sooner we can educate ourselves with regard to this fact, the sooner we can institute appropriate supply-side policies to counter this problem, leaving demand-side policies to their correct function, namely to maintain $\phi(z, Dz)$ close to its equilibrium value and thus stabilize the rate of wage inflation. Even this recommendation has distributional consequences which may not be spread equitably across the diverse regions of the economy.

Once again, stabilization policy is the key to an improvement in the overall performance of the economy. If the average rate of utilization is to be maximized without acceleration in the rate of wage inflation, it is essential to minimize the amplitude of cyclical fluctuations around the equilibrium condition, $\phi(z, Dz) = 0$. This implies that stabilization policy should be designed to close the gap between the natural and actual rates of utilization and the natural and real rates of interest. Again, it is to be noted that these gaps are dual to each other and opposite in sign. Since neither the natural rate of interest nor the natural rate of utilization is directly observable, however, it follows that the design of appropriate stabilization policies will always be a matter of judgment. Nevertheless, it is evident from Sec. C of chapter 10 that there are strong grounds for recommending that the authorities pursue a policy of reasonable stability in the growth rate in the nominal stock of money.

In addition to this, any shift in the natural rate of interest that occurs for demographic or technological reasons will be associated with a shift in the natural rate of utilization. By way of example, since the acceleration in inflation that has occurred over the last few years has coincided with an acceleration in the growth rate of the labor supply, it is instructive to trace the impact of a temporary expansion in the growth rate of the supply of labor through our basic model. The consequences of this expansion bear a formal similarity to the impact of a temporary expansion in the rate of improvement of labor efficiency, given the assumption of Harrod-neutrality. In both cases, the natural rate of economic growth is temporarily increased.

It has been shown in Part Two of this book (and especially in chapters 5 and 9) that an expanded rate of improvement in labor efficiency is associated with a higher rate of capital accumulation and a higher rate of profit. In the analytical framework of pure competition and certainty on which Part Two was based, the rate of profit may be equated with the natural rate of interest. The relevant conclusion to draw for present purposes is, therefore, that the natural rate of interest must rise. It follows that the real wage rate per efficiency unit of labor must (temporarily) fall. In addition, in these circumstances $\phi(z, Dz)$ must also shift and a decrease in the natural rate of utilization is implied.[29]

If labor market equilibrium is to be maintained in these circumstances, there must necessarily be a decrease in the actual rate of utilization, whether the initial expansion occurs in the rate of improvement of labor efficiency or in the rate of growth of the labor supply. Despite the "neo-classical synthesis," there is such a thing as "technological unemployment," and it can only be averted through an acceleration in the rate at which money wage rates are increasing. In other words, if the actual utilization rate, z, either remains constant or increases at the same time as a temporary expansion occurs in the rate of improvement in labor efficiency or in the rate of growth of the labor force, the inevitable consequence is an accelerated rate of wage inflation. Although this acceleration is entirely warranted in real terms in the case of a higher rate of improvement in labor efficiency, it is clearly inflationary in the case of a higher rate of growth in the labor force.

Something of this kind has been occurring in North America, and particularly in Canada, over the last few years as the surge of postwar babies became graduates of our educational institutions and emerged as participants in the labor force. The satisfaction of the demands of this new generation for gainful employment, and the pressures put on the markets for houses and consumer durables in response to high rates of family formation, could well have induced a policy response designed to promote lower real interest rates, particularly on mortgages, and higher employment growth rates. Against a demographic background which implied a temporary increase in the natural rate of interest and a temporary decrease in the natural rate of utilization, it is not surprising that the permissive policies followed from mid-1970 until the end of 1973 inevitably led to higher rates of inflation.[30] The dual combination of a negative gap between the real and natural rates of interest and a positive gap between the actual and natural rates of utilization necessarily generated a series of positive values for $\phi(z, Dz)$, which resulted in an acceleration in wage inflation.[31]

In the context of any model with cyclical tendencies, such as that described in the earlier sections of this chapter, government stabilization policies are faced with two basic questions. First, how can these policies be used to move the equilibrium levels of the underlying variables, in this case w, z, and c, to some desired or target levels. Second, how can these policies be used to reduce or remove

29. On this point, compare Mortenson, *op. cit.*, pp. 167–211.

30. It would be interesting to examine the opposite interaction of demographic and technological events with monetary events that led to the great depression of the 'thirties in the same light. A recent paper by my colleague, C. L. Barber, "On the Origins of the Great Depression," unpublished mimeograph, 1976, attempts to do precisely this.

31. This brief comment on recent events should not be taken to imply the judgement that the permissive policies were wrong, but simply the judgement that a somewhat tighter run coupled by an appreciation of the Canadian dollar could have avoided some of the more obvious inflationary excesses and consequential instabilities that have emerged. For further comment, see chapter 13 of this book.

the cyclical momentum in such an economy around its equilibrium position. In the context of the present model, therefore, stabilization policy entails that the actual levels of w, z, and c be made to converge on their target levels with a minimum amount of cyclical fluctuation.[32]

The mention of target levels automatically raises the question, "Is there an optimal rate of inflation?" The answer to this question is not a simple one,[33] and a detailed treatment of it would lead us too far afield. A cursory treatment, however, would begin with the observation that the basic question of an optimal inflation rate may be separated into two subordinate questions. First, is there an optimal rate of anticipated (or expected) inflation? Second, is there an optimal rate of actual inflation, given the anticipated rate of inflation?

It is probably fair to say that the economic impact of unanticipated inflation outweighs the impact of anticipated inflation, and that most of the social costs and benefits of inflation as well as its distributional consequences are associated with unanticipated inflation. Accordingly, one can be quite agnostic on the question whether there is an optimal anticipated or expected rate of inflation while still recommending to a government that is concerned about the social costs of inflation that its short run stabilization policies should be designed to reduce the potential of the economy to experience unanticipated inflation. This implies the policy recommendation that from a short run stabilization viewpoint the expected rate of inflation should be treated as the optimal or target rate of inflation. Although this might seem to be an odd recommendation, in the context of our simple model economy it carries the important implication that the only rational target level for $\phi(z, Dz)$ over any reasonable period of time is the equilibrium level $\phi(z, Dz) = 0$, since it is only in this way that the gap between the actual and expected rates of wage inflation, $w - w^*$, can be reduced. The basic objective of stabilizing the domestic rate of inflation cannot be achieved unless the target and equilibrium values of $\phi(z, Dz)$ coincide. A basic corollary of the condition $\phi(z, Dz) = 0$, of course, is that there exists an optimal path for z which leads monotonically towards the natural rate of utilization.

It was suggested in the previous paragraph that, from the viewpoint of short run stabilization policy, the optimal rate of wage inflation is simply the expected or "going" rate of wage inflation. When different individuals have different expectations, the expected rate of inflation has no clear meaning. However, there will exist a mean value to these individual expectations. This mean value is influenced by the media, and it is comparable in conception to the consensus forecasts that are thrashed out in meetings of economic policy makers. Assuming that these forecasts are based upon more recent and consistent information and upon more rigorous analytical frameworks than are readily available to the average decision making unit, the mean expected rate of inflation should respond to observed inflation rates with a longer lag than do these consensus forecasts. If

---

32. Compare chapter 1, Sec. E, of this book.
33. This can be evidenced by the voluminous discussion contained in a recent book by E. S. Phelps. See Phelps, *Inflation Policy and Unemployment Theory*, New York, Norton, 1972.

this assumption is false, however, it would indeed be difficult for policy makers to stabilize the rate of inflation.

However one chooses to cross-classify the income recipients who fall into each particular category of the size distribution of income, whether it is by ownership of particular inputs into the production process, by the geographical location of their principal residence, by their main occupation or industry of employment, or by the generation in the normal life cycle to which they belong, the distribution of income and wealth in any actual economy is continuously in a state of flux. This will be so no matter what the actual rate of change of the overall inflation indicator happens to be whether or not this rate of change is generally anticipated.

Inflation occurs over any period of time in which the totality of income claims adds to a greater sum than the overall real volume of output produced. If this inflation is correctly anticipated by every individual decision making unit *and* reflected in all contractual arrangements, then there is no reason why it should have any significant effect on the distribution of income. In fact, however, the inflationary expectations of individual decision making units may differ widely at any point of time. Since these expectations are inconsistent, they cannot all be realized simultaneously. Most, if not all, of them will turn out to be falsified with the passage of time, and will subsequently be revised in the light of experience.

The falsification of inflationary expectations necessarily implies unanticipated gains and losses in real terms on both income and capital accounts. The degree of frustration and disappointment associated with unanticipated losses, as well as the degree of pleasant surprise associated with unanticipated gains, may depend upon the extent to which inflationary expectations are falsified. In addition, the social consequences of the falsification of inflationary expectations may depend upon which groups in society are the net gainers and which are the net losers.[34] Since the majority of individuals receive most of their income in the form of wages and salaries which are only renegotiated at infrequent intervals (though the discrete nature of wage changes is being eroded as the use of indexing schemes and escalator clauses becomes more widespread), a generally unanticipated increase in the continuous rise in the cost of living may create a majority view that people are being cheated by inflation even if, on balance, they are managing to stay ahead of the game. Of course, if the unanticipated inflation is associated with a lower overall volume of output than anticipated or with a significant deterioration in the terms of international trade, the problem of sharing the *real* distributional burden of unanticipated inflation may have serious social consequences. The impact of

---

34. Of course, the gainers might be able to compensate the losers, especially if compensatory transfers were costless. However, an all inclusive system of compensatory transfers is not feasible (nor would it necessarily be desirable), even if the inflationary expectations of every individual were directly observable. The composition of the complete inventory of decision making units is constantly changing as individuals and generations of individuals pass through their life cycle. One cannot compensate the aged after they are dead for the previously unanticipated erosion of the real value of their life savings. The frustrations and disappointments resulting from the falsification of expectations, and the associated failure of the plans to which these expectations give rise, are an unalterable feature of the irreversible time span of human life.

recent upheavals in the world prices of foodstuffs and energy fuels bears witness to this possibility.

Ultimately, therefore, we must face up to the fact that the problem of inflation is seriously intertwined with distributional questions; indeed, it is this fact that makes it so intractable. All that it may be possible to achieve is to stabilize the rate of inflation and, thereby, reduce the scale of frustrations and surprises associated with the inevitable losses and gains that result from unanticipated inflation. Of course, many groups in society are either (a) able to protect their real income claims in the face of inflation or (b) protected by governmental or private indexing schemes. Nevertheless, since it is not possible to index everything, it will often be the case that the introduction of indexation simply transfers the risk burden associated with uncertainty about the future rate of inflation from one group in society to another. In addition, some of these transfers are likely to be intergenerational in nature.[35]

From the point of view of stabilizing the rate of inflation, the inclusion of cost of living escalator clauses in labor contract settlements has one major advantage and one major disadvantage. The advantage is associated with a reduction in the discrete nature of individual wage changes. This reduction allows the wage adjustments received by each occupational group to occur in a somewhat more simultaneous or "across the board" fashion, thus generating the appearance of greater equity. In consequence, some reduction in the importance of "wage-wage" leapfrogging ought to occur. The disadvantage, on the other hand, is associated with an increase in the speeds of response in the lags involved in the "price-wage" spiral. High speeds of response in this inflation transmission process increase the likelihood of upwards instability and, therefore, of trajectories culminating in hyper-inflation.[36]

Some simple arithmetic illustrates the dangers of instability involved in wage indexing schemes, particularly if they involve one for one adjustment for the percentage increase in the cost of living. Let the rate of price inflation in a closed

---

35. Serious problems of intergenerational equity arise in the area of pension plans, where for formula plans at least (simple money purchase plans apart) it is impossible to know what the term "fully funded" means when there is considerable uncertainty about the future value of money.

36. Trajectories leading to hyper-inflation usually emerge out of a situation in which the economy has already experienced a series of inflation cycles of increasing amplitude. Moreover, these trajectories are always associated with falling output growth rates and rising unemployment. They project, therefore, an inflationary recession with a vengeance. Furthermore, policy shifts which are sharp enough to reverse the tendency towards hyper-inflation run a distinct danger of producing an economic depression. In terms of the trade-off function developed in Sec. A of this chapter, hyper-inflation could develop if the coefficient attached to the expectations term, w^*, became greater than unity as inflation progressed. In this case, hyper-inflation would necessarily be associated with a series of negative values for $\phi(z, Dz)$. In the language of traditional trade-off models, the long run "trade-off" relation between inflation and unemployment would then be positively sloped. Of course, without worldwide hyper-inflation, for an open economy all such trajectories must imply escalating currency depreciations. For a rigorous treatment of such trajectories see Scarfe, *Price Determination and the Process of Inflation in Canada*, chapter 2, pp. 16–21, and especially the phase diagram on p. 19.

economy be equal to the rate of wage inflation less the overall rate of growth of labor productivity. Let the rate of wage inflation be equal to the rate of price inflation in the previous period (as in a one for one wage indexing scheme) plus a positive real wage demand. In such an arithmetical world, both the rate of price inflation and the rate of wage inflation must accelerate without bound if the real wage demand always exceeds the overall rate of growth of labor productivity.[37]

Of course, no actual economy operates in exactly this arithmetical way. Real demands must eventually be reconciled with the overall increase in labor productivity by a squeeze of those on relatively fixed incomes who fall behind in the inflationary scramble, by greater unemployment, or by the collapse of the system. However, the problems involved are always particularly acute whenever labor productivity growth is slow, or (in an open economy) whenever the terms of international trade deteriorate. It is an unfortunate fact that, over the period 1973–75, wage indexing formulas in the presence of a significant deterioration in the terms of trade necessarily generated a rapid escalation in wage inflation in many countries before policy makers had time to think their way to sensible policy reactions. Of course, the indexation schemes only reduced the time lag in a response that was, in any case, going to occur.

Analysis of these kinds of situations leads to two conclusions. First, the indexation of the personal income tax is a desirable institutional change, not only because it forces the government to finance the growth in its expenditures in a less automatic and more open way, but also because it may reduce the propensity of wage demands to reflect the rise in the cost of living with a coefficient that is greater than unity. Second, the fundamental goal of incomes policy should be to minimize the future portion of new labor contract settlements that is *not* tied to cost of living adjustments, that is, the part which has just been called the "real wage demand." This conclusion is not inconsistent with the longer run maximization of the real wage rate per efficiency unit of labor (a concept which refers to a level as opposed to a rate of change), since it is only by stabilizing the rate of inflation that this longer run objective can be achieved, given the current institutional constraints. Indeed, if the rate of inflation is to be stabilized without a long period of excessive unemployment, the average "real wage demand" that is granted must not be allowed to exceed the overall increase in labor productivity in the economy. For otherwise, these "real wage demands" cannot, in the aggregate, be realized.

Apart from the indexation of the personal income tax, further indexation should only be introduced as a means of reducing real demands on the economy,

37. I am reminded of the fact that university faculty associations often ask for salary increases which reflect the sum of (a) a full cost of living adjustment, (b) an amount related to the annual increase in national productivity, and (c) a strictly positive award for "merit." Of course, they do not normally receive increases based on this formula. However, if the whole economy operated on this principle, a most "meritorious" acceleration in inflation would occur, except in so far as the merit pool is derived from the retirement of the "old guard" on low pensions and their replacement by "young turks" on low salaries.

particularly "real wage demands." Since these demands become inflated in the first place precisely because of the greater uncertainty about future rates of inflation that is generated through the experience of accelerating inflation, it may be possible to reduce them once again by advocating an extension of the prevalence of wage indexation as a guarantee against future erosion of real purchasing power by accelerating inflation. If one embarks on this course, however, it is crucially important that the economy be insulated by exchange rate appreciation from any further acceleration in the rate of world price inflation.

The overall policy conclusions arising from this chapter are not new.[38] Macro-economic stabilization policies should be designed to aim for some reasonable and explicit targets for such variables as the overall rate of resource utilization, the overall rate of growth, and the pace of price inflation. Unless these targets are compatible it will be impossible to attain them.[39] There are three fundamental conditions for compatibility. First, a realistic appraisal should be made of the average levels of demand pressure that the economy can withstand without suffering excessive and probably accelerating inflation, giving due recognition to the considerable limitations of the national unemployment rate as an adequate proxy for the overall pressure of demand. Second, recognition should be given to the strong probability that the failure to maintain the economy on a path consistent with the eventual achievement of targets which appear to be compatible from the vantage point of the current time period may well set in motion expectational, behavioral, and institutional shifts that render these same targets incompatible in future time periods, from which it follows that appropriate "aiming" requires a consideration of "optimal trajectories" and complete time paths. Third, the exchange rate should be allowed to vary continuously through

38. Compare Scarfe, *Price Determination and the Process of Inflation in Canada*, p. 55, and Scarfe, *"A Model of the Inflation Cycle in a Small Open Economy,"* pp. 201–203. The excerpts contained in this paragraph are reproduced by permission of the Minister of Supply and Services, Canada, and Oxford University Press, respectively.

39. For example, in its Tenth Annual Review, the Economic Council of Canada set out a new performance indicator for the Canadian economy. This "relative inflation" indicator called for domestic prices, as measured by the Consumer Price Index (C.P.I.), to remain in line with a trade-weighted average of foreign consumer price indexes. (See Economic Council of Canada, *Shaping the Expansion, Tenth Annual Review*, Ottawa, Information Canada, 1973, pp. 64–68.) Although this new performance indicator is rationalized on the grounds that "Canada is not in a position to apply a price policy that is significantly different from that of its partners" (*ibid.*, p. 57), it can be analyzed critically from at least three points of view. One may question (a) the choice of foreign inflation indicators, (b) the omission of exchange rate considerations, and (c) the consistency of the relative inflation performance indicator with the maintenance of other desirable policy goals, such as economic stability. This critical analysis leads to the conclusion that the desirability of the relative inflation indicator depends very much on the stability of the external environment with respect to prices in particular; there is no inherent magic about foreign price performance that makes it desirable to emulate it under all circumstances (by the maintenance of a relatively constant exchange rate). In particular, the relative inflation indicator is inconsistent with domestic stabilization objectives when the economy is subjected to foreign inflationary shocks; it makes sense only in the context of a stable external environment. Of course, it is possible that one may underestimate the "political power" of dollar-for-dollar parity.

time to prevent the varying rates of foreign inflation from becoming domestic inflation. Indeed, the only effective tool for insulating a small open economy from fluctuations in the rate of world price inflation is an appropriately managed flexible exchange rate; without this tool, it would be exceedingly difficult, it not impossible, to stabilize the economy around its specified target levels.

The following chapter is designed to illustrate the analytical developments of this and earlier chapters via a brief exploration of the common causative forces lying behind the recent instability in world monetary arrangements and the recent acceleration in rates of price increase common to most advanced Western economies. In particular, it describes how the events leading to the depreciation of the US dollar in world currency markets—the unsticking of the numeraire— provided a major thrust to the acceleration of the pace of price inflation in industralized countries in the West. Although this discussion will no doubt appear somewhat dated as well as somewhat out of context with the chapters which have gone before, until someone actually lays the foundations of monetary theory[40] it will have to suffice. Its inclusion is perhaps justified by the conclusions that are drawn in the penultimate section of chapter 13.[41]

40. Perhaps this is unfair. In particular, one might cite D. Patinkin, *Money, Interest and Prices*, New York, Harper and Row, 1965, and J. L. Stein, *Money and Capacity Growth*. In a different (neo-classical) framework, one should also cite D. K. Foley and M. Sidrauski, *Monetary and Fiscal Policy in a Growing Economy*, New York, Macmillan, 1971.

41. Its inclusion may also be justified by a quotation from Hicks, *Critical Essays in Monetary Theory*, pp. 156–7: "Monetary theory is less abstract than most economic theory; it cannot avoid a relation to reality, which in other economic theory is sometimes missing. It belongs to monetary history, in a way that economic theory does not always belong to economic history. Indeed it does so in two ways which need to be distinguished.... It is noticeable, on the one hand, that a large part of the best work on Money is topical.... Throughout the whole period—back before Ricardo, forward after Keynes—money itself has been evolving."

THIRTEEN

INFLATION AND ECONOMIC EXPANSION
IN A FINITE WORLD

A: CAPITAL MOBILITY AND THE DEPRECIATION
OF THE NUMERAIRE

It is now twenty-three years since the publication of Hicks' "Inaugural Lecture"[1] which introduced a lively discussion of the apparent dollar shortage of the early postwar period, and fifteen years since the publication of the volume edited by Harris, *The Dollar in Crisis*,[2] which discussed the birth of the apparent dollar surplus of the later postwar period. But despite this elapse of time, economists are not in full agreement about the underlying causes of this considerable swing in the payments fortunes of the United States of America. Nevertheless, a consensus viewpoint based upon an appropriate blending of "stylized facts" and theoretical analysis would suggest that the central ingredients in the swing from dollar shortage to dollar surplus in the postwar period are (a) the pattern of productivity growth in competitor countries relative to the United States (technological convergence), (b) the size of long term investment flows to these (and other) countries from the United States (capital mobility), and (c) the lack of coordination of the targets set by the various monetary and fiscal authorities of advanced Western economies. This consensus viewpoint emphasizes the importance of technological convergence in the explanation of differences in growth rates and changes in trade patterns, and indicates how the process of technological convergence interacts with long term international capital mobility to produce movements in the balances of payments of major open economies through time. It suggests, however, that the

---

1. J. R. Hicks, "An Inaugural Lecture," *Oxford Economic Papers*, vol. 5, June, 1953, pp. 117–125. See also J. R. Hicks, *Essays in World Economics*, Oxford, Oxford University Press, 1959, chapter 4 and Appendix B, and G. D. A. MacDougall, *The World Dollar Problem*, London, Macmillan, 1957.

2. S. E. Harris (ed.), *The Dollar in Crisis*, New York, Harcourt Brace and World, 1961.

lack of coordination of the monetary and fiscal policies of advanced Western economies is responsible for turning a "dollar problem" into a "dollar crisis."

One of the remarkable features of the postwar period has been the expansion of *per capita* real incomes in Western Europe and Japan relative to *per capita* real incomes in the United States and Canada. Associated with this "catching up" phenomenon, or reduction in the productivity gap between Europe and the United States, has been a convergence in broad patterns of production costs and commodity consumption in Europe towards those of the United States. The connection between this convergence and the emergence of the US balance of payments problem may be established by means of two propositions that were developed in Sec. D of chapter 9 of this book.

Proposition one suggests that the process of technological convergence involves the diffusion of the usage of "best practice" techniques across the various producers of a particular commodity, in whichever countries these producers are located. This diffusion process normally implies some degree of "anti-import bias" in the pattern of productivity improvements introduced by countries which are, on the whole, importers of new techniques of production, and makes it progressively more difficult for a country which is largely an exporter of new productive techniques to continue exporting relatively large quantities of commodities in the production of which it initially possesses a comparative cost advantage.

Proposition two suggests that, in addition to this, economies growing rapidly through the reduction of an existing productivity gap will experience higher rates of profit and higher rates of capital accumulation than a slower growing economy with a higher level of productivity. If long term direct foreign investment responds to relative profit rates, capital will flow from a slower growing more advanced economy to faster growing less advanced economies, this flow tending to equalize profit rates among the countries under consideration.

That the United States has been not only a technological leader but also a major long term capital exporter to other advanced Western countries in the postwar period is unquestionable. Although part of this foreign investment from 1958 onwards has been associated with the establishment of market orientated subsidiaries behind the common tariff wall of the European Economic Community, in the main it has probably been triggered by the relatively higher profit rates that could be obtained by combining more advanced technologies with lower European labor costs. International technological migration and international capital mobility go hand in hand, the major vehicle being the multinational corporation.

In addition to the "anti-import bias" problem associated with the process of technological convergence, the United States has been faced with a transfer problem associated with its long term capital outflows. The appropriate response to these two related problems is an overall movement in the terms of trade against the United States. To bring this about under fixed exchange rates would have required a *slower* rate of inflation in the United States than elsewhere, at least in the costs of producing tradeable goods. Largely due to the inflationary overshoot from 1965 to 1970 associated with the Vietnam War, the rate of inflation has not been sufficiently slower in the United States than elsewhere.[3] The result has therefore been that US long term capital outflows have been financed in part by a diminution of the US gold stock and in part by short term borrowing from foreign banking systems, thus giving the appearance that the United States has been buying up foreign assets with foreign money.

Neither the "anti-import bias" problem nor the transfer problem, however, would necessarily have led to a substantial balance of payments deficit in the United States since 1958 (even when the important direct effects on the balance of payments of the war in Vietnam are included) had US money incomes grown more slowly relative to money incomes in Western Europe and Japan. Despite the importance of technological convergence and long term capital mobility as underlying factors in the emergence of the US balance of payments deficit, therefore, this deficit developed into crisis proportions in 1970–71 largely for monetary reasons. Indeed, the emergence of the dollar crisis in 1970–71 resulted from the previous mismanagement of domestic demand in the United States in the face of the Vietnam War and from the malfunctioning of the exchange rate system at that time.

The collapse of the gold exchange standard is associated with the over-valuation of the US dollar and the refusal of European (and Japanese) monetary authorities to abandon their chronic surpluses by freely appreciating their domestic currencies. Under the gold exchange standard, Gresham's Law dictates that it is crucial to maintain a stable dollar price of gold. If the US gold stock must be used to maintain this price, then the system is inherently unstable since the United States cannot preserve confidence in the dollar while continuing to sell gold.[4] It was, therefore, inevitable that if the US balance of payments deficit were not substantially reduced the system would collapse. This collapse occurred in two basic stages, first the agreement in March, 1968, to abandon the attempt to stabilize the price of gold on the free London market which led to the two tier gold pool system, and second the announcement in August, 1971, that the United States would no longer exchange dollars for gold with foreign central banks. Whereas it was formerly possible for European central banks to put contractionary pressure on the US monetary authorities by trading in dollars for

3. This is especially so when foreign inflation rates are adjusted for exchange rate changes prior to the fall of 1971. The main exchange rate changes between the 1949 devaluation of the pound sterling (and associated currencies) and the autumn of 1971 include (a) the two French devaluations of 1957 and 1958 amounting in total to 29 percent, (b) the 5 percent upwards revaluation of the Deutschemark and the Netherlands guilder in 1961, (c) the 14.3 percent devaluation of the pound sterling in 1967, (d) the 12.5 percent devaluation of the French franc in 1969, (e) the 9.3 percent upwards revaluation of the Deutschemark in 1969, (f) the 7.0 percent upwards revaluation of the Swiss franc in the spring of 1971, and (g) the continuous floating of the Canadian dollar prior to mid-1962 and again from June, 1970. The Deutschemark was allowed to float prior to its revaluation in 1969, and again, along with the Netherlands guilder, from May, 1971. On balance, therefore, the US dollar had appreciated relative to other currencies in the postwar period up until the fall of 1971.

4. For a useful discussion of the inherent instability of the gold exchange standard, see R. A. Mundell, *International Economics,* chapter 20.

gold, this option is no longer available to them. This suspension of convertibility, which came after a year of rapid monetary expansion in the United States, placed the Western world formally on a dollar standard. Informally, of course, it had been on such a standard for some time.

Under the dollar standard, it is just as necessary for the reserve currency country to maintain a non-inflationary monetary stance as it is under the gold exchange standard. In actual fact, the US economy did provide a price stable anchor to the world monetary system in an exemplary fashion prior to the middle of the 'sixties. However, US price stability started to become unstuck in the 1965–66 expansion, and it is this more than anything else which led eventually to the apparent overvaluation of the US dollar in 1971.[5] The recession of 1970 may be regarded as an abortive attempt to resist the inflationary process which had become firmly established in the earlier expansionary period.

Although the expansionary monetary and fiscal policies of the US authorities beginning in early 1970 were ostensibly related to the attempt to catch up with the "game plan" before the presidential election in November 1972, the fact that US interest rates (and particularly short term rates) fell dramatically (and to a level lower than likely inflationary expectations would warrant) worsened the balance of payments deficit by inducing a substantial outflow of short term portfolio capital. Moreover, the continuation of the monetary expansion through the presidential announcement of August 1971, and the Smithsonian agreement of December, 1971, prevented short term capital from flowing back into the US economy.

In retrospect, the novel feature of US monetary and fiscal policies in this period is that they appear to represent an attempt *to inflate* one's way out of a balance of payments deficit, but with a twist.[6] The twist is that the expansionary policies appear to have been designed to have their dominant inflationary effect on the US dollar price of foreign produced commodities, either through further exchange rate adjustments or through the inflationary effects of foreign monetary expansion, while the US dollar price of US produced commodities was supposed to be contained by a system of wage and price controls. One reason for doing this appeared to be to bring about relative price adjustments that eventually

5. On these points, compare R. I. McKinnon, "Monetary Theory and Controlled Flexibility in the Foreign Exchanges," *Princeton Essays in International Finance*, no. 84, Princeton University Press, April, 1971, p. 27: "American price-level behaviour and otherwise unstable policies over the past five years have undoubtably been inconsistent with appropriately specified rules of a dollar standard and should be subject to international censure. On the other hand, American economic performance over the whole postwar period has been reasonably good as an international balance wheel—even in some periods when American economic policy has been quite heavily censured by foreign and international official agencies." On a similar theme, see W. D. Nordhaus, "The Worldwide Wage Explosion," *Brookings Papers on Economic Activity*, Washington, Brookings, 1972, pp. 431–465.

6. The orthodox way of correcting a balance of payments deficit via exchange rate depreciation entails some deflation of domestic demand, particularly by fiscal means, to make room for an expansion in the trade balance. This is especially the case if the economy is operating in the neighborhood of full employment. Of course, the unsticking of the numeraire is not an orthodox case.

generate a real transfer of resources that justifies whatever amounts of long term direct foreign investment that US based multinational corporations wish to carry out; the demand for concessions on the commercial policy front was simply an important ancillary to this basic policy stance.[7] These appearances, however, probably reflect the faulty vision of hindsight, since it is thoroughly unlikely that the US authorities anticipated the extent to which planned speculative conversions of privately held, short term dollar liabilities into foreign currencies would mushroom in 1971 as foreign exchange markets reacted to the fundamental signal provided by the first recorded US deficit on merchandise trade for many years.

B: MONETARY INSTABILITY AND WORLD INFLATION

The primary options available to foreign central banks in the face of these vastly expanded planned speculative conversions of privately held, short term dollar liabilities were (a) to inflate their surpluses away by not sterilizing their foreign exchange acquisitions, (b) to hold larger and larger portfolios of short term dollars, sterilizing their foreign exchange acquisitions, and (c) to let their currencies appreciate relative to the dollar. Whereas option (a) does not attempt to wall out the monetary effects of the currency conversions, option (b) cannot succeed in walling out these pressures indefinitely because the relative interest rate effects (as well as speculative effects) on short term capital flows will eventually lead to the breakdown of the sterilization operation. Option (c) would therefore remain as the only effective way of combating these planned speculative conversions. Unfortunately, this last option was not used in many cases until it was too late to prevent excessive domestic monetary expansion.

The inexorable monetary linkages of the dollar standard world transferred the excessive supply of dollars to the foreign exchange reserves of other advanced Western countries as these countries responded only in part by appreciating their currencies. In order to maintain their interest rates at a level low enough to prevent further large scale inflows of short term portfolio capital from the United States, considerable expansion of their money supplies was required. The total monetary expansion, coupled with the inevitable breakdown of the US wage and price control scheme, has left in its wake a world price inflation of very serious magnitude. At least in part, therefore, the considerable increase in the rate of world price inflation results from a series of mercantilistic attempts either to

---

7. Of course, it might well be argued that *in net terms* US long term direct investment outflows should diminish in importance through time as the process of technological convergence runs its course, simply because the higher rates of profit attainable in other advanced Western countries are directly associated with this process. In addition, the readjustment of exchange rates itself should to some degree increase profit rates in the United States relative to profit rates in other advanced Western countries, thus serving to reduce the volume of *net* US long term capital outflows.

depreciate the domestic currency or to avoid its appreciation, attempts which have involved the manipulation of short term capital movements through the reduction of interest rates,[8] and which have eventually led to an upwards readjustment of nominal interest rates as financial markets have adapted to expectations of further inflation.

The magnitude of the total world monetary expansion depends upon the monetary aggregates used. Indeed, it is difficult to obtain monetary aggregates on a wholly consistent basis across the countries comprising (say) the Group of Ten. Nevertheless, from an examination of international monetary growth figures it is difficult to refute the view that one causal element in the recent acceleration of inflation can be found in the monetary and fiscal policies of the US authorities beginning in the middle of 1970, policies which appear to be overly permissive when considered in the light of the fact that the previous inflationary pressures resulting from the mismanagement of domestic demand in the face of the Vietnam War had not been eradicated from the system. And it is certainly not possible to refute the view that the mercantilistic attempts by foreign monetary and fiscal authorities not to appreciate their currencies much earlier has led to unbelievably large increases in their own domestic liquidity.

Different countries have, of course, suffered different rates of inflation depending in part upon (a) the initial pressure of domestic demand, in part upon (b) the degree to which various forms of wage and price controls have been successful in repressing inflationary tendencies in the short term, and in part upon (c) the degree to which they have followed the overly permissive monetary expansion in the United States. Abstracting from (a) and (b), those which have monetized least and appreciated their currencies most are likely to have suffered less pressure towards accelerated inflation than those which have managed their money supplies to keep their currencies at par with the depreciating US dollar. One must, of course, beware of simple statistical correlations. The money supply of a country whose currency is *expected* to appreciate will grow rapidly simply because of large scale, short term capital inflows that the authorities may not be able to sterilize effectively. Rapid monetary growth *and* currency appreciation are then simultaneously forced upon an economy by external pressures, though it remains true that the authorities are still able to opt for more or less currency appreciation with more or less restrictive monetary responses.

The aftermath of the depreciation of the US dollar has been to leave in its wake a considerably higher rate of world price inflation, an aftermath which is the inevitable consequence of the means used to achieve this depreciation in a world of inconsistent balance of payments objectives. The basic difficulty is that, in August 1971, in the face of a hemorrhage of short term capital outflows, the United States had no choice but to abandon its passive balance of payments

---

8. As the author wrote in the spring of 1972: "Quite obviously, however, a competitive game to see who can get the lowest interest rates may well lead to a world inflation of very serious magnitude." See Scarfe, "Technological Convergence, Capital Mobility and the Dollar Crisis," a paper presented to the annual meetings of the Canadian Economics Association in June, 1972, p. 22.

strategy of "benign neglect,"[9] thus joining the list of countries actively seeking balance of payments surpluses and running headlong into the persistent refusal of a small number of other countries, notably Germany and Japan, to abandon their chronic surpluses by freely appreciating their domestic currencies.[10]

Judging by the most recent figures, the depreciation of the US dollar in world currency markets has had the effect of generating a surplus in the current account of the United States balance of payments, though after allowing both for the initially perverse effects of currency depreciation caused by substantial adjustment lags, and for the substantial adverse effects of the so-called "energy crisis" it has taken considerable time for the surplus to emerge. In addition, there has been a reduction in net long term capital outflows from the United States (though it is not clear whether this would be so if one ignored long term capital inflows that are accounted for by the investment of the surplus revenues accruing to the Organization of Petroleum Exporting Countries). In part, therefore, the US balance of payments has adjusted through an expansion of the current account surplus of the United States (as desired by Washington) and in part through a contraction in the capital account deficit (as desired by European capitals).[11] This adjustment should not be taken to imply that the US dollar should strengthen in world currency markets, since there remains the important possibility that investors will continue to diversify their portfolios away from US dollars and towards a wider range of currencies in anticipation of continued uncertainty about exchange rates.[12]

In summary, while the rates of inflation in existence in 1970–71 might have perpetuated themselves through institutional mechanisms and cost push pressures, to a substantial degree the acceleration in these rates from 1972 to 1974 is a consequence of demand-pull factors and results from excessive monetization. Of course, some specific shortages notably (beginning in 1972) in the foodstuffs area, and more recently (beginning in 1973) in energy resources, have seriously worsened the problem. These shortages are the combined result of (a) the world population explosion, (b) some particular harvest failures, (c) the cartelization of world petroleum production, and (d) some prudent stockpiling by those with surplus

9. See L. B. Krause, "A Passive Balance-of-Payments Strategy for the United States," *Brookings Papers on Economic Activity*, Washington, Brookings, 1970, pp. 339–368.

10. Compare J. H. Makin, "Capital Flows and Exchange Rate Flexibility in the Post-Bretton Woods Era," *Princeton Essays in International Finance*, no. 103, Princeton University Press, February, 1974, p. 15: "The basic difficulty is that, in August 1971, the United States joined the majority of major trading nations in adopting an active surplus-orientated balance-of-payments policy."

11. On this point, compare J. C. Ingram, "The Dollar and the International Monetary System: A Retrospective View," *Southern Economic Journal*, vol. 40, April, 1974, pp. 533–4: "In my opinion the so-called 'dollar problem' can be more accurately and adequately interpreted as a result of unresolved political issues between a few industrial nations and the United States. In particular, it reflects a basic disagreement about the role and nature of capital movements."

12. For an enlightening discussion of this point, see W. S. Salant, "The Post-Devaluation Weakness of the Dollar," *Brookings Papers on Economic Activity*, Washington, Brookings, 1973, pp. 481–497.

dollars of falling value. The global importance of these shortages should not be minimized.

Some common features of the recent acceleration of world price inflation have been (a) the flight from money (and particularly dollars) into commodities (and especially land and real estate), resulting from the expectation of further inflation, (b) the distortion of individual markets due not only to controls but also to the threat of controls and the expectation of decontrol,[13] (c) the degree to which it was initially an acceleration of price inflation rather than (until somewhat later) an acceleration of wage inflation, leading to the temporary erosion of the real incomes of the wage earning populace and to an equally temporary expansion in profits and profit related incomes, and, as a consequence, (d) the increasing degree of industrial unrest. The clamor has been for new or refurbished wage and price controls to protect the "fixed income recipient" and the "common man," despite the fact that the protection of the former is better handled through the much more widespread use of escalator clauses, and the fact that the protection of the latter through controls may well be a misnomer, though this probably depends upon the exact details of the control scheme and, in particular, the exact time with respect to the inflation cycle at which the controls are imposed.

For example, the US control scheme was originally imposed in the early stages of an economic expansion.[14] For this reason, the view that controls reduced the expansion in the share of profits which would ordinarily have accompanied a cyclical recovery with a time profile similar to the US experience from 1971 to 1973 may well contain an important element of the truth, particularly when one considers the rapidity of the cyclical recovery.[15] However, it is possible to argue that the rapidity of the upswing and the fact that controls were imposed as part of the revised "game plan" of the US administration are not independent

13. For an illustration, one has only to remember the behavior of meat prices in the summer of 1973. One should also remember that leakages to control systems beget additional control systems. Rising world prices for soyabeans and other protein feeds coupled with a depreciating US dollar and internal price controls inevitably led the United States in 1973 to impose export controls, worsening the price problem for other countries and reducing the effectiveness of US efforts to generate a trade surplus.

14. Somewhat but not entirely fortuitously, it was precisely this case that was analyzed for the Canadian Prices and Incomes Commission in the spring of 1971. See Scarfe, "On the Economic Implications of a Short-Term Wages Freeze," p. 80–83.

15. For an important, well-documented statement of this view, see R. J. Gordon, "The Response of Wages and Prices to the First Two Years of Controls," *Brookings Papers on Economic Activity*, Washington, Brookings, 1973, pp. 765–779. See especially pp. 777–8: "Most important, the data that suggest that price controls checked inflation in the 1971–73 period are not clear evidence that the controls 'succeeded.' Controls worked not by moderating the behaviour of wages relative to prices, but rather by squeezing profit margins sufficiently to hold prices below their free market levels. This is not a situation that can be expected to last indefinitely, and hence the very fact of short-run 'success' for the control program guarantees its long-run failure. Only if factors other than the control program kept profit margins from exhibiting their usual cyclical rebound during 1971–72 can one expect that the profit squeeze will be maintained after the price controls are eliminated. If instead profit margins eventually return to their no-controls level, there will be a catch-up period

events. As pointed out previously by the author,[16] the motivation leading to the imposition of controls may well have been precisely to suppress, albeit temporarily, the inflationary consequences of an expansion that was unfortunately designed to be more rapid than a longer term view of stabilization policy would have permitted. A slower expansion without controls might well have had a smaller redistributionary effect away from the average American worker than the actual combination of rapid expansion and controls, with its aftermath of an unanticipated acceleration of inflation.

The problems for the administration of a wage and price control scheme that are created by fluctuations in import prices are seriously amplified if the currency is simultaneously allowed to depreciate. Thus, in the explanation of the breakdown of the US wage and price control scheme, one must add the distortionary pressures created by the import price effects associated with the depreciation of the US dollar to the shortages and excess demand pressures created by the expansionary policy itself. As the control scheme was abandoned, it became evident that the internal inconsistencies of the threefold program of rapid expansion, wage and price controls, and the depreciation of the numeraire of the international monetary system has led to a considerable expansion in world liquidity and to a simultaneous and unsustainable inflationary boom in the countries of the Western world. The socio-economic consequences of this unanticipated acceleration of inflation are still in the process of unfolding.

More recently, in 1973–74, an attempt was made to restrain the rate of inflation through a reduced rate of monetary expansion. Coming on top of the upwards adjustment in interest rates associated with higher expected rates of inflation, this belated restraint sent interest rates to all time highs, leading to the widespread suspicion that monetary overkill coupled with underkill everywhere else would only lead to further distortions in the economy. There can

---

after the controls are lifted during which the rate of inflation will be substantially faster than it would have been had the controls not been imposed. On the assumption that profit margins will eventually be reestablished, one can cite at least four reasons for concluding that the controls were a failure:

1. Controls will have had no long-run effect on inflation.
2. The removal of controls will cause an extra, 'catch-up,' inflation at some point; the timing of this catch-up may be awkward, if, for example, non-farm prices are simultaneously escalating because of the energy shortage.
3. Controls have caused shortages and misallocations of resources in several sectors.
4. The administration of controls has consumed real resources."

16. "On the Economic Implications of a Short-Term Wages Freeze," p. 82: "The main advantage to be had from the wage control alternative is that it allows one to start moving back towards the natural rate (of unemployment) at a faster pace than the unemployment alternative.... While it is precisely because one wishes to get back to the natural rate more quickly that one might introduce wage controls, it is also precisely for the same reason that greater future instability will be imparted to the system by the wage control alternative than by the unemployment alternative. And greater future instability involves greater future costs either through the inefficiency of excess unemployment or through the inefficiency of wage controls."

This quotation has been reproduced by permission of the Minister of Supply and Services, Canada.

be no doubt, however, that tighter monetary policies, coupled with the sub-stantial quantity deflationary as opposed to price inflationary effects of the quadrupling of the international price of petroleum, have checked the overheated boom conditions that prevailed in 1973. This fact is well illustrated by develop-ments in housing markets, stock markets, and primary commodity markets in 1974. Thus, the real output component of the boom, which had previously been expanding at an unsustainable rate, was sharply cut back and a widespread inflationary recession of major proportions evolved. The excesses of the boom, however, have left a permanent legacy of faster inflation and output lost through industrial unrest as trades unions have attempted to restore their relative position at the expense of profits and profit related incomes, non-unionized employees and, inevitably, a larger pool of unemployed workers.

C: THE LESSONS OF EXPERIENCE

There are several lessons for macroeconomic policy that can be drawn from the experience of monetary instability and world inflation recounted in the previous sections. It is useful to illustrate these lessons by describing very briefly the response of the Canadian economy to this experience. It would be idle to suggest that the Canadian economy could have been insulated fully from the disturbances created by the internal inconsistencies of the threefold (expansion, controls, and depreciation) policy of the US administration, or from the more or less mer-cantilistic responses of other foreign governments. This is particularly true of the distortion of individual markets (due not only to controls but also to the threat of controls and the expectation of decontrol) that resulted from the characteristic chops and changes of the various phases of the US wage and price control scheme. Complete insulation from such microeconomic disturbances is never possible. Nevertheless, from a macroeconomic perspective, the response of the Canadian monetary and fiscal authorities to the acceleration of world price inflation was unduly permissive, as evidenced in particular by the fact that the Canadian dollar was allowed to depreciate by four and one half percentage points on a trade weighted basis, and by about two and one half percentage points in terms of the falling US dollar, from the late summer of 1972 to the late summer of 1973 just at the time when world price inflation was accelerating dramatically and the terms of international trade were moving strongly in Canada's favor. Whereas a significant appreciation of the exchange rate would have been a necessary ingredient in any attempt to insulate the Canadian economy from the acceleration in world price inflation, the impact of this depreciation was an unnecessary addition to the domestic rate of price inflation.[17]

17. Movements in Canadian price series strongly suggest that the recent acceleration of inflation really got underway in the late summer of 1972. Although the rate of inflation also accelerated from the end of 1970 through to the late summer of 1972, this acceleration can be attributed to the normal cyclical rebound in profit margins that had been strongly squeezed by the appreciation of the

One of the consequences of these events was a considerable (but temporary) expansion in the share of profits and profit related incomes, as the increase in world commodity prices expressed in Canadian dollars outstripped the rise in Canadian wage rates adjusted for productivity increases. More recently, however, an acceleration in the rates of wage increase agreed to in new wage settlements has occurred, particularly in those sectors in which profits have been most buoyant. The built-in rate of inflation has therefore been ratcheted upwards once again as labor markets have responded to the recent acceleration of price inflation by a gradual upwards adjustment of the going rate of wage settlements. In consequence, in 1974–75 an inflationary recession with steadily rising unemployment emerged; and in such a situation significant exchange rate appreciation is neither likely nor desirable.[18] Nevertheless, had a gradual attempt to tighten monetary policy been begun early enough (no doubt as early as 1972), the resulting appreciation of the currency would definitely have been of service to the cause of price stability in Canada.

There are at least two important reasons why the federal government found itself unable to insulate the Canadian economy against the acceleration in world price inflation from the late summer of 1972 until the beginning of 1974. The first of these reasons concerns the unemployment picture in the autumn of 1972, as perceived by a minority government that had only narrowly missed defeat in the general election of October 1972. The seasonally adjusted unemployment rate, which peaked at 6.8 percent in September, 1972, was judged to be unacceptably high, and the permissive monetary and fiscal policies which had been launched much earlier were allowed to continue with at least the same expansionary force. Coupled with a strongly expansionary external environment, the

Canadian dollar in 1970. (One must assume that an avoidable inflation rate of about five percent had been built-in by the eight percent pattern of wage settlements solidly established in the 1966 to 1972 period.) Indeed, the events leading to the 1970 appreciation indicate how futile it is to fight inflation in Canada without using the big lever of the exchange rate, while the impact that the appreciation itself had on prices indicates how potent an instrument the exchange rate is.

18. Envisioning circumstances of this kind, the Economic Council of Canada has stated that: "Canada is not in a position to apply a price policy that is significantly different from that of its partners. If attempts were made to reduce rates of price and cost increase below those being experienced in other countries, monetary restriction would likely lead to higher interest rates, an influx of capital, and an increase in the exchange rate, well before costs had in fact been lowered. The result would be a deterioration in the competitive position of the export industries and, consequently, lower output and higher unemployment. Canadian developments at the end of the 1950's, and again 10 years later, provide ample support for such a conclusion." (Economic Council of Canada, *Tenth Annual Review*, 1973, p. 57.)

It must be remembered, however, that the cyclical phase of inflationary recession is normally preceded by an inflationary boom. This boom phase is one in which it generally would have been feasible to have a better price performance than one's trading partners, provided that the exchange rate was allowed to appreciate to offset some of the impact of excessive foreign inflation. For in this phase, it is not a matter of reducing domestic rates of price and cost increase below their foreign counterparts, but rather one of preventing domestic inflation rates from increasing to match the higher rates of world price inflation. Here again, important asymmetries between upside and downside responses should be kept in mind.

impact of these policies was to reduce the seasonally adjusted unemployment rate to 5.3 percent in July 1973, a figure which was repeated in April 1974. At the same time, the labor force was growing very rapidly and the labor force participation rate rose to a level unprecedented in peacetime. Moreover, job vacancy rates were also running at high levels. Thus, from the point of view of the short run objective of employment creation, the permissive monetary and fiscal policies of recent years can hardly be faulted, particularly when the recent changes in the Unemployment Insurance Act may have created incentives in some quarters that lead, in the aggregate, to higher unemployment numbers.

The second of these reasons concerns the composition of the balance of payments. In order to decrease the dependence of the Canadian economy on long term capital inflows, it is necessary to reduce the deficit generated in the current account of the balance of payments. To achieve this end, it is usually argued that monetary policy should be loose enough to ensure a low external value of the Canadian dollar, thus making export and import competing industries highly profitable. This argument is further strengthened in a period such as the autumn of 1972, when it appeared that unit labor costs in Canada might become excessive relative to unit labor costs in the United States. Thus, both the short run employment objective and the balance of payments objective are served, it is argued, by loose monetary policy.

Unfortunately, both of these arguments are short run in nature, and depend for their longer run validity on the faulty assumption that the expected rate of inflation will not adapt to the permissive monetary and fiscal policies. Once the expected rate of inflation adapts to the actual experience of higher inflation rates that accompanies the permissive policies, however, the reduction in the unemployment rate may turn out to be largely ephemeral. Moreover, once wage rates adjust to reflect the inevitable increase in the cost of living, so may the improvement in the current account of the balance of payments. Indeed, it would appear that the only sound way of reducing the current account deficit through time, and thus decreasing the dependence of the economy on foreign capital inflows, is to ensure that the total current expenditure of all levels of government is reduced in relationship to the corresponding tax revenues. The resulting reduction in the overall budgetary deficit would then enable a larger proportion of total long term investment to be financed from domestic sources, while releasing the resources necessary to allow exports of goods and services to expand relative to imports. The argument that permissive monetary policy can achieve this same result is based upon a mis-specified view of the determinants of long term capital inflows, and may have contributed to the degree of foreign ownership and control of Canada's real resources in two ways, namely, by resulting in these resources being priced cheaply in terms of foreign currencies and by providing via short term capital outflows the finance required for foreigners to acquire ownership of these real assets.

Thus, there is some evidence that the Canadian monetary and fiscal authorities attempt in a somewhat mercantilistic (and self-defeating) way to keep the Canadian economy in a phase of the business cycle where profit margins are expanding and the unemployment rate is falling. To remain in any one phase of the cycle perpetually is, of course, impossible, no matter how undesirable other phases, such as inflationary recession, might be. Even if it proves to be impractical to suggest a policy of continuous appreciation of the currency through time, so that in the long run domestic inflation rates must adapt to foreign inflation rates, the short run stabilization of the economy requires that the exchange rate be allowed to appreciate, at least temporarily, whenever cyclical bursts of world price inflation occur. Although in the short run such an appreciation will result in an unemployment rate which may be slightly higher than it would have been without this attempt at insulation, it has been shown in the previous chapter that the gain in cyclical stability so achieved will permit a lower *average* rate of unemployment to be maintained through time.

The main lesson to be drawn from this experience is that until governments come to realize that the mercantilistic attempt to get into *and remain in* a phase of the business cycle where profit margins are expanding and the rate of unemployment is contracting is doomed to longer run failure, the economies of the Western world will continue to experience an upward ratcheting of the pace of inflation. For such a phase of expansion is inevitably followed by a phase of inflationary recession, where output growth moderates but the pace of price inflation remains roughly at the new higher level reached through the excesses of the boom. To expect moderation on the part of governments, which are naturally interested in re-election and therefore reflect the overt aspirations and more vocal opinions of their electorate, may well be a pipedream. But governments may also lead public opinion and temper the expectations of their electorates, *provided that* they understand the dynamic processes in which they are enmeshed. These processes may well indicate that serious resource shortages and consequent price inflation could occur in the not too distant future. Now is the time to plan so that the impact of these shortages can be softened; now is the time to begin molding expectations so that mankind's apparently insatiable appetite can be reconciled with the finite globe on which he lives.

One should, therefore, end with a warning. Our real consumption standards cannot be expected to grow exponentially forever. The resources of this planet are finite. Although many of them can be conserved, others are definitely non-renewable. How they are distributed among present and future generations is a matter of social choice. Our continual failure to face up to this problem of choice, no matter how unpalatable it may be, is ultimately responsible for the distributional problem of inflation. High utilization rates for labor resources can only be sustained without accelerating inflation if the natural rate of interest (or social rate of discount) can be lowered. This implies a deliberate social choice to weigh more heavily the need to conserve our scarce natural resources for future generations. It also implies, for an open economy like Canada, that our natural resources should never be underpriced to foreigners through the mercantilistic and self-defeating device of an undervalued exchange rate. The following section is devoted to some final comments on these and other problems associated with the analysis of economic expansion in a finite world.

D: A FINAL ATTEMPT AT PERSPECTIVE

This survey of contemporary macrodynamics has come a long way from the humble beginnings of the original inventory cycle model of chapter 1. The road has not always been easy, nor (one would be quick to remark) has it always been consistent. Indeed, an astute critic might well add that the topics we have chosen to include or exclude reflect no more than the author's personal prejudice. Nevertheless, there are a variety of themes and interrelationships that are worth pursuing further in subsequent analytical work.

One of these themes is the impact of the emerging scarcity of non-renewable natural resources on macroeconomic behavior and the models economists build to interpret that behavior in a dynamic setting. In particular, the conditions under which a macrodynamic system may be said to be continuously viable, "productive," or capable of generating a non-negative growth rate of consumption per head (the Hawkins-Simon conditions) may turn out to be much more important in a world of scarce natural resources with substantial but limited substitution possibilities than in a "never-never land" where economic growth is unconstrained by the finiteness and vulnerability of the ecological system in which actual economies are necessarily imbedded.

In addition to this, bilaterally coupled flex-price dynamic systems of the kind discussed in chapter 11 of this book may also turn out to be of considerable analytical usefulness; for natural resources and land may be treated as the ultimate fixed (but perhaps depleting) capital of the system, while what we usually consider to be fixed capital equipment may be treated as inventories of circulating capital goods in the manner of chapters 7 to 9 of this book. In this way, the short run model of chapter 11 may be converted into a useful long run model with particular natural resource inputs (including energy resources) being required in each productive sector. Nevertheless, a great deal of more analytical work is required in order to make these thoughts operative.

This book has been concerned with an analysis of how macrodynamic systems function. It has taken stock of the progress made in macrodynamic analysis in the postwar period (though perhaps it has been unnecessarily elliptical with respect to developments integrating monetary theory with the theory of longer run growth equilibrium paths), and has pointed out at least' three directions for further analytical work. These are (a) the formulation of appropriately co-ordinated stabilization policies in response to cyclical fluctuations, (b) the consequences of the existence of scarce and non-renewable natural resources, and (c) the causes and consequences of the problem of inflation.

Although this book has explored a wide variety of analytical developments, it has paid little attention to comparisons among alternative schools of thought. Perhaps this lack of emphasis on controversy and division is appropriate in an attempt to present these analytical developments in a connected, if not formally integrated, manner. Moreover, to present them with a more critical and interpretative eye would have substantially increased the length of this book and would, perhaps, have pre-empted the desire of each individual reader to interpret recent developments in macrodynamic analysis in his own way. I sincerely hope that this book has provided the basic framework for a variety of meaningful interpretations.

BIBLIOGRAPHY

1. Allen, R. G. D., *Mathematical Economics*, London, Macmillan, 1960.
2. Allen, R. G. D., *Macro-Economic Theory, A Mathematical Treatment*, London, Macmillan, 1967.
3. Arrow, K. J., "Alternative Proof of the Substitution Theorem for Leontief Models in the General Case," pp. 155–164 in T. C. Koopmans (editor), *Activity Analysis of Production and Allocation*, New York, Wiley, 1951.
4. Arrow, K. J., S. Karlin, and P. Suppes (editors), *Mathematical Methods in the Social Sciences*, Stanford, Stanford University Press, 1960.
5. Ayres, R. U., and A. V. Kneese, "Economic and Ecological Effects of a Stationary Economy," *Resources for the Future, Inc.*, Reprint 99, Washington D.C., 1972.
6. Baldwin, R. E., "The Role of Capital-Goods Trade in the Theory of International Trade," *American Economic Review*, vol. 56, September, 1966, pp. 841–848.
7. Barber, C. L., "On the Origins of the Great Depression," unpublished mimeograph, 1976.
8. Blaug, M., *The Cambridge Revolution, Success or Failure?*, London, The Institute of Economic Affairs, 1974.
9. Bliss, C. J., "On Putty-Clay," *Review of Economic Studies*, vol. 35, April, 1968, pp. 105–132.
10. Boulding, K., "The Economics of the Coming Spaceship Earth," pp. 3–14 in H. Jarrett (ed.), *Environmental Quality in a Growing Economy*, Baltimore, Johns Hopkins Press, 1966.
11. Brown, M., *On the Theory and Measurement of Technological Change*, Cambridge, Cambridge University Press, 1966.
12. Bruno, M., E. Burmeister, and E. Sheshinski, "The Nature and Implications of the Reswitching of Techniques," *Quarterly Journal of Economics*, vol. 80, November, 1966, pp. 526–553.
13. Bruno, M., "Fundamental Duality Relations in the Pure Theory of Capital and Growth," *Review of Economic Studies*, vol. 36, January, 1969, pp. 39–53.
14. Burmeister, E., R. Dobell, and K. Kuga, "A Note on the Global Stability of a Simple Growth Model with Many Capital Goods," *Quarterly Journal of Economics*, vol. 82, November, 1968, pp. 657–665.
15. Burmeister, E., and A. R. Dobell, *Mathematical Theories of Economic Growth*, London, Collier-Macmillan, 1970.
16. Burmeister, E., C. Caton, A. R. Dobell, and S. A. Ross, "The 'Saddle Point Property' and the Structure of Dynamic Heterogeneous Capital Good Models," *Econometrica*, vol. 41, January, 1973, pp. 79–95.
17. Burmeister, E., and D. A. Graham, "Multi-Sector Economic Models with Continuous Adaptive Expectations," *Review of Economic Studies*, vol. 41, July, 1974, pp. 323–336.
18. Champernowne, D. G., "The Production Function and the Theory of Capital: A Comment," *Review of Economic Studies*, vol. 21, no. 55, 1953–1954, pp. 112–135.

19. Cragg, J. G., "Structural Aspects of Price Inflation," unpublished mimeograph, 1976.
20. Dasgupta, P., and G. M. Heal, "The Optimal Depletion of Exhaustible Resources," *Review of Economic Studies,* Symposium on the Economics of Exhaustible Resources, Special Issue, 1974, pp. 3–28.
21. Deardorff, A. V., "The Gains from Trade In and Out of Steady-State Growth," *Oxford Economic Papers,* vol. 25, July, 1973, pp. 173–191.
22. Debreu, G. and I. N. Herstein, "Non-negative Square Matrices," *Econometrica,* vol. 21, October, 1953, pp. 597–607.
23. Denison, E. F., *Why Growth Rates Differ,* Washington, The Brookings Institution, 1967.
24. Domar, E. D., "Capital Expansion, Rate of Growth, and Employment," *Econometrica,* vol. 14, April, 1946, pp. 137–147.
25. Dunn, R. M., "Flexible Exchange Rates and Oligopoly Pricing: A Study of Canadian Markets," *Journal of Political Economy,* vol. 78, Jan/February, 1970, pp. 140–151.
26. Dunn, R. M., *Canada's Experience with Fixed and Flexible Exchange Rates in a North American Capital Market,* Washington, Canadian-American Committee, 1971.
27. Economic Council of Canada, *Tenth Annual Review: Shaping the Expansion,* Ottawa, Information Canada, 1973.
28. Fisher, F. M., "Embodied Technical Change and the Existence of an Aggregate Capital Stock," *Review of Economic Studies,* vol. 32, October, 1965, pp. 263–288.
29. Foley, D. K., and M. Sidrauski, *Monetary and Fiscal Policy in a Growing Economy,* New York, Macmillan, 1971.
30. Fortin, P., "Can Economic Policy Pair Instruments and Targets? (Or Should It?)," *Canadian Journal of Economics,* vol. 7, November, 1974, pp. 558–577.
31. Friedman, M., *The Optimal Quantity of Money and Other Essays,* London, Macmillan, 1969.
32. Friedman, M., "The Role of Monetary Policy," pp. 95–110 in M. Friedman, *The Optimal Quantity of Money and Other Essays.*
33. Frisch, R., "On the Notion of Equilibrium and Disequilibrium," *Review of Economic Studies,* vol. 3, February, 1936, pp. 100–106.
34. Gale, D., and H. Nikaido, "The Jacobian Matrix and Global Univalence of Mappings," *Mathematische Annalen,* Bd. 159, Heft 2, 1965, pp. 81–93.
35. Goodwin, R. M., "The Non-Linear Accelerator and the Persistence of Business Cycles," *Econometrica,* vol. 19, January, 1951, pp. 1–17.
36. Gordon, R. J., "The Response of Wages and Prices to the First Two Years of Controls," *Brookings Papers on Economic Activity,* Washington, Brookings, 1973, pp. 765–779.
37. Gorman, W. M., "Capital Aggregation in Vintage Models," unpublished paper, Oxford, 1965.
38. Hahn, F. H., "The Stability of Growth Equilibrium," *Quarterly Journal of Economics,* vol. 74, May, 1960, pp. 206–226.
39. Hahn, F. H., and R. C. O. Matthews, "The Theory of Economic Growth: A Survey," *The Economic Journal,* vol. 74, December, 1964, pp. 779–902.
40. Hahn, F. H., "Equilibrium Dynamics with Heterogeneous Capital Goods," *Quarterly Journal of Economics,* vol. 80, November, 1966, pp. 633–646.
41. Hahn, F. H., "On Warranted Growth Paths," *Review of Economic Studies,* vol. 35, April, 1968, pp. 175–184.
42. Hahn, F. H., "Some Adjustment Problems," *Econometrica,* vol. 38, January, 1970, pp. 1–17.
43. Hahn, F. H., "On the Foundations of Monetary Theory," pp. 230–242 in J. M. Parkin and A. R. Nobay (eds.), *Essays in Modern Economics,* London, Longman, 1973.
44. Harcourt, G. C., *Some Cambridge Controversies in the Theory of Capital,* London, Cambridge University Press, 1972.
45. Harcourt, G. C., "The Cambridge Controversies: Old Ways and New Horizons—or Dead End?," *Oxford Economic Papers,* vol. 28, March, 1976, pp. 25–65.
46. Harris, S. E. (ed.), *The Dollar in Crisis,* New York, Harcourt Brace and World, 1961.
47. Harrod, R. F., *Towards a Dynamic Economics,* London, Macmillan, 1948.
48. Hatanaka, M., "Note on Consolidation within a Leontief System," *Econometrica,* vol. 20, April, 1952, pp. 301–303.

49. Hawkins, D., and H. A. Simon, "Note: Some Conditions of Macroeconomic Stability," *Econometrica,* vol. 17, July-October, 1949, pp. 245–248.
50. Hayek, F. A., *Prices and Production,* London, Routledge, 1935.
51. Hayek, F. A., *The Pure Theory of Capital,* London, Routledge and Kegan Paul, 1941.
52. Heckscher, E. F., "The Effect of Foreign Trade on the Distribution of Income," pp. 272–300 in H. S. Ellis and L. A. Metzler (editors), *Readings in the Theory of International Trade,* London, Allen and Unwin, 1950.
53. Helliwell, J. F. *et al., The Equations of RDX2 Revised and Estimated to 4Q 1970,* Ottawa, Bank of Canada, 1974.
54. Hicks, J. R., *A Contribution to the Theory of the Trade Cycle,* Oxford, Oxford University Press, 1950.
55. Hicks, J. R., "An Inaugural Lecture," *Oxford Economic Papers,* vol. 5, June, 1953, pp. 117–125.
56. Hicks, J. R., "A 'Value and Capital' Growth Model," *Review of Economic Studies,* vol. 26, June, 1959, pp. 159–173.
57. Hicks, J. R., *Essays in World Economics,* Oxford, Oxford University Press, 1959.
58. Hicks, J. R., *International Trade: The Long View,* Cairo, National Bank of Egypt, 1963.
59. Hicks, J. R., *Capital and Growth,* Oxford, Oxford University Press, 1965.
60. Hicks, J. R., *Critical Essays in Monetary Theory,* Oxford, Oxford University Press, 1967.
61. Hicks, J. R., *The Crisis in Keynesian Economics,* Oxford, Blackwell, 1974.
62. Ingram, J. C., "The Dollar and the International Monetary System: A Retrospective View," *Southern Economic Journal,* vol. 40, April, 1974, pp. 531–543.
63. Johnson, H. G., *Inflation and the Monetarist Controversy,* Amsterdam, North-Holland, 1972.
64. Jorgenson, D. W., "A Dual Stability Theorem," *Econometrica,* vol. 28, October, 1960, pp. 892–899.
65. Jorgenson, D. W., "The Structure of Multi-Sector Dynamic Models," *International Economic Review,* vol. 2, September, 1961, pp. 276–293.
66. Jorgenson, D. W., and J. A. Stephenson, "Investment Behaviour in U. S. Manufacturing, 1947–1960," *Econometrica,* vol. 35, April, 1967, pp. 169–220.
67. Jorgenson, D. W., "Linear Models of Economic Growth," *International Economic Review,* vol. 9, February, 1968, pp. 1–13.
68. Kaldor, N., "Hicks on the Trade Cycle," pp. 193–209 in Kaldor, N., *Essays on Economic Stability and Growth,* London, Duckworth, 1960.
69. Kaldor, N., "A Model of Economic Growth," *The Economic Journal,* vol. 67, December, 1957, pp. 591–624. Reprinted as pp. 259–300 in N. Kaldor, *Essays on Economic Stability and Growth.*
70. Kaliski, S. F., and D. C. Smith, "Inflation, Unemployment and Incomes Policy," *Canadian Journal of Economics,* vol. 6, November, 1973, pp. 574–591.
71. Kemp, M. C., and P. C. Thanh, "On a Class of Growth Models," *Econometrica,* vol. 34, April, 1966, pp. 257–282.
72. Keynes, J. M., *A Treatise on Money,* London, Macmillan, 1930.
73. Keynes, J. M., *The General Theory of Employment Interest and Money,* London, Macmillan, 1936.
74. Kindleberger, C. P., *International Economics,* Homewood, Irwin, 1963.
75. Krause, L. B., "A Passive Balance-of-Payments Strategy for the United States," *Brookings Papers on Economic Activity,* Washington, Brookings, 1970, pp. 339–368.
76. Kurz, M., "The General Instability of a Class of Competitive Growth Processes," *Review of Economic Studies,* vol. 35, April, 1968, pp. 155–174.
77. Leijonhufvud, A., *On Keynesian Economics and the Economics of Keynes,* New York, Oxford University Press, 1968.
78. Levhari, D., "A Nonsubstitution Theorem and Switching of Techniques," *Quarterly Journal of Economics,* vol. 79, February, 1965, pp. 98–105.
79. Lindahl, E., *Studies in the Theory of Money and Capital,* London, Allen and Unwin, 1939.
80. Lutz, F. A., *International Payments and Monetary Policy in the World Today,* Stockholm, Almqvist and Wiksell, 1961.
81. MacDougall, G. D. A., *The World Dollar Problem,* London, Macmillan, 1957.

82. Machlup, F., "Equilibrium and Disequilibrium: Misplaced Concreteness and Disguised Politics," *The Economic Journal,* vol. 68, March, 1958, pp. 1–24.

83. Makin, J. H., "Capital Flows and Exchange-Rate Flexibility in the Post-Bretton Woods Era," *Princeton Essays in International Finance,* no. 103, February, 1974.

84. Matthews, R. C. O., "The New View of Investment: A Comment," *Quarterly Journal of Economics,* vol. 78, February, 1964, pp. 164–172.

85. McKenzie, L. W., "Specialisation and Efficiency in World Production," *Review of Economic Studies,* vol. 21, no. 56, 1953–1954, pp. 165–180.

86. McKenzie, L. W., "Matrices with Dominant Diagonals and Economic Theory," pp. 47–62 in Arrow, Karlin, and Suppes (editors), *Mathematical Methods in the Social Sciences.*

87. McKinnon, R. I., "Monetary Theory and Controlled Flexibility in the Foreign Exchanges," *Princeton Essays in International Finance,* no. 84, April, 1971.

88. Meier, G. M., *International Trade and Development,* New York, Harper and Row, 1963.

89. Mirrlees, J. A., "The Dynamic Nonsubstitution Theorem," *Review of Economic Studies,* vol. 36, January 1969, pp. 67–76.

90. Morimoto, Y., "Aggregation Problems in Input-Output Analysis," unpublished D. Phil. dissertation, Oxford University, 1967.

91. Morishima, M., *Equilibrium, Stability and Growth,* Oxford, Oxford University Press, 1964.

92. Mortenson, D. T., "A Theory of Wage and Employment Dynamics," pp. 167–211 in E. S. Phelps (editor), *Micro-Economic Foundations of Employment and Inflation Theory.*

93. Mundell, R. A., *International Economics,* New York, Macmillan, 1968.

94. Negishi, T., "Existence of an Under-Employment Equilibrium," unpublished mimeograph, 1975.

95. Newman, P. K., "Some Notes on Stability Conditions," *Review of Economic Studies,* vol. 27, October, 1959, pp. 1–9.

96. Nordhaus, W. D., "The Worldwide Wage Explosion," *Brookings Papers on Economic Activity,* Washington, Brookings, 1972, pp. 431–465.

97. Nordhaus, W. D., "The Political Business Cycle," *Review of Economic Studies,* vol. 42, April 1975, pp. 169–190.

98. Ogata, K., *State Space Analysis of Control Systems,* Englewood Cliffs, Prentice-Hall, 1967.

99. Ohlin, B., *Interregional and International Trade,* Cambridge, Harvard University Press, 1933.

100. Oniki, H., and H. Uzawa, "Patterns of Trade and Investment in a Dynamic Model of International Trade," *Review of Economic Studies,* vol. 32, January, 1965, pp. 15–38.

101. Patinkin, D., *Money, Interest and Prices,* New York, Harper and Row, 1965.

102. Phelps, E. S., "The New View of Investment: A Neoclassical Analysis," *Quarterly Journal of Economics,* vol. 76, November, 1962, pp. 548–567.

103. Phelps, E. S., and M. E. Yaari, "Reply," *Quarterly Journal of Economics,* vol. 78, February, 1964, pp. 172–176.

104. Phelps, E. S. (editor), *Microeconomic Foundations of Employment and Inflation Theory,* New York, Norton, 1970.

105. Phelps, E. S., "Money Wage Dynamics and Labour Market Equilibrium," pp. 124–166 in E. S. Phelps (editor), *Microeconomic Foundations of Employment and Inflation Theory.*

106. Phelps, E. S., *Inflation Policy and Unemployment Theory,* New York, Norton, 1972.

107. Phillips, A. W., "Stabilisation Policy in a Closed Economy," *Economic Journal,* vol. 64, June, 1954, pp. 290–323.

108. Robinson, J., *The Accumulation of Capital,* London, Macmillan, 1956.

109. Robinson, J., "Accumulation and the Production Function," *The Economic Journal,* vol. 69, September, 1959, pp. 433–442. Reprinted as pp. 132–144 in J. Robinson, *Collected Economic Papers,* vol. II.

110. Robinson, J., *Collected Economics Papers,* vol. II, Oxford, Blackwell, 1960.

111. Robinson, J., "The Real Wicksell Effect," *Collected Economic Papers,* vol. II, pp. 185–190.

112. Robinson, J., "Some Problems of Definition and Measurement of Capital," *Collected Economic Papers,* vol. II, pp. 197–208.

113. Rosenbluth, G., "Economists and the Growth Controversy," *Canadian Public Policy,* vol. 2, Spring, 1976, pp. 225–239.

114. Salant, W. S., "The Post-Devaluation Weakness of the Dollar," *Brookings Papers on Economic Activity,* Washington, Brookings, 1973, pp. 481–497.
115. Salter, W. E. G., *Productivity and Technical Change,* Cambridge, Cambridge University Press, 1960.
116. Samuelson, P. A., "Interaction between the Multiplier Analysis and the Principle of Acceleration," *Review of Economics and Statistics,* vol. 21, May 1939, pp. 75–78.
117. Samuelson, P. A., *Foundations of Economic Analysis,* Cambridge, Harvard University Press, 1947.
118. Samuelson, P. A., "Prices of Factors and Goods in General Equilibrium," *Review of Economic Studies,* vol. 21, no. 54, 1953–1954, pp. 1–20.
119. Samuelson, P. A., "Abstract of a Theorem Concerning Substitutability in Open Leontief Models," pp. 142–146 in T. C. Koopmans (editor), *Activity Analysis of Production and Allocation,* New York, Wiley, 1951.
120. Samuelson, P. A., "Efficient Paths of Capital Accumulation in Terms of the Calculus of Variations," pp. 77–88 in Arrow, Karlin, and Suppes (editors), *Mathematical Methods in the Social Sciences.*
121. Samuelson, P. A., "A New Theorem on Nonsubstitution," pp. 407–423 in H. Hegeland (editor), *Money, Growth and Methodology, and Other Essays in Economics in Honour of Johan Akerman,* Lund, CWK Gleerup, 1961.
122. Samuelson, P. A., "Parable and Realism in Capital Theory: The Surrogate Production Function," *Review of Economic Studies,* vol. 29, June, 1962, pp. 193–206.
123. Samuelson, P. A., "Equalization by Trade of the Interest Rate along with the Real Wage," pp. 32–52 in R. E. Caves, *Trade, Growth, and the Balance of Payments, Essays in Honour of Gottfried Haberler,* Amsterdam, North-Holland, 1965.
124. Scarfe, B. L., "Capital Accumulation and Comparative Advantage: A Critical Appraisal," unpublished D. Phil. dissertation, Oxford University, 1970.
125. Scarfe, B. L., "Multi-sectoral Growth and Technological Change," *Canadian Journal of Economics,* vol. 4, August, 1971, pp. 299–313.
126. Scarfe, B. L., *Price Determination and the Process of Inflation in Canada,* Ottawa, Information Canada, 1972.
127. Scarfe, B. L., "On the Economic Implications of a Short-Term Wages Freeze," Appendix C, pp. 80–83 of B. L. Scarfe, *Price Determination and the Process of Inflation in Canada.*
128. Scarfe, B. L., "Technological Convergence, Capital Mobility and the Dollar Crisis," unpublished paper presented to the annual meetings of the Canadian Economics Association in June 1972.
129. Scarfe, B. L., "A Model of the Inflation Cycle in a Small Open Economy," *Oxford Economic Papers,* vol. 25, July, 1973, pp. 192–203.
130. Scarfe, B. L., *Inflation and the Exchange Rate,* unpublished monograph, Ottawa, Bank of Canada Research Department, 1974.
131. Schumpeter, J. A., *The Theory of Economic Development,* New York, Oxford University Press, 1961.
132. Shell, K., and J. E. Stiglitz, "The Allocation of Investment in a Dynamic Economy," *Quarterly Journal of Economics,* vol. 81, November, 1967, pp. 592–609.
133. Shinkai, Y., "A Model of Imported Inflation," *Journal of Political Economy,* vol. 81, July/August, 1973, pp. 962–971.
134. Smith, A., *An Inquiry into the Nature and Causes of the Wealth of Nations,* Cannan or fifth edition, London, Methuen, 1904.
135. Solow, R. M., "The Production Function and the Theory of Capital," *Review of Economic Studies,* vol. 23, no. 61, 1955–1956, pp. 101–108.
136. Solow, R. M., "A Contribution to the Theory of Economic Growth," *Quarterly Journal of Economics,* vol. 70, February, 1956, pp. 65–94.
137. Solow, R. M., "Investment and Technical Progress," pp. 89–104 in Arrow, Karlin, and Suppes (editors), *Mathematical Methods in the Social Sciences.*
138. Solow, R. M., *Capital Theory and the Rate of Return,* F. DeVries Lectures, Amsterdam, North-Holland, 1963.

139. Solow, R. M., "The Interest Rate and Transition Between Techniques," pp. 30–39 in C. H. Feinstein (editor), *Socialism, Capitalism and Economic Growth, Essays Presented to Maurice Dobb,* Cambridge, Cambridge University Press, 1967.

140. Solow, R. M., *Growth Theory: An Exposition,* Oxford, Oxford University Press, 1970.

141. Solow, R. M., "Intergenerational Equity and Exhaustible Resources," *Review of Economic Studies,* Symposium on the Economics of Exhaustible Resources, Special Issue, 1974, pp. 29–45.

142. Stein, J. L., *Money and Capacity Growth,* New York, Columbia University Press, 1971.

143. Stiglitz, J. E., "Factor Price Equalization in a Dynamic Economy," *Journal of Political Economy,* vol. 78, May/June, 1970, pp. 456–488.

144. Stiglitz, J. E., "Growth with Exhaustible Natural Resources: Efficient and Optimal Growth Paths," *Review of Economic Studies,* Symposium on the Economics of Exhaustible Resources, Special Issue, 1974, pp. 123–137.

145. Swan, T. W., "Economic Growth and Capital Accumulation," *The Economic Record,* vol. 32, November, 1956, pp. 334–361.

146. Tobin, J., "Monetary Policy in 1974 and Beyond," *Brookings Papers on Economic Activity,* Washington, Brookings, 1974, pp. 219–232.

147. Turnovsky, S. J., and A. Kaspura, "An Analysis of Imported Inflation in a Short-Run Macroeconomic Model," *Canadian Journal of Economics,* vol. 7, August, 1974, pp. 355–380.

148. Usher, D., "Traditional Capital Theory," *Review of Economic Studies,* vol. 32, April, 1965, pp. 169–186.

149. Uspensky, J. V., *Theory of Equations,* New York, McGraw-Hill, 1948.

150. Viner, J., *Studies in the Theory of International Trade,* New York, Harper, 1937.

151. Wicksell, K., *Interest and Prices,* London, Macmillan, 1936, (*Geldzins und Güterpreise,* 1898).

152. Wicksell, K., *Value, Capital and Rent,* London, Allen and Unwin, 1954, (*Über Wert, Kapital und Rente,* 1893).

INDEX